C000256598

Milton and the Culture of Violence

OTHER WORKS BY MICHAEL LIEB

The Dialectics of Creation: Patterns of Birth and Regeneration in "Paradise Lost"

Poetics of the Holy: A Reading of "Paradise Lost"

The Sinews of Ulysses: Form and Convention in Milton's Works

The Visionary Mode: Biblical Prophecy, Hermeneutics, and Cultural Change

MILTON
and the Culture
of Violence

MICHAEL LIEB

Cornell University Press

ITHACA AND LONDON

CORNELL UNIVERSITY PRESS GRATEFULLY ACKNOWLEDGES A SUBVENTION
FROM THE UNIVERSITY OF ILLINOIS, CHICAGO, WHICH AIDED IN THE
PUBLICATION OF THIS BOOK.

First published 1994 by Cornell University Press.

Library of Congress Cataloging-in-Publication Data

Lieb, Michael, 1940-
    Milton and the culture of violence / Michael Lieb.
        p.   cm.
    Includes bibliographical references and index.
    ISBN 0-8014-2903-X
    1. Milton, John, 1608-1674—Political and social views.
    2. Violence—England—History—17th century.   3. Violence in
literature.   I. Title.
PR3592.V56L54   1994
821'.4—dc20   93-32279

Printed in the United States of America

⊗ The paper in this book meets the minimum requirements
of the American National Standard for Information Sciences—
Permanence of Paper for Printed Library Materials, ANSI Z39.48-1984.

In memory of my parents, Saul and Adele Lieb

Contents

PART III   STAGING THE BODY

Acknowledgments

This book has benefited immeasurably from the counsel of several individuals. Two readers for Cornell University Press, David Loewenstein and Paul Morrison, were extremely helpful in their comments, criticism, and close attention to detail. For their wise judgments and their astute observations, I am indeed grateful. I also thank Bernhard Kendler and Kay Scheuer of Cornell University Press for their continuing support and encouragement. In addition to the Press's readers, John T. Shawcross read the manuscript in its entirety and offered invaluable suggestions concerning matters both large and small.

Portions of the book were presented before several gatherings, including the Newberry Library Milton Seminar and the University of Central Florida First Biennial Conference on the Arts and Public Policy. These lively and memorable meetings proved immensely helpful to me in working out the thesis of my book and in fostering the development of the argument as a whole. Whether in the context of these meetings or in informal discussion, I have had the opportunity to benefit from the good offices of friends and colleagues whom I acknowledge here. These include Diana Treviño Benet, Robert Fallon, Stephen M. Fallon, Achsah Guibbory, Alan Hager, Albert C. Labriola, Helen Marlborough, Donald G. Marshall, Janel Mueller, Michael Murrin, Annabel Patterson, Mary Beth Rose, and Regina M. Schwartz.

I am also indebted to Yale University Press for permission to quote from *The Complete Prose Works of John Milton*, 8 vols. in 10, ed. Don M. Wolfe et al. (1953–82), copyright © 1953, 1959, 1962, 1966, 1971, 1973, 1980, 1982, by Yale University Press; to William Kerrigan for permission to quote from his unpublished essay "John Milton, Poetess"; and to Hakim O. Merrill to quote from his father's unpublished doctoral dissertation "Milton's Secret Adversary: Du Moulin and the Politics of Protestant Humanism" (University of Tennessee, Knoxville, 1959).

Finally, I extend yet once more both my profound thanks and deep affection to my wife, Roslyn, with whom I have shared everything for nearly three decades. The book itself is dedicated to the memory of my parents.

MICHAEL LIEB

Chicago, Illinois

Notes on Sources

Throughout this book, line references to Milton's poetry are to *The Complete Poetry of John Milton*, ed. John T. Shawcross (Garden City, N.Y.: Doubleday, 1971), abbreviated as *Complete Poetry*. References to Milton's prose by volume and page number are to *The Complete Prose Works of John Milton*, 8 vols. in 10, gen. ed. Don M. Wolfe et al. (New Haven: Yale University Press, 1953–82), indicated by *YP*. Corresponding references to the original Latin (and on occasion to the English translations) are to *The Works of John Milton*, 18 vols. in 21, ed. Frank Allen Patterson et al. (New York: Columbia University Press, 1931–38), cited as *CM*.

Other sources cited throughout this book are abbreviated as follows:

Early Lives   *The Early Lives of Milton*, ed. Helen Darbishire. New York: Barnes and Noble, 1933.

Facsimile   *John Milton's Complete Poetical Works Reproduced in Photographic Facsimile*, 4 vols., ed. Harris Francis Fletcher. Urbana: University of Illinois Press, 1943–45.

Life of Milton   David Masson, *The Life of John Milton*, 6 vols. plus index. London: Macmillan, 1881, 1894; reprinted Gloucester, Mass.: Peter Smith, 1965.

Life Records   J. Milton French, *The Life Records of John Milton*, 5 vols. New Brunswick, N.J.: Rutgers University Press, 1956.

Milton Biography   William Riley Parker, *Milton: A Biography*, 2 vols. Oxford: Clarendon Press, 1968.

Milton Encyclopedia   *A Milton Encyclopedia*, 9 vols., ed. William B. Hunter, Jr. Lewisburg, Pa.: Bucknell University Press, 1978–83.

Milton and the Culture of Violence

Introduction:
The Poetics of Violence

In the remarkable passage that concludes *Mansus* (ll. 85–100), Milton envisions the aftermath of his own death. What he offers is a fantasy of wholeness, fulfillment, and the solicitous endeavors of a close friend who attends upon him in these crucial moments to keep his body safe and unviolated. Bequeathing (*relinquam*) to death (*cineri*) that which is owed to it, Milton has no concern about what will happen to his body. His friend will make certain that his limbs (*artus*), no longer animated by life, are deposited with due care and respect in an appropriate receptacle. So deposited, Milton's body will be accorded all the rites that accompany the veneration of one who has achieved such acclaim. His friend will erect a memorial in Milton's honor. As a sign that the poet will endure, his features (*vultus*) will be engraved in marble, a memorial that will depict his flowing hair (*comas*) wreathed with myrtle or laurel, foliage befitting his poetic vocation. Because of the care, indeed veneration, exhibited in these burial rites, the poet, so nobly and solicitously interred, will be entirely at peace (*at ego secura pace quiescam*). Fully satisfied that such care has been taken with his remains, the poet is then able to undergo an apotheosis to the celestial realms. There, "suffused with brilliant light" on his "serene face," he shall congratulate himself (*plaudam mihi*) on all he has accomplished, as he observes his body so well attended to in its final state of rest.

Such is the fantasy of one determined to create the circumstances by which his body will be appropriately preserved.[1] It is a fantasy, we might say, that deliberately eliminates any possibility of potential violation by refusing to acknowledge the presence of such destructiveness in the universe it envisions. Wholeness, safety, and soundness, accompanied by the rites of veneration, are the distinguishing characteristics of the fantasy of death and burial which culminates Milton's poem to Manso.[2] Such a consummation is devoutly to be wished.

But does the fantasy come true, and, if not, is the poet of the lines that project it aware of the extravagance of what they project? For the sake of argument, let us say he is. If so, we are tempted to observe that these lines mask a certain anxiety about what the future holds for the body they would have the world honor. Whatever the source of that anxiety, the lines themselves are ironically an invitation to disaster. With their appeal to wholeness, soundness, and indeed veneration, they reflect a self-assurance (*plaudam mihi*) that is almost certain to provoke the gods to give the poet his comeuppance. His determination to make certain that a violation of his sacred limbs does not occur is the surest way of guaranteeing that it does. As if this culminating moment in *Mansus* were written with a degree of prescience, the desire to protect one's body from harm leaves it subject to victimization by that which is most feared. At the very point this

1. Accounts of Milton's death and burial can be found, among other places, in *Life Records*, 5:98–100. According to William Riley Parker, "in early November, probably on Sunday, 8 November [1674], one month before his sixty-sixth birthday, John Milton died at night 'in a fit of gout, but with so little pain or emotion that the time of his expiring was not perceived by those in the room.'...On Thursday, 12 November, he was buried at St. Giles, Cripplegate, in the upper end of the chancel, at the right hand. Since his own father was also lying in this church, he 'had this elegy in common with the patriarchs and kings of Israel—that he was gathered to his people' " (*Milton Biography*, 1:640). See also the accounts in *Early Lives*, pp. 33, 76, 193. According to George Vertue, the eighteenth-century engraver, "there was a grave stone for Milton in St. Giles Cripplegate, where he was buried; but in repairing the church lately they have taken it away and it is lost, though there are people that know perfectly the spot of ground where it stood, which was shown to me. Upon that gravestone was cut only J. M." Vertue's comments are preserved in some manuscript jottings now in the British Library (MS Harleian 7003, ff. 1754–56, dated 12 August 1721, in a letter to Charles Christian). For background, see A. C. Howell, "Milton's Mortal Remains and Their Literary Echoes," *Ball State Teachers College Forum* 4 (1963), 17–30.

2. Milton exhibits similar concern for the bodies of others throughout his own elegies on such individuals as Richard Ridding, Lancelot Andrewes, Nicholas Felton, Dr. John Gostlin, Anne Phillips (the child of Milton's sister Anne), Jane Paulet, Edward King, and Charles Diodati. In these elegies one finds an attention to the ultimate disposition of the body and the treatment to which the body is subjected.

fear is repressed, it is most pronounced. The poet thereby becomes vulnerable to the actualization of that which he would at all costs avoid.

I offer this reading simply to appropriate *Mansus* as a frame to introduce a story. Doing so, I suggest that the culminating passage of *Mansus* is prescient in masking an anxiety about what the poet might well have known would be the opposite of that which he has fantasized. The passage portrays precisely what was not the ultimate fate of the poet's body. If one can give credence to the reports of what occurred during the century following Milton's burial, the nightmare of bodily violation visited upon Milton's corpse did in fact come about.

In all its gruesome detail, this violation is fully delineated in Philip Neve's *Narrative of the Disinterment of Milton's Coffin, in the Parish-Church of St. Giles, Cripplegate, on Wednesday, 4th of August, 1790; and of the Treatment of the Corpse, during that, and the following day* (London, 1790).[3] Assuming the validity of Neve's account, the poet's deepest anxieties were realized as a result of the disinterment of his body by the curious rabble. Almost as if in response to Milton's own extravagant desire for a monument (as recorded in *Mansus*), the disinterment was initially prompted by intentions that were noble enough: Milton's admirers wished to erect "a monument to the memory of *Milton*, and the par-

---

3. Unless otherwise noted, the following summary of the circumstances surrounding the disinterment and its aftermath is taken from Neve's second edition, which also contains a postscript written in response to those who attempt to call the accuracy of Neve's account into doubt, and from Howell, "Milton's Mortal Remains," pp. 19–20. For a collection of Neve's account; responses to the account in the St. James Chronicle, September 4–7, 1790, and in the *European Magazine* 28 (1790), 205–9; and Neve's postscript, see John Ashton, "Milton's Bones," in *Eighteenth Century Waifs: Essays on Social Life and Biography of the Eighteenth Century* (London: Hurst and Blackett, 1887), pp. 55–82. Neve's account and the incident that inspired it are discussed in *Gentleman's Magazine* 60 (1790), 837; *Critical Review* 70 (1790), 343; and *Monthly Review* 3 (1790), 350. See also Clement Mansfield Ingleby's study *Shakespeare's Bones. The Proposal to Disinter Them, Considered in Relation to Their Possible Bearing on His Portraiture: Illustrated by Instances of the Living to the Dead* (London: Trübner, 1838), which recounts cases of exhumation, including Cromwell, Milton, Swedenborg, and Schiller, among many others. For additional commentary, see Corrie Leonard Thompson, "John Milton's Bones," *Notes and Queries*, 7th series, 9 (1890), 361–64; John Walter Good, *Studies in the Milton Tradition* (Urbana: University of Illinois, 1913); Allen Walker Read, *PMLA* 45 (1930), 1050–68; and Howell, "Milton's Mortal Remains." Perhaps because of their distasteful nature, the events surrounding the disinterment receive scant (if any) attention in the biographies. In the nineteenth century, see Charles Symmons, *The Life of Milton* (London, 1810), pp. 569–70, n. 2; and Henry John Todd, *Some Account of the Life and Writings of John Milton*, 2d ed. (London, 1809), pp. 139–41. In the twentieth century, the disinterment receives little or no notice at all. See the brief descriptions in James Holly Hanford, *John Milton, Englishman* (New York: Crown, 1949), p. 249; and A. N. Wilson, *The Life of John Milton* (Oxford: Oxford University Press, 1983), p. 259. See also *Life Records*, 5:136.

ticular spot of his interment." To erect such a monument, however, they needed "incontestable evidence of its exact position" (p. 7). Accordingly, orders were given the workmen who were repairing the church at the time to search for the coffin. On August 3, 1790, a leaden coffin believed to be Milton's was discovered. The overseer, Mr. Thomas Strong, and the churchwarden, Mr. John Cole, were informed of the discovery. "They went immediately to the church; and, by help of a candle, proceeded under the common-council-men's pew, to the place where the coffin lay. It was in a chalky soil, and directly over a wooden coffin, supposed to be that of *Milton's* father" (p. 11). Strong and Cole cleaned and washed the coffin, which was very corroded, but they found no inscription specifically indicating that it contained Milton's body. Because no identifying marks were present, and out of respect for the contents of the coffin, they reintered the coffin without opening it.

That same evening, however, a "*merry meeting*" ensued at the home of one Fountain, a tavern keeper of Beech Lane. At this gathering were John Laming (a pawnbroker), Mr. Taylor (a Derbyshire surgeon), and William Ascough (a coffin maker), as well as Cole and Fountain. Because of the desire of the merrymakers to see the body, Cole was prevailed upon to open the coffin the following morning. With the assistance of Holmes, Ascough's apprentice, they managed to "cut open the top of the coffin, slantwise from the head, as low as the breast; so that, the top being doubled backward, they could see the corpse." Although Neve himself was not present at the time, he gathered the firsthand details from those who were: "Upon first view of the body, it appeared perfect, and completely enveloped in the shroud, which was of many folds: the ribs standing-up regularly." The dismemberment then followed. "Mr. *Fountain* told me," Neve writes, "that he pulled hard at the teeth, which resisted, until some one hit them a knock with a stone, when they easily came out. There were but five in the upper-jaw, which were all perfectly sound and white." They then shared the teeth among them. "Mr. *Laming* told me," Neve continues, "that he had at one time a mind to bring away the whole under-jaw with the teeth in it; he had it in his hand, but tossed it back again. Also, that he lifted up the head, and saw a great quantity of hair." They then poked the head with a stick to get a better look at it, after which they tore out clumps of the hair. There was a "sludge" at the bottom of the coffin that emitted "a nauseous smell" (pp. 15–21). The coffin was replaced but not covered. Now Elizabeth Grant the gravedigger took possession of it. According to Neve, she kept a tinderbox at hand to strike a light so that she might exhibit the remains to the curious. At first, she charged six pence but later lowered her price to three pence and finally to two. (Milton's body, in short, was marked down.) The workmen claimed a share of the profits and refused to allow anyone into the church who did not give them "the price of a pot of beer." Later, one Mr. Ellis, comedian of the Royalty-Theatre, visited the church and made off with some "souvenirs," including a rib. Other parts of the body that were removed were later sold off.

Responding to the dismemberment, Neve concludes with the following observation: "In recording a transaction, which will strike every liberal mind with horror and disgust, I cannot omit to declare, that I have procured those relics, which I possess, only in hope of bearing part in a pious and honorable restitution of all that has been taken: the sole atonement, which can now be made, to the violated rights of the dead" (pp. 32–33). Horrified by the desecration, Neve attempted to collect the stolen bones and hair. He interviewed all those suspected of making off with Milton's body parts, and he was able to purchase some of them back (including a tooth, some hair, and a few "small bones," possibly the ribs) for a few shillings. A sad friend of Milton's body, Neve, in the language of *Areopagitica*, imitated "the careful search that *Isis* made for the mangl'd body of *Osiris*," by going "up and down gathering up limb by limb still as . . . [he] could find them" (*YP*, 2:549). As with Osiris, so the Milton: desecration is followed by the search for the dismembered body of one who has fallen victim to a group of merrymakers. These merrymakers become in effect the followers of Bacchus come to life in order to perform their outrageous deed.

Assuming that Neve's account is accurate, we are made to conclude that the body in question is none other than Milton's. If the culminating lines of *Mansus* do suggest the fantasy of one determined to keep his body intact in the face of a possible violation, the fears this fantasy masks may very well have been realized in subsequent years. In its violated state, the torn body of the poet thereby becomes a sign of the destructive forces a culture is capable of unleashing. Focused upon the body of the dead poet as powerless victim, those forces are released to perform the utmost that mindless acts of violence are able to inflict. As much as the poet might see to the care of his body during his own time, it is nonetheless victimized by forces beyond his control after his interment. No friend is present here to keep the poet's body safe, no one to watch over it. The desire to memorialize it by way of a monument results ultimately in its desecration. If (as projected in *Mansus*) an apotheosis to the celestial realms does occur, Milton no doubt looks down not in serenity but in horror at his own mutilation.

With something of this idea in mind, an anonymous poet was shortly thereafter prompted to publish an elegy entitled "Milton's Ghost," in which the spirit of Milton returns to lament the terrible fate of his body: "With hands profane my tomb they now disclose, / My bones torn rudely from their grave deface, / And rob my ashes of their due repose" (ll. 30–32). "Are these mighty honours they bestow— / With sacrilegious hands my corpse to raise, / My bones expose a mercenary show?" the spirit asks. It concludes by placing a curse on those responsible for the desecration. The spirit charges the poet "To brand the wretches, who the dead invade / With shame and fell remorse be thine the care" (ll. 42–46). This is only one of several such literary responses.[4] They all reveal that Neve's horror and fascination were shared by others.

As might well be expected, several individuals were skeptical that the disinterred body was really Milton's. In a response to Neve's account, there appeared anonymous refutations such as "Reasons why it is impossible that the Coffin lately dug up in the Parish Church of St. Giles, Cripplegate, should contain the reliquies of MILTON."[5] According to the author of this refutation, counterarguments are available— some concerning the coffin and some the body. The coffin, argues the respondent, is unlikely to have been either the one in which Milton was

4. "Milton's Ghost: An Elegy" (1790) is reprinted in Good, *Studies*, pp. 101–2. This poem was printed in John Almon's *Asylum for Fugitive Pieces* (London, 1795). See also William Cowper's "Stanzas on the late Indecent Liberties taken with the Remains of the Great Milton— Anno 1790. August, 1790," cited in Howell, "Milton's Mortal Remains," p. 23. Cowper's poem is interesting in part because it adopts and translates Milton's lines on his burial in Mansus as its point of departure. Along with this poem, Howell also cites a letter by Cowper which, although later than the poem, addresses a similar theme. Dated February 24, 1793, the full text of the letter can be found in *The Letters and Prose Writings of William Cowper*, 5 vols., ed. James King and Charles Ryskamp (Oxford: Clarendon Press, 1979–86), 4:297–98. Compounding Cowper's reaction, the London literary scene was also abuzz with notice of the event. A cantata was to have been performed at one of the London theaters in which the following lines were to be sung by three antiquaries: "1ST ANTIQUARY: But where so long did linger / These relics rare and rum? 2ND ANTIQUARY: I filched the monarch's finger. 3RD ANTIQUARY: I stole the poet's thumb" (Howell, "In Milton's Remains," p. 22).

5. This responce appeared September, 1790, in the *St. James's Chronicle* and the *European Magazine* (see note 3).

buried or the one deposited where that which was unearthed was found; the body parts moreover, are not conformable to what is known of Milton's own body. Because of the quality and placement of the coffin and the nature of the body parts, the respondent argues that the remains belong to the "Smith family." Specifically, the respondent maintains that the body in question belongs not to a male but rather to a female member of the Smith family, no doubt one Elizabeth Smith, buried, according to an inscription on an adjacent wall, in 1665.[6]

In a postscript responding to these allegations, Neve argued at length that the body was male and Milton's. Neve first confirms the fact of a second disinterment, one in which an experienced surgeon, one Mr. Dyson, examined the corpse on August 17. Neve's account is as follows: "On Wednesday, September the 1st, I waited on Mr. *Dyson*, who was the gentleman sent for on the 17th to examine the corpse. I asked him simply, whether from what had then appeared before him, he judged it to be male or female? His answer was, that, having examined the pelvis and the skull, he judged the corpse to be that of a man. I asked what was the shape of the head? He said that the forehead was high and erect, though the skull was of that shape and flatness at the top, which . . . is observed to be common, and almost peculiar, to persons of very comprehensive intellects." Having established gender and intellectual capacity, the surgeon then proceeds to confirm that, in his professional opinion, the head was certainly that of Milton. "On a paper, which he shewed me, enclosing a bit of the hair," Neve observes, the surgeon "had written '*Milton's hair.*'" As further confirmation of Mr. Dyson's findings, yet another surgeon, one Mr. Taylor, and a gravedigger in the parish also judged the corpse to be that of a male. "With as little hesitation [the gravedigger] pronounced another, which had been thrown out of the ground in digging, to be that of a woman." On the part of the gravedigger, this determination, Neve suggests, is "obviously the result of practical, rather than of scientific knowledge; for, being asked his reasons, he

6. Ashton, "Milton's Bones," pp. 70–76. So the respondent argues: "There is reason to believe that the aforesaid remains are those of a young female . . . ; for the bones are delicate, the teeth small, slightly inserted in the jaw, and perfectly white, even, and sound. From the corroded state of the pelvis, nothing could, with certainty, be inferred; nor would the surgeon already mentioned pronounce *absolutely* on the sex of the deceased" (pp. 71–72). According to Ingleby, "Mr. George Steevens, the great editor of Shakespeare . . . , satisfied himself that the corpse [putatively Milton's] was that of a woman of fewer years than Milton" (p. 19).

could give none, but that observation had taught him to distinguish such subjects." Practical knowledge of this sort, argues Neve, "is not to be too hastily rejected.... To any one acquainted with those who are eminently skilled in judging of the genuineness of ancient coins, it will be perfectly intelligible" (pp. 45–48).

Whatever credence one wishes to bestow upon Neve's conclusions, it is significant that the identity of the body is only putatively Milton's. The trace of its actualization in the exhumed and torn remains of what was once the true Miltonic body is all but erased by those who, like the merrymakers that dismembered it in the first place, are determined to appropriate it, to authenticate it, to make it theirs. Its parts now belong to them. These are the exhumers of that which has been exhumed: the surgeons, the gravediggers, the critics. In their act of authentication, they are bound to place an inscription on the coffin that contains its mangled remains. They are bound to bestow upon it a name for the sake of memorializing it properly. The bestowal of this name eventuates in the bestowal of a gender. Is that gender male? Or is it female? If male, is the doubly exhumed body that of "John Milton" or is it that of one "Elizabeth Smith"? The metaphysics of such speculation invites further reflection. If the gender is indeed female and the body that of Elizabeth Smith (an appropriately nondescript surname), is she after all Milton's alter-ego, his bogey?[7] The act of (re)exhumation for the sake of authenticating results in a metaphysics of (re)embodiment, a (re)presenting of Milton as gendered other. The poor, dismembered corpse of the exhumed, finally unidentified body is made to shift genders just as it shifts identities. Such, as I argue in this book is as crucial to the act of configuring Milton as the fact of dismemberment itself.

Whether or not the body exhumed was Milton's, the fact of its disinterment, the violence perpetrated upon it, and, finally, the debate

---

7. The word "bogey" alludes to Virginia Woolf's use of the term in *A Room of One's Own* (1929; San Diego: Harcourt Brace Jovanovich, 1989). The word is used in the context of Woolf's discussion of Shakespeare's "sister": "If we look past Milton's bogey... the dead poet who was Shakespeare's sister will put on the body which she has so often laid down. Drawing her life from the lives of the unknown who were her forerunners, as her brother did before his, she will be born" (pp. 113–14). The same, I would argue, can be said of Milton. See "Milton's Bogey: Patriarchal Poetry and Women Readers," in Sandra M. Gilbert and Susan Gubar, *The Madwoman in the Attic: The Woman Writer and the Nineteenth-Century Literary Imagination* (New Haven: Yale University Press, 1979), pp. 187–212. For an astute examination of the premises underlying "Milton's Bogey," see Joseph Wittreich, *Feminist Milton* (Ithaca: Cornell University Press, 1987).

over its gender raise significant issues bearing upon the subject of this book. I do not wish for a moment to suggest that that subject has anything to do with the actual afterlife of Milton's body. I simply invoke the postburial circumstances of that body to devise a metaphor, indeed, a poetics, for raising the issues of violence and gender that are the primary concerns of my enterprise. At the forefront of those concerns is Milton's body during the course of his life and the world his body comes to inhabit in his works. In my exploration of this theme, I do not wish simply to venture another theory about Milton's blindness, his gout, or his other putative ailments. As Kester Svendsen long ago pointed out, there is already a surfeit of that sort of analysis. To the great relief of the reader, I am not about to endorse the Mutschmannian madness inclined to see in the poet the body of one who bears the discreet marks of the albino.[8] I leave that sort of endeavor for others.

What I do explore in some depth is a pervasive concern in Milton's thinking with his own body: what constitutes it, how it appears to others, how it is to be preserved, what the forces are that threaten to undo it, and how those forces are to be overcome. Specifically, I argue that underlying Milton's sensibility is an anxiety about the body faced with the horrifying prospect of mutilation and dismemberment, an anxiety that brings to bear in his own time what might have been realized in the century after his death. This is an anxiety deeply rooted in the Miltonic psyche, one intimately tied to Milton's sense of his own sexuality, his notion of gendered self, and the culture out of which his selfhood emerges.

Crucial to these concerns is the personality of Milton, as strong as any personality the culture of his times could have produced.[9] Despite its strengths (perhaps because of them), this personality finds itself constantly besieged, constantly threatened, constantly under attack. Because of the extent to which the body in Miltonic terms is to be seen as a manifestation of self, the fate of one finds its correspondence in the fate of the other. To destroy the one is to destroy the other: to preserve the one is to preserve the other. Milton's need to keep his body whole and sound in the face of an alien world that threatens to undo it, to mutilate and dismember it, is the obverse of

8. I refer to Heinrich Mutschmann, *The Secret of John Milton* (1925; Folcroft, Pa.: Folcroft Press, 1969).

9. The term "strong" has been made current by Harold Bloom; among his many books, see in particular *The Anxiety of Influence* (New York: Oxford University Press, 1973). My use of the term is essentially psychological.

an equal need to preserve the self, to ballast it, against the potential encroachments of an ever-threatening Chaos "blustring round."[10]

As a result of those encroachments, the body is victimized, rent asunder beyond all recognition. So decimated, the body is confronted with the devastating prospect of attempting to renew itself, to generate a new form, a new configuration, from the violence that has destroyed it. Reborn from a violence that is at once destructive but potentially regenerative, this new form would in fact be made stronger by the forces Chaos has unleashed. Such, as I argue, is the essential paradox inherent not only in the Miltonic view of self but in the nature of violence as a cultural phenomenon.

Particularly in the criticism of *Paradise Lost*, this theme has been asserted numerous times. It has, one might suggest, assumed the status of a commonplace. Although I have written about the theme at length, I defer to Regina M. Schwartz, whose superb analysis of Milton's diffuse epic sums up the situation nicely: "Only after we meet the fallen angels in Books I and II do we hear Uriel's account of creation in Book III; the war in heaven and fall of the rebel host in Book VI is followed by Raphael's creation account in Book VII; and the fall of Adam and Eve in Books IX and X is followed by Michael's disclosure of the new creation in the final books of the poem."[11] To be sure, re-creation is at the heart of Milton's thought. But in the "re-membering" of the body I project, I am concerned with a darker, more unsettling side of Milton's personality. The struggle to preserve the body in its wholeness and soundness, on the one hand, and the attempt to re-configure it once it has been dismembered, on the other, are ongoing processes that we would like to think capable of ultimate resolution but perhaps remain unresolved or at best only occasionally resolved as the Miltonic anxiety over mutilation and dismemberment continues to assert and reassert itself throughout his works.

10. The reference here is to *Paradise Lost* 3.424–25.
11. Regina Schwartz, *Remembering and Repeating: Biblical Creation in "Paradise Lost"* (Cambridge: Cambridge University Press, 1988), pp. 2–3. See also Michael Lieb, *The Dialectics of Creation: Patterns of Birth and Regeneration in "Paradise Lost"* (Amherst: University of Massachusetts Press, 1970), as well as John T. Shawcross, *With Mortal Voice: The Creation of "Paradise Lost"* (Lexington: University of Kentucky Press, 1982), esp. pp. 1–20.

Part I

RENDING THE BODY

1

The Slaughter of the Saints

I

To explore the presence of bodily mutilation and dismemberment in Milton's works, we must first attempt to delineate a theory of violence. As cultural historians appear to concur, any attempt to delineate such a theory is to recognize the primacy of violence as a religious category. In his seminal study, René Girard observes that "violence is the heart and secret soul of the sacred." The sacred for Girard consists of all those forces whose power over the individual increases in proportion to one's effort to master them. These forces refuse to be contained: the more one attempts to keep them in check, the more they are unleashed. "The very weapons used to combat violence are turned against their users. Violence is like a raging fire that feeds on the very objects intended to smother its flames." Locating violence first at the elemental level in such events as tempest, fire, and earthquake, Girard moves to the human level, where violence in its various forms manifests itself as "a part of all the other outside forces that threaten mankind."[1]

If this form of violence is essentially negative, Girard sees another

1. René Girard, *Violence and the Sacred*, trans. Patrick Gregory (Baltimore: Johns Hopkins University Press, 1977), p. 31.

side to it that is essentially positive: "At times violence appears to man in its most terrifying aspect, wantonly sowing chaos and destruction; at other times it appears in the guise of peacemaker, graciously distributing the fruits of sacrifice."[2] This is what Gerard calls "generative violence." Restorative in nature, generative violence is that through which a surrogate victim is sacrificed as a means of terminating "the vicious and destructive cycle of violence" and initiating a "constructive cycle" that protects the community from destructive violence and allows culture to flourish. If such is the case, then generative violence may be seen as the source of renewed order in society. This idea, observes Girard, is affirmed by the many etiological myths that recount the murder of one mythological character by other mythological characters. Such an event is conceived as the origin of cultural order and stability.[3]

In the universe of violence that expresses itself in both destructive and generative terms, that which assumes utmost prominence is mankind's penchant for bodily mutilation and dismemberment. Such a penchant appears to be fundamental not only to the individual psyche but to the notion of violence as a religious category. In either case, bodily mutilation and dismemberment is, as Girard makes clear, of seminal importance to the history of culture. In the realm of Greek mythical thought, this idea is designated *sparagmos*, and its principal inspiration appears to spring from the figure of Dionysus.[4] Known as *anthroporraistes*, "render of men," Dionysus embodies a spirit of violence reflected both in the festivals that commemorate this deity and in the literature through which the concept of sparagmos assumes dramatic form.[5] Thus, in the cult sacrifices made to Dionysus, sparagmos is carried out in a ritual manner, as the *pharmakos*, or sacrificial victim (either human or beast), is torn apart (and at times even devoured) by the worshipers.[6] These are normally women (the Maenads)

2. Girard, *Violence and the Sacred*, p. 37.
3. Girard, *Violence and the Sacred*, p. 93.
4. Girard, *Violence and the Sacred*, pp. 131, 119–42. See *Thesaurus Graecae Linguae*, 9 vols. comp. H. Stephanus (Graz: Akademische Druck-U. Verlagsanstalt, 1954), s.v. "sparagmos." (This is a reproduction of the 1572 *Thesaurus* of Stephanus [Estienne].) See also *A Greek-English Lexicon*, comp. Henry George Liddell and Robert Scott (Oxford: Clarendon Press, 1968), s.v. "sparagma."
5. Walter F. Otto, *Dionysus, Myth, and Cult*, trans. Robert B. Palmer (Bloomington: Indiana University Press, 1965), pp. 103–9.
6. The rending that underlies sparagmos, then, finds its counterpart in the cannabalism that underlies *omophagia*. Both are aspects of the frenzy associated with Dionysus. So E. R.

seized with the madness of Dionysus. In its most brutal form, this savagery possesses mothers, who tear apart and devour the flesh of their infants. Such is a reflection of Dionysus's own history, which involved the danger he faced as a newborn child who would have been torn to pieces by his fostermothers, the daughters of Lamos, had he not been snatched away by Hermes and placed in the care of Ino. In other versions of the myth, Dionysus is in fact torn to pieces by the Titans or as the result of Hera's orders. In these versions, however, Dionysus is invariably resurrected, a fact commemorated in those seasonal festivals that celebrate the return of growth and vegetation.[7] A salient feature of those festivals, once again, is the ritual sparagmos undertaken to promote the coming of the new year. Whatever form this sparagmos assumes, the brutality attendant upon the impulse to bodily mutilation and dismemberment is ever present. As Walter F. Otto suggests, "the same brutality speaks to us out of the cult as out of the myth. We feel its presence clearly; the infinity which the ecstasy of life inhabits threatens with the ecstasy of destruction everyone who approaches it."[8] This is the essence of Dionysian frenzy.

Complementing the cultural and mythic perspective represented by René Girard is what might be called the psychogenetic perspective of Carl Gustav Jung. From this perspective, sparagmos is seen to be of such fundamental importance that it assumes the status of an archetype. For Jung, sparagmos is a symbol of the means by which the unconscious self undergoes the process of individuation in its quest for wholeness. Although initially destructive, this is essentially a creative process, one in which the unconscious self is subjected to a kind of dismemberment in preparation for its reintegration in the world of consciousness. This Jung calls the "repristination or apocatastasis" of the self. "Ancient philosophy," observes Jung, "paralleled this idea with the legend of the dismembered Dionysus, who as creator is the *ameristos* (undivided) *nous*, and, as the creature, the *memerismenos* (divided) *nous*." As the *memerismenos nous*, Dionysus is "distributed

---

Dodds comments in the Introduction to his edition of Euripides' *Bacchae* (2d ed.; Oxford: Clarendon Press, 1960): "The culminating act of the Dionysiac winter dance was the tearing to pieces, and eating raw, of an animal body, *sparagmos* and *omophagia*. Symbolically, this is the day when the infant Dionysus was himself torn to pieces and devoured" (pp. xvi–xvii).

7. Otto, *Dionysus*, p. 107. For a a detailed account of the myths surrounding the dismemberment of Dionysus, see Sir James Frazer, *The Golden Bough: A Study in Magic and Religion*, 12 vols., 3d ed. (New York: Macmillan, 1935), 7:12–16.

8. Otto, *Dionysus*, p. 106.

throughout the whole of nature," and "just as Zeus once devoured the throbbing heart of the god, so his worshippers tore wold animals to pieces in order to reintegrate his dismembered spirit." From the psychological point of view, this is "the integration of the self through conscious assimilation of the split-off contents." It is a "self-recollection" that entails "a gathering together of the self." Such is the "urge to individuation," an urge founded upon the potentially generative implications of sparagmos.[9]

As the observations of Girard and Jung suggest, then, violence is essentially paradoxical. Destructive at its core, it is capable of being transformed into a source of renewal and stability, indeed, into a means of attaining a new level of harmony and order. As such, destructive violence has the potential for becoming generative violence in a dialectic through which the annihilative and the restorative may be seen as counterbalancing and fostering each other. At the heart of this dialectic is the all-important notion of sparagmos.

II

The extent to which bodily mutilation is fundamental to the Miltonic point of view may be seen in an analysis of its enactment in both his poetry and prose. There, one discovers the emergence of what might be called a "sparagmatic mentality" so pervasive that its presence underlies every aspect of his thinking and personality. Sparagmos is at the heart not only of Milton's conduct as a writer but of the way he views himself in relation to the world. Its impact, in short, is inescapable. Infusing itself into his outlook as a poet, it makes itself felt everywhere in his vocation as a polemicist. For Milton, it becomes an experience felt on his pulses and formulated and reformulated in numerous ways throughout his long career. It is possible here to suggest only some of the main lines of its influence, but these should be sufficient to indicate how the culture of violence that finds its antecedents in the kind of milieu established above is discernible in his writings.

Because it is so immediately germane to the present discussion,

9. Carl G. Jung, "Transformation Symbolism in the Mass," in *Psychology and Religion: West and East,* quoted from *The Collected Works of Carl Gustav Jung,* 20 vols., ed. Sir Herbert Read et al., Bollingen Series 20, 2d ed. (New York: Pantheon Books, 1953–79), 9:264–65.

Milton's account of the dismemberment of Truth in *Areopagitica* serves as an appropriate point of departure. A locus classicus of Milton's sparagmatic mentality, this account becomes a means of moving to other related considerations. As is well known, Milton's account finds its antecedent in Plutarch's *Moralia.*[10] There, Plutarch allegorizes the dismemberment of Osiris by associating it with the rending of the body of Truth (*aletheia*). In that act of sparagmos, Typhon (a symbol of pride, *typho*) in effect "tears to pieces and scatters to the winds the sacred writings," which Isis (symbol of knowledge, *oida*) "collects and puts together and gives into the keeping of those that are initiated into the holy rites" (5:9).[11] What in Typhon begins as destructive violence becomes in Isis a means of regeneration. Searching for the limbs of Osiris, whose bodily form she would restore, Isis performs the highest possible service. Hers is as much a religious as a philosophical act. Plutarch makes it clear that Osiris is to be identified with Dionysus: the fate of each is comparable (5:69). That fate is finally transformative. The destructive violence of sparagmos eventuates in renewal.

Drawing in *Areopagitica* upon the Plutarchan portrayal of the myth of Isis and Osiris, Milton makes it a centerpiece of his argument on behalf of the liberty of unlicensed printing:

> Truth indeed came once into the world with her divine Master, and was a perfect shape most glorious to look on: but when he ascended, and his Apostles after him were laid asleep, then strait arose a wicked race of deceivers, who as that story goes of the *Aegyptian Typhon* with his conspirators, how they dealt with the good *Osiris*, took the virgin Truth, hewd her lovely form into a thousand peeces, and scatter'd them to the four winds. From that time ever since, the sad friends of Truth, such as durst appear, imitating the carefull search that *Isis* made for the mangl'd body of *Osiris*, went up and down gathering up limb by limb still as they could find them. We have not found them all, Lords and Commons, nor ever shall doe, till her Masters second comming; he shall bring together every joynt and member, and shall mould them into an immortall feature of loveliness and perfection. (*YP*, 2:549) *

10. References are to *Plutarch's Moralia*, 15 vols., trans. Frank Cole Babbit (Harvard: Cambridge University Press, 1957).

11. For Typhon as a symbol of pride and Isis as a symbol of knowledge, see the notes to the *Moralia*, 5:8–9.

* Milton p 263

Milton's version of the myth contextualizes it in Christocentric terms. Drawing upon what is already a troping of the Osiris myth in Plutarch's act of allegoresis, Milton ventures his own layering. What results is a convergence and indeed an interlocution of myths. As in Plutarch, sparagmos operates at the base level of the Isis-Osiris myth; it is allegorized into the fable of Truth; and, finally, it is given a Christocentric setting through the reference to the divine master and the events surrounding his advent and ministry in this life and beyond. All this, in turn, is projected first into apostolic history, next into Reformation history, and finally into apocalyptic history. This ultimate event is delineated in the context of the attempt of the sad friends of Truth to reconstitute the "mangl'd body of *Osiris*" by "gathering up limb by limb still as they could find them."[12]

From the perspective of the Isis-Osiris myth and its allegorical reinterpretation into the fable of Truth, Milton emphasizes in particular the "shape" of Truth. This is a figure of perfection, the "inward" beauty of which is manifested in its "outward" form. One recalls Milton's depiction of the figure of Discipline in the *Reason of Church-Government*: "If any visible shape can be given to divine things," Discipline is "the very visible shape and image of vertue, whereby she is not only seene in the regular gestures and motions of her heavenly paces as she walkes, but also makes the harmony of her voice audible to mortall eares" (*YP*, 1:751–52). For Milton, she is clearly a transcendent figure of great beauty and grace.

The same may be said of Truth: her physical presence is that of supreme loveliness and perfection. To mutilate and dismember her "lovely form" amounts accordingly to a desecration. It is a rape of the most heinous sort. With the tearing and mangling of her body in this manner, the sad friends of Truth attempt to recreate her original beauty, to restore her purity. Theirs is as much a devotional, indeed religious act as it is an aesthetic one. In this respect, the two (that is, the religious and the aesthetic) are synonymous for Milton, who views himself as a votary engaged in the act of worship, as he performs his "obsequies to the torn body of...[his] martyr'd Saint" (*YP*, 2:549–50), that virgin of virgins who has been so brutally violated by the

---

12. Milton's allegoresis upon Plutarch's allegoresis of the Isis-Osiris myth finds its antecedent in that of Clement of Alexandria, who conceives the dismemberment of truth through the corresponding myth of the sparagmos of Pentheus by the Bacchantes; see *The Stromata* (1.13).

brutal and wicked race of deceivers. Such is Milton's allegoresis upon Plutarch's allegoresis of the Isis-Osiris myth.

Milton's allegoresis assumes even greater complexity, moreover, if one considers that the convergence and interlocution of myths enacted in his portrayal of Truth involves an implicit androgyny. By means of that androgyny, the male-female relationship between the divine master and his manifestation in that being through which he disseminates his divinity overlaps. This overlapping makes itself apparent from the very outset of Milton's sparagmatic portrayal. Although we may immediately assume that the perfect shape to which Milton initially alludes is Truth in all her female beauty, the reference also suggests the master of whom she is a manifestation. His maleness is forever a part of her presence, just as her femaleness is forever a part of his presence. The blurring, indeed interchangeableness, of gender distinctions makes itself apparent in the allegoresis of the Miltonic account. If Milton is consistent with Plutarch in the association of the fate of Osiris with the fate of *aletheia*, the Miltonic portrayal is conceived in a manner that invites an androgynous reading of the violence perpetrated upon the female body of Truth.[13] Such a reading insists upon the sparagmos endured by Osiris as an event that is forever kept in the foreground of the Miltonic account. It is both Osiris and the fate of Osiris that cause our understanding of the dismemberment of Truth to move between the femaleness of Truth and the maleness of the divine body enunciated in the reference to the master of whom Truth is a manifestation.

The dynamic implicit in that movement is articulated in the syntax through which the sparagmos of Truth is enacted. The bare outlines of that enactment are simple enough: a wicked race of deceivers "took the virgin Truth, hewd her lovely form into a thousand peeces, and scatter'd them to the four winds." The articulation of the enactment, in contrast, is exceedingly complex. Introduced through a dependent clause, the sparagmos of Truth is immediately conceived in junction with (in fact, intervolved with) the fate of Osiris ("a wicked race of deceivers, who as that story goes of the Aegyptian Typhon with his conspirators, how they dealt with the good Osiris"): "who" yields to "as," which yields to "of," which yields to "how," which yields to "with,"

---

13. In his *Adversus Haereses* (1.14.2–4), Irenaeus portrays the body of Truth (Aletheia) as both male and female.

which moves us imperceptibly from the female body of Truth to the male body of Osiris. Taking up the momentum of this movement, the sentence that follows places us squarely within the milieu of Osiris, whose experience assumes that of the foreground, as tenor becomes vehicle and vehicle tenor: "From that time ever since, the sad friends of Truth, such as durst appear, imitating the carefull search that *Isis* made for the mangl'd body of *Osiris*, went up and down gathering up limb by limb still as they could find them." The effect is to suggest the blurring of gender distinctions: female becomes male, male female. Sparagmos comes to exist in a world of androgyny, an idea that ironically returns us to the dismemberment of Pentheus, whom Dionysus attires in the clothing of a woman in preparation for the fate that befalls him. In the Miltonic account, one might suggest that the opposite occurs: the female is attired as male. Truth assumes the form of Osiris, whose myth exists in the foreground of the sparagmos Milton delineates.

Recalling Plutarch's account of this event, it is perhaps significant to note that the attempt to reassemble the body of Osiris is successful except for the inability of Isis to find one part: the phallus. Once that part was tossed in the river, Plutarch informs us, fish devoured it. To commemorate the phallus, Isis made a replica of it and consecrated it, "in honour of which the Egyptians even at the present day celebrate a festival" (5:47). Although Milton makes no reference to the lost phallus, his conviction that we shall never find all the lost members of Truth until the Second Coming speaks as much to the maleness represented by Osiris as it does to the femaleness represented by Truth. In either case, the master "shall bring together every joynt and member, and shall mould them into an immortall feature of loveliness and perfection." Keeping in mind that one member tossed in the river and devoured by fish, we might suggest that the reinstallation of the phallus on the androgynous figure represented by Truth-Osiris is an attestation to the ability of violence ultimately to assume generative form. Milton's androgyne is a figure in whom the ritualized pursuit of the lost members (particularly that member which is the very source of renewal) is confirmation of not only the beauty but the generative power of the repristinated body. In our exploration of the contexts that help to define this body, we are made aware of precisely how complex the convergence and interlocution of myths can become in the allegoresis that underlies Milton's account of the dismemberment and ultimate apocatastasis of Truth.

Underscoring that allegoresis, Christocentrism is all-important. This Christocentrism moves Milton's sparagmatic myth first into the context of Jesus' advent and ministry and then into those events (apostolic history, Reformation history, apocalyptic history) following upon his death, resurrection, and ascension. As Milton makes clear in his portrayal of this succession of events, human history is sparagmatic history. With Jesus' advent and the fulfillment of his ministry as preface and with his apostles "laid asleep," the brutality of destructive violence follows. History destroys. The only way to reclaim it, that is, to transform destructive violence into generative violence, is to make sparagmos meaningful through a reconstituting of the form of Truth as pharmakos. Such is the function of Reformation history: its purpose is to re-form. As a result of this reformative process, that which has been destroyed is given new life.

This idea had already been sounded earlier in Milton's tract in his portrayal of books as objects imbued with a life of their own. Containing "a potencie of life in them to be as active as that soule was whose progeny they are," they have the potential for dynamic renewal. In a reference that anticipates his account of the dismemberment and eventual repristination of Truth, Milton confirms his faith in this generative potential by alluding to the legend of Cadmus. Arguing on behalf of the potency with which books are imbued, Milton compares that potency to the generative power released through the act of sowing "those fabulous Dragons teeth." "Being sown up and down," these teeth, like the ideas they symbolize, "may chance to spring up armed men" (*YP*, 2:492).[14] The allusion recalls the third book of Ovid's *Metamorphoses*.[15] There, it is recounted how Cadmus slays the serpent responsible for the slaying of his own men. Having destroyed the serpent, Cadmus is then commanded by Minerva "To plow the earth, to sow the teeth of the serpent / Which would become the seed

14. For a discussion of the political dimensions of this idea, see Michael Wilding, *Dragons Teeth: Literature in the English Revolution* (Oxford: Oxford University Press, 1987).

15. References in my text are to Ovid, *Metamorphoses*, trans. Rolfe Humphries (Bloomington: Indiana University Press, 1955). This translation is used in conjunction with the Latin text and translation in the *Metamorphoses* of Ovid, 2 vols., trans. Frank Justus Miller (Cambridge: Harvard University Press, 1976). Citations of the Latin in my text are to this edition.

of future people." With the sowing of the "mortal seed," we are told, "The covered earth broke open, and the clods / Began to stir, and first the points of spears / Rose from the ground, then colored plumes, and helmets, / Shoulders of men, and chests, arms full of weapons, / A very harvest of the shields of warriors" (3.101–9).

For Milton, this myth of sowing and regeneration underscores his argument that, as vital things, books, like the authors who create them, must be accorded utmost respect, even reverence; in them resides that Truth which will be otherwise destroyed if not allowed to flourish. Containing "the pretious life-blood of a master spirit, imbalm'd and treasur'd up on purpose to a life beyond life," books may be subject to the same kinds of persecutions as human beings (*YP*, 2:492–93). Drawing upon his knowledge of the sufferings endured by those committed to the fostering of Truth, Milton moves from the tribulations imposed upon the authors of books to the books themselves. "We should be wary," he admonishes, "what persecution we raise against the living labours of publick men, how we spill that season'd life of man preserv'd and stor'd up in Books; since we see a kinde of homicide may be thus committed, sometimes a martyrdome, and if it extend to the whole impression, a kinde of massacre" (*YP*, 2:493). As a result of such persecutions, books will be deprived of their ability to propagate. They will be denied the opportunity to fulfill their destiny of sowing ideas that will spring up like "Dragons teeth."

Underlying Milton's application of the language of suffering to books as the embodiment of that life and potency infused in their creators is an awareness of the nature of the persecutions the seekers after Truth were in fact bound to endure in their attempts to advance her cause. The very language of the licensing orders to which *Areopagitica* responds makes clear the extent to which Milton's allegoresis is founded upon actual circumstance. One need only examine the Star Chamber Decree of 1637 and the Licensing Order of 1643 to verify this fact. According to the Star Chamber Decree, any person who is responsible for the publication of books that violate the decree shall, among other censures, "*suffer such correction*, and *severe punishment*, either by Fine, imprisonment, or *other corporall punishment* ... as shall be thought fit to be inflicted on him" (*YP*, 2:793; italics mine). Elaborating still further, the Licensing Order not only confirms the harshness of the Star Chamber Decree but warns that the implements of publication ("printing Presses Letters, together with the Nut, Spindle, and other materialls") will be "defaced and made unserviceable according to Ancient Custom." In the case of opposition of search and seizure, the authorities are empowered "to break open Doores and Locks" (*YP*, 2:798–99).

What is so striking about the official documents themselves is the *violence* they portend against the offenders. This is a violence of a particularly physical sort. At its center, we discover not merely the implements of publication and the books and pamphlets these implements produce. Of equal importance are the bodies of those involved in the violation.

This idea strikes at the heart of the historical subtext of Milton's allegoresis. Envisioning the multitude of tribulations the violated figure of Truth must undergo, Milton looks upon the "torn body" of the "martyr'd Saint" as a symbol of the travails those who suffer for Truth's sake encounter in their homage to her sacred body. The narrative of the plight of Truth and her votaries encodes a narrative of the sufferings experienced by the martyrs to its cause during Milton's own time. As a subtext of Milton's allegoresis, the fact of actual mutilations extends the interlocution of myths into the realm of historical enactment. Extant accounts of such enactment constitute a martyrology, the details of which have been minutely and dramatically recorded. Occurring within the recent memory of the composition of *Areopagitica* and yet recalling an earlier period of tyranny from which those addressed in Milton's tract would wish to distance themselves, the sufferings endured by Henry Burton, John Bastwick, and William Prynne, among others, are a case in point.[16]

Any attempt to invoke the tribulations of Burton, Bastwick, and Prynne (or any other contemporary tribulations, for that matter) must be immediately qualified by the realization that Milton's portrayal of the sparagmos of Truth in *Areopagitica* defies localization. In the case of Prynne, such localization is especially problematic because of the extremely ambivalent view Milton held of Prynne as a reformer. This "marginal" figure is one in whose sufferings Milton himself might be

---

16. The mutilations of Burton, Bastwick, and Prynne on June 30, 1637, were witnessed by crowds assembled to view the event. The possible association of the mutilations with the dismemberment of Truth in *Areopagitica* has already been suggested by Michael Wilding, "Milton's *Areopagitica*: Liberty for the Sects," *Prose Studies* 9 (1986), esp. pp. 12–13. See also *YP*, 1:39–45. In " 'Trembling Ears': The Historical Moment of *Lycidas*," *Journal of Medieval and Renaissance Studies* 21 (1991), 59–81, John Leonard associates the mutilations recounted here with the imagery of bodily violence and mutilation in Milton's pastoral elegy.

said to have participated through ridicule, a fact that Milton sought
to erase from memory but that remains all the more vivid because of
that attempt at erasure.[17] With these qualifications in mind, I nonetheless adopt the tribulations of Burton, Bastwick, and Prynne as a
means of offering a backdrop for Milton's sparagmatic portrayal in
Areopagitica. To recall the mutilations endured by these reformers is
to provide a renewed sense of the sparagmatic culture from which
the Miltonic portrayal of the dismemberment of Truth arose and out
of which the "re-formation" of the divine body was ultimately to be
made possible.

As a result of the censure of the Star Chamber in 1637, Burton,
Bastwick, and Prynne were condemned to endure terrible torture.
During the trial, this torture was justified by Archbishop Laud himself,
whose justification is appropriately and ironically couched in the language of sparagmos. The libelous writings of these three, Laud declares, have amounted to a "tearing and rending" of the reputations
of those gentle and generous individuals made to suffer the re-
proaches of their enemies. Accordingly, Laud implies, this mutilation

17. See William B. Hunter's entry on Prynne in *Milton Encyclopedia*, s.v. Although Milton
as a temporary Calvinist may have welcomed Prynne as an ally in 1642, by 1644 the *Doctrine
and Discipline of Divorce* had occasioned public outrage, and Milton's disillusionment with the
Presbyterians had occurred. In *Twelve Considerable Serious Questions touching Church Government*
(1644), Prynne attacked Milton's book by claiming that Independency supported "divorce at
pleasure." This, Milton immediately answered in the first paragraph of Colasterion. Acknowledging Prynne "as one above others who hath suffer'd much and long in the defence
of Truth" at the very point of taking him to task for his views, Milton demonstrated both a
responsiveness to his tribulations and a willingness (at least initially) to associate him with the
cause of Truth (*YP,* 2:723). Although Prynne was elected to Parliament in 1948, he was
immediately removed by Colonel Pride. He responded by writing a series of pamphlets
attacking the Army, Commonwealth, and later the Protectorate. Toward the end, he supported the cause of Charles II. As one of the members of the Long Parliament who reassembled shortly before the Restoration, Prynne endorsed the effort to punish the supporters
of the Interregnum (Hunter, s.v.). As secretary of the council, Milton was ordered to search
Prynne's rooms at Lincoln's Inn (*Milton Biography,* 1:377). Milton's attitude toward Prynne,
however, remained ambivalent. As late as *Considerations Touching the Likeliest Means to Remove
Hirelings out of the Church* (1659), Milton took Prynne to task for his views but also referred
to him as "a fierce reformer once" (*YP,* 7:293–94). Milton's ambivalence toward the mutilation
is discernible in the changes he made in his sonnet "On the Forcers of Conscience," esp. ll.
15–17: "That so the Parliament / May with their wholsom and preventive sheares / Clip your
Phylacteries though bauk your eares." The original version of these lines in the Trinity
College Manuscript is brutally specific: "Clip ye as close as marginal P——'s ears" (*Facsimile,*
1:454–55). Milton participates poetically in the defacement of Prynne and then, as it were,
defaces his own lines. As an indication of Milton's evolving responses toward the fact of
Prynne's mutilation, the revision is significant. See Annabel Patterson's analysis of Milton's
revision, as well as her discussion of *Areopagitica,* in *Censorship and Interpretation: The Conditions
of Writing and Reading in Early Modern England* (Madison: University of Wisconsin Press,
1984), pp. 111–19, 178.

of clerical reputation as the result of an enforced schism deserves to be met with the kind of bodily schism or rending the perpetrators of abusive acts visit upon their victims.[18] Literalizing metaphor, the Star Chamber obviously took Laud at his word.

In this respect, the mutilations endured by William Prynne are illustrative. Having already sustained the cropping of his ears for earlier offences, Prynne was to suffer the removal of whatever yet remained of his ears, as well as the branding on each cheek with the letters s.l. for "Seditious Libeller." The account of his sufferings may be looked upon as a drama of sparagmos endured by one who viewed himself as a martyr in the cause of liberty:

> Now the Executioner being come, to seare him and cut off his eares, Mr. Prynne spake these words to him: Come friend, Come, burne mee, cut mee, I feare it not. I have learned to feare the fire of Hell, and not what man can doe unto mee: Come seare mee, seare mee, I shall beare in my body the markes of the Lord Iesus: Which the bloody Executioner performed with extraordinary cruelty, heating his Iron twice to burne one Cheeke: And cut one of his eares so close, that hee cut off a peice of his Cheeke. At which exquisit torture hee never mooved with his body, or so much as changed his countenance, even to the astonishment of all the beholders. And uttering (as soone as the Executioner had done) this heavenly sentence: *The more I am beate downe, the more I am lift up.*[19]

The account is interesting for several reasons. Gruesome in its details, it enacts a kind of hagiographic drama in which torture is ritualized and its principal actors (the victim and the executioner) admirably perform their respective roles. The stage is set; the audience looks on; the executioner approaches, fulfills his mission in as cruel, un-

---

18. In *A Complete Collection of State Trials and Proceedings for High Treason and Other Crimes and Misdemeanors from the Earliest Period to the Year 1783*, 21 vols., comp. Thomas Bayley Howell (London: Longman, 1816–26), 3:725–45. An account of the trial in its entirety may be found at 3:711–70; see also in this volume the accounts of the trials of others accused of seditious writings, including the Earl of Bedford, the Earl of Clare, the Earl of Somerset, Sir Robert Cotton, and John Selden.

19. *A Briefe Relation of certain speciall and most materiall passages, and speeches in the Starre-Chamber, occasioned and delivered Iune the 14th 1637, at the censure of those three worthy Gentlemen, Dr. Bastwicke, Mr. Bvrton and Mr. Prynne, as it hath been truely and faithfully gathered from their owne mouthes by one present at the sayd Censure* ([London], 1637), pp. 21–22. Compare the detailed account of the butchery endured by Henry Burton in the same tract (p. 30). Correspondingly, see also Burton's own portrayal in *A Narration of the Life of Mr. Henry Burton* (London, 1643), pp. 12–14.

feeling, and bloody a manner as possible; the victim as martyr wel-
comes his torture not just with equanimity but with a kind of theatrical
flare. The scene amounts to what Michel Foucault calls "the theatrical
representation of pain" within a "festival of torture."[20]

The drama enacted in that festival, moreover, becomes the occasion of triumph, the means by which the victim transforms his
defacement into the stigmata of martyrdom. As a sign of that transformation, the s.l. is made to be interpreted "STIGMATA LAVDIS,"
that is, "STIGMATA maxillis bajulans insignia LAVDIS Exultans remeo,
victima grata Deo." This, the account avers, has since been "Englished"
as "s.l. LAVDS SCARS," accompanied by the verse "Triumphant I
returne, my face descries,/LAVDS scorching SCARS, Gods gratefull
sacrifice."[21] By interpreting his defacement in this manner, the victim
performs a poetic act that associates his mutilation and dismemberment with that of the consummate sacrifice, Christ himself. In that
imitatio Christi, the victim offers himself as a *pharmakos* through whom
destructive violence becomes generative: "*The more I am beate downe,
the more I am lift up*." Like that of Christ, his *sparagmos* becomes a
means of ultimate apocatastisis. As a result of such a triumph, the
body will once again be made whole, re-formed in its entirety. Such
is the nature of Reformation history as emblematized in the poetic
transformation of the stigmata inscribed in the bodies of its saints,
and such is the outlook reflected in Milton's allegoresis on the tribulations endured by the figure of Truth in *Areopagitica*.

Culminating that allegoresis is a declaration of Milton's antipathy
toward those, like Laud, who hold schism in such contempt and who
literalize the meaning of schism by visiting its effects upon the actual
bodies of those it seeks to mutilate. Unwittingly subscribing to the
brutal policies espoused by the very prelatical tyranny they seek to
disavow, such individuals delay the onset of true Reformation as a
result of their intolerance of what they call schism. "There be," Milton
observes, those "who perpetually complain of schisms and sects, and
make it such a calamity that any man dissents from their maxims. 'Tis

20. Michel Foucault, *Discipline and Punish: The Birth of the Prison*, trans. Alan Sheridan
(New York: Random House, 1977), pp. 9, 14. During this period (as opposed to the later
periods Foucault explores), one finds the spectre of "the tortured, dismembered, amputated
body, symbolically branded on face or shoulder, exposed alive or dead to public view" (p.
8).

21. *A Briefe Relation*, p. 22. The pun on Archbishop Laud as the one who has caused
those scars is obvious.

their own pride and ignorance which causes the disturbing." Such, he says, are themselves the "troublers," the creators of schism: "They are the dividers of unity, who neglect and permit not others to unite those dissever'd peeces which are yet wanting to the body of Truth." It is the act of uniting the dissevered pieces that Milton's allegoresis most passionately celebrates. For Milton, this act involves what he calls "closing up truth to truth as we find it (for all her body is *homogeneal*, and proportional)" (*YP*, 2:550–51). Those who are branded (both figuratively and literally) schismatics, then, are paradoxically the means by which that which has been divided, mutilated, and rent will once again assume perfect form.

In *Areopagitica*, Milton conceives of that perfect form in several ways. Extending the Pauline notion of the body as the temple of God (1 Cor. 3:16–17, 6:19), for example, Milton views those who are "cry'd out against for schismaticks and sectaries" as in fact re-formers engaged in the enterprise of rebuilding the temple anew: "some cutting, some squaring the marble, others hewing the cedars."[22] In that transformative process, however, they themselves must divide, engage, as it were, in a schism of sorts, in order to achieve greater unity. So Milton observes: "There must be many schisms and many dissections made in the quarry and in the timber, ere the house of God can be built." In his plea for the tolerance of those involved in the re-creation of the body as temple, Milton allows for the presence of what he terms "brotherly dissimilitudes" in this world as an anticipation of the ultimate perfection, the ultimate repristination of the body in the next. "Let us therefore be more considerat builders, more wise in spirituall architecture, when great reformation is expected" (*YP*, 2:555).

As already suggested in my discussion of Milton's account, however, the promise of Reformation history will not be fulfilled in this life. Although the sad friends of Truth have made a noble effort in gathering up limb by limb and of rebuilding the body as far as their talents enable them, the perfect form will be realized only as a result of the *parousia*. With the fulfillment brought about by this event, Christ "shall bring together every joynt and member, and shall mould them into an immortal feature of loveliness and perfection."

Apocalyptic in bearing, the idea once again is fundamentally Pau-

---

22. For Milton's indebtedness to the Pauline point of view, see Timothy J. O'Keefe, *Milton and the Pauline Tradition: A Study of Theme and Symbolism* (Lanham: University Press of America, 1982), esp. pp. 203–54.

line. Drawing upon the Pauline association of the body with the temple, it finds its basis in an allegiance to the veneration of the sacred body of Christ as both the symbol and embodiment of the body of those incorporated into the holy church of Christ. Proclaiming with Paul that *"the body is for the Lord and the Lord for the body"* (*YP*, 1:892; 1 Cor. 6:13), Milton held firmly to the Pauline tenet that "as the body is one, and hath many members, and all the members of that one body, being many, are one body: so also *is* Christ" (1 Cor. 12:12). "Now," says Paul, "ye are the body of Christ, and members in particular." So incorporated, "there should be no schism in the body." It should be kept comely, and all the members "should have the same care for one another" (1 Cor. 12:23–27).[23] As long as we are bound to the "natural body" sown in corruption, there will be forms of division that no amount of re-formation in this life can amend.

Ultimate repristination must await the next life. As members of Christ's spiritual body, we know that we shall be raised in glory and power in the form of that perfect body represented by Christ's own bodily perfection.[24] "Behold," Paul declares, "I shew you a mystery"; we shall be changed "in a moment, in the twinkling of an eye, at the last trump: for the trumpet shall sound, and the dead shall be raised incorruptible, and we shall be changed." "For this corruptible must put on incorruption, and this mortal must put on immortality" (1 Cor. 15:51–53). At that point, all those who have undergone the effects of sparagmos will finally be reunited in one comely and perfect body.[25] Reflecting such an outlook, Milton conceives of the parousia as the ultimate occasion through which the divine master will effect a complete reconstitution of the dismembered body of Truth, a process begun in human history but not fully realized until time stands fixed. Such is the apocalyptic bearing of sparagmos in Milton's thought. In the working out of that view, the transformation of destructive violence into a generative experience commences historically but is

23. Compare Romans 12:4–5: "For as we have many members in one body, and all members have not the same office: So we, being many, are one body in Christ, and every one members one of another."

24. "So also *is* the resurrection of the dead. It is sown in corruption; it is raised in incorruption" (1 Cor. 15:42).

25. The idea is recapitulated in the common Renaissance belief that with the Second Coming "the numberless infinities of souls would arise to join their scattered bodies"; see C. A. Patrides, *Milton and the Christian Tradition* (Oxford: Clarendon Press, 1966), p. 276. Patrides's reference, of course, is to John Donne's Holy Sonnet "At the round earths imagined corners."

consummated eschatologically. Sparagmos assumes the form of apocalypsis. Only in that apocalypsis can the Reformation as a re-formation truly occur. From an apocalyptic perspective, this point of view underlies Milton's rendering of sparagmos in *Areopagitica*.

III

The sparagmatic mentality made evident in *Areopagitica* finds expression elsewhere in Milton's writings. As a reflection of that mentality, Sonnet 18 ("Avenge O Lord thy slaughter'd Saints") comes immediately to mind. There, one discovers precisely the kind of transformative dialectic that distinguishes René Girard's view of the relationship between violence and the sacred. As a result of this dialectic, the nihilistic elements implicit in the bodily mutilation and dismemberment suffered by the Vaudois become the source of the quest for renewal. Paradoxically, the effect of sparagmos is to transform destructive violence into generative violence. In Miltonic terms, that transformation occurs within the apocalyptic context delineated in Areopagitica. To appreciate the full extent of the transformative process, it might first be advisable to suggest something of the circumstances surrounding the composition of Sonnet 18. A glance at these circumstances provides a historical perspective through which we might better understand the function of sparagmos in the sonnet itself. At the same time, an awareness of the historical contexts confirms once again the sparagmatic basis of the culture that informs the Miltonic outlook.

As we are well aware, Sonnet 18 was written in response to the massacre of the Vaudois by the army under the Marquis of Pianezza, who was sent by Charles Emmanuel II, Duke of Savoy, on April 24, 1655, to expel the noble adherents of the Protestant Waldensian church from the Piedmont after they refused to convert to Catholicism. What the Vaudois suffered in this massacre at Piedmont is not only officially registered in the Miltonic state papers but graphically depicted in the surviving accounts. According to these accounts, victims of the massacre, "being naked were tyed neck and heels together, and rowled down from the tops of great Mountains." "There is scarce any thing now to be seen," declares another account, "but here a Head, and there a Body; here a Leg, and there an Arm; here a hand, and there a foot." "Amongst so many furious assaults . . . did resound nothing else but the Cries, Lamentations, and fearful Scriechings, made yet more pitiful by the multitude of those Eccho's, which are in those Mountains and Rocks."[26] Reflecting these sentiments, Samuel Morland, Cromwell's official envoy to the Duke of Savoy on the occasion of the massacre, provides his own impassioned portrayal of what transpired.[27] That portrayal assumes the form of a poetic outcry:

> Oh the fired houses which are yet smoking, the torn limbs, and ground defiled with bloud! Virgins being ravished, have afterwards had their wombs stuffed up with gravel and Rubbish, and in that miserable manner breathed out their last. Some men an hundred years old, decrepit with age, and bed-rid, have been burnt in their beds. Some infants have been dashed against the Rocks, others their throats cut, whose brains have with more than Cyclopsean cruelty, being boiled and eaten by the Murtherers! . . . Angels are surprised with horrour! men are amazed! Heaven it self seems to be astonied with the cries of dying men, and the very earth to blush, being

26. Portions of these contemporary accounts, drawn from newsletters, are reprinted in *Milton's Sonnets*, ed. E. A. J. Honigmann (London: Macmillan, 1966), pp. 164–66. See also J[eanne] B[aptiste] Stouppe, *A Collection of Several Papers Sent to His Highness the Lord Protector . . . Concerning the Bloody and Barbarous Massacres* (London, 1655). In "A Note on the Piedmont Massacre," *Milton Quarterly* 6 (1972), 36, John T. Shawcross calls attention to a pamphlet entitled *The Barbarous & Inhumane Proceedings Against the Professors of the Reformed Religion within the Dominion of the Duke of Savoy. April the 27th, 1655* (London, 1655), which contains a detailed account of the atrocities. Finally, of interest is a letter of intelligence addressed to John Thurloe, dated April 27, 1655, in *A Collection of the State Papers of John Thurloe, Esq.*, 7 vols., ed. Thomas Birch (London, 1742), 3:384–85.

27. What follows is a contemporary translation of the second version of the speech of Morland. This version is headed as follows: "Copy of Mr. Morlands Speech to the Duke of Savoy, at His First Audience, in Quality of Envoy from His Highness the Lord Protector of England, in the Behalf of the Poor Distressed Protestants in the Vallies of Piemont." Both versions (Latin and English) are compiled under the Additional State Papers in *CM*, 13:476–89. The speech is also printed in Morland's *History of the Evangelical Churches of the Valleys of Piemont* (1658), pp. 568–71. In its original form, the speech was attributed to Milton by W. Douglas Hamilton, *Original Papers Illustrative of the Life and Writings of John Milton*, Publications of the Camden Society, no. 75 (1859), pp. 18–20, a view shared by David Masson (*Life of Milton*, 5:186–88), and cautiously endorsed by J. Milton French (*Life Records*, 4:24–30). Although Milton's authorship has been discounted, the debate continues. More recently, see Robert T. Fallon's "Milton in Government: Denmark and Savoy," *Milton Quarterly* 23 (1989), 45–57, esp. 52–54. For further information, see *CM*, 13:633–34, as well as the note in *Milton Biography*, 2:1035, n. 108; and William B. Hunter, "Milton and the Waldensians," in *The Descent of Urania: Studies in Milton, 1946–1988* (Lewisburg, Pa.: Bucknell University Press, 1989), pp. 169–78. See also John T. Shawcross, "A Survey of Milton's Prose Works," in *Achievements of the Left Hand: Essays on the Prose of John Milton*, ed. Michael Lieb and John T. Shawcross (Amherst: University of Massachusetts Press, 1974), p. 351. For Sir Samuel Morland and the Waldenses, see the respective entries in the *Milton Encyclopedia*, s.v.

discoloured with the gore-bloud of so many innocent persons! (*CM*, 13:484–87)

What is so striking about Morland's depiction, as well as those of the contemporary accounts, is the uncompromising delineation of the physical atrocities the Vaudois were made to endure: the tearing of limbs, the defilement of bodies, the cutting of throats, cannibalism, the violation of innocence in all its forms. This is violence at its most brutal and savage extreme. It is violence totally oblivious to considerations of age, gender, station, or propriety. It is violence that defiles. Above all, it is violence of the body: it mutilates and rends the body. It commits atrocities on the body which horrify both humans and angels; it causes the very earth to blush at its bloody affront to the body. From the cultural perspectives explored earlier, it may, in short, be seen as a most primal manifestation of *sparagmos*, inflicted here upon innocent victims, *pharmakoi*, in the purest sense. As such, it cries out not just for revenge but for a kind of ritual cleansing.

Aware of the religious implications of his own description, Morland accordingly concludes his outcry with an appeal not so much for divine vengeance as for divine purification: "Do not, O thou most high God, do not thou take revenge which is due to so great wickedness and horrible villanie!" Rather, Morland proclaims, "Let thy bloud, O Christ, wash away this bloud!" (*CM*, 13:486–87). Although retribution would be entirely justified, Morland counters barbarism with a sense of the need to cleanse as a means of effecting renewal. The consummate expression of such a cleansing is the purification wrought by the blood of Christ's own body. Only in that way will the defilement brought about by sparagmos in its most extreme form be rectified.

In Oliver Cromwell's letter to Gustavus Adolphus on the occasion of the massacre, one discovers the intense awareness that the massacre represents a mutilation not just of individual bodies but of the body of Christ itself: "Assuredly, if there is any religious bond between us, any love of religion or any communion of belief and worship, so great a multitude of our most innocent brethren, who are part of the body of Christ, cannot endure such inhuman treatment without the whole of His body suffering in the same way and being affected by the same emotion" (*YP*, 5[ii]:690). Given the extent of his direct involvement in the composition of such sentiments, Milton both as Secretary for

Foreign Tongues and as poet might certainly be said to be committed in the most profound way to this outlook.

That commitment is nowhere more profoundly expressed than in Sonnet 18. At the forefront of Milton's call for divine vengeance is his painful awareness of what God's "slaughter'd Saints" have been made to undergo. The brutality to which the Vaudois have been subjected becomes the initial point of focus in the reference to the "bones" that "Lie scatter'd on the Alpine mountains cold" (ll. 1–2). Corresponding to the language that distinguishes the descriptions in the contemporary accounts, bodily dismemberment in Milton's poem is conceived as an act of carnage that bestows upon violence a life of its own, totally unresponsive to and dissociated from the life of those it destroys.

We witness the effects of violence as a brutal force that rends limb from limb, joint from joint, after which it scatters the remains of its handiwork indiscriminately over a cold and unfeeling landscape. Coming upon the lifeless effects of this carnage, we are made to behold the act itself perpetrated in the form of "the bloody *Piemontese* that roll'd / Mother with Infant down the Rocks." Witnessing this as we move in the octave from the effects of carnage to the source of carnage, we are then made to hear the redoubling of the moans of the slaughtered as they echo and reecho from vale to hill and from hill to heaven (ll. 7–10). As with the contemporary accounts, so with the sonnet: sight is complemented by sound, as that which is too unbearable for sight resolves itself into the reiterated outcries of those who are slaughtered.

It is the grand articulation of these outcries that Milton's sonnet seeks to express in its outrage at the perpetration of such a massacre. Throughout the poem, we hear the reverberation of the groans of the "slaughter'd Saints" in the form of those moans that gain phonetic intensity in a kind of onomatopoetic and finally symphonic iteration of the agony that accompanies sparagmos. Whether in the form of full rhyme, near rhyme, end rhyme, internal rhyme, or a variation of the foregoing, this agony is recorded in the unrelenting repetition of the archetypal biblical "woe" oracle (e.g., Isa. 5:8–22, Luke 11:42–52, Rev. 8:13) which Milton anticipates phonetically in the "o" sounds of words such as "bones," "cold," "old," "stones," "groans," "fold," "roll'd," "moans," "sow," "grow" and "hunderd-fold" and which culminates in the final trumpet blast of "Babylonian wo" (l. 14). As Milton was well aware, this "woe" oracle is what Claus Westermann would call one of the basic forms of prophetic speech: it is a formulaic signature of the "judgment proclamation" that underlies prophetic utterance.[28] In Sonnet 18, it signals the outcome of a sparagmos that cries out for an appropriate response. That response is to memorialize sparagmos in a form through which violence may become ultimately generative and restorative. This is what Milton's sonnet presumes to do.

By memorializing bodily mutilation and dismemberment in poetic form, Milton's sonnet causes the destructive elements of sparagmos to resolve themselves generatively. Such a resolution occurs within a distinctly apocalyptic framework. So the initial reference to the "slaughter'd Saints" immediately recalls Saint John the Divine's vision of "the souls of them that were slain for the word of God, and for the testimony which they held." These are the faithful under God's sacrificial altar who cry with a loud voice, saying, "How long, O Lord, holy and true, dost thou not judge and avenge our blood on them that dwell on the earth" (Rev. 6:9–10). Aligning himself with these saints, Milton opens his sonnet from the perspective of the Enthroned Deity in His celestial court. Residing within His throne room, this regal figure holds in his right hand the book of judgment "written within and on the backside, sealed with seven seals" (Rev. 5:1). In its own way, Milton's sonnet reenacts the opening of the seals, particularly the fifth, which reveals the souls of the "slaughter'd Saints" who cry out under God's altar. Just as Milton would have God "record their groans" in His book (l. 5), the poet himself offers his poem as a memorial to their sacrifice.

Doing so, he calls in the sestet upon God to cause the blood of that sacrifice and the ashes that remain from their holocaust to become a source of renewal and new life: "Their martyr'd blood and ashes sow / O're all th' Italian fields where still doth sway / The triple Tyrant" (ll. 10–12). The reference to the sowing of the martyr'd blood recalls Tertullian's apothegm, "The blood of the martyrs is the seed of the Church."[29] The possibility of renewal implicit in such an idea counters

---

28. Claus Westermann, *Basic Forms of Prophetic Speech*, trans. Hugh Clayton White (Philadelphia: Westminster Press, 1967), pp. 190–94. For a discussion of this idea from the perspective of *Lycidas*, see Michael Lieb, *The Sinews of Ulysses: Form and Convention in Milton's Works* (Pittsburgh: Duquesne University Press, 1989), pp. 52–67.

29. Cited in *A Variorum Commentary on the Poems of John Milton*, 3 vols., gen. ed. Merritt

the destructive assocations envisioned by the seer of Revelation, who beholds the whore of Babylon as one "drunken with the blood of the saints, and with the blood of the martyrs of Jesus" (Rev. 17:10). She is the handmaid of the "triple Tyrant," for Milton a symbol of the pope with his triple crown.[30] From the political perspective Milton's poem embodies, such is the Babylonian woe of Roman Catholicism that Milton hopes to overcome.

To do so, Milton implies, is to take refuge in the blood of Christ as a means of renewal. For Milton, as for Morland, the blood of the martyrs finds its source in Christ's own blood, which not only washes away "the gore-bloud of so many innocent persons" but transforms the blood of the *pharmakoi* into that *semen* through which the destructive elements of sparagmos become generative. In the dialectic implicit in such an idea, blood operates to suggest the paradoxical nature of violence as both a source of destruction and a means of renewal. From the apocalyptic perspective suggested by Saint John the Divine, that dialectic is pervasive. Prophesying the destruction of Babylon, the seer of Revelation beholds the fallen city covered with "the blood of prophets, and of saints, and of all that were slain upon the earth" (Rev. 18:24; cf. Psal. 137:8–9 and Jer. 51). Within the celestial confines of God's throne room, on the other hand, the saints of God "are they which came out of great tribulation, and have washed their robes, and made them white in the blood of the Lamb" (Rev. 7:14). Blood encodes both points of view: the destructive and the generative. With the sowing of the blood, Milton transforms the one into the other.

That transformation, in turn, is reinforced by the effects of the sowing. From the seeds of that which is sown, Milton hopes to see "grow / a hunderd-fold" those who, having learned God's way, will perpetuate the line of His saints and be delivered from the tribulations wrought by the papacy (ll. 12–14). Significantly positioned as the hundredth word in the sonnet, "hunderd-fold," with its sense of finality and completion, focuses our attention most immediately on the parable of the sower in the Gospels (see Matt. 13:1–23, Mark 4:3–20,

---

Y. Hughes (New York: Columbia University Press, 1970–), 2:440. See also John S. Lawry, "Milton's Sonnet 18: 'A Holocaust,'" *Milton Quarterly* 17 (1983), 11–14.

30. I am indebted to Shawcross, Complete Poetry, p. 242, n. 6, for the network of allusions cited here. For an earlier reference to the pope's triple crown, see Milton's "In Eandem (In Proditionem Bombardicam)" (l. 3).

Luke 8:5–18).[31] According to the common strand of thought running throughout the various accounts, the sowing of the seed is the sowing of the word of God, which is also the word of the kingdom.

There are those who, receiving this word, do not understand it and make no use of it, and there are those who do understand it and make use of it. In these latter, the seed will become fruitful and multiply a hundredfold. They and their offspring will have access to the kingdom of heaven. Correspondingly, those who look upon Milton's sonnet as a parable that portrays the sowing of the word of God will understand and act accordingly. They will be able to view the very words that constitute Milton's sonnet as themselves seeds with the potential to germinate an awareness of how to respond to the Babylonian oppression that confronts. Fleeing the power of the "triple Tyrant," who continues to hold sway "O're all th'*Italian* fields," they will be in a position to attain to that kingdom promised in the parable of the sower.[32] This parabolic dimension, in turn, finds its counterpart in and is reinforced by that which approximates the apocalyptic dimension so crucial to the action of the sonnet from the very outset.

A sense of that dimension has already made itself felt with the idea of the re-formation of the body of Truth in *Areopagitica*. There, the figure of Osiris, whose body was torn apart and then reassembled, served as the mythic paradigm upon which Milton founded his allegoresis. What is true of *Areopagitica* is likewise true of Sonnet 18: in the execution of the myth of renewal, we are reminded once again of the legend of Cadmus, who is commanded by Minerva to plow the earth and sow the teeth of the serpent, after which the ground breaks open and releases armed warriors. The event results ultimately in the founding of Thebes.[33]

31. Shawcross makes note of this positioning in *Complete Poetry*, p. 242, n. 8. According to Shawcross, the final eleven words of the poem suggest regeneration and thus salvation. Compare other sowing parables, for example, that in Matthew 13:24–44. See also George Walton Williams, "The Manifold Massacre in Piedmont," *Milton Quarterly* 24 (1990), 82.

32. According to the beliefs of the Fifth Monarchy Men, the Apocalypse was supposed to occur in 1657. Placing Milton's sonnet against this belief, we can see the urgency of the need to flee the Babylonian woe, since the apocalyptic destruction of the Roman Catholic world would also entail the destruction of all those (including the true Protestant believers) caught within sway of papal authority. I owe this insight to John T. Shawcross (letter to the author dated Thursday, January 17, 1991).

33. See Kester Svendsen, "Milton's Sonnet on the Massacre in Piedmont," *Shakespeare Association Bulletin* 20 (1945), 147–55. For corresponding, important readings of the poem, see, among other studies, Anna K. Nardo, *Milton's Sonnets and the Ideal Community* (Lincoln:

A corresponding biblical text for this idea, Ezekiel 37: 1–14, draws upon the all-important notion of the scattered bones with which Sonnet 18 begins and which is so important to the sparagmatic concept of the torn body that is ultimately made whole. There, the prophet, set down by the hand of the Lord "in the midst of the valley which was full of bones," is made to behold how these bones are reanimated through the power of God's word: "Thus saith the Lord God unto these bones; Behold, I will cause breath to enter into you, and ye shall live: And I will lay sinews upon you, and will bring up flesh upon you, and cover you with skin, and put breath in you, and ye shall live; and ye shall know that I am the Lord." Acting through his prophet, God then proceeds to reanimate the bones. He reassembles them, endows them with sinews and flesh, and breathes life into them. So animated, they are seen to stand upon their feet, "an exceeding great army." In that disciplined formation, they are conceived as "the whole house of Israel," representations of the new kingdom of God. A proto-apocalypse in its own right, this event looks forward to a time when the graves of the dead will be opened and those whose bodies have been torn asunder will arise from the graves whole again and be brought by God into the land of Israel. Such is the fate of those whose prospect is that of ultimate reanimation as the result of continued faith in the ways of God.

It is with the fervent hope and even promise of such reanimation that Milton's sonnet ends. But the elation this hope brings is mitigated by the immediate awareness that during this particular historical moment the "triple Tyrant" continues to hold sway. The sparagmos that may result from the destructive violence attendant upon the power of such a tyrant is an ever-present threat. All one can do is to seek to be delivered from the tribulations wrought by that tyrant and look forward to a period when the kingdom of God is realized in perfect wholeness and completeness, when the bodies of those who have been torn asunder will ultimately be reassembled like the body of Truth at the Second Coming. Such is the basis of Milton's sparagmatic mentality throughout his works. From the perspective this treatment of the

University of Nebraska Press, 1979), pp. 127–36; and the essays by John R. Knott, Jr., "The Biblical Matrix of Milton's 'On the Late Massacre in Piemont,' " *Philological Quarterly* 62 (1983), 259–63; and " 'Suffering for Truths Sake': Milton and Martyrdom," in *Politics, Poetics, and Hermeneutics in Milton's Prose*, ed. David Loewenstein and James Turner (Cambridge: Cambridge University Press, 1990), pp. 153–70.

Miltonic outlook offers, we can now explore corresponding dimensions of his sparagmatic sensibility. Those dimensions involve Milton's configuration of himself as poet and the implications of that configuration as a reflection of his attempt to overcome the forces of sparagmos.

2

The Fate of the Poet

A s a shaping force in Milton's outlook, sparagmos assumes a compelling presence in his sense of poetic vocation. That vocation is founded upon the awareness of the fate of the archetypal poet, the Thracian Orpheus, a figure whose influence on Milton's works proved to be pervasive.[1] We need only glance at the earliest writings to determine the nature and extent of that influence. Doing so provides a context against which to place Milton's treatment of Orpheus's terrible fate and its bearing on Milton's sparagmatic point of view.

As early as his first Prolusion ("Whether Day or Night Is the More Excellent"), Milton cited the Orphic "Hymn to the Dawn" in support of his own celebration of light as a source of birth and fruition (*YP*,

---

1. For an analysis of the importance of the Ovidian Orpheus to Milton's works, see, among other studies, Richard DuRocher, *Milton and Ovid* (Ithaca: Cornell University Press, 1985), pp. 64–74. For the impact on Milton of the Renaissance version of Ovid's myth, see Davis P. Harding, *Milton and the Renaissance Ovid* (Urbana: University of Illinois Press, 1946), and Charles Martindale, "Paradise Metamorphosed: Ovid in Milton," *Comparative Literature* 37 (1985), 301–33. See also Mason Tung's entry on Orpheus and Milton in the *Milton Encyclopedia*, s.v. Also of interest is Patricia Vicari, "The Triumph of Art, the Triumph of Death: Orpheus in Spenser and Milton," in *Orpheus: The Metamorphoses of a Myth*, ed. John Warden (Toronto: University of Toronto Press, 1982), pp. 207–30.

1:229), and in the seventh Prolusion ("Learning Brings More Blessings to Men than Ignorance"), he celebrated the ability of Orpheus to invigorate the natural world (*YP*, 1:305).[2] In both cases, Orpheus is viewed as a poet whose transcendent and transformative powers are able to bring order out of chaos, light out of darkness, and to imbue that which is otherwise inert with new life. By means of his powers, Orpheus places all things under his spell. Descending to the underworld, he succeeds in enchanting even the overseers of that realm to grant him his desires. Alluding to these abilities in *L'Allegro* (ll. 145–50) and *Il Penseroso* (ll. 105–8), Milton commemorated them throughout his works.[3]

Ad Patrem is a case in point. Attempting in that eloquent poem to convince his father of the nobility of the poet's calling, Milton engages in what amounts to an Orphic declaration of the divinity of poetry and the exalted nature of the poetic vocation. After an initial exordium, he addresses his father with the following *propositio*:

> Nec tu vatis opus divinum despice carmen,
> Quo nihil aethereos ortus, et semina caeli,
> Nil magis humanam commendat origine mentem,
> Sancta Promethéae retinens vestigia flammae.
> Carmen amant superi, tremebundaque Tartara carmen
> Ima ciere valet, divosque ligare profundos,
> Et triplici duros Manes adamante coercet. (ll. 15–23)

> [You should not despise the poet's task, divine song, /
> than which nothing commends more completely the
> offspring of heaven / to their ethereal origins, or the
> human mind to its lineage, / for song preserves a holy
> spark of Promethean fire. / The gods love song, and

---

2. For Milton, Orpheus had more than mythical status. See Milton's references to Orpheus in such works as *Of Education*, in which he groups Orpheus with Hesiod, Theocritus, Aratus, Nicander, Oppian, and others as poets "counted most hard" but of great importance to be read (*YP*, 2:394).

3. Both *L'Allegro* and *Il Penseroso* focus on Orpheus's descent to the underworld to reclaim Eurydice. But the nuances implicit in the reference to Orpheus's descent are different in the two poems. In *L'Allegro* the emphasis is upon what amounts to the ultimate failure of Orpheus, who is left with a "half-regained Eurydice" (ll. 145–50), whereas in *Il Penseroso* the emphasis is upon the initial success of Orpheus, who is able to draw "Iron tears down *Pluto's* cheek" and thereby to make "Hell grant what Love did seek" (ll. 105–8). See Marilyn L. Williamson, "The Myth of Orpheus in *L'Allegro* and *Il Penseroso*," *English Literary Renaissance* 1 (1971), 165–77.

song has power to stir / the trembling depths of
Tartarus, and to bind the lower gods;/ and it restrains
the stern shades with triple adamant.]

This elevation of the role of the poet to the level of the gods is
reinforced by the assertion not only of the great appeal poetry has in
the celestial realms but of the indomitable power (*valet*) poetry exerts
in the underworld. If it inspires the love of the gods, it causes the
underworld to be responsive to its will. With its emphasis upon *valet*,
the allusion is implicitly Orphic.[4] This allusion, in turn, underlies the
remainder of the encomium, with its detailed account of the poet's
functions and its copious citation of the poet's attainments (composing
songs at altars, embellishing regal banquets, singing deeds of heroes,
recounting the creation of the universe, infusing the universe with
song; ll. 26–50).

At the forefront of the encomium stands Orpheus, a figure replete
with power. This power is celebrated at the culminating moment of
the encomium. There, Orpheus is invoked by name as one "who
restrained the rivers and gave ears to the oaks / by his song...and
singing stirred / the shades of the dead to tears [*Qui tenuit fluvios et
quercubus addidit aures / Carmine...simulachraque functa canendo / Com-
pulit in lacrymas*]" (ll. 52–55). The naming of Orpheus concretizes what
had before been only implied. All that can be associated with poetry
as a divine phenomenon of utmost power is embodied in the figure
of Orpheus.

Complementing this aura of divine power is a sacralizing of Orpheus's role to the extent that he becomes for Milton, in effect, a
priest of the gods. The idea is already enunciated in the sixth Elegy
("To Charles Diodati, Sojourning in the Country"). As both *vates* and
sacerdos (l. 77), Orpheus is placed in the company of Pythagoras, Tiresias, Linus, Calchas, and Homer, the most exalted of figures.[5] The
placement is significant not only because of the distinguished company

4. See Louis L. Martz's discussion of the passage in these terms; *Milton: Poet of Exile*,
2d ed. (New Haven: Yale University Press, 1986), pp. 41–42.
5. See my discussion of this dimension of the poet's role in Michael Lieb, *Poetics of the
Holy: A Reading of "Paradise Lost"* (Chapel Hill: University of North Carolina Press, 1980),
pp. 43–63. The priestly view of Orpheus is the product of Renaissance neoplatonism. There,
Orpheus is transformed from civilizer and symbol of the "beautiful voice" (*Oraia phone*) into
theologian. In this regard, see in particular D. P. Walker, "Orpheus the Theologian and
Renaissance Platonism," *Journal of the Warburg and Courtauld Institutes* 16 (1953), 100–120.

Orpheus as archetypal poet is made to keep but because of the way he is depicted. He is described as "old / Orpheus with the vanquished beasts among the forsaken caves [*senemque / Orpheon edomitis sola per antra feris*]" (ll. 69–70).[6] The mode of depiction is significant because it is at pains to portray Orpheus, like those whose company he shares, as an old, sequestered, and experienced individual. In the language of *Il Penseroso*, he is one through whom "old experience" has been able to "attain / To somthing like Prophetic strain" (ll. 173–74). Projecting himself onto this aged yet still powerful figure, Milton looks upon Orpheus as a sacred poet whose entire life has been governed by a strict code of conduct. It is just such a code that Milton—aspiring young poet of celestial battles, divine heroes, supreme gods, and the doings of the other world—would embrace: "His youth void of crime and chaste [*Additur huic scelerisque vacans, et casta juventus*]" is distinguished "by stern morals and without stain of hand. / With like nature, shining with sacred vestment and lustral waters, / does the priest rise to go to the hostile gods [*Et rigidi mores, et sine labe manus. / Qualis veste nitens sacra, et lustralibus undis / Surgis ad infensos augur iture Deos*]" (ll. 61–66).[7] It is by this rule, Milton says, that Orpheus, among such priestly figures as Tiresias, Linus, Calchas, and Homer, lived (ll. 67–70).[8] Viewing himself in this manner, Milton concludes that he, as Orphic poet, is "sacred to the gods, and priest of the gods, / And his hidden heart and lips breathe Jove [*Diis etenim sacer est vates, divumque sacerdos, / Spirat et occultum pectus, et ora Jovem*]" (ll. 77–78).

As much as Milton throughout his earlier works fostered a vision of Orpheus that portrayed him both as replete with indomitable power (*valet*) undiminished even by advanced age (*senemque / Orpheon edomitis sola per antra feris*), this fantasy of an old but unconquerable poet could not be sustained. Milton was well aware of the sparagmatic fate of

6. For the sources of this depiction, see *A Variorum Commentary on the Poems of John Milton*, 3 vols., gen. ed. Merritt Y. Hughes (New York: Columbia University Press, 1970–), 1:123.

7. The original has *Stet prope fagineo pellucida lympha catillo, / Sobriaque è puro pocula fonte bibat. / Additur huic scelerisque vacans, et casta juventus / Et rigido mores, et sine labe manus*" (ll. 61–64). Milton's emphasis upon the importance of himself as a *casta juventus* is to be seen everywhere in his early works. See, for example, the lines appended to the seventh Elegy. For a discussion of these lines, see J. W. Saunders, "Milton, Diomede, and Amaryllis," *ELH* 22 (1955), 254–86.

8. So Milton likewise portrays the other figures as imbued with age and experience: "By this rule it is said wise Tiresias lived / after his eyes were put out, and Ogygian Linus / And Calchas fugitive from his appointed house" (ll. 67–69).

Orpheus, of his failure to tame the uncontrolled and overwhelming strength of those whose savagery was too powerful to be contained. As Milton knew, the tragedy of Orpheus was his ultimate frailty, his vulnerability in the face of insuperable odds. That very chaos he was accustomed to tame, those very forces of darkness he was known to overcome, finally enveloped him. More than any other event in the career of Orpheus, his dismemberment struck at the heart of Milton's sense of himself and of his vocation.

Among the various renderings of the myth of Orpheus that influenced Milton most profoundly, none provides a more detailed portrayal of the sparagmos that Orpheus underwent than Ovid's *Metamorphoses* (ll. 1–84).[9] Having already prepared us for this sad event through his earlier depiction of Orpheus's initial success but ultimate failure to retrieve Eurydice from the underworld, Ovid proceeds to relate Orpheus's dismemberment at the hands of the Bacchantes.[10] The description is graphic and unrelenting. With the strength of creatures who are able to slay oxen limb from limb (*divulsere boves*), the mad Ciconian women release their savagery upon the defenseless poet. His hands outstretched in supplication, he cries out for mercy but to no avail. His voice, as Ovid says, "moved no one [*nec quicquam voce moventem*]." His divine poetic powers prove utterly futile. Disregarding those powers completely, the sacrilegious Maenads "struck him down [*sacrilegae perimunt*], / And through those lips to which the

9. References in my text are to Ovid, *Metamorphoses*, trans. Rolfe Humphries (Bloomington: Indiana University Press, 1955). This translation is used in conjunction with the Latin text and translation in the *Metamorphoses* of Ovid, trans. Frank Justus Miller, 2 vols. (Cambridge: Harvard University Press, 1976). Citations of the Latin in my text are to this edition. For a corresponding account, see Virgil's *Georgics* (4. 454–527). The figure of Orpheus in Virgil and Ovid is depicted entirely differently. For an enlightening comparison of the Virgilian and Ovidian renderings, see W. S. Anderson, "The Orpheus of Virgil and Ovid: *flebile nescio quid*," in *Orpheus*, ed. Warden, pp. 25–62. As Anderson observes, the Orpheus of Ovid is little more than a flawed lover and a shallow orator-poet who deserves his fate. Even more damnable, Ovid's Orpheus is guilty of pederasty, homosexuality, and misogyny (pp. 36–48). Although this perverse dimension of Orpheus was hardly given wide currency in the later traditions, it certainly does survive. In the Renaissance, it can be seen in the works of Dürer, for whom Orpheus becomes "the first homosexual [*Orpheus der erst puseran*]." See Giuseppe Scavizzi, "The Myth of Orpheus in Italian Renaissance Art, 1400–1600," in *Orpheus*, ed. Warden, p. 121, and, most important, D. P. Walker, *Spiritual and Demonic Magic from Ficino to Campanella* (London: Warburg Institute, 1958).

10. In its most ancient form, the *sparagmos* of Orpheus was the subject of a lost play of Aeschylus, the *Bassarids*, probably composed early in the fifth century B.C. See Emmet Robbins, "Famous Orpheus," in *Orpheus*, ed. Warden, p. 13. As an expression of the Dionysian sparagmos, the fate of Orpheus has its roots in that of Dionysus himself.

rocks had listened, / To which the hearts of savage beasts responded, / His spirit found its way to winds and air."

Ovid's description vividly reinforces both the poignancy and the futility of the sorrowful occasion. Totally dismembered,

> Membra iacent diversa locis, caput, Hebre, lyramque
> excipis: et (mirum!) medio dum labitur amne,
> flebile nescio quid queritur lyra, flebile lingua
> murmurat eanimis, respondent flebile ripae.
> iamque mare invectae flumen populare relinquunt
> et Methymnasae potiuntur litore Lesbi.

> [The poet's limbs lay scattered,
> Where they were flung in cruelty or madness,
> But Hebrus River took the head and lyre
> And as they floated down the gentle current
> The lyre made mournful sounds, and the tongue murmured
> In mournful harmony, the banks echoed
> The strains of mourning. On the sea, beyond
> Their native stream, they came at last to Lesbos
> And grounded near the city of Methymna.][11]

The brutal dismembering of the body by the Bacchantes, the scattering of the limbs, the reverberation of the mournful cries: these are all motifs encountered earlier and reiterated in the Miltonic canon. Assimilating and transforming the myth of Orpheus within his oeuvre, Milton caused it to become the basis of his own view of the poet as one perpetually threatened by the sparagmos Orpheus himself was made to undergo. As John Carey comments, "the myth of his [Orpheus's] dismemberment by Thracian women during orgies of Bacchus seems to have focused some of Milton's deepest fears."[12] Such

---

11. In the Ovidian account in the *Metamorphoses*, Bacchus punishes the Maenads: "Mourning his singer's loss, he bound those women,.../ Twisted their feet to roots, and thrust them deep / Into unyielding earth" (11.66–71). Iconographic depictions of the sparagmos of Orpheus can be found in the Renaissance. See Scavizzi, "Myth of Orpheus," p. 119.

12. John Carey, in *The Poems of John Milton*, ed. John Carey and Alastair Fowler (London: Longman Group, 1968), p. 777n. From a psychological perspective, such fears might well have their basis in an underlying dread associated with the female gender as potential threat. According to Karen Horney, this dread is one experienced by both genders in the process of maturation. In Milton's case, it might have been particularly pronounced. See Horney's "The Dread of Women: Observations on a Specific Difference in the Dread Felt by Men and by Women Respectively for the Opposite Sex," *International Journal of Psycho-Analysis* 13 (1932), 348–60.

fears are ones Milton sounded as early as *Lycidas* and as late as *Paradise Lost.*

As a way of addressing those fears in the context of *Lycidas*, we might well begin by acceding to William Riley Parker's observation that Milton's elegy on the death of Edward King is one of the most autobiographical of all Milton's poems and that, to understand his elegy, we must in some way recreate Milton's state of mind at the time of composing it.[13] Although such an approach carries with it obvious perils, I think it appropriate here to adopt it momentarily to suggest what this state of mind might have been on the occasion of the composition of *Lycidas*. Doing so provides something of a psychological context for determining the nature of the fears that underlie this most autobiographical of poems.[14] Certain facts are clear. The twenty-nine-year-old poet is at a pivotal point in his career in 1637. Having undergone "the wearisome labours and studious watchings wherein . . . [he] has spent and tired out almost a whole youth," he is very much conscious of the severity of the demands that he has placed upon himself since his graduation from Cambridge in 1632.[15] Perhaps on a return visit to Cambridge he first learns of the shipwreck and unfortunate drowning of Edward King *"in his passage from* Chester *on the* Irish *Seas"* and of the proposal for a volume of memorial verses to honor King.[16] As Parker observes, death was very much on Milton's mind.[17] On the horizon loomed his plans to undertake a perilous journey by sea to the continent. Such circumstances were no doubt much in Milton's thoughts when he undertook the sad and difficult task of writing an elegy on King. In the enactment of that task, Milton, it has been

13. *Milton Biography*, 1:157.

14. For the significance of *Lycidas* as a revelation of personality, see the essays of John Crowe Ransom, "A Poem Nearly Anonymous," and Stanley Fish, *"Lycidas*: A Poem Finally Anonymous," both anthologized in *Milton's "Lycidas": The Tradition and the Poem*, 2d ed., ed. C. A. Patrides (Columbia: University of Missouri Press, 1983), pp. 68–85, 319–40.

15. See Milton's reference to his "wearisome labours and studious watchings" in the *Apology* for Smectymnuus (1642) (*YP*, 1:869). In his letter to an unknown friend (1633), Milton had earlier referred to his "studious retirement" (*YP*, 1:319). For a discussion of Milton's periods of retirement, see John T. Shawcross's entry "Retirement" in the *Milton Encyclopedia*, s.v.

16. *Milton Biography*, 1:155. The italicized line is from the headnote prefixed to the poem in the 1645 edition of the *Poems*.

17. *Milton Biography*, 1:155. Death was in the air. As Parker observes, the plague (with its attendant ravages) had visited Horton shortly after the death of Milton's mother Sara, on April 3, 1637. During that period, the Countess Dowager of Derby had died, and on August 9 Ben Jonson was buried in Westminster Abbey.

argued, projected himself and his uncertainties onto King as a kind of Miltonic other.

The nature of that projection and the creation of a Miltonic counterpart in the figure of Edward King are most eloquently described in the account offered by E. M. W. Tillyard:

> When he [Milton] heard of King's death, and still more when by consenting to write the elegy he had to make his mind dwell on it, he cannot but have felt the analogy between King and himself. Milton and King had been at the same college in the same University. Their careers and interests had been similar there. Milton was a poet, King had written verse too. King had made a voyage on the sea, Milton was about to make voyages. How could Milton have missed the idea that *he* might make the analogy complete by getting drowned, like King, also?[18]

Faced with such uncertainties, as well as with the realization that he had "sacrificed so much to his great ambition" during this long period of preparation now drawing to an end, Milton "must have dwelt on the thought that it might be all for nothing." It is little wonder that under such circumstances Milton's "fears must have come crowding on him."[19] This is all conjecture, of course, but it does provide a context for coming to terms with Milton's conceptualization of such fears in the terrible fate that beset Orpheus.

In Milton's elegy on the death of Edward King, then, the dismemberment of Orpheus might be viewed as a mythic reformulation not only of King's own sparagmos but as a projection of Milton's deep-seated fears of a similar fate. Confronting his sense of powerlessness in the face of the overwhelming forces of nature, Milton seeks to reconcile himself to the demands placed upon him by his onerous task. Embarking upon that quest, he moves through a series of crises in response to the body of the drowned figure floating upon "his watry bear" and weltering "to the parching wind" (ll. 12–13). The movement is reinforced by the establishment of the relationship between the speaker as budding poet and Lycidas, the counterpart of the drowned figure commemorated by the poem. The intimacy of that relationship

---

18. E. M. W. Tillyard, *Milton* (New York: Collier-Macmillan, 1967), p. 71.
19. Tillyard, *Milton*, p. 71. See Parker's account (*Milton Biography*, 1:156), which elaborates further.

is fostered by the memory of the nurturing it received during an earlier time of innocence and bliss in a world of pastoral harmony (ll. 25–36). Such innocence and bliss were not to last: harmony gave way to dissonance, joy to sorrow in the recognition that Lycidas is "gon, and never must return!" (l. 38).

The response is to seek out causes, to place blame, as the poet turns to the world of myth in a vain desire for answers. Invoking the protective divinities of the natural world that has nurtured the poet in the past, he exclaims: "Where were ye nymphs when the remorseless deep / Clos'd or're the head of your lov'd Lycidas?" (ll. 50–51).[20] As if realizing the futility of such an exclamation, he then concludes on a note of painful resignation that moves him dramatically to the sparagmatic point of crisis in the poem, the dismemberment of Orpheus:

p 41

> Ay me, I fondly dream!
> Had ye bin there, for what could that have don?
> What could the Muse her self that Orpheus bore,
> The Muse her self for her inchanting son
> Whom universal nature did lament,
> When by the rout that made the hideous roar
> His goary visage down the stream was sent,
> Down the swift *Hebrus* to the *Lesbian* shoar. (ll. 56–63)

As a passage of crucial import to Milton's entire poetic enterprise in *Lycidas*, these lines and their manifold implications serve as the basis for a discussion of the nature of sparagmos in Milton's pastoral elegy.

II

The Orpheus passage is among the most thoroughly revised in *Lycidas*. A glance at the Trinity College Manuscript confirms the extent to which Milton worked and reworked the passage before it reached its present form.[21] In the first version of the passage, we encounter

20. For the identity of the nymphs and their association with the classical Muses, see the *Variorum Commentary*, 2:655–56.

21. *Facsimile*, 1:436–43. The annotations in and the section on *Lycidas* in John Milton, *Poems, Reproduced in Facsimile from the Manuscript in Trinity College, Cambridge* (Menston Ilkley: Scolar Press, 1972), pp. 29–34, have also been consulted.

the following: "what could the golden hayred Calliope / for her in-chaunting son / when shee beheld (the gods farr sighted bee) / his gorie scalpe rowle downe the Thracian lee." The last two lines are then canceled and "whome universale nature might lament / and heaven and hel deplore / when his divine head downe the stream was sent / downe the swift Hebrus to the Lesbian shore" inserted. On another leaf, this version reappears, accompanied by the following changes: "might lament" is corrected to "did lament," and "divine visage" is corrected to "gorie visage."[22] Such alterations reveal a good deal about the importance of the dismemberment of Orpheus to Milton's sparagmatic point of view.[23]

In the evolution of that point of view from the manuscript versions to the printed text, Milton made the decision first to emphasize and thereby universalize the role of Calliope as Muse and second to underscore the generative relationship between mother and son.[24] In the first instance, this act of emphasis serves to reinforce the transition that the poet of *Lycidas* undergoes between the means of inspiration in the pagan world and the means of inspiration in the Christian world he ultimately comes to embrace. That is, the poem is concerned not so much with the identity and characteristics of Calliope (with her golden hair and her farsightedness) as it is with the function of Calliope specifically as Muse, indeed, "the Muse her self" (an epithet twice invoked).[25] In the second instance, the underscoring of the generative relationship ("the Muse her self that *Orpheus* bore") serves to establish the importance of the Muse as the maternal source of her son's birth. From this second point of view, the role of the Muse as mother intensifies the sense of anguish that arises out of the awareness of her

22. I am indebted to John Carey for sorting out the possible sequence of alterations (*Poems of John Milton*, p. 244n.).

23. In "The Revision of the Orpheus Passage in 'Lycidas,'" *Notes and Queries* 5 (1958), 335–36, David S. Berkeley examines and suggests reasons for the changes. See also J. B. Leishman, *Milton's Minor Poems* (London: Hutchinson, 1969), pp. 295–310; Caroline W. Mayerson, "The Orpheus Image in *Lycidas*," in *Milton's "Lycidas,"* ed. Patrides, pp. 116–28; and Balachandra Rajan's full entry on *Lycidas* in the *Milton Encyclopedia*, s.v.

24. Orpheus is traditionally viewed as the son of Calliope (the Muse of epic poetry) and Oeagrus (a Thracian river god) or Apollo.

25. According to David Berkeley, " 'Golden hayrd' the Greeks epithetically applied to Dionysus, Eros, and Apollo, absolutely . . . to the latter. Milton probably means the terms not only to be decorative but also to imply divinity and close association with Apollo Mousagetes. But because the Greeks did not use this epithet specifically of Calliope, and, more urgent, since 'golden hayrd' belonged also to Dionysus . . . , and hence might be associated with the Bacchantes, enemies of Calliope, Milton removes this blurred effect" ("Revision of the Orpheus Passage," p. 335).

powerlessness to save her own offspring from the violence of his attackers. Absent from the sources, this poignant maternal dimension is one that Milton established at the very outset in the manuscript versions and that evolved into its present powerful form in the printed text.[26]

Beyond these considerations in the evolution of the passage from manuscript to text, others of corresponding importance emerge. Those considerations have to do with the details through which Orpheus's dismemberment is conceived. Milton is particularly concerned with the decapitation of Orpheus. A symbol of sorts for the dismemberment of the body as a whole, the decapitation, followed by the passage of the head down "the swift Hebrus," drives home the sense of horror (accompanied by wonder) Milton no doubt associated with the beheading of Orpheus.[27] In his attempt to recreate the aura of that beheading, Milton struggled with the need to portray the horror and anguish its brutality engenders, on the one hand, and the need to be responsive to the propriety imposed by the demands of his task, on the other. For this reason, the original version simply would not do. Depicting a gory scalp rolling down the Thracian lea is finally self-defeating.[28] With consummate tact, Milton preferred instead to focus on the aftermath of the decapitation, an aftermath much more nearly in keeping with the vocation of Orpheus as archetypal poet.

One is at once able to recoil in horror at the fact of the decapitation and respond in wonder at the ability of the severed head to produce those mournful sounds customarily associated with the myth as Milton

26. As the editors of the *Variorum Commentary* observe, neither Ovid in *Metamorphoses* nor Virgil in the *Georgics* mentions the Muse's inability to save her son. But Ovid does mention this detail in his elegy on Tibullus (*Amores* 3.9.21; *Variorum Commentary*, 2:657).

27. Compare Virgil's account in the *Georgics*. After describing the dismemberment of Orpheus by the Bacchantes, Virgil relates the effects of the decapitation in poetic and eerie detail. We first perceive the head, "plucked from the marble-pale / Neck rolling down midstream on the river Hebrus," and next we hear "that voice" produced by "that cold, cold tongue" that "cried out 'Eurydice!' / Cried 'Poor Eurydice!' as the soul of the singer fled, / And the banks of the river echoed, echoed 'Eurydice!' " *The Eclogues and Georgics of Virgil*, trans. C. Day Lewis (Garden City: Doubleday, 1964), ll. 522–26.

28. Berkeley quips that, in the original version, Milton conceived of the Bacchantes using Orpheus's head as a bowling ball ("Revision of the Orpheus Passage," p. 335). There is a touch of unintentional comedy in the original version. For a Derridean reading of the dismemberment of Orpheus in *Lycidas*, see Herman Rappaport's important study *Milton and the Postmodern* (Lincoln: University of Nebraska Press, 1983), esp. pp. 114–19. For additional and important discussion, see Elizabeth Hanson, "To Smite Once and Yet Once More: The Transaction of Milton's *Lycidas*," *Milton Studies* 25 (1990), 69–88.

knew it. In his rendering of the movement of the head downstream, Milton made two particularly significant alterations. Rather than retain any reference to the "scalp" of Orpheus, Milton adopted the term "visage," and rather than employing the phrase "divine visage," as originally planned, he chose "goary visage." These alterations are very much to the point. The use of "scalp" would have overly localized and rendered prosaic the fact of the decapitation. The substitution of "visage" for "scalp" is much more appropriate. With its connotations of seeing (as well as being seen), "visage" (from *videre*) elevates the event to a level of visionary import. "Goary" (as opposed to the rather flat "divine"), however, retains that sense of brutality and horror so crucial to the conception as a whole. No matter how much Milton desired to elevate the event, he was constantly aware of the bloody circumstances that produced it. These circumstances remain at the center of his rendering. Changing "might lament" to "did lament," finally, represents an acknowledgment of the momentous impact the event had on the natural universe: this is an event that "universal nature" *did* indeed lament. Focusing on the evolution of the passage from manuscript to printed text offers a heightened sense not only of Milton's artistry but of the way his sparagmatic point of view worked itself out at this pivotal moment in the poem.

At this moment, the poet is made painfully aware of all the fate of Orpheus implies for one who would seek to prevent the disintegration of a world upon which he has come to depend but which is no longer able to sustain the violence that has brought about its own undoing. The Muse has failed her son, whose power to enchant has lost its former efficacy. The pagan world, with all its charming accoutrements, has proven itself insufficient. By means of the mutilation and dismemberment of Orpheus, the poet of *Lycidas* comes to know what the poem in its entirety reveals: as an event subject to and unable to transcend the forces that define the pagan world, sparagmos offers no possibility of renewal. Confined within the economy of a pagan sparagmos, one has no hope of transforming destructive violence into generative violence. Rather, one must face the terrible realization of an economy that rewards self-denial in the cause of poetic vocation with nothing but indiscriminate and self-destructive turmoil, a turmoil in which the expectation of bursting out into sudden blaze is undermined by "the blind *Fury* with th'abhorred shears" who "slits the thin-spun life" (ll. 72–76).[29] Were the poet made to depend solely upon the efficacy of the pagan world, he would forever be searching for the remains of one who has been washed far away by "the shoars and sounding seas" and whose bones have been hurled "beyond the stormy *Hebrides*" (ll. 154–56). There would be no reclamation of the body, no reconstitution of the lost members. As a sad friend of an *aletheia* that has revealed its essential emptiness and its ultimate illusoriness, the poet of *Lycidas* may attempt to imitate the careful search Isis made for the mangled body of Osiris, but the effort would be futile. With the hideous roar of the wild Bacchantes ringing in his ears, he would be left only with the memory of false enchantments and the knowledge of severed parts.

Such, however, is not the case. As the poet of *Lycidas* comes to learn, the fate of Orpheus is to find its fulfillment in that of Christ.[30] Those equipped with the revealed knowledge of what the Christo-centric worldview affords are able to read Orpheus's fate in prefi-gurative terms. The idea is a Renaissance topos.[31] In the words of Alexander Ross:

29. In the reference to "the blind *Fury* with th'abhorred shears," Milton not only conflates Atropos, the third of the Fates, with the Furies but adds the quality of blindess as well (see the *Variorum Commentary*, 2:664). Compare Milton's reference to the "wholsom and preventive sheares" in the sonnet "On the Forcers of Conscience," discussed earlier. As a reflection of Milton's sparagmatic mentality, the lines that follow the reference to "the blind *Fury* with th'abhorred shears" who "slits the thin-spun life" are correspondingly significant: "But not the praise, / *Phoebus* repli'd, and touch't my trembling ears" (ll. 76–77). As mentioned in Chapter 1, John Leonard has ably demonstrated the extent to which the political context of the passage in its entirety (ll. 72–77) is that of the mutilation of Bastwick, Burton, and Prynne. Leonard contends, moreover, that the concept of the dangerous voyage implicit throughout *Lycidas* as a whole, is in keeping with the post-mutilation experiences of the "martyrs"; " 'Trembling Ears': The Historical Moment of *Lycidas*," *Journal of Medieval and Renaissance Studies* 21 (1991), 59–81. Leonard too agrees that Milton's lines on the dismemberment of Orpheus "emerge from deep, quite possibly repressive, roots in his psyche." In fact, he suggests, "one possible source of Milton's anxiety about dismemberment is a fear of the hangman" (p. 69).

30. The idea has a long history both as a medieval and as a Renaissance commonplace. For the medieval traditions, see in particular J. B. Friedman, *Orpheus in the Middle Ages* (Cambridge: Harvard University Press, 1970), the standard work in the field. Additional commentary can be found in Eleanor Irwin, "The Songs of Orpheus and the New Song of Christ," and Patricia Vicari "*Sparagmos*: Orpheus among the Christians," in *Orpheus*, ed. Wardem, pp. 52–62, 63–83. In the later Middle Ages, the complex working out of the Orpheus-Christ parallel is particularly discernible in such works as the anonymous *Ovid Moralisé* (thirteenth century), which Christianizes every detail of the story.

31. For the Renaissance dimensions, see Kenneth Louis Gross, "The Triumph and Death of Orpheus in the English Renaissance," *Studies in English Liberature* 9 (1969), 63–80.

Christ is the true *Orpheus*, who by the sweetness and force of his Evangelical musick caused the Gentiles, who before were stocks and stones in knowledge, and no better than the beasts in Religion, to follow after him: it was he only who went down to hell to recover the Church his Spouse, who had lost her self ... What was in vain attempted by *Orpheus*, was truly performed by our Saviour, for he alone hath delivered our souls from the nethermost hell; and at last was he torn with whips, and thorns, and pierced with nails, and a spear, upon the Cross, for our transgressions.[32]

Ross articulates overtly what Milton's poem implies: the prefigurative relationship between Orpheus as symbol of the pagan world and Christ as the fulfillment of the new economy is one of type to antitype. The relationship manifests itself on all fronts. Orpheus as pagan poet finds the ultimate expression of his craft in Christ as consummate poet who endows his followers with new knowledge and new life. If Orpheus descended to the underworld, so did Christ. Whereas the descent of Orpheus resulted in failure, however, the descent of Christ proved eminently successful, for he was able to recover not only the Church his Spouse but the souls of all those who might otherwise be lost to perpetual damnation. Finally, just as Orpheus was made to undergo a terrible and painful sparagmos, so was Christ. Whereas the sparagmos of Orpheus appeared to occur to no end, that of Christ was undertaken as an expression of his voluntary willingness to sacrifice himself for our transgressions. A manifestation of God's providence, this sacrifice results in that reclamation through which we are reborn into a new life. With Christ as the "true Orpheus," we undergo the renewal of redemption brought about by the transformation of violence into that which is ultimately generative.

III

In *Lycidas* the transformation from destructive to generative violence is given eloquent expression, as the reclamation and reconsti-

32. Alexander Ross, *Mystagogus Poeticus or the Muses Interpreter: Explaining the Historical Mysteries, and Mystical Histories of the Antient Greek and Latin Poets* (London, 1675), pp. 338–39.

tution of the body are made possible by the new economy the Christocentric worldview affords. Within that worldview, sparagmos gives rise to the possibility of renewal. Destructive violence can become the source of its opposite, as mutilation and dismemberment result in a generative transformation of apocalyptic proportions. The idea is sounded prefiguratively in what begins as the poet's desperate search for the remains of the body washed far away by the shores and sounding seas and in what ends as an appeal first to the angel to look homeward and "melt with ruth" and second to the dolphins to "waft the hapless youth" (ll. 154–64). Moving to the utmost bounds of English soil in his pursuit of a means to find and restore the dismembered body, the poet culminates his pilgrimage at the top of St. Michael's mount in Land's End, Cornwall. On that high point, the "great vision" of the angelic guard Michael looks over the waters toward the Spanish stronghold of Bayona and the mountain range of Namancos (ll. 161–62). On watch against all who might threaten the homeland, he becomes a "Genius of the shoar" in his own right. He likewise fulfills his role as one traditionally viewed as the patron of mariners who wander in the "perilous flood" of the high seas.[33] In that capacity, Michael receives the call to turn his attention homeward. Implicitly heeding the call, he performs an act that signals the experience of reclamation with which the poem culminates. That experience, in turn, is indicated in the reference to the wafting of the hapless youth by the dolphins. As an event that finds its counterpart in the sparagmos of Orpheus, the allusion to the hapless youth who is finally reclaimed becomes part of the pervasive dialectic through which destructive violence resolves itself in a generative form.

To understand the nature of this dialectic in the mythic universe Milton envisions for *Lycidas*, one must attend to the complex of fables that underlie the reference to the hapless youth. As it is already fairly well recognized, the reference in question includes any one of several possible figures, among them Coeranus, Phalanthus (Taras), Enalus, Palaemon (Melicertes), Arion, and Icadius.[34] In a plethora of ancient sources ranging from Lucian, Pausanius, and Philostrastus to Apuleius and Ovid, these figures come to be associated with acts of violence

---

33. Compare *Lycidas*, ll. 183–85.
34. See the *Variorum Commentary*, 2:723–25, for an overview of prevailing critical opinion. The fullest account of the sources may be found in Eunice Burr Stebbins, *The Dolphin in the Literature and Arts of Greece and Rome* (Manasha, Wis.: George Banta, 1929), pp. 63–94.

perpetrated upon an innocent youth who is then borne upon a dolphin's back to ultimate safety. Although the dolphin is not necessarily present in all accounts, early mythographers generally tend not only to include the dolphin as a symbol of reclamation and renewal but to conflate the myths surrounding the youthful figures who have undergone violence and are finally reclaimed. Once again, Dionysus is crucial to the whole process. Founded upon the concept of violence and ultimate renewal, his epiphany is at the heart of the notion of the youth who is first made to suffer but is then reborn.[35]

In this respect, Palaemon (Melicertes) and Arion are pivotal figures. Placing these figures in the context of his discourse on Dionysus, Philostratus, for example, draws upon the myths associated with both of them to suggest how the destructive power of violence can have a generative outcome.[36] His account focuses first on the plot of evil Tyrrhenian pirates to attack Dionysus, who responds by transforming them appropriately into dolphins. The effect of this transformation for Philostratus is paradoxical: that which is evil becomes the source of that which is good. He concludes his account in the following manner: "Dionysus on the prow of his ship laughs at the scene and shouts orders to the Tyrrhenians as fishes in shape instead of men, and as good in character instead of bad." (I.19) Having made this observation, Philostratus conflates the myths of Palaemon and Arion as figures through whom the paradox of destructive violence giving rise to a generative outcome is realized. Though subjected to violence, both are ultimately saved by dolphins. So, he asserts that Palaemon "will ride on a dolphin's back, not awake, but lying prone upon it sound asleep," and Arion "makes it clear that dolphins are the companions of men, and fond of song, and worthy to take the field against pirates in defence of men and the art of music" (I.19).[37] Represented

---

35. According to Eunice Burr Stebbins, the dolphin legends in their association with the epiphany of Dionysus "belong to the cycle of myths symbolizing the battle between winter and summer. The winter is represented by the death of Dionysus who disappears into the water whence he is brought back as the returning springtime either in a chest, on a ship, or on the back of a dolphin" (*Dolphin in Greece and Rome*, pp. 60–61). Furthermore, the dolphin is seen to be "the conveyor of the living and of the dead in the legends and folk-tales which have sprung from the myth of Dionysus." Apollo is also looked upon as such a conveyor, either as a god or in the form of a dolphin (p. 81).

36. References are to Philostratus, *Imagines*, trans. Arthur Fairbanks (Cambridge: Harvard University Press, 1960).

37. Compare *A Mask*: "*Bacchus*, that first from out the purple grape / Crush't the sweet poyson of mis-used wine / After the *Tuscan* mariners transform'd/ Coasting the *Tyrrhene shore*, as the winds listed / On *Circe's* Iland fell" (ll. 46–50).

by the Tyrrhenian pirates, destructive violence is potentially generative. Dionysus is at the source of this idea, and the figures of Palaemon and Arion, saved by dolphins, are the beneficiaries of it. The myths that surround both figures attest to this fact.

In the case of Palaemon, for example, the destructiveness of violence makes itself felt from the outset. In her desire to be avenged on Ino, votary of Bacchus (Dionysus), Juno arranges to have Ino and her husband Athamas driven mad through the influence of the hellish Tisiphone. As Ovid recounts the myth, Athamas in his madness tears his son Learchus from his mother's arms, swings him around his head, and flings him head-first at a wall of rock. In her grief and madness, Ino takes up the other son Melicertes and, crying out to Bacchus, climbs to the top of a cliff and "launche[s] herself and her burden / Far out into the ocean, and the wave / Churned with white foam." In response to the pleas of Venus, Neptune "Took from the victims all their mortal being, / Gave them divinity, and changed both name / And form, gave the new god a name, Palaemon, / And called the goddess-mother Leucothea" (4.414–542).[38] Although Ovid makes no mention of dolphins, these bearers of lost souls are, as we have seen, customarily associated with the Palaemon myth, which in turn finds its counterpart in that of Arion.

Offering fit comparison with Orpheus, Arion is looked upon as consummate poet and musician. His ties to Dionysus may be seen in the tradition that associates him with the invention of the dithyramb, the hymn in honor of Dionysus, "with the circumstances of whose birth the word is somewhat fancifully connected."[39] Like Orpheus, Arion as poet has the power to charm the very elements. According to Ovid's account in the *Fasti*, he is able "to stay the running waters" through his song.[40] "Often at his voice the wolf in pursuit of the lamb stood still, often the lamb halted in fleeing from the ravening wolf; often hounds and hares have couched in the same covert, and the

38. References are to the *Metamorphoses*. See also Ovid's *Fasti* (6.485–502). In that account, Ino and Melicertes are received by Panope and her sisters and bore mother and child through their realms.

39. In Herodotus, *The Persian Wars*, trans. George Rawlinson (New York: Random House, 1942), p. 13, n. 30. According to Rawlinson, the invention of the dithyramb, or cyclic chorus, was attributed to Arion, not only by Herodotus, but also by Aristotle, Hellanicus, Dicaearchus, and, implicitly, Pindar. See Herodotus's account of Arion in *The Persian Wars* (1.23–24).

40. References are to the *Fasti*, trans. James George Frazer (Cambridge: Harvard University Press, 1976).

hind upon the rock has stood beside the lioness." "By the music of his lyre," Arion "had charmed the Ausonian land." Heading toward home on one occasion, Arion boards a ship filled with pirates who are determined to rob and kill him. To gain time, Arion persuades them to listen to his music. Donning his singing robes, "twice dipped in Tyrian purple," he plays his final song upon his lyre, then leaps into the sea. The power of his music, however, saves him. So Ovid observes: "A dolphin did submit his arched back to the unusual weight; seated there Arion grasped his lyre and paid his fare in song, and with his chant he charmed the ocean waves" (2.79–116). According to the earliest versions of the legend, Arion is even carried safe to shore.[41]

In response to the legend of Arion, scholars traditionally see a striking resemblance to the story of the Tyrrhenian pirates and conclude that the Arion story represents a version of the Dionysian myth.[42] If such is the case, one is able to discern in the Palaemon-Arion association the way violence as a destructive phenomenon is transformed into something positive, indeed generative. In that transformation, the figure of Dionysus once again becomes the source of renewal and reclamation. Conceived destructively in the terrible fate that befalls Orpheus, the effects of the power of Dionysus in the remarkable fate that befalls Palaemon and Arion suggest the extent to which violence lends itself to both points of view. As a poem that embodies the full range of meanings implicit in this outlook, *Lycidas* conceives a mythic world in which the destructive elements implicit in acts of violence are ultimately and triumphantly metamorphosed into a new order.

As I have argued elsewhere, such an idea is already encoded within the opening phrase of the poem: "Yet once more."[43] A formula that recalls biblical concepts of violence, on the one hand, and the promise of restoration, on the other, "Yet once more" finds its antecedents in both the Old Testament and the New. In the Old Testament, it is to be seen in Haggai's prophecy concerning the restoration of the temple as tantamount to an event of cosmic proportions: "For thus saith the

41. See the *Variorum Commentary*, 2:723. The idea is present, for example, in Herodotus's account.

42. Stebbins, *Dolphin in Greece and Rome*, p. 67.

43. Michael Lieb, *The Sinews of Ulysses: Form and Convention in Milton's Works* (Pittsburgh: Duquesne University Press, 1989), pp. 52–66.

Lord of hosts; Yet once, it is a little while and I will shake the heavens, and the earth, and the sea, and the dry *land*; and I will shake all nations, and the desire of all nations shall come; and I will fill this house with glory, saith the Lord of hosts" (Hag. 2:6–7). In the New Testament, it is to be seen in the author of Hebrews' transformation of the Haggai prophecy into an event that signals the advent of the new kingdom: "And this *word*, Yet once more, signifieth the removing of those things that are shaken, as of things that are made, that those things which cannot be shaken may remain. Wherefore we receiving a kingdom which cannot be moved, let us have grace, whereby we may serve God acceptably with reverence and godly fear: for our God *is* a consuming fire" (Heb. 12:26–29). Both proclamations encode that fundamental idea upon which Milton bases the notion of sparagmos as correspondingly destructive and generative.

In *Lycidas*, the transition from the destructive to the generative implications of the "Yet once more" formula, in turn, is delineated in the climactic phrase "Weep no more" (l. 165). This moment of peripeteia marks the occasion through which all that has been subject to the destructive forces that threaten the shepherd in his quest for permanence are now provided with a new order, a new understanding, and a new vision. In the generative economy the moment of peripeteia inscribes, sparagmos assumes a decidedly apocalyptic bearing. That fact is reinforced by the biblical contexts in which "Weep no more" appears. Those contexts have their most immediate source in the Book of Revelation. In this respect, the locus classicus of the formula is Revelation 7:16–17: "They shall hunger no more, neither thirst any more; neither shall the sun light on them, nor any heat. For the Lamb which is in the midst of the throne shall feed them, and shall lead them unto living fountains of waters: and God shall wipe away all tears from their eyes" (cf. Rev. 21:4). It is the aura that surrounds the ultimate promise of renewal embodied in this apocalyptic proclamation that is portrayed in those lines of *Lycidas* that give full expression to the significance of "Weep no more."

Following hard upon the series of allusions that encompass the fate of Orpheus, on the one hand, and the fate of such figures as Palaemon and Arion, on the other, the lines through which the peripeteia is dramatized recount, in effect, that repristination or apocatastasis associated with the resurrection and ascension of Christ:

Weep no more, wofull shepherds weep no more,
For *Lycidas* your sorrow is not dead,
Sunk though he be beneath the watery floar,
So sinks the day star in the Ocean bed
And yet anon repairs his drooping head
And tricks his beams, and with newspangled ore
Flames in the forehead of the morning sky:
So *Lycidas* sunk low but mounted high
Through the dear might of him that walkt the waves. (ll. 165–73)

If the drowning of Lycidas is tantamount to a dismemberment in which the bones of the shepherd are scattered beyond the stormy seas, the reclamation of the torn body is tantamount to an apotheosis in which all the features are restored to their original form. This repristination is portrayed mythically through a cycle of descent and reascent. In that cycle, the commonplace association of Sun and Son assumes the form of a drama of expectation and fulfillment. Sparagmos becomes only the first step in the realization of a new order. Within the providential framework Milton provides for it, the fact of dismemberment represents the occasion through which that which is torn asunder may prepare itself for a glorious reunification that is correspondingly a divinization. Reinscribing the resurrection and ascension of Christ in cosmic terms, this event is conceived as the explosive moment through which all that the body has been made to suffer is triumphantly realized. In this moment, the agony of sparagmos gives way to the apotheosis of renewal, as the day star "with newspangled ore / Flames in the forehead of the morning sky."

Such is the outcome of the "reparation" of the dismembered body. Submerged beneath the "watry floar," the body is able to prepare itself to be reborn. The act of preparation is dramatized through the synecdoche of the head that is "repaired." This reparation figures the regenerative experience of reclaiming the body as a whole. Underlying that experience, once again, is the dismemberment of Orpheus, whose "goary visage" is sent down the stream as a mythic reenactment of the fate of Lycidas, one whose head is likewise subject to the destructive forces of "the remorseless deep" (ll. 49–50). To counter those destructive forces, one must embrace a new order, a new economy. That economy is founded upon the concept of renewal, of repristination centered in Christ. It is only by means of the power embodied in his revelation that the destructive forces of the remorseless deep can finally be overcome: "So *Lycidas* sunk low but mounted high / Through the dear might of him that walkt the waves" (cf. Matt. 14:24–31).

Through the power of Christ, the dismembered body is given the opportunity to experience new life, to undergo a transformation tantamount to the assumption of a new form. With that assumption, the redeemed body finds itself among "other groves and other streams" than it has known before. In its new surroundings, it experiences the bliss of ultimate purification, as its "oozy locks" are washed with "nectar pure" and its eyes are forever cleansed of its tears (ll. 174–81). So cleansed, the regenerated figure of Lycidas may now assume its protective position as "the Genius of the shoar." In this position, Lycidas "shalt be good / To all that wander in that perilous flood" (ll. 183–85).

As a poem that reenacts the fate of one who undergoes both the violence of that flood and the reclamation to which this violence can give rise, *Lycidas* represents a profound statement of the paradoxical bearing that sparagmos assumes in Milton's thought. Having explored the nature of Milton's sparagmatic mentality in his elegy on the death of Edward King, we may turn to an examination of its impact on his outlook in *Paradise Lost*. There, we shall see a renewed emphasis on sparagmos as an experience of utmost importance to the point of view that underlies his epic.

3

The Dismemberment of Orpheus

Particularly as it centers upon the figure of the poet, *Paradise Lost* is a poem in which the concept of sparagmos is fully articulated. Within the world of the poet, the sparagmatic perspective already encountered in *Lycidas* assumes renewed significance in *Paradise Lost*. We need only attend to the proem to Book 7 of Milton's epic to confirm this observation. Culminating the proem is a passage that brings into focus the epic implications of all I have discussed in the earlier treatment of *Lycidas*:

> But drive farr off the barbarous dissonance
> Of *Bacchus* and his revellers, the Race
> Of that wild Rout that tore the *Thracian* Bard
> In *Rhodope*, where Woods and Rocks had Eares
> To rapture, till the savage clamor dround
> Both Harp and Voice; nor could the Muse defend
> Her Son. So fail not thou, who thee implores:
> For thou art Heav'nlie, shee an empty dream. (7.32–39)

Adopting this passage as a point of departure, I explore its bearing on Milton's sense of his role as Orphic poet. From the perspective of this self-portrayal, I proceed to some "extrapoetic" speculations. These involve the construction of what might be called (and in fact has been called) a piece of "Secret History" underlying Milton's composition of the proem in question. At issue throughout the discussion is the notion of sparagmos, Milton's abiding fear of it, and the function of the Miltonic body faced with the prospect of having to sustain its ravages.

As an inset piece within the larger proem, the passage on Bacchus and his revellers embodies an appeal, in effect an urgent prayer to that celestial source of salvation, the Christian Muse Urania. The poet calls upon her to protect him as her child from the ravages the archetypal pagan poet Orpheus was made to undergo and from which he could not be protected by his mother, the pagan Muse Calliope. The circumstances here recall those earlier examined in *Lycidas*. Indeed, they extend those circumstances and implicitly comment upon them. At the forefront of the prayer, once again, is the realization of the inability of the pagan world to sustain that being in whom its values had been so admirably embodied. Here, as in *Lycidas*, the powers of Orpheus are seen to fail utterly, as the bard is torn asunder by the disruptive forces of "that wild Rout," the Bacchantes. As violent as the description is in *Lycidas*, however, that in *Paradise Lost* is even more so. Because of the form in which the description is cast, one finds in Milton's epic an intensification (and, by implication, an elevation) of the violence. This intensification operates in several ways. Rather than name the individual who must endure the sparagmos, Milton simply offers the epithet "the *Thracian* Bard." The allusion takes for granted a shared knowledge of the name. Not to know the name (and the history it encodes) is to risk undergoing the same fate. A similar circumstance surrounds the reference to "that wild Rout," an ascription that encodes the Bacchantes and their history. In the epic account, however, Milton is at pains to elaborate on the background of the Bacchantes. Their genealogy derives from Bacchus, just as Orpheus derives from the Muse Calliope. In either case, Milton pits one against the other, just as he pits the Muse of "the *Thracian* Bard" against the Muse of the Christian bard, that is, the poet of *Paradise Lost*. This results in a pairing and a balance not discernible in *Lycidas*.

There are other differences as well. Whereas the account in Milton's pastoral elegy focuses in lyric fashion upon the severed head and its passage down "the swift *Hebrus*," the account in Milton's epic focuses implicitly upon the torn body in its entirety and the barbarous effects engendered by the act of tearing. Here, one finds no lamentations by a "universal nature" for the passing of its "inchanting son," whose "goary visage" elicits dulcet moans. Drawing upon the implications of "hideous roar" that the poet of *Lycidas* mentions almost as an aside, the poet of *Paradise Lost* features it as the central theme in his epic account. There, that roar is transformed into a "barbarous dissonance" that destroys by its sound as much as those who produce it destroy by their violent act of dismemberment.[1] All possibility of beauteous music produced by "Harp and Voice" is drowned out by the "savage clamor" of those whose physical abominations find their counterpart in the savagery and barbarity of the sounds they produce. Nature is in no position to lament. "Where Woods and Rocks had Eares / To rapture," now there are only the appalling effects of "barbarous dissonance." If there is rapture now, it is the rapture brought on by the din of devastation. As the result of his undoing, the Thracian bard is silenced; he all but disappears. Nature is deafened. There is only the barbarity of noise, what Milton earlier in his epic calls "a universal hubbub wild / Of stunning sounds and voices all confus'd" (2.951–952). Orpheus's sparagmos results in the return to the world of Chaos. It is this return the poet of *Paradise Lost* is desperate to avoid. To realize his quest, however, he must be successful in establishing the new genealogy that places him in the direct lineage not of the Muse who failed her son but of the Muse who is able to protect her children from devastation. Whereas the first is nothing more than an "empty dream," the second is truly "Heav'nlie." This distinction underlies Milton's address to the Muse in the proem to the seventh book of his epic.[2]

The distinction is one that suggests the importance of the placement of the Orpheus allusion to the proem as a whole. If the proem to Book 7 is an *Ad Matrem* of sorts which celebrates the heavenly Muse

---

1. Compare the Attendant Spirit's reference to the barbarous dissonance of Comus and his crew in *A Mask*. Meditating his "rural minstrelsie," the Attendant Spirit suddenly hears "the wonted roar" rise "up amidst the woods." It "fill'd the air with barbarous dissonance" (ll. 547–50). See also Sonnet 11: "I did but prompt the age to quit thir clogs / By the known rules of ancient liberty, / When strait a barbarous noise environs me / Of Owls and cuckoes, asses, apes and dogs" (ll. 1–4).

2. Compare the comments of William Kerrigan in *The Prophetic Milton* (Charlottesville: University Press of Virginia, 1974), p. 134.

as a source of divine inspiration, sustenance, and protection, allusion
to the sparagmos of Orpheus represents a culminating moment in
what amounts to a highly personal and profoundly moving appeal.
This appeal develops through a complex network of allusions that
contextualize the myth of dismemberment in which the proem culminates. These allusions commence with the invocation to Urania and
her celestial lineage and conclude with the all-important distinction
between Urania as "Heav'nlie" and Calliope as "empty dream." In a
poem of genealogies, this allusive structure is in keeping with the
outlook Milton's epic embodies. Within the context established by the
proem to Book 7, the opening invocation offers the opportunity to
delineate the nature of the heavenly Muse, to explore her origins,
and to suggest her relationship to the poet who later claims her as his
"Celestial Patroness" (9.21), that mother who is the source of his own
poetic being.

The precise identity of the Muse whose very name means "heavenly" but whom Milton is at pains to dissociate from the "the Muses
nine" (7.5–7) of classical mythology is not of immediate concern.[3]
What is of concern is Milton's insistence upon her celestial origins as
one who is "Heav'nlie born." This lineage places her in the biblical
realm of Wisdom and in the environment of "th'Almightie Father,"
whom she entertains with her "Celestial Song" (7.5–12).[4] This realm
and environment Milton associates with his own poetic vocation and
lineage as epic poet. His invocation to Urania at the outset of the
proem is a testament to his abiding faith in the divine source of
inspiration with whom he has aligned himself. That alignment represents a choice made as early as *Lycidas* not to place his trust in the
pagan economy embodied in the Muse of Orpheus. That way destruction lies: just as much in the epic as in the pastoral elegy, the
Muse will fail to save her son. Milton opts instead to place his trust
in the truly divine (and ultimately Christian) economy embodied in

3. Among the many studies that deal with this subject, see E. R. Gregory, *Milton and
the Muses* (Tuscaloosa: University of Alabama Press, 1989), pp. 94–124; William B. Hunter,
"Milton's Muse," in Hunter, C. A. Patrides, and J. H. Adamson, *Bright Essence: Studies in
Milton's Theology* (Salt Lake City: University of Utah Press, 1971), pp. 149–56; John M. Steadman, *Milton's Biblical and Classical Imagery* (Pittsburgh: Duquesne University Press, 1984),
pp. 88–120; and Steadman's entry on Urania in the *Milton Encyclopedia*, s.v.
4. The most complete study of the role of Wisdom in Milton's epic is John Reichert,
Milton's Wisdom: Nature and Scripture in "Paradise Lost" (Ann Arbor: The University of Michigan
Press, 1992).

the Muse whose origins are traceable to "th'Almightie Father."[5] He through her will be the source of the poet's inspiration, sustenance, and indeed his very survival.

The urgency through which Milton declares his faith in the heavenly Muse, as opposed to the pagan world represented by the Muse of Orpheus, is established from the very outset of his proem. As Barbara Kiefer Lewalski has demonstrated, the subtext of the opening invocation of Milton's proem ("Descend from Heav'n *Urania*"; 7.1), as well as the action of the proem as a whole, is Horace's fourth ode of the Third Book, which commences *Descende caelo ... Calliope* (ll. 1–2).[6] The implicit allusion to Horace suggests not only the odic basis of Milton's proem but the extent to which Milton is at pains to distinguish his Muse from that pagan source of inspiration on whom one may no longer depend. In effect, Milton's odic proem represents a denial and a revision of Horace's. On the surface, the two "odes" share the same structural and thematic assumptions. They contain, says Lewalski, "the same structural elements—prayer and praise to the muses and the gods, myths from the heroic past, personal references—and they explore the same themes: the poet's calling, the muse as embodiment of wisdom, light, and reason, the muse as guardian of the poet against the forces of chaos and disorder." Invoking his Muse as divine protectress, Horace, moreover, "proclaims himself Calliope's darling, miraculously protected from several near-catastrophes in childhood, and ready to dare future exploits with full confidence in her continuing protection."[7] In response to such assertions, Milton calls upon his Muse to afford him protection in the face of his own perilous situation. Knowing full well how baseless a faith in that "empty dream" Calliope can be, he "implores" Urania to sustain him during a period of great danger and uncertainty.

---

5. For the Christianization of the Muse during the Renaissance, see Lily B. Campbell, "The Christian Muse," *Huntington Library Bulletin* 8 (1935), 29–70, and *Divine Poetry and Drama in Sixteenth-Century England* (Berkeley: University of California Press, 1959).

6. Barbara Liefer Lewalski, *"Paradise Lost" and the Rhetoric of Literary Forms* (Princeton: Princeton University Press, 1985), pp. 34–35. References to Horace in my text are to *Horace: The Odes and Epodes*, trans. C. E. Bennett (Cambridge: Harvard University Press, 1921).

7. Lewalski, *"Paradise Lost,"* p. 34. Thus, Horace relates how, through the protection of his Muse, he was able as a child to sleep "safe from bears and black serpents" and how he was "overspread with sacred bay and gathered myrtle, with the gods' help a fearless child" (ll. 17–20). He also suggests other occasions when he was kept safe by the Muse: "Friends to your springs and dancing choirs, not Philippi's rout destroyed me, nor that accused tree, nor the Sicilian wave near Palinurus' headland" (ll. 25–28).

That perilous period assumes several forms. In epic terms, it encompasses both the infernal and celestial voyages upon which Milton had embarked in the first half of his narrative (Books 1–6). These voyages he conceives through the myths of Orpheus, on the one hand, and Bellerophon, on the other. The Orphic dimension is addressed in the proem to Book 3 of his epic, that having to do with Bellerophon, in the proem to Book 7.

Having journeyed down to Hell in the first two books, Milton opens his third book with a celebration of his ascent to celestial light and the heavenly spheres. The celebration is enacted in a manner that at first suggests the way the voyage corresponds to its Orphic prototype and then insists upon the way the voyage departs from that prototype. Addressing the "holy Light" to which he has finally attained after his arduous journey, he declares:

> Thee I revisit now with bolder wing,
> Escap't the *Stygian* Pool, though long detain'd
> In that obscure sojourn, while in my flight
> Through utter and through middle darkness borne
> With other notes then to th' *Orphean* Lyre
> I sung of *Chaos* and *Eternal Night*,
> Taught by the heav'nly Muse to venture down
> The dark descent, and up to reascend,
> Though hard and rare. (3.13–21)

The address aligns him with Orpheus in recalling that poet's own descent to the underworld to reclaim Euridyce. As we have seen, it is a descent that Milton long admired, not only because of its dangers but because of Orpheus's remarkable poetic ability to enchant the powers of the underworld. As the result of his sojourn, Orpheus became, in effect, the poet of the underworld and the devotee of its powers.

Milton, however, dissociates himself from Orpheus. First, he suggests that he does not intend to celebrate the realm of "*Chaos* and *Eternal Night*," an act that he might well have associated with the various hymns attributed to Orpheus in the traditions surrounding him.[8] Second, Milton suggests that he will be ultimately successful in

---

8. According to Merritt Y. Hughes, "Milton may have thought of the Orphic hymn to Night where Night is treated as a beneficent goddess. He surely thought of the tradition of

his quest, because he has been "Taught by the heav'nly Muse to venture down / The dark descent, and up to reascend, / Though hard and rare." As a result of the protection afforded him in this divine instruction, he has been able to escape "the *Stygian* Pool." So escaped, he finds himself safely before the beams of the "sovran vital Lamp" of the celestial light (3.21–22).[9] Even here, however, the poet's experience is precarious. If Milton has been taught by his heavenly Muse to "venture down / The dark descent, and up to reascend" to the realms of light, he is very much aware of the "ever-during dark" that continues to surround him and of his own experience of being cut off from the "chearful wayes of men" (3.45–47). Like an Orpheus faced with the irretrievable loss of past joys, Milton too is sequestered with his own torment. With the fate of Orpheus ever before him, the poet of this new song must appeal for continued sustenance and protection, lest he, like Orpheus, be forever "cut off." Prompted by the knowledge of his own darkness in the face of his ascent to light, Milton culminates his proem with a plea for an apocatastasis that only spiritual wholeness and divine illumination can afford: "So much the rather thou Celestial light / Shine inward, and the mind through all her powers / Irradiate, there plant eyes, all mist from thence / Purge and disperse, that I may see and tell / Of things invisible to mortal sight" (3.51–54). In this way, the Orphic poet who has been able to reascend to the realms of light from the darkness of the underworld will be spared the pain of a sparagmos his forebear could not escape.

As a counterpart to this Orphic experience of descent and reascent, Milton invokes the figure of Bellerophon within the context of his appeal to the Muse to be returned to his earthly station from the

---

Orpheus as the first interpreter of the physical and spiritual secrets of hell"; *John Milton: Complete Poems and Major Prose*, ed. Merritt Y. Hughes (New York: Macmillan, 1957), p. 258, n. 18. Compare Lewalski: Milton "has not sought love or esoteric knowledge in the dark places: instead of an Orphic 'Hymn to Night' he offers his 'Hymn to Light' " ("*Paradise Lost*," p. 32). In the first Prolusion, Milton alludes to the Orphic "Hymn to the Dawn" to support his defense of light as a source of generation.

9. See my full discussion of this aspect in Michael Lieb, *The Dialectics of Creation: Patterns of Birth and Regeneration in "Paradise Lost"* (Amherst: University of Massachusetts Press, 1970), pp. 37–55, and *Poetics of the Holy: A Reading of "Paradise Lost"* (Chapel Hill: University of North Carolina Press, 1981), pp. 185–211. For a contemporary mockery not only of Milton's self-portrayal in the proem to the third book of *Paradise Lost* but of his other works, see [Richard Leigh], *The Transproser rehears'd: of the fifth act of Mr. Bayes's play* (Oxford, 1673). The author refers to Milton's image of the "vital Lamp" as his having "lighted a Christmas Candle in his brain." Full excerpts are cited by William Riley Parker, *Milton's Contemporary Reputation* (1940; Folcroft, Pa.: Folcroft Press, 1969), pp. 113–16.

precarious heights to which he had ascended in the earlier books (3–6). There, he dramatized not only the heavenly council but the celestial warfare involving the overthrow of Satan and his forces.[10] From the perspective of these events, he appeals to the Muse:

> Up led by thee
> Into the Heav'n of Heav'ns I have presum'd,
> An Earthlie Guest, and drawn Empyreal Air,
> Thy tempring; with like safetie guided down
> Return me to my Native Element:
> Least from this flying Steed unrein'd (as once
> *Bellerophon*, though from a lower Clime),
> Dismounted, on th' *Aleian* Field I fall
> Erroneous there to wander and forlorn. (7.11–19)

The passage returns us to the spirit of the proem to the first book of his epic. In that inaugural moment, Milton invoked the heavenly Muse to aid his "adventrous Song, / That with no middle flight intends to soar / Above th' *Aonian* Mount, while it pursues / Things unattempted yet in Prose or Rime" (1.12–16). As a representation of the Miltonic act of transcendence signaled there, Bellerophon in the proem to Book 7 becomes an emblem of aspiration bordering upon presumption. If Milton follows the divine voice of his Muse "above th'*Olympian* Hill" and "above the flight of *Pegasean* wing" (7.2–4), he does so at tremendous danger to himself, for his journey exceeds even that of Bellerophon upon Pegasus.[11]

Transcending the topography of the classical world represented by Bellerophon and his voyage, Milton's journey risks far more than even Bellerophon's perils. At the very least, Milton faces the prospect of becoming a Bellerophon in his own right, and he is well aware that the journey of Bellerophon ultimately resulted in disaster. Offending the gods in his presumptuous flight, Bellerophon was undone. As a

10. Compare once again Horace's ode: "Full well we know how the impious Titans and their frightful horde were struck down with the descending bolt by him who rules the lifeless earth" (3.4.42–46). In his address to Calliope Horace focuses on concerns similar to Milton's.

11. Milton had earlier associated himself with Pegasus as an expression of his poetic aspirations. See his letter to Charles Diodati (November 23, 1637): "You ask what I am thinking of? So help me God, an immortality of fame. What am I doing? Growing my wings and practising flight. But my Pegasus still raises himself on very tender wings" (*YP*, 1:327). Ironically, Pegasus is the product of violence. The winged horse springs from the Gorgon's blood after Perseus slays her (Ovid, *Metamorphoses* 4.785–87).

reward for his aspirations, he was cast from Pegasus onto the Aleian plain in Lycia, where, according to tradition, he was made to wander crazed and blind until his death.[12] Desiring to avoid such a fate as the result of even greater aspirations, Milton calls upon his Muse to be guided down in safety and returned to his "Native Element." Failing to receive the aid of his Muse, he will be made to suffer at the very least what Bellerophon was made to endure.

Drawing upon the association of "Aleian" with the idea of wandering, Milton underscores his own sense of anomie at the prospect of being made to undergo the experience of a fallen Bellerophon.[13] If he can be returned safely, he will be able to avoid wandering aimlessly, erroneously, and forlornly on that field of wandering, a field fraught with all the perils a crazed and blinded individual can expect under such circumstances. Returned safely to his "Native Element," he will be able to find comfort in that place of origins, that place from which he was sired and in which he now seeks refuge. Calling upon the heavenly Muse to guide him to that place, he remains painfully aware of what the failure to realize his destination will entail.

As the foregoing discussion suggests, the voyages of Orpheus and Bellerophon underscore the abiding fear that pervades the proems to Books 3 and 7.[14] As manifestations of that fear, Orpheus embodies the concept of descent and reascent, and Bellerophon the concept of unlicensed ascent followed by a disastrous return. Bellerophon undoes Orpheus, just as Orpheus will undo himself in the form of the Bacchantes' savagery. Faced with this prospect, the poet calls upon his heavenly Muse to aid him in avoiding it. Nonetheless, it remains a perpetual possibility that causes the poet to articulate it not only in

12. For the sources of the myth, see Charles Grosvenor Osgood, *The Classical Mythology of Milton's English Poems* (New York: Henry Holt, 1900), pp. 16–17. The myth finds its antecedents in Homer (*Iliad* 6.200–2) and Pindar (*Olympian Odes* 13 and *Isthmian Odes* 6). For an excellent discussion of Bellerophon, see Stephen M. Fallon, "Milton and Bellerophon: Intention and Its Limits in *Paradise Lost* 7," in *Literary Milton: Text, Pretext, Context*, ed. Diana Treviño Benet and Michael Lieb (Pittsburgh: Duquesne University Press, 1994).

13. According to the entry on Bellerophon in *The Oxford Classical Dictionary*, 2d ed., ed. N. G. L. Hammond and H. H. Scullard (Oxford: Clarendon Press, 1970), s.v.: *pedion Aleion* in Homer (*Iliad* 6.200–2) signifies the "plain of wandering." See Alastair Fowler's comments in *The Poems of John Milton*, ed. John Carey and Alastair Fowler (London: Longman Group, 1968), p. 776 n. Milton plays upon the idea of wandering in "Aleian" and combines it with the notion of wandering in *errare*. The Aleian Field is Milton's answer to Spenser's Wood of Error.

14. From the perspective of modern philosophy, the whole question of anxiety in Milton's epic is explored in depth by John S. Tanner in *Anxiety in Eden: A Kierkegaardian Reading of "Paradise Lost"* (New York: Oxford University Press, 1992).

his invocation to the Muse in the proem to Book 7 but in his invocations in general.

Milton is never able to dispel the anxiety of sparagmos entirely. One would like to see the same sense of confidence, indeed mental tranquility, in Milton's address to Urania which Horace evinces in his address to Calliope, but that confidence and tranquility are finally missing. As much as Milton would like to believe that Urania is "Heav'nlie" and Calliope is nothing but an "empty dream," his intense awareness of the sparagmatic fate of Orpheus and his own deep-seated fears of a similar fate keep getting in the way.[15] Milton's abiding faith in the powers of his heavenly Muse requires constant reaffirmation.

Depending upon that reaffirmation to sustain him, he gives the proem to his seventh book a pivotal status. Transitional in nature, the proem looks backward to scenes of divine councils and grand warfare and forward to scenes of cosmic and human creation. From the poet's perspective this transition, as we have seen, requires a repositioning. Seeking to return to his "Native Element" from "the Heav'n of Heav'ns" into which he has "presum'd" as "an Earthlie Guest," he is no longer "rapt above the Pole," as he was earlier in his epic. Aware that "half yet remains unsung," he now finds himself "standing on Earth" within "the visible Diurnal Sphear." There, he will sing "with mortal voice" (7.13–24).[16] In this moment of transition from one point to the next, he once again confirms his desire for safety.

At the very juncture at which he declares the fact of his safety ("More safe I sing with mortal voice"), however, he qualifies the immediate sense of confidence it projects by insisting upon the precariousness of his own present circumstances: "though fall'n on evil dayes, / On evil dayes though fall'n, and evil tongues; / In darkness, and with dangers compast round, / And solitude" (7.25–28). The anxiety that pervades these lines is heightened as the result of how they are articulated and of how they are framed by the lines that surround them. Their articulation emphasizes the poet's own sense of isolation, his feeling of being surrounded by alien forces that threaten to engulf him. He is veritably "compast round" by those forces ("darkness,"

15. In this regard, see Don Parry Norford, "The Devouring Father in *Paradise Lost*," *Hebrew University Studies in Literature* 8 (1980), 98–126.

16. For the bearing of that "mortal voice" on all aspects of Milton's epic, see John T. Shawcross, *With Mortal Voice: The Creation of "Paradise Lost"* (Lexington: University Press of Kentucky, 1982).

"dangers," "solitude") and is fearful of being besieged by them at any moment.[17] In an epic about the devastating effects of the Fall, he finds that he himself is "fall'n" on evil days that encompass him on all sides, right ("though fall'n on evil dayes") and left ("on evil dayes though fall'n"). Faced with these dangers, he appears to be a prisoner in his own world of isolation. Within that world, the "I" of the poet is obliterated, erased. It seeks refuge in a power beyond itself. It declares its faith in a celestial being whose name is "Heav'nlie" but whose presence fails to dispel the persistent dread that manifests itself at precisely those points the poet attempts to subdue it most. If the poet feels himself "more safe" by singing "with mortal voice, unchang'd / To hoarce or mute," that feeling is immediately compromised by the recognition that follows in the lines through which the dread of "evil dayes," "evil tongues," "darkness," "dangers," and "solitude" irresistibly erupts.

But even the confidence projected by the lines immediately preceding this eruption is expressed with a certain disquietude, a whistling in the dark. The safety is only comparative ("more safe"), the voice itself qualified by an awareness of its own mortality ("mortal voice"), the vocal resonance of the poet's song, although presently unabated ("unchang'd / To hoarce or mute"), subject to the "barbarous dissonance" of those "evil tongues," the "savage clamor" of which constantly threatens to drown "both Harp and Voice." The poet may declare himself "not alone" in the lines that follow his expression of disquietude and solitude, but his hope for a "fit audience" to hear him is itself muted by the recognition that this audience will be "few" (7.28–31).

The point is that, in the act of repositioning himself in his return to the "narrower bound / Within the visible Diurnal Sphear," he finds himself stationed within a realm fraught with dangers equally as great as those that confronted him when he was "rapt beyond the Pole." Recalling that rapture as he is "standing on Earth," he now faces the terrible prospect of the tearing of "the Thracian bard," who com-

17. As Barbara Kiefer Lewalski makes clear, the poet's desire for protection finds its antecedents in biblical psalms of lament and prayer. "In passage after passage, the Psalmist calls for or rejoices in God's protection as he is beleaguered by darkness, dangers, and many enemies." Lewalski cites corresponding passages from Psalms 17:3, 8–9 and 109:2 (*"Paradise Lost,"* p. 35). The passage suggests other biblical parallels as well, for example, Ecclesiastes 12:1 and Ephesians 5:16–19.

municated a "rapture" of his own to the woods and rocks until the means of that communication were silenced utterly.[18] The Bacchantes are an ever-present threat: they are forever waiting to perform their terrible act upon the poet, who may implore the higher powers to protect him and whose faith in those powers may be passionate and abiding but who nonetheless is unable to rid himself of the dread that continues to surface at the very point when his protestations to the contrary are most confidently expressed.

II

The situation in which the Orphic poet of *Paradise Lost* finds himself at the pivotal juncture in the proem to the seventh book has about it the immediacy and urgency of personal crisis. The anguish expressed here is a reflection of what Milton might well have experienced personally and directly as he faced the prospect of a terrifying and uncertain future immediately after the restoration of Charles II. To make connections of this sort, of course, carries with it the distinct danger of founding an argument upon biographical and compositional speculation that ultimately has no basis in demonstrable fact. Although the assumption is that the proem in question is of later, rather than of earlier, origin, there is no conclusive evidence regarding the specifics of its chronology or its topicality.

The prevailing assumption, however, is that the lines "though fall'n on evil dayes, / On evil dayes though fall'n, and evil tongues; / In darkness, and with dangers compast round, / And solitude," followed by the allusion to "*Bacchus* and his revellers, the Race / Of that wild Rout that tore the *Thracian* Bard," refer to Milton's situation brought upon by the Restoration.[19] Whether or not such is precisely

18. In *Naming in Paradise: Milton and the Language of Adam and Eve* (New York: Oxford University Press, 1990), John Leonard explores the various meanings of "rapt" and "rapture" in *Paradise Lost*. Implicit in Milton's use of these terms in the proem to Book 7 is that sense of brutality and violence we have come to associate with the dismemberment of Orpheus (pp. 236–41).

19. According to William Riley Parker, "at some point not long after the Restoration, he [Milton] had been able to dictate 'Half yet remains unsung', and resolutely closing his ears to 'the barbarous dissonance / Of Bacchus and his revellers', he had addressed the heavenly Muse that continued to inspire him" (*Milton Biography*, 1:587). The association of the proem with this period of Milton's life has a long history. Among earlier attestations, see *The Poetical Works of John Milton: With Notes of Various Authors*, 6 vols., 3 ed., ed. H. J. Todd (London: C. and J. Gilbert, 1826), 3:10n., and *The Poetical Works of John Milton*, 3 vols., ed. David Masson (London: Macmillan, 1890), 3:487n. More recent confirmation can be found

the case, I work with this assumption in order to extend the implications of the lines into the biographical and historical arena in which
Milton's own sparagmatic point of view was forged at that point in
his career when all hopes for the Good Old Cause had been completely
undermined and the noble champion of that cause was left alone,
blind, and bereft.[20] Proceeding on this assumption, I am not claiming
one-to-one correspondences or venturing chronological observations
concerning precise dates of composition. Rather, I am suggesting the
possibility of the milieu out of which Milton's sparagmatic mentality
arose in the creation of his proem in particular and of his epic in
general. Doing so, I am creating my own historical fiction in order to
provide both a biographical and a psychological context for Milton's
proem. In the creation of that context, I hope to be able to to engage
still further the terrible sense of urgency and anguished immediacy
embodied in Milton's references to his personal dilemma at that critical
moment in the life of his poem.

The historical fiction I have in mind is one propounded at least
as early as Jonathan Richardson the elder in his biography of Milton.
Addressing himself to Milton's circumstances after the Reformation,
Richardson observes:

> Well it was for Him that he had So Fine an Amusement, and a Mind
> Stor'd with Rich Ideas of the Sublimest Kinds: for besides what
> Affliction he Must have from his Disappointment on the Change of

---

in the standard modern editions. In his edition of the *Complete Poetry*, John T. Shawcross
notes that "evil dayes" and "evil tongues" are a temporal reference to the period of the
Restoration, from 1660 (p. 388, n. 8). This is in accord with Hughes (*Complete Poems and
Major Prose*, p. 346n) and Carey and Fowler (*The Poems of John Milton*, p. 776n). Hughes
warns, however, against "an over-positive identification" of the biographical and historical
circumstances underlying Milton's references. Such is particularly true in any attempt to
establish the chronology of composition. In this regard, see what are possibly the "over-
positive" speculations of Grant McColley, *"Paradise Lost": An Account of Its Growth and Major
Origins* (Chicago: Packard, 1940), pp. 294–325, esp. pp. 300–302. Such speculations are called
into question by J. B. Broadbent, "Links between Poetry and Prose in Milton," *English Studies*
37 (1956), 49–62. On the whole subject of the dating of *Paradise Lost*, among Milton's other
major poems, see the definitive study of John T. Shawcross, "The Chronology of Milton's
Major Poems," *PMLA* 76 (1961), 345–58. According to Shawcross, "neither the entire epic
nor any one of its books ... exhibits a clear-cut chronological ordering from its start to its
finish" (p. 350). Shawcross elaborates and extends these conclusions in *With Mortal Voice*,
pp. 173–77. The fullest account of the composition of *Paradise Lost* is to be found in Allan
H. Gilbert, *On the Composition of "Paradise Lost": A Study of the Ordering and Insertion of Material*
(Chapel Hill: University of North Carolina Press, 1947). Gilbert supports a Restoration context for the passage in question (pp. 84, 154).

20. On the eve of the Restoration, Milton in the *Ready and Easy Way* (1660) characterized
the royalist court as inhabited by the "tigers of Bacchus ... inspir'd with nothing holier then
the Venereal pox" (*YP*, 7:452–53).

the Times, and from his Own Private Losses, and probably Cares for Subsistence, and for his Family; he was in Perpetual Terror of being Assassinated; though he had Escap'd the Talons of the Law, he knew he had Made Himself Enemies in Abundance. [H]e was So Dejected he would lie Awake whole Nights. He then kept Himself as Private as he could. . . . and This is what is Intimated by Himself, VII. 26. *On Evil Daies though fall'n and Evil Tongues, in Darkness, and with Dangers compast round, and Solitude.*[21]

The context Richardson establishes is one in which the poet of *Paradise Lost*, finding himself in the direst of circumstances, is not only put to the expense of attempting to bear up under the weight of the losses he was made to sustain as a result of the changing times but faced with the prospect of the terrible physical harm encountered by those regicides who did not, in fact, escape the law. Subject to the perpetual terror of assassination, he would lie awake in a state of worry, dejection, and self-imposed confinement. As much as he might claim in his epic that he is not alone as long as his Muse visits his slumbers nightly, his condition of solitude and sleeplessness belies such assertions. Such for Richardson are the circumstances upon which the evil days and evil tongues, the darkness and dangers of Milton's proem, are founded. This, as it were, is Richardson's historical fiction.

Although it is obviously impossible to verify Richardson's account, it is perhaps worth noting that it is reiterated and further elaborated in the annotations that appear in the Richardsons' accompanying edition of *Paradise Lost* as the combined efforts of father and son. There, the events surrounding the composition of the proem in question are founded upon what the Richardsons call a "Secret History" for which they have "Good Authority."[22] To be sure, the Rich-

---

21. References to the biography are to J. Richardson, Father and Son, *Explanatory Notes and Remarks on Milton's "Paradise Lost"*. . . *With the Life of the Author, and Discourse on the Poem. By J. R. Sen.* (London, 1734), in *Early Lives*, pp. 275–76.

22. References to the annotations are to the Richardsons' *Explanatory Notes and Remarks on Milton's "Paradise Lost"* (London, 1734), p. 291. In their annotations, which supplement the comments in the biography, the Richardsons gloss *Paradise Lost* 7.32–39 as follows: "This is explained by a piece of Secret History for which we have Good Authority. *Paradise Lost* was written after the Restoration when *Milton* Apprehended himself to be in Danger of his Life, first from Publick Vengeance (having been very Deeply engag'd against the Royal Party) and, when Safe by a Pardon, from Private Malice and Resentment He was Always in Fear; Much Alone, and Slept Ill; when Restless he would Ring for the Person who Wrote for him (which was his Daughter Commonly) to Write what he Compos'd, which Sometimes flow'd with Great Ease."

ardsons never divulge the source of their authority, so the reliability of their secret history eludes confirmation. In our response to the text under consideration, however, I would argue, however, that such matters finally are not at issue. What is at issue is the extent to which our own understanding of the terrors portrayed at this poetic moment are conditioned by our willingness to believe that they in fact encode a crisis of the most personal sort, a crisis that is very much the product of historical exigencies that bestow upon Milton's epic an urgency and immediacy of profound significance. For the sake of argument, I adopt the Richardsons' secret history as the basis of my own biographical and psychological speculations.

Such speculations invite one to elaborate further on my historical fiction by exploring in greater detail Milton's circumstances during these especially trying times. Here, David Masson's account is very much to the point. Alluding to Milton's removal from Petty France to Bartholomew Close in May 1660 to avoid the dangers of the Restoration, Masson describes the place of Milton's "retirement and abscondence" in vivid terms:

> The narrow passage so named was entered from West Smithfield by a very old arch, part of the church of the Priory of St. Bartholomew, which dated from the twelfth century. It was a row or labyrinth of tenements that must have been old and quaint even in Milton's time.... To Milton, who may have known the close and its neighbourhood in his Aldersgate Street days, what mattered it now, in his blindness, in what dingy recess from any of the city thoroughfares, or in what room or garret there, they cooped him up for safety.... And so, in some small room, the walls of which he could feel round in his darkness, much alone, and hearing of the outside world only through the family [that harbored him], or through some faithful stealthy visitor, ... Milton waited to know his fate.[23]

Almost as if written under the inspiration of Milton's own account of himself as enveloped "in darkness" and "compast round" with dangers

---

23. *Life of Milton*, 6:162–63. Masson's account elaborates that of Edward Phillips: "His next removal was, by the advice of those that wisht him well, and had a concern for his preservation, into a place of retirement and abscondence, till such time as the current of affairs for the future should instruct him what farther course to take; it was a Friend's House in *Barthomew-Close*, where he liv'd till the Act of Oblivion came forth"; see Phillips, "The Life of Mr. John Milton," in *Early Lives*, ed. Darbishire, p. 74.

and with solitude, the description recreates the sense of foreboding confinement, enclosure within enclosure, which pervades the self-portrayal in the proem to the seventh book of *Paradise Lost*. In Masson's portrayal, the very name Bartholomew Close is made to inscribe the sense of enforced confinement delineated with such elaborate care, as the description moves from one enclosure to the next: the narrow passage, the labyrinth of tenements, the dingy recess, the room or garret, all culminating in Milton's own blindness as the ultimate enclosure. Here, in this world of topographical, physical, and implicitly spiritual confinement, the frightened recluse hides from an alien and threatening universe.

"Three months and three weeks," observes Masson, Milton lived in that room, "listening for footsteps and uncertain whether he was to be hanged or not." As Masson points out, the fear he attributes to Milton is not at all exaggerated. "There had been exulting prophecies by royalist pamphleteers on the eve of the Restoration that Milton would soon be going to Tyburn in a cart." This was fully the expectation of all who anticipated the fate of the regicides. "As surely as if he had left the statement on record, the imagination of his own execution, to the last ghastly particular of cart, ladder, hangman, rope, and the yelling multitude that should see him, though unseen by him, must have passed through Milton's mind again and again during those three months and three weeks of his hiding in Bartholomew Close."[24]

The world on the outside was no doubt for Milton one of deafening jubilation and noise. "Englishmen released their pent-up emotions in countless ways—in singing and shouting, in drinking, toasts, ringing bells, and building bonfires, in firing guns and cannon, in hanging effigies of Oliver and other hated rebels." In short, there must have been more than sufficient "savage clamor" to drown out "both Harp and Voice."[25] On the occasion of the festivities surrounding the Restoration itself, Milton, suggests William Riley Parker, "probably heard the wildly cheering crowds, the trumpets and the kettledrums, as the royal progress moved through the streets of the city. The restored monarch slept at Whitehall that night for the first time in eighteen years. He was physically and emotionally exhausted, and doubtless slept soundly on the down bolster and the velvet bed,

24. *Life of Milton*, 6:163.
25. *Milton Biography*, 1:568.

under the satin and fustian quilts so hurriedly prepared for him. Elsewhere in his capital there were men who lay stark awake, wondering what the morrow held for them."[26] Secluded in "retirement and abscondence," Milton was alone and afraid.

The ordeal of this self-imposed confinement over that terrible period was further compounded by other indignities. Although Milton's body may have "Escap'd the Talons of the Law" (or at least the worst those talons might have been disposed to inflict), his works became subject to the mutilations his body managed to escape. Books into which had been poured the "pretious life-blood" of a "master spirit" were faced with the order to be burned by the common hangman.[27] Moreover, the talons of the law did extend to Milton's own person to the extent that he was actually imprisoned (presumably in the Tower) some time between September and November 1660.[28] As Parker observes, "for the first time in his life, and quite unexpectedly, Milton experienced the inside of a jail."[29] Even after his release, he remained in constant danger. So Masson conjectures that "the resentment of some fanatic royalist at his escape from the gallows might easily have taken the form of knocking the blind man down in the streets or stabbing him in his house."[30]

Self-imposed imprisonment, followed by actual imprisonment and the ever-present specter of unanticipated violence to his person: Milton was indeed enveloped "in darkness" and "compast round" with dangers, as well as with solitude. Confronted with a darkness and a solitude that continued to replicate and intensify itself, Milton must have enacted and reenacted within his own mind the sufferings of those whose fate he might very well have shared. In those moments, "the imagination of his own execution" was no doubt given free reign.

---

26. *Milton Biography*, 1:569.

27. These books included *Eikonoklastes* and Milton's *Pro Populo Anglicano Defensio* (or *Defensio Prima*) against Salmasius (*Milton Biography*, 1:570). According to Masson, "such burnings in London and Westminster were but the signal for burnings that were to continue for some time in different parts of the country" (*Life of Milton*, 6:193). See Charles II's *A Proclamation For calling in, and suppressing of two Books written by John Milton* (August 13, 1660), in *Life Records*, 4:328–32.

28. This occurred some time after the issuing of the Act of Oblivion and Milton's removal to Red Lion Fields in Holburn. See the entry "Imprisonment, Milton's" by John T. Shawcross in the *Milton Encyclopedia*, s.v. See also Godfrey Davies, "Milton in 1660," *Huntington Library Quarterly* 18 (1954–55), 351–63. Milton's mental outlook during this trying period is explored by Frank Kermode, "Milton in Old Age," *Southern Review* 11 (1975), 513–29.

29. *Milton Biography*, 1:575.

30. *Life of Milton*, 6:215.

In a very real sense, he became the victim of a culture that sought not only his undoing but the undoing of others with whom he had held an intimate bond.

That culture was among the most barbarous one can imagine. One need only attend to the trials and executions of Milton's compatriots to see the extent of the brutality. The experience of Maj. Gen. Thomas Harrison is a case in point. Arrested, tried, and condemned by the Commissioners of the Court as a regicide for his participation in the beheading of Charles I, he received a sentence deemed appropriate for those found guilty of having committed so heinous a crime.[31] The language of the sentence is executed in a manner to suggest the exquisite care with which the particulars of the punishment were conceived:

> The Judgment of this Court is, and the Court doth award, That you be led back to the place from whence you came, and from thence to be drawn upon an hurdle to the place of execution; and there you shall be hanged by the neck, and being alive shall be cut down, and your privy members to be cut off, your entrails to be taken out of your body, and, you living, the same to be burnt before your eyes, and your head to be cut off, your body to be divided into four quarters, and head and quarters to be disposed of at the pleasure of the king's majesty, and the Lord have mercy upon your soul.[32]

As the language of the sentence makes clear, the particulars of the punishment are such that the victim upon whom the sentence has been placed becomes a participant in the drama of the undoing of his own body. He is both subject and object of that undoing. As subject, he takes center stage in the unfolding drama. Drawn upon a hurdle or sledge, he makes his grand entrance from the place of his confinement to the place of his execution. Brought up to the platform

31. The punishments described here are by no means unique to English culture. We need only recall the multiple accounts of torture, mutilation, and burnings at the stake described in John Foxe's *Actes and Monuments of the Church* (1563) and Raphael Holinshed's *Chronicles of England, Scotland, and Ireland* (1586–87) to confirm this fact.

32. In *A Complete Collection of State Trials and Proceedings for High Treason and Other Crimes and Misdemeanors from the Earliest Period to the Year 1783*, 21 vols., comp. Thomas Bayley Howell (London: Longman, 1816–26), 5:1034. For the rationale underlying the sentence for high treason, see William Blackstone, *Commentaries on the Laws of England*, A Facsimile of the First Edition of 1765–69, 4 vols. (Chicago: University of Chicago Press, 1979), 4:370.

of the execution, before the watchful eyes of the audience, he is hanged by the neck. From that point forward, he becomes not so much the subject as the object of his undoing. In that transition, he is made to behold with his own eyes the degradation and mutilation of his body parts. His privy members are cut off, an emasculation that fully deprives him not only of his manhood but of that selfhood and self-respect through which he might have otherwise maintained any semblance of honor and worth. Compounding that indignity, he is next disemboweled and then forced to witness the burning of his entrails. So emasculated and eviscerated in this festival of cruelty and torture, he witnesses his body as a vehicle or representation of self totally obliterated. No longer able to claim manhood, selfhood, and self-respect, he is deprived of identity: both as subject and as object, his beingness is erased. Following that mutilation and degradation, he finally undergoes the ultimate erasure. He is beheaded, and his body is divided into four quarters. He undergoes the most extensive form of sparagmos imaginable. Such was the fate of Maj. Gen. Thomas Harrison. It was, to be sure, a fate he shared with others.[33]

As Milton well knew, such brutality was imposed not only upon those made to sustain such mutilations as a prelude to death. Dismemberment was actually imposed upon those who had already died. The desecration of such horrors followed the dead into their very graves. Thus, on January 30, 1661, to commemorate the anniversary of King Charles the Martyr, the order of the two Houses for disinterring the corpses of Bradshaw, Cromwell, and Ireton was fully implemented. The account in the *Mercurius Politicus* is sufficient to suggest the outcome of that event:

---

33. See Masson's account of the execution, which occurred at Charing Cross on October 13, 1660. According to Masson, John Cook, Hugh Peters, Thomas Scott, Gregory Clements, Adrian Scroope, and John Jones were similarly executed at Charing Cross. None of the condemned was executed with less pity than Hugh Peters. "The execution of Peters, said the newspapers of the day, 'was the delight of the people, which they expressed by several shouts and acclamations when they saw him go up the ladder, and also when the halter was putting about his neck' " (*Life of Milton*, 6:96–97). As witness to these events, Samuel Pepys is, as usual, unwittingly revealing. Here is his entry for October 18, 1660: "This afternoon, going through London and calling at Crowes the upholster in Saint Bartholmew—I saw the limbs of some of our new Traytors set upon Aldersgate, which was a sad sight to see; and a bloody week this and the last have been, there being ten hanged, drawn, and Quarterd. Home; and after writing a letter to my Uncle by the post, I went to bed"; *The Diary of Samuel Pepys*, 11 vols., ed. Robert Latham and William Matthews (Berkeley: University of California Press, 1970–83), 1:269–70.

This day, Jan. 30 (we need say no more, but name the day of the month) was doubly observed,—not only by a solemn fast, sermons, and prayers, in every parish church, for the precious blood of our late pious sovereign King Charles the First, of ever glorious memory, but also by publicly dragging those odious carcases of Oliver Cromwell, Henry Ireton, and John Bradshaw, to Tyburn. On Monday night Cromwell and Ireton, in two several carts, were drawn to Holborn from Westminster, where they were digged up on Saturday last; and the next morning Bradshaw. To-day they were drawn upon sledges to Tyburn. All the way (as before from Westminster), the universal outcry and curses of the people went along with them. When the three carcases were at Tyburn, they were pulled out of their coffins, and hanged at the several angles of that triple tree, — where they hung till the sun was set; after which they were taken down, and their heads cut off, and their loathsome trunks thrown into a deep hole under the gallows.[34]

According to Masson, the heads of Cromwell, Bradshaw, and Ireton were immediately placed by the common hangman on poles on the top of Westminster Hall, with the head of Bradshaw in the middle. They were to remain there for years, "people looking up at them for a while with whatever thoughts might be convenient, and soon with no thoughts at all, and the heads themselves looking down, with their empty eye-sockets, on what was passing underneath."[35] Although one does not know precisely where Milton was during the acting out of these festivities, it is highly unlikely that he was in his house in Holborn.[36] "For it was up Holborn that the mob ran that morning, howling round the hurdle on which the corpses were laid; and it was actually

34. *Mercurius Politicus*, January 24–31, 1660–61, cited in *Life of Milton*, 6:123. See John Evelyn's entry for January 30, 1661, in *The Diary of John Evelyn*, 6 vols., ed. E. S. de Beer (Oxford: Clarendon Press, 1955), 3:269.

35. *Life of Milton*, 6:123–24.

36. In a letter to me of December 15, 1991, John T. Shawcross suggests the possibility that Milton may have been hiding at Edward Millington's house. Shawcross raises this possibility based on the observation of Jonathan Richardson: "about 1670 I have been told by One who Then knew him, that he Lodg'd Some time at the House of *Millington* the Famous Auctioneer Some Years ago, who Then Sold Old Books in *Little Britain*"; see Darbishire, ed. *Early Lives*, p. 275. According to Shawcross, "Parker [in his Biography] has no explanation for this, for there was no reason at the time [that is, in 1670] for Milton to be anywhere except in his own house. Millington was in Duck Lane, Little Britain, not far from Red Lion Square and Holborn (west of Little Britain) where Milton was until early 1661 when he moved to Jewin Street (just east of Little Britain). It could have been easy enough for Richardson or his informant to get the date [that is, 1670, rather than 1660] wrong, or even for some kind of error in writing or printing: a 7 for a 6."

in the Red Lion Inn, Holborn, close to Milton's house" that "the corpses had been deposited, since they had been dug up in Westminster, with a view to that day's finishing spectacle." Overrun by howling mobs, this vicinity, Masson observes, "would not have been a safe one for Milton, had it occurred to anyone that he was at hand."[37]

Such was Milton's situation after the restoration of Charles II. In the darkness of his seclusion and blindness, Milton became an unwilling witness to all the ferocity and barbarity an alien culture could inflict. In the release of the forces underlying that ferocity and barbarity, sparagmos was given free reign. In its most extreme form, it was realized once again as a datum of history, a datum which, in its various manifestations, must certainly have underscored for Milton what Masson so aptly called the "imagination of his execution." From the psychological perspective his outlook has been seen to embody, this datum must have profoundly influenced his sparagmatic sensibility. Dismemberment, after all, was of crucial import to the very culture in which he found himself both participant and potential victim. Milton no doubt saw himself suffering in his imagination the fate of those regicides who, like Harrison, were mutilated, emasculated, eviscerated, beheaded, and dismembered; he no doubt projected his own deepest fears, compounded by equal amounts of revulsion, onto the corpses of Cromwell, Bradshaw, and Ireton, disinterred, hanged, and beheaded for the masses to gaze at. In the midst of these atrocities, he no doubt heard the deafening din of the masses as they celebrated such acts in what he would have considered a rapturous frenzy of delight. In memory of such atrocities, he might well have implored his Celestial Patroness to save him from the horrors of a similar fate.

Such is the context through which I have read the passage that culminates the proem to the seventh book of *Paradise Lost*. I offer this context not as a way of establishing a causal relationship between historical circumstance and poetic creation. I frankly do not think that such a relationship established conclusively. Rather, I propose a historical fiction (a piece of secret history) that dates back to Milton's earliest commentators and forward to some of his latest interpreters. Doing so, I hope to provide a context through which it might be possible to understand in greater depth the psychological foundations for John Carey's astute observation that the idea of dismemberment,

37. *Life of Milton*, 6:215.

centered in the figure of Orpheus, seems to have focused some of Milton's deepest fears.

For Milton, the sparagmos of Orpheus became the focal point for all those horrors he feared might be visited upon his own body. Anticipated in *Lycidas*, such fears assumed consummate form in *Paradise Lost*. Particularly as they are manifested in Milton's configuration of self and the relationship between self and body in his thought, these concerns are of immense importance to the issues of gender addressed in Part II of this book.

Part II

GENDERING THE BODY

4

The Pursuit of the Lady

I

We have explored in depth the mythic and historical dimensions that underlie the Miltonic horror of sparagmos as expressed in the proem to the seventh book of *Paradise Lost*. With this as our point of departure, we have moved not only into other areas of Milton's epic but into his personal circumstances after the period of the Restoration. From that perspective, we have explored the culture of violence that threatened to victimize Milton at every turn, to engulf him, and to rend him savagely, as it had his compatriots both living and dead. As I have attempted to demonstrate throughout, Milton's fears of sparagmos were well founded. Centered in those myths he imbibed from his early youth and drew upon throughout his career, they came to full historical realization in the world around him. What Milton in his darkness witnessed as being perpetrated not only upon the living bodies of Thomas Harrison and Hugh Peters but upon the dead bodies of Cromwell, Ireton, and Bradshaw, he knew might very well become his own fate.

As we have seen, one of the great ironies is that this fate may have actually come to pass over a century after Milton's interment. Compounding this irony is that concerning the precise gender of the body that was disinterred and barbarously desecrated in this final act of sparagmos. In its postburial form, the body alleged to have been Milton's is viewed as male by some, female by others. The torn body in the inscriptionless coffin has bestowed upon it the double name John Milton/Elizabeth Smith. It is bisexual.

The event becomes a fitting symbol for the exploration of the issue of gender identity in the living body. Applying the postburial event to our present act of critical disinterment, we might observe that what is true of the dead body is no less true of the living body: it too is bisexual. In both forms, it is subject to the ravages of an alien world. If the proem to the seventh book of *Paradise Lost* is in effect an *Ad Matrem* that calls upon the Muse to defend her son against the ravages of Bacchus, this appeal is made all the more complex by virtue of the poet's association of himself not only with the figure of a violated Orpheus but with the presence of that other of which the poet is likewise a prime representative—the feminine the poet of *Paradise Lost* comes to subsume.[1]

This is an other that has prompted William Kerrigan to apply the title "poetess" to Milton. At the core of Milton's being, asserts Kerrigan, lies a woman, a female entity crucial to his psychic makeup. As Kerrigan observes, this creator of male figures (Satan, Adam, the Son, Jesus, Samson) is also an individual whose outlook betrays at once "an agitated concern with keeping the genders separate" and, "beneath the dogmatic planks of his work, in the nooks and crannies of its symbols and its suggestiveness," a subconscious inclination toward bisexuality. As a result of that inclination, the genders he portrays (particularly as the result of the act of self-gendering) undergo intriguing variations, so much so that not only the existence but the excellence of such poems as *Paradise Lost* "owe a good deal to the submerged refiguring of womanliness."[2] In a world that bore witness

---

1. For enlightening discussions of the bisexual aspect reflected in the poet and his Muse, see, in particular, William B. Hunter (with Stevie Davies), "Milton's Urania: 'The Meaning, Not the Name I Call,'" in *The Descent of Urania: Studies in Milton, 1946–88* (Lewisburg, Pa.: Bucknell University Press, 1989), pp. 31–45; Stevie Davies, *The Feminine Reclaimed: The Idea of the Woman in Spenser, Shakespeare, and Milton* (Lexington: University Press of Kentucky, 1986); Virginia Mollenkott, "Some Implications of Milton's Androgynous Muse," Bucknell Review 24 (1978), 27–36. See also James Turner, *One Flesh: Paradisal Relations in the Age of Milton* (Oxford: Oxford University Press, 1987), esp. pp. 65–71, 142–48.

2. The citations are from Kerrigan's unpublished paper, "John Milton, Poetess" (presented before the SUNY, Binghamton, Renaissance Conference, October 1987), which explores the bisexual implications of Milton's personality in *Paradise Lost*. Of corresponding

to what Thomas Laqueur calls "the fundamental incoherence of stable, fixed categories of sexual dimorphism, of male and/or female," the gender shifting Kerrigan sees in the Miltonic personality is very much consistent with a frame of mind extending back to the world of classical physiology and forward into the Renaissance.[3] Applying this frame of mind to Milton, I here extend my discussion of the mythic dimensions of Milton's sparagmatic sensibility to the notion of gender shifting that is an essential constituent of his outlook. To gain a renewed sense of this outlook, I first examine the Miltonic other as it emerges in his earliest works.

In particular, I have in mind those works in which Milton was made to respond, either directly or implicitly, to his special identity as "the Lady of Christ's College."[4] Codified in the form of an epithet, this became a signature of his being from the period of his Cambridge schooldays (a time when such epithets burn most and are thereafter branded on the memory). It was a signature of castigation imposed from without as a derisive form of typecasting. In his brilliant study of the implications of this epithet (indeed, sobriquet) within the context of Milton's fragile sense of self-identity, John T. Shawcross has astutely observed: "What no one seems to have remarked is that at Christ's, a community of about 265 people in those days, Milton was called *the* Lady of Christ's, indicating no slight notoriety and probably no localization to that one college only." In short, this was a person with a reputation, one resulting from the universal "penchant for assigning certain attributes to the male or to the female" as the result of appearance or behavior.[5] *The* Lady of Christ's was therefore an

---

significance is Kerrigan's "Gender and Confusion in Milton and Everyone Else," *Hellas* 2 (1991), 195–220, which served as the basis of discussion at the Newberry Library Milton Seminar, October 1990. Kerrigan's major statement concerning the complexities of the developing Miltonic personality is to be found in *The Sacred Complex: On the Psychogenesis of "Paradise Lost"* (Cambridge: Harvard University Press, 1983).

3. Thomas Laqueur, *Making Sex: Body and Gender from the Greeks to Freud* (Cambridge: Harvard University Press, 1990), esp. p. 22.

4. The ascription is found in John Aubrey, "Minutes of the Life of Mr John Milton," in *Early Lives*, p. 3: "He had light browne hayre, his complex[ion]...exceeding faire....He was so faire y[t] they called him the Lady of X[ts] coll." See the comments in Henry John Todd, *Some Account of the Life and Writings of John Milton*, 2d ed. (London, 1809): "Milton, in his youth, is said to have been extremely handsome. He was called the Lady of his College; an appropriate appellation which...he could not relish; and I may add that he might be less inclined to be pleased with the title, as, at that period, the appearance of effeminacy was attacked from the pulpit: 'We live in an age,' says bishop Lake, 'wherein it is hard to say, whether in cloathes *men grow more womannish*, or women more mannish!' " (pp. 141–47).

5. John T. Shawcross, "Milton and Diodati: An Essay in Psychodynamic Meaning," in

identity through which Milton became known to others and as a result of which he was made to struggle with the whole notion of femininity such a designation implied. As an aspect of that struggle, Milton was in a sense obliged to justify himself not only to his compeers but to himself as an individual at once male and yet exhibiting characteristics that would prompt others to identify him as a female. Milton took the epithet to heart. At stake for him was what became the dilemma of an incipient bisexuality crucial to his own sense of self and essential to his formative outlook.

In no other work are the implications of this dilemma more dramatically portrayed than in his sixth Prolusion, a document of essential importance to the development of Milton's formative outlook.

Most probably composed in 1628 when Milton was entering his senior year, the sixth Prolusion was delivered (according to the headnote) "In the college summer vacation, but in the presence of almost the whole body of students, as is customary [*In Feriis aestivis Collegii, sed concurrente, ut solet, tota fere Academiae juventute*]." Divided into three parts, the Prolusion is structured formally with an *oratio*, a *prolusio* proper, and a concluding poem ("At a Vacation Exercise in the Colledge").[6] The *oratio* bears a title that is applicable to the argument of the Prolusion as a whole: "Sportive Exercises on occasion are not inconsistent with philosophical Studies [*Exercitationes Nonnumquam Ludicras Philosophiae Studiis non Obesse*]" (YP, 1:266; CM, 12:204).[7]

In defense of that assertion, Milton undertakes to address his

---

"*Eyes Fast Fixt*": *Current Perspectives in Milton Methodology*, ed. Albert C. Labriola and Michael Lieb (Pittsburgh: University of Pittsburgh Press, 1975), pp. 127–63 (Vol. 3 in the Milton Studies series). In revised form, this essay has been integrated into Shawcross's magisterial study, *John Milton: The Self and the World* (Lexington: University Press of Kentucky, 1993), pp. 33–66. My analysis is much indebted to Shawcross's insights.

6. The full title of the poem in effect contains its own headnote: "At a Vacation Exercise in the Colledge, part Latin, part English. The Latin speeches ended, the English thus began." At the end of the poem is a postscript: "The rest was prose." As Shawcross notes in his edition of the *Complete Poetry*, the Latin speeches referred to in the "headnote" are lost. Judging by the postscript, there were apparently prose sections following the poem, but these are also lost (p. 52, n. 1). See the entries on the sixth Prolusion and "At a Vacation Exercise" in *Milton Encyclopedia*, 7:37–39, and 1:109–10, respectively. Informative are Masson's account of the Prolusion and its occasion in *Life of Milton*, 1:285–96, and Harris Francis Fletcher, *The Intellectual Development of John Milton*, 2 vols. (Urbana: University of Illinois Press, 1961), 2:443–52, as well as the commentary, text, and translation in John Milton, *Private Correspondence and Academic Exercises*, trans. Phyllis B. Tillyard, introd. and comment. by E. M. W. Tillyard (Cambridge: Cambridge University Press, 1932).

7. Fletcher, *Intellectual Development*, 2:444, renders *Ludicras* more accurately as "jesting or scornfully laughing."

classmates in what amounts to a "summer saturnalia" during the annual vacation exercises at the college. As master of ceremonies, he finds himself called upon to engage in a "salting," that is, an initiation of his fellow students by a senior sophister. In the salting, the senior customarily performed as a "Father" instructing his "Sons." The function of the Father was to burlesque with his Sons the exercises and subscriptions to the oaths required for entrance to the university.[8] The nature of the Father's role was variously conceived. In Milton's case, it assumed the form of the Aristotelian *ens* (absolute being) or "Father of the Predicaments," that is, the progenitor of the categories into which all knowledge is reduced (*YP*, 1:285; *CM*, 12:242). As the Prolusion itself makes clear, Milton's particular predicament extended well beyond the metaphysical circumstances his adopted role implied. It engaged his very sense of self, as well as his sexuality, in the midst of a potentially alien environment.

This sense of alienation and indeed hostility is discernible from the outset of the Prolusion and persists until the very end. At the outset, it is discernible in the self-conscious and finally ambivalent posture Milton adopts in response to his audience. Addressing that audience in a tone of forced jocularity, Milton makes it clear that he is really not like his fellow students. Appalled by the lusts (*libidinis*) he sees all about him, he is obliged to "disguise his almost godlike mind [*animum prope Diis immortalibus parem*]" under the "semblance of idiocy" (*vecordiae*) and play the wise fool (*morosophos*) in order to accommodate the demands of the occasion and to satisfy the desires of those who insist that he make a "spectacle" of himself in the performance of a solemn show (*solennes ludos*) on their behalf (*YP*, 1:266–268; *CM*, 12:204–8). This solemnity is more than a frivolous romp, an Erasmian jeu d'esprit: it is a serious game, one in which the stakes are high.

On the occasion of this summer saturnalia, Milton finds himself in a difficult situation. Having earlier been rejected by his peers, he

---

8. Roslyn Richek, "Thomas Randolph's *Salting* (1627), Its Text, and John Milton's Sixth Prolusion as Another Salting," *English Literary Renaissance* 12 (1982), 103–31. According to Richek, the term "salting" perhaps refers to the idea that those who misbehaved had to drink a salted beer (p. 105). One suspects that in spirit at least what was then known as a salting might today come close to what we would call a roasting. The phrase "summer saturnalia" is Parker's; see his discussion of the occasion of the sixth Prolusion in *Milton Biography*, 1:44–45. Parker argues that the ceremony took place in July of 1628 (2:739, n. 55). Richek argues for October rather than midsummer (p. 129, n. 5).

is now in his aloofness determined at once to maintain his distance
and to be accepted as "one of the boys." Although he admits having
anticipated a cold reception from his fellow students, Milton expresses
mock-surprise at the new-found friendliness toward him among those
who had previously shown him nothing but hostility and dislike (*pror-
sus infenso*) (*YP*, 1:266–68; *CM*, 1:204–8). Theirs has been a record of
disruption and misrule, a record that persists in Milton's address to
them throughout the Prolusion. Later beset by their shouting (*clamorem*) and their malice (*maledicant*), Milton alludes to the fact that on
a previous occasion some fifty of his fellow students (themselves so-
phisters), "armed with short staves, [marched] across Barnwell Field,
and, as a step toward laying siege to the town . . . destroyed the aq-
ueduct, in order to force the townsfolk to surrender through shortage
of water." (Apparently, the leader of that siege was originally supposed
to have assumed Milton's role as master of ceremonies at this present
occasion, but because of his "recent departure" Milton himself was
enlisted to perform it.) In any case, this is a rowdy group indeed, one
Milton characterizes as a commonwealth of fools (*stultorum*) and one
over which he has been made Dictator (*meo Dictator sum creatus*)
charged with the commemoration of an April Fools festival (*stultorum
festa*) "sacred to the god of Laughter" (*Deo Risui*) (*YP*, 1:277, 284–86;
CM, 12:226–28, 242–46).[9]

On the occasion of this *stultorum festa*, Milton places himself on
display for all to see. Beheld by all, he opens himself up, lays himself
bare, with an awareness of the potentially threatening position in
which he has situated himself and the knowledge that he stands to be
victimized again by the "keen and biting enmity" of his compeers in
an outburst of renewed hostility. It is with a sense of grim irony, then,
that he refers to them as the most learned individuals (*doctissimorum
hominum*). They are indeed "the very flower" of the University. So
profound is Milton's "admiration" for them that he boasts himself
more fortunate than Orpheus or Amphion, "who used to attract an
audience consisting only of rocks and wild beasts and trees, and if
any human beings came, they were at best but rude and rustic folk."
Milton, in contrast, discovers before him "the most learned men al-
together engrossed in listening to [his] words and hanging on [his]

9. The phrase *stultorum festa* comes from Ovid's discussion of the Feast of Fools in the
Fasti (2.512); see *Ovid's Fasti*, trans. Sir James Frazer (Cambridge, Mass.: Harvard University
Press, 1959).

lips."[10] Such praise is little more than a ruse, one of which Milton's students are well aware, as they "nod" to each other knowingly while they gather to witness the senior sophister perform as Dictator of the Commonwealth of Fools (*YP*, 1:268–69, 274; *CM*, 12:208–10, 220).

If this is all great fun, one wonders where the levity ends and the anxiety over self begins. For *this* we recall is an Orpheus / Amphion with a reputation, one that renders him defensive throughout his performance and that prompts him to draw upon his considerable rhetorical skills as a desperate means of holding the wolves at bay.[11] Whatever the sweetness of the Orphic (or Amphionic) music here, its ultimate outcome, as Milton knew, could be disastrous in the face of the hostile and disruptive throng that surrounds the "poet" on all sides (*circumfusum me*), as it threatens to undo him. Despite these dangers, Milton takes upon himself the task of "entertaining" this throng. As suggested by his choice of words to describe what he is about, his self-exposure becomes an act of undressing. Departing from the "the strict rules of modesty [*rigidas verecundiae leges transversum*]" that customarily distinguish his behavior, he "unclothes" (*exuisse*) himself, as he descends to the level of those whose behavior he himself would call into question. Doing so, he looks upon himself as one of those comic actors (*Comoedi*) that implore (*implorare*) their audience for acceptance. He seeks, that is, applause and laughter (*plaudite, & ridete*) (*YP, 1:268–277; CM*, 12:208–27). What results is a remarkable performance, an act of self-exhibitionism and finally self-denigration in which the psyche laid bare at once exposes itself to and defends itself against the encroachments of the outside world.

Anyone familiar with Milton's performance in the second part of the Prolusion (the so-called *Prolusio* proper) knows only too well how enthusiastically this Dictator of the Commonwealth of Fools carries out his function. As if in direct reaction to prevailing university statutes against "improper jesting moving to theatrical laughter," Milton engages in an act of crude and obscene theater that has traditionally

---

10. See the notes on Orpheus and Amphion in *YP*, 1:269, nn. 13–14. Both references allude to these figures ironically as civilizing influences.

11. Ironically, Milton speaks of those who are always concerned that the witticisms of others are made at their own expense. "It would indeed serve them right," Milton maintains, "if their unreasonable suspicions were to be realised, and if they should find themselves the butt of everyone's witticisms, till they were almost driven to suicide" (*YP*, 1:272; *CM*, 12:218). The harshness of this statement is interesting in light of Milton's own determination not to be "the butt of everyone's witticisms."

caused his staunchest defenders to blanch.[12] There is no need to
rehearse in detail his antics here, except to observe that they serve an
important purpose in suggesting the extent to which Milton was determined to demonstrate that he too could be one of the boys. One
senses in that determination a willingness (perhaps even a compulsion)
to go to any lengths to elicit from his audience in all their raucousness
both *plaudite, & ridete*. Judging by the crudeness with which the *prolusio*
opens, Milton as rabble-rouser was successful in his cause.

Calling upon his audience to "raise loud laughter from [their]
saucy spleen [*petulanti splene*]," he wishes to hear the whole place
"resound with most immoderate laughter."[13] Like a stand-up comic,
he insults with crudeness in order to provoke even more laughter:
"If I see anyone not opening his mouth as wide as he should to laugh,
I shall say that he is trying to hide teeth which are foul and decayed,
and yellow from neglect, or misplaced and projecting, or else that at
today's feast he has so crammed his belly that he dares not put any
extra strain upon it by laughing, for fear that not the Sphinx but his
sphincter anus [*non Sphinx sed Spincter anus*] should sing a second part
to his mouth's first and accidentally let out some enigmas." Oral humor
is reinforced by anal humor: "For I should not like the cheerful sound
of laughter to be drowned by groans from the posterior [*posticus*] in
this assembly. I leave it to the doctors, who can loosen the bowels, to
loosen up all this" (*YP*, 1:277–79; *CM*, 12:226–29). Accompanied by
additional insults to those present, such humor serves in its crudeness
to align the fool with those whose folly he would share, in whose
grossness he would participate. In that alignment, the Dictator of the
Commonwealth of Fools demonstrates his manhood: he becomes, as
indicated, one of the boys.

The need to reinforce the act of making oneself over into the
identity of those from whom he seeks acceptance and recognition is
reinforced by the performance that follows hard upon the heels of
this gross appeal to laughter.[14] In that performance, Milton as con-

12. See *YP*, 1:277, n. 39; and *Life of Milton*, 1:288, n. 1.
13. The translation here is that of *CM*, 12:229, which comes closer, I think, than *YP*
to the sense of the original.
14. In his execution of the *prolusio*, Milton follows the call to laughter with additional
pointed humor presumably concerning the porters posted at the entrance of the hall in which
the performance took place. Punning upon the names of these porters, Milton conceives this
section as a descent to Hell, a descent he characterizes as a difficult and dangerous journey
(*YP*, 1:278–80; *CM*, 12:230–33).

summate chef prepares a banquet for his compeers. Although the banquet is sumptuous (and sumptuously described), there is something wrong with almost every dish. These include "fifty fatted boars which have been pickled in beer for three years, and yet are still so tough that they may well tire out," Milton laments, "even our dog-teeth." Next, appear the same number of oxen with "magnificent tails" (*insigniter caudatos*); only, Milton says, "I am afraid all the juice has gone into the dripping-pan." After these, there are as many calves' heads, "fat and fleshy enough, but with so little brains as not to be enough for seasoning." Then, there are about a hundred kids, but they are too lean "from over-indulgence in the pleasures of love [*crebriori Veneris usu nimium macros*]." It would be nice to have "a few rams with fine spreading horns [*speciosis & patulis cornubus*]," Milton continues, but the cooks have not yet delivered them from the town.

Such "sumptuous" dishes are followed by others, including fowls of various sorts. As delicious as these might appear, they unfortunately are not edible, for they produce rashes and even lice. Nonetheless, Milton offers up with gusto "an enormous turkey, so fat and stout after three years' fattening that one vast dish is scarcely big enough for it, and with such a long and horny beak [*rostro eousque praelongo & eduro*] that it could attack an elephant or a rhinoceros with impunity." We have "rightly slaughtered it on this day," Milton declares, "because it had begun, after the custom of the huge apes, to lie in ambush for the girls and to offer violence to the women [*propterea quod praegrandium Simiorum more incepit puellis insidiari, & vim inferre mulieribus*]."[15]

Having concluded his account of the feast he would offer his compeers, Milton invites them to help themselves to whatever they desire. That cannot be much, for what is so striking about the banquet is the sense of unpleasantness and finally revulsion it provokes. Whether it is the tough-skinned boars unsuccessfully chewed by dog-teeth, oxen depleted of all their juices, fat and fleshy (but brainless) calves' heads, lean, undigestible goats, or birds that produce rashes and lice, this is hardly a banquet one would relish. With a certain amount of amusement, Milton concedes that his fellow students will probably go away even hungrier than they arrived (*YP*, 1:280–82;

---

15. Once again, the translation here is that of *CM*, 12:237, which comes closer than *YP* to the sense of the original.

CM, 12:234–39).[16] If such is true, then Milton will have achieved precisely the effect he seeks: that of disgusting and in effect assaulting his fellow students in the act of presuming to cater to their appetites. The purpose of this turnabout is significant. It encapsulates Milton's own deep-seated feelings about those he himself (either implicitly or overtly) views with such disgust and revulsion. The humor thereby becomes double-edged: it cuts those it would amuse (indeed sustain) with the feast it sets out before them.

But even more is at stake than the sense of disgust and revulsion implicit in Milton's description of the feast. Crucial to that description (and consistent with the distaste it provokes) is its repeated emphasis upon the gross sexuality it associates with the various dishes it serves up. One thinks, for example, of the "magnificent tails" of the oxen, of which, Milton says, "I am afraid all the juice has gone into the dripping-pan." This loss of potency is reinforced by the corresponding references to those figures of lust, the skinny goats depleted of their virility "from over-indulgence in the pleasures of love." Nothing will reclaim this loss of virility, not even rams "with fine spreading horns." Then, of course, there is that turkey with its "long and horny beak." This is a wild and virile bird indeed; however, it is also a dangerous fowl, not to be trusted, because of the threat it poses to all those innocent and unsuspecting girls and women for whom it lies in ambush like a predatory ape. Beware of such violent and rapacious turkeys given to sexual assault! The best recourse for them is sudden death, an expeditious slaughtering to deprive them of their power to do harm, to attack with their long and horny beaks. If such is Milton's attitude toward the dishes he would serve up, it reflects in repugnant and loathsome form his attitude toward those he would serve. They become an extension of the banquet, their perverse and aggressive (but ultimately impotent) sexuality a reflection of the dishes they would be loath to devour. Milton sends them away hungry, for the sexuality they embody finally does not satisfy.

A culminating moment in what might be considered the first part of the *prolusio* proper, Milton's banquet is crucial to an understanding not only of his problematic relationship with those he addresses but

16. The illusory quality of the banquet is reinforced at this point by Milton's comparison of his feast to "the nocturnal feasts offered by the devil to witches" (*YP*, 1:282; *CM*, 12:238).

to his establishment of his own sense of self as a being whose sexuality is potentially under attack and who finds himself both on show and on the defensive. It is this attitude that assumes concrete and dramatic form in the second part of the *prolusio*. The transition to that part is signaled by the statement: "I will now turn to what concerns me more closely [*Vereum ad ea pergo quae ad me propius attinent*]" (*YP*, 1:282; *CM*, 12:238). The wording of the transition is revealing: it suggests that everything Milton has been about in the earlier part of the Prolusion has been preparatory to this moment. If you have been wondering what I have been getting at with all the foregoing nonsense, Milton appears to be saying, I am now prepared to put my cards on the table. For what I am about to disclose will show you what is really on my mind. It is something that concerns me more closely. That which concerns him more closely is what he has been talking about all along: his own sexuality.

That sexuality Milton projects onto his role as Father obliged to address his Sons. His discomfort with this role is immediately discernible in his mode of "conceiving" it. Somehow, that assumption is immediately looked upon as suspect, a feeling that is projected by the Father onto the children he has ironically begotten: "We, gentlemen, in our desire to come as near as may be to paternity [*ad paternitatem*], are eager to play in pretence a part which we should not dare really to play unless in secret [*in occulto*]." Be careful about displaying the desire for fatherhood too openly, Milton warns: such public display might get you into trouble. Indeed, it might compromise your manhood, for you will then be looked upon as too openly desiring that which is customarily associated with the occupations of girls, who, Milton says, "are wont to invent games of weddings and births, striving to catch and hold the shadows of those things for which they long and yearn" (*YP*, 1:282–283; *CM*, 12:238). At issue is Milton's conflict over his own sexuality. As a "Lady" who has been transformed not only into a man but into a "Father," that is, the progenitor of offspring, he projects onto those responsible for his transformations his own discomfort at being obliged to assume a role that places him in an untenable and potentially threatening situation. This is a gender conflict upon which he elaborates in some detail.

In a statement of dramatic self-revelation, Milton brings the terms of this conflict graphically to the fore:

But, I ask, how does it happen that I have so quickly become a Father [*subito factus sum Pater*]? Good heavens, what a prodigy this is, more astonishing than any recorded by Pliny [*Quid hoc est prodigii Pliniana exuperantis portenta*]! Have I slain some serpent and incurred the fate of Tiresias [*numnam ego percusso angue Tyresiae fatum expertus sum*]? Has some Thessalian witch poured magic ointment over me [*ecqua me Thassala saga magico perfudid unguento*]? Or have I been violated by some god, like Caeneus of old [*an denique ego a Deo aliquo vitiatus, ut olim Caeneus*], and won my manhood as the price of my dishonour [*virilitatem pactus sum stupri pretium*], that I should be thus suddenly changed from woman into man? Some of late called me "the Lady" ' [*A quibusdam, audivi nuper Domina*]. But why do I seem to them too little of a man [*At cur videor illis parum masculus*]? . . . It is, I suppose, because I have never brought myself to toss off great bumpers like a prize-fighter, or because my hand has never grown horny with driving the plough, or because I was never a farm hand at seven or laid myself down full length in the midday sun; or last perhaps because I never showed my virility in the way these broth-ellers do. But I wish they could leave playing the ass as readily as I the woman [*verum utinam illi possint tam facile exuere asinos, quam ego quicquid est feminae*]. (*YP*, 1:283–84; *CM*, 12:240)

Complex in its implications, this vivid passage strikes at the heart of Milton's self-consciousness concerning his sexual identity and the way that identity has been configured by his compeers.

At issue in the passage is the fact of Milton's strange metamorphosis, one that causes him to rival in appearance the monstrous prodigies to be found in Pliny's *Natural History*. As a woman become a man (indeed, a Domina become a Pater), he is a prodigy to confound all prodigies, a monster that is a genuine source of astonishment to those who behold him. It is as if he has been besmeared with the magic ointment of some Thessalian witch, an act that has occasioned his prodigious transformation. Responding to this act, Milton must defend himself, cleanse his reputation. Although Milton adopts a tone of apparent jocularity in response to such a metamorphosis, it is of crucial importance to his sense of self. Underlying that sense is, as we have seen, a bisexuality arising from the transformation from one gender to the next. To use the language of the Prolusion, such once again is Milton's special predicament. In the passage under consid-eration, Milton represents the predicament in a variety of ways, among them the allusions to Tiresias and Caeneus, two figures that represent in mythological form the basis of what is involved in Milton's sense of self, his sexual identity, and the extent to which he feels his identity has come under attack and must be championed, if not cleansed of imputed blame.

As we have seen from our discussion of the sixth Elegy, Tiresias is one among several figures with whom the Orphic poet comes to associate his own divine calling. The seer Tiresias appears throughout Milton's poetry and prose as the embodiment of prophetic discourse and knowledge. The poet of *Paradise Lost* extols this blind figure in the highest terms possible.[17] Identifying himself with Tiresias and his plight, Milton, however, establishes an uneasy relationship. For if Tiresias as blind seer possessed the power of foresight, he came by that knowledge as the result of an offense to the gods, an offense that was the direct result of a violation of gender propriety. In the traditions surrounding Tiresias, that violation assumes several forms.[18] In the passage under consideration, that form has to do with Tiresias's experience of having undergone a transformation from the male gender to the female gender and from the female to the male.

As related by Ovid and others, this transformation occurred as the result of Tiresias's having come upon two serpents coupling one day. Seeing them in the act, he struck them apart with a stick. Because of this act, he was transformed into a woman, a fate he endured for seven years. Thereafter, he saw the serpents coupling once again and once more struck them apart with a stick; as a result, he was returned to the form of a man. This transformation, in turn, became useful to Jupiter and Juno. According to the myth, they appealed to Tiresias to settle a dispute they were having concerning who gets more pleasure out of loving, the male or the female. (Jupiter opted for the female, Juno for the male.) Having experienced both genders, Ti-

17. So Milton declares in the proem to the third book of Paradise Lost: "nor somtimes forget / Those other two equal'd with me in Fate, / So were I equal'd with them in renown, / Blind *Thamyris* and blind *Maeonides*, / And *Tiresias* and *Phineus* Prophets old" (3.32–36). In *De Idea Platonica*, Milton refers to Tiresias as "the Dircean seer, to whom blindness yielded a profound light" (l. 25). Milton's references in the prose reflect this deep admiration. In his dedicatory poem to *Paradise Lost*, Andrew Marvell bestows upon Milton the highest praise through an allusion to Tiresias: "Just Heav'n thee like Tiresias to requite / Rewards with Prophesie thy loss of sight"; "On *Paradise Lost*," ll. 43–44 (*CM*, 2:3–5).

18. According to one version of the story, for example, Tiresias was blinded as a result of having seen Athena bathing. The story is related by Callimachus (*Hymns*, 5:57 ff., *Bath of Pallas*).

resias, they felt, was in the best position to provide the answer. His authority would be unimpeachable. Unfortunately, his judgment was not, for he took the side of Jupiter in the debate and was immediately blinded by Juno for his efforts.[19] Although he received the gift of prophecy in recompense, his prophetic ability, as Milton was aware, always had about it an aura of blame, stemming from the impropriety associated with the act of offending the gods.[20] Throughout his later writings, Milton was at pains to dissociate the fact of his own blindness from the idea that this affliction was visited upon him as the result of an offense to the higher powers. Protestations to the contrary, Tiresias for Milton remained a problematic figure, at once exalted for his visionary powers but also implicated in some disturbing way in the gender transformations that were so much a part of the Miltonic outlook. At a deep level, these transformations could assume a quality of impropriety that put Milton himself on the defensive regarding the feminine other that found itself open to attack.

This other is projected in the figure of Caeneus, "violated," as Milton says, "by some god [*a Deo aliquo vitiatus*]" and made to win his "manhood as the price of . . . [his] dishonour [*virilitatem pactus sum stupri pretium*]." For Milton, Caeneus was particularly interesting because his transformation was accompanied by a corresponding change in names. As a woman, Caeneus was known as Caenis, as a man Caeneus. This fact must have been particularly telling for one whose identity moved between Domina and Pater. According to the Ovidian account of Caeneus, Caenis was the loveliest girl in Thessaly and the object of the attention of many suitors, who were attracted to her beauty and sought her favors. Maintaining her virginity and her honor, she refused to yield herself to any of them. Upon seeing her, Neptune, however, became enamored. One day, as she was walking the lonely shore, he raped her. Moved by her plight and in recompense for her lost honor, he offered to grant her any request in his power. Caenis replied that she wished to be changed to a man. In that way, she would

---

19. See Ovid's *Metamorphoses* (3.316–38), as well as Hyginus, *Fabulae*, 75.

20. In his illuminating essay "Courting Urania: The Narrator of *Paradise Lost*," Noam Flinker demonstrates that the concept of offending the gods is implicit in the Miltonic account not only of Tiresias but of Phineus as well. In these cases, the act of effrontery toward a divine being is exacerbated by the fact that the offended divinity is normally female. Crucial to Miltonic thought, the idea is discernible in both the earlier and the later works; in *Milton and the Idea of Woman*, ed. Julia M. Walker (Urbana: University of Illinois Press, 1988), pp. 86–99.

never again be forced to suffer such an indignity. Neptune immediately complied, and she thereafter lived as a man.[21]

The transformation strikes at the heart of the dilemma that underlies Milton's own bisexuality. Fiercely devoted to the exalted cause
of his honor and indeed his virginity, he is nonetheless defensive about
those qualities that prompt his detractors to mock him as Domina.[22]
At once proud of qualities that others might deem unmanly, he is at
pains to maintain his masculinity: "Some of late called me 'the Lady.'
But why do I seem to them too little of a man [*At cur videor illis parum
masculus*]?" In its mock defensiveness, Milton's attestation to his manhood (*masculus*) reveals a great deal about his role as Domina. As much
as his detractors might accuse him of being "too little of a man," he
is just as much a man as they. Not to put too fine a point on it, the
implied sexuality of "too little" (*parum*) returns us to all that phallic
punning (oxen with magnificent tails, rams with spreading horns,
turkeys with long and horny beaks) that distinguishes Milton's feast.
Although his fellow students might consider him *parum masculus*, his
is as big as theirs, Domina or no Domina.

Such a defensive posture, moreover, is reinforced by the final
reference in the passage: "I wish they could leave playing the ass as
readily as I the woman [*verum utinam illi possint tam facile exuere asinos,
quam ego quicquid est feminae*]." Attributing "asshood" to those who
attack him, he avers that he has far less trouble in laying aside or
baring himself (*exuere*) of his feminine qualities (*feminae*), that is, the
woman within him, than they that quality of asinos within them.[23] His
feminine qualities, he implies, should not be construed as a manifestation of his *ens*. Although he may strike others as effeminate, the
differences they observe, he argues, are only apparent. Simply because
he does not make a practice of excessive drinking or because his hands

21. See the account in Ovid's *Metamorphoses* 12.189–210.
22. Shawcross's explanation is most telling: "The most obvious pun—amazingly not
recognized before—is the equation of 'Lady' with 'Mother,' suggested not only by the re-
placement of 'Father' but by its qualifying phrase 'of Christ's.' That is, Milton to his fellow
students was like the Virgin Mary, most apparently because of his virginity.... For the term
'Lady' suggests hauteur, and the term 'Father' not only indulges his 'return' to maleness but
requires sexual intercourse resulting in a pregnancy" ("Milton and Diodati," pp. 137–38).
23. The translation in *YP* does not do the original justice. The translation in *CM* is
more to the point: "But would that they could as easily lay aside their asshood as I whatever
belongs to womanhood" (12:241). Masson is even truer to the spirit of the original: "I would
they could as easily doff the ass as I can whatever of the woman is in me" (*Life of Milton*,
1:292). As Shawcross comments, the pun on "exuere ['uncover' or 'lay bare'] asinos ['asses']"
is both obvious and bawdy ("Milton and Diodati," p. 138).

are not rough with driving the plough, or because he never worked on a farm, or because he does not frequent brothels, the lack of these supposedly manly qualities should not cause him to be derided as effeminate.

Indeed, he maintains, the so-called qualities of effeminacy for which he is derided are the very ones upon which he prides himself. In that pride, he associates himself with earlier notables, great men who were likewise deemed effeminate, among them the orators Demosthenes and Hortensius. These also were branded by their adversaries as being "too little" (*parum*) or suffered the ignominy of having bestowed upon them female names such as Dionysia. Enlisting the aid of earlier notables, Milton turns upon his own adversaries by declaring that he utterly dismisses the attempts at character assassination to which he has been subjected and maintains that his spiteful adversaries are beneath contempt (*YP*,1:284; *CM*, 12:240–42).

Here Milton goes on the attack. Reminding the raucous crowd of students before him that, if he is the Father in this "comic" drama, they are his sons, his brood. As Domina/Pater, he gave birth to them, an act that in itself caused him no little discomfort and pain. Veiled in mock comedy, his response reflects a desire to return pain with pain, violence with violence, savagery with savagery. In the very act of disclaiming any intention of perpetrating violence upon his raucous brood, he in effect threatens to do just that. The threat returns him to the trope of the banquet that initiated the *prolusio* proper. That banquet is no longer one of such sumptuous fare as oxen and fowl. Rather, it now becomes the very offspring of the Domina/Pater: it is the Sons themselves. In accord with the brutality of Tantalus and Lycaon, on the one hand, and the frenzy of Dionysus, on the other, Milton threatens to serve his brood up as a feast to be devoured (*YP*, 1:285–86; *CM*, 12:242–44).[24] Because Milton's Sons are ironically manifestations of his own being, his *ens*, however, the trope of the banquet turns upon itself, becomes potentially self-devouring, in what might well amount to a final act of carnage. Although Milton is at pains to avoid such an outcome, the prospect of its occurrence even in jest contributes a cautionary note to the Prolusion as a whole and

---

24. In an act of *omophagia*, Tantalus killed his son Pelops and served his limbs to the gods as food; Lycaon served up human flesh to Zeus. The idea of the Father eating the Sons is consistent with the tradition of the saltings, see Richek, "Thomas Randolph's *Salting*," pp. 109, 130.

underscores the sense of disquietude and anxiety with which Milton conducts himself as Dictator, indeed *morosophos*, in this *stultorum festa*.

Within the context established by the sixth Prolusion, such a feast accordingly became for Milton an arena for the display of his own deep-seated feelings regarding the whole issue of self-portrayal which constituted his very being. At the heart of that self-portrayal is an incipient bisexuality that distinquished his acknowledged role as Domina/Pater. Defending this role in the face of potential victimization, Milton came under attack on all sides, an attack he threatened to return in kind. Whatever comic qualities one might wish to ascribe to the Miltonic configuration of self on this so-called occasion of laughter, a sense of sparagmos lurks in the background, prepared to manifest its disruptive forces at any moment unless held in check. These are forces of which Milton was painfully aware and to which he responded with a full display of his rhetorical prowess as the Lady of Christ's.

II

The anxiety made evident in the gender reversals of the sixth Prolusion, coupled with the terrible sense of being victimized by an alien universe, finds ample and indeed dramatic representation in *A Mask*. There, the Lady of Christ's assumes his role as the Lady of the masque, and the threatening forces against which the Lady of Christ's defended his personality on the occasion of the college festivities becomes the ragged and unruly crew headed by Comus, that master of revelry and deceit. As such, the solemnity presented September 29, 1634, to celebrate the Earl of Bridgewater's election as Lord President of Wales is the perfect vehicle for the Domina of the sixth Prolusion to project himself and his situation into a new arena with a new audience some six years later.

Whereas in the sixth Prolusion Milton asked his audience to imagine that they were celebrating a festival sacred to the god of laughter, in *A Mask* he adopts the calendrical occasion of Michaelmas Night to reinforce the "solemnity" of what he is about.[25] In keeping with the

25. For a discussion of these festivals, see, among other works, Howard V. Harper, *Days and Customs of All Faiths* (New York: Fleet, 1957). Coming at the end of the harvest season (September 29), St. Michael's Day is a festive occasion, marked by overindulgence (pp. 242–43). Its higher purpose is to commemorate the ministry of the angels in celebrating

decorum of that occasion, Milton was conscious of both its social and liturgical contexts, notably those that emphasize the need to demonstrate restraint and order in the face of all misrule.[26] It is as if the sometime Dictator of the *stultorum festa* has now taken it upon himself to reconfigure the terms of his Prolusion in order to reclaim that reputation, that sense of self, he was obliged to lay bare as *morosophos* in the earlier work. Confronted by the onslaught of the new *morosophos* in the form of Comus and his crew, the Domina of *A Mask* counters the forces of misrule against her person.

What results is a battle for self-preservation, one in which the ability to remain chaste in the face of overwhelming odds is at the very center of the *agon*.[27] Chastity assumes this centrality as the result of its elevation to the level of a theological virtue. Substituting chastity for charity in the Pauline paradigm ("And now abideth faith, hope, and charity, these three; but the greatest of these is charity"; 1 Cor. 13:13), Milton bestows upon chastity not only a theological prominence but a supremacy that places it first in the hierarchy of virtues. There, it is distinguished by a visionary status as a virtue that must not be sullied under any circumstances. So the Lady proclaims,

> O Welcom pure-ey'd Faith, white-handed Hope
> Thou flittering Angel girt with golden wings
> And thou unblemish't form of Chastity,

the victory of Saint Michael over the dragon (Rev. 12). See the entry on Michaelmas in the *Encyclopaedia of Religion and Ethics*, 12 vols., ed. James Hastings (New York: Charles Scribner's Sons, 1926), s.v., as well as *The Book of Days: A Miscellany of Popular Antiquities in Connection with the Calendar*, 2 vols., ed. Robert Chambers (Edinburgh: W. & R. Chambers, 1862–64), 2:393.

26. See William B. Hunter's discussion of the liturgical backgrounds to the feast of Michaelmas in "The Liturgical Context of Comus," *English Language Notes* 10 (1972), 11–15, and in *Milton's "Comus": Family Piece* (Troy, New York: Whitston, 1983), esp. pp. 30–32. See also James Taaffe, "Michaelmas, the 'Lawless Hour,' and the Occasion of Milton's *Comus*," *English Language Notes* 6 (1968–69), 257–62, which provides a detailed account of the customs associated with Michaelmas, especially those having to do with misrule. In connection with Michaelmas, Taaffe discusses the practice of "ganging," which involved assaults on individuals who came in the path of the revelers, and the "lawless hour," during the exchange of power when the reins of authority were held by no one.

27. In the consideration of these matters, one must be aware of the changes made between the manuscript versions and the printed texts. The text that serves as the basis of my discussion is that in the Shawcross edition. For a treatment of the complexities surrounding the text, see Shawcross, "Certain Relationships of the Manuscripts of *Comus*," *Papers of the Bibliographical Society of America* 54 (1960), 38–56, 293–94; and the Introduction to *A Maske: The Earlier Versions*, ed. S. E. Sprott (Toronto: University of Toronto Press, 1973), pp. 3–33.

I see ye visibly, and now beleeve
That he, the supreme good, t' whom all things ill
Are but as slavish officers of vengeance,
Would send a glistring guardian if need were
To keep my life and honour unassail'd. (ll. 214–20)

Reinforcing this belief in the supremacy and purity of chastity is an association of the virtue with warriorlike characteristics. In the words of the Elder Brother, it contains a "hidden strength." Whoever possesses such a strength is "clad in compleat steel." Armed with the weapons chastity affords and imbued with the aura of its "sacred rayes," the warrior may "trace huge forests, and unharbour'd heaths, / Infamous hills, and sandy perilous wilds," with the full assurance that "No savage feirce, bandite, or mountaineer / Will dare to soyl her virgin purity." In this respect, the chaste virgin as warrior with her "arms" becomes Diana-like in her aspect. Bearing her "dred bow," she is the "Fair silver-shafted Queen for ever chaste": "gods and men / Fear'd her stern frown, and she was queen o'th woods." More than that, she possesses the "snaky-headed *Gorgon* sheild / That wise *Minerva* wore, unconquer'd virgin, / Wherwith she freez'd her foes to congeal'd stone" through "rigid looks of chast austerity / And noble grace that dash't brute violence / With sudden adoration, and blank aw" (ll. 419–52). As such, she is not just a formidable figure but a frightening one as well. Enemies fear her ability to overcome and unnerve them at will.

In this fantasy of power that endues the chaste person, Milton projects his own needs as an individual fully committed to the ideals of chastity he seeks to uphold. As the Lady of *A Mask*, he at once transforms the Pauline triad of theological virtues into an ideal of the highest form of ethical conduct and mythologizes that transformation to accommodate his view of the chaste person as an awesome and invincible warrior. Bestowing these qualities of awesomeness and invincibility upon his warrior, Milton as Lady assumes a fearsome aspect, one capable of defending himself against any enemy who might attempt to assault. In the fantasy Milton creates at this juncture, there is no room for any possibility of "feminine" vulnerability. That which is customarily associated with masculine strength and prowess is embodied in female form. Such a tactic is a Renaissance commonplace.[28]

28. See in particular the figure of Britomart as a representation of the virtue of chastity

Drawing upon that commonplace, Milton reconceptualizes the Pauline triad through a mythology of power centered in his female warrior. As such, the Lady becomes the new warrior par excellence. From the theological perspective Milton adopts, the Lady's assumption of the role of warrior gives new meaning to the Pauline notion of the individual who is called upon to defend himself against the evils of this world. "Finally, my brethren," Paul exhorts, "be strong in the Lord, and in the power of his might. Put on the whole armour of God, that ye may be able to stand against the wiles of the devil. For we wrestle not against flesh and blood, but against principalities, against powers, against the rulers of the darkness of this world, against spiritual wickedness in high *places*" (Eph. 6:10–12). If Milton so arms himself, he does it in the form of a Domina prepared to risk all in the defense of her chastity.

Milton cultivated such a posture throughout his career as poet and polemicist. His *Apology* for Smectymnuus is a case in point. Faced with the disruptive and noisy threats of the adversary "barking at the doore," he defends his chastity in a manner that bears directly upon the distinctions to which his self-portrayal in the masque gives rise. Here is the Lady of *A Mask* justifying that sense of moral righteousness and indeed aloofness in response to any affront that might cause her to compromise her standards of propriety. That justification takes into account Milton's deportment as much as it does his convictions. At the same time, it reflects an intense awareness of the gender-related issues that assume paramount importance in such figures as the Lady of his masque. Alluding to a "reserv'dnesse of naturall disposition, and morall discipline," he maintains in the *Apology* that he is proud of having been infused with those "chaste and high mysteries" espoused in holy Scripture that "*the body is for the Lord and the Lord for the body* [1 Cor. 6:13]." These mysteries have taught him "that if unchastity in a woman whom Saint *Paul* termes the glory of man, be such a scandall and dishonour, then certainly in a man who is both the image and glory of God, it must, though commonly not so thought,

---

in the third book of *The Faerie Queene*. The Lady is very much patterned after Spenser's lady warrior. In an entirely different vein, compare Milton's discussion of Boadicea in *The History of Britain*: "She was of Stature big and tall, of visage grim and stern, harsh of voice, her hair of bright colour flowing down to her hipps; she wore a plighted Garment of divers colours, with a great gold'n Chain; button'd over all a thick robe." Milton has contempt for those who see her as an example of a conflict of genders that underlies the British sense of identity, "as if in *Britain* Woemen were Men, and Men Woemen" (*YP*, 5:79–81).

be much more deflouring and dishonourable [1 Cor. 11:7]" (*YP*, 1:892). Willing to sacrifice all for the sake of his chastity, he dedicates himself and his body to the cause of his Lord. In this act of dedication, he sees himself as appropriating that virtue customarily associated with woman and incorporating it into himself, into his body, into his very being. Implicit in this appropriation is the all-important male-female relationship that underlies the Pauline hierarchy. It is a relationship Milton accommodates to his own needs as a way of reinforcing his outlook: if man is the image and glory of God and woman the image and glory of man, so unchastity in the man is that much more "deflouring and dishonourable" than unchastity in the woman.

Expressing the relationship in these terms, Milton invites us to view that which has been "commonly not so thought" (that is, the association of chastity with maleness) as consummately male. In this association, we are to see the chastity that defines maleness not only as encompassing femaleness but as moving it to a higher plane. From this perspective, chastity becomes the means by which male and female are at once subsumed into one whole and incorporated into a new form. If "the body is for the Lord and the Lord for the body," the body in question is decidedly bisexual by virtue of that quality through which its maleness is informed by and brings to perfection its femaleness. Milton gives new meaning to the Pauline doctrine "Neither is the man without the woman, neither the woman without the man, in the Lord. For as the woman *is* of the man, so *is* the man also by the woman: but all things of God" (1 Cor. 11:11–12). Applying such texts to his own notion of sexuality, Milton consummates within himself as it were the characteristics of both genders. As the very embodiment of chastity, he incorporates both that maleness he views as crucial to his identity and that femaleness whose characteristics he seeks to sublimate. It is just such characteristics that are reflected in the Domina who resists the wiles of Comus in *A Mask*.

As the action of *A Mask* makes clear, however, the fantasy of power through which the Lady's strength and prowess are defined is subject to assaults of the most threatening sort. Despite all claims to the contrary, the chastity that empowers the Lady does not render her completely invulnerable. In the domain of the purely physical, her hidden strength can be overmatched by superior powers. As one who remains vulnerable to powers over which she has no control, she can be immobilized: her body can be made to succumb to forces capable of subjecting her to their will. Led by the enchanter Comus, those forces are formidable indeed. Tracing his lineage to Bacchus and Circe, Comus has the power both to overcome his victim forcibly and, given the opportunity, to transform his victim into "the inglorious likeness of a beast" (ll. 520–30, 559–662). As his name implies, he is the very embodiment of the forces not just of revelry but of unbridled riot and chaos against which even the most potent forces of order are powerless.[29]

Confronted by such destructive forces within the "wild surrounding wast" of the "hideous wood" (ll. 403–520) which threaten the unwary traveler, the Lady finds herself in a precarious situation. With the "corporal rind" of her physical being "immanacl'd," she is placed against her will in an "*inchanted Chair*" (that manifestation of the body as flesh bound to its own corporality). There, Comus attempts to overwhelm her entirely (ll. 660–65; stage directions).[30] What she faces in this situation is the possible devastation brought about by that "deflouring" of innocence (to use Milton's term) that the virgin is made to undergo as the result of an attack by a superior force. In short, she faces the specter of rape.

Such a possibility is implied rather than overtly stated, but it remains a distinct possibility nonetheless. The context of the Lady's immobilization and the language through which it is described are clearly sexual and indeed violent in orientation. They imply rape. Leah Marcus, among others, has argued most persuasively for such a reading.[31] The Lady, she observes, "is placed in an atmosphere of seemingly gratuitous sordidness and increasing sexual menace." Comus compares her first to a "near victim of rape"—Daphne fleeing Apollo (ll. 661–62). Accompanied by a "cordial Julep heere / That flames, and dances in his crystal bounds" (ll. 672–73), he then offers

---

29. For the most illuminating discussion of this aspect, see Cedric C. Brown, *John Milton's Aristocratic Entertainments* (Cambridge: Cambridge University Press, 1985), esp. pp. 57–77. Brown provides a complete background for coming to terms with the etymological associations of Comus as *Komos*. See also Georgia B. Christopher, "The Virginity of Faith: *Comus* as a Reformation Conceit," *ELH* 43 (1976), 479–99.

30. The suggestion of the "inchanted Chair" as a manifestation of the flesh as chair is inescapable here. As "corporal rind," the body in its "fleshliness" has been completely immobilized.

31. Leah Marcus, "The Milieu of Milton's *Comus*: Judicial Reform at Ludlow and the Problem of Sexual Assault," *Criticism* 25 (1983), 293–327. I have also had occasion to consult the excellent unpublished essay of Julia M. Walker, "Textual Assault: Milton's Mask of Pornography."

her a chance to surpass "*Jove*-born *Helena*," a victim of abduction who complied with her abductor. When it becomes clear that he has failed to move her, he suggests physical aggression against her. The full sordidness of the Lady's dilemma is made apparent only at the moment of her release, with the implication that the "marble venom'd seat" in which she has been imprisoned has been "smear'd with gumms of glutenous heat" (ll. 916–17). Although the precise meaning of these lines is open to question, writes Marcus, "most readers seem to agree that there is something distinctly seamy about them: Milton's vagueness, if anything, heightens the atmosphere of sexual innuendo by allowing our imaginations to work on the images."[32]

One might well reconfirm the view of those inclined to apply a sexual interpretion to the Lady's dilemma of being "smear'd with gumms of glutenous heat" by recalling Milton's own predicament in the sixth Prolusion of having been assaulted by "some Thessalian witch" who has "poured magic ointment" over him. As we have seen, such an assault is specifically conceived in the context of a sexual violation (*vitiatus*), indeed, a rape. The dilemma is no less compelling in Milton's masque. There, Comus with his false magic assumes the role of the Thessalian witch, one whose new ointment has correspondingly subjected the Lady to the grossest of indignities, tantamount, at least symbolically, to the perpetration of a rape.

As several of scholars have persuasively demonstrated, this situation of potentially forced compromise finds its counterpart in actual contemporary circumstances concerning rape, circumstances with which Milton would certainly have been familiar and as the result of which the action of his masque assumes a renewed urgency. There is no need to reiterate the findings of these scholars here.[33] What is at issue is the importance, as well as the nature, of the sexual threat Comus represents. Underlying Comus's assault upon the Lady is a

32. Marcus, "Milieu of Milton's *Comus*," p. 317. As Marcus notes (p. 327, n. 29), *Milton Quarterly* is the source for the exchange of views that resulted in this interpretive approach: see J. W. Flosdorf, "Gums of Glutenous Heat: A Query," *Milton Quarterly* 7 (1973), 5; followed by John T. Shawcross and Stanley Archer, " 'Glutenous Heat': A Note on Comus, l. 917," *Milton Quarterly* 7 (1973), 99; Edward Le Comte, "By Sex Obsessed," *Milton Quarterly* 8 (1974), 55–57, and Shawcross's response, p. 57; and Jean-Francois Camé, "More about Milton's Use of the Word 'Gums,' " *Milton Quarterly* 9 (1975), 51–52.

33. See in particular Barbara Breasted, "*Comus* and the Castlehaven Scandal," *Milton Studies* 3 (1971), 201–24; Marcus, "Milieu of Milton's *Comus*"; and Marcus, "Justice for Margery Evans: A 'Local' Reading of *Comus*," in *Milton and the Idea of Woman*, ed. Walker, pp. 66–85.

heightened sense of the violence he would perpetrate upon her. Although portrayed symbolically in her immobilization in the chair and in the language and imagery that underscore her dilemma, the aura of violence is very much part of the scene both as it conceived and as it is executed.

Faced with the prospect of this violence, the Lady is put to the expense of relying upon whatever power she has available to her as one whose bodily mobility has been effectively obliterated. In that position, she resorts to the power of language. The way her claim to verbal power is executed and its effect upon her assaulter bring into sharp focus her precarious situation. The claim to verbal power highlights an ability to perform that which never really comes to pass:

> To him that dares
> Arm his profane tongue with contemptuous words
> Against the Sun-clad power of Chastity,
> Fain would I somthing say, yet to what end?
> Thou hast nor Ear, nor Soul to apprehend
> The sublime notion, and high mystery
> That must be utter'd to unfold the sage
> And serious doctrine of Virginity. (ll. 780–87)

Clearly at stake here is a conflict of power, one that involves the attack of the profane upon the sacred. The conflict is conceived in verbal terms, as an assault of the sullied language of contempt upon that which is so pure and so sublime that the very language required to unfold its meaning transcends the ability and the worth of the attacker to apprehend its mysteries. This is what is at stake in the Lady's defense of her identity as a being totally chaste and virginal. So committed is she to "the uncontrouled worth / Of this pure cause" that the "sacred vehemence" through which she is prepared to champion it would move "dumb things" to "sympathize" and "the brute Earth" to "lend her nerves, and shake" (ll. 794–96). In short, her claims to verbal power rival those of Orpheus himself: she is, in fact, the female counterpart of the archetypal poet. Such is the extent of the Lady's ability, as well as her commitment to the cause.

Momentarily at least, her effect on Comus is daunting: "She fables not," Comus concedes; "I feel that I do fear / Her words set off by som superior power; / And though not mortal, yet a cold shuddring dew / Dips me all o're" (ll. 780–803). His hesitation is temporary, however, and his determination redoubled in the renewal of his assault. The threat continues unabated, and the Lady's condition remains precarious. She may claim access to a sacred vehemence that has the power to move dumb things to sympathize and the brute Earth to lend her nerves, and shake, but she remains immobilized nonetheless. As a being able to elicit the response of that which is otherwise dumb and to control the natural world through the power of her utterance, she is faced with the terrible fact of her inability to liberate herself. No one doubts her claims to power, but her claims are insufficient to ward off the attack. This is an Orpheus whose magic is once again in need of a superior force to counter the effects of one who derives his power from his Bacchanalian, as well as his Circean, heritage.

The superior force in question assumes the form of the Attendant Spirit as Thyrsis initially and as the nymph Sabrina ultimately. Although an understanding of the symbolism reflected in both figures is important to an appreciation of the means by which the Lady is finally liberated, an assessment of those complexities lies beyond our immediate concerns. What is important for our purposes is an awareness of the extent to which the Lady remains subject to powers beyond her control. As chaste and virtuous as she is, the environment in which she finds herself continues to be threatening. Despite all his powers, the Attendant Spirit does not possess within his own means the ability to liberate the Lady: by implication, his "thyrsus" fails to perform adequately against the thyrsus of Comus. Even equipped with "haemony," the brothers, as emissaries of the Attendant Spirit, are unable to "sease" Comus's "wand" (ll. 647–52; 814–15). "Without his rod revers't / And backward mutters of dissevering power," the Attendant Spirit laments, "We cannot free the Lady that sits heer / In stony fetters fixt and motionless" (ll. 816–19). The lament is an acknowledgment not only of the Lady's immobilization but in some sense of her subjection to the "dissevering power" of the enchanter.[34]

The Lady has, as it were, undergone a dissevering, a sparagmos of sorts. It requires the power of language to reverse the enchantment,

34. That dissevering is symbolized in the power of Comus's thyrsus: "Nay Lady sit; if I but wave this wand, / Your nervs are all chain'd up in alabaster / And you a statue" (ll. 659–61). Comus presumably does wave his wand, and the Lady is chained up. The chaining is tantamount to a symbolical dissevering.

that is, to repristinate her, to make her whole. To achieve that repristination, the Attendant Spirit must call upon the aid of Sabrina,
one who has correspondingly undergone a "dissevering" and has herself been repristinated. Marcus offers the following summary: "According to standard accounts, among them Milton's own, she [Sabrina]
had herself been the guiltless product of a forced sexual relationship,
her mother a hostage of war, the daughter cast into the flood despite
her own innocence, and transformed into the goddess of the Sev-
ern."[35] In short, the guiltless product of a forced sexual relationship
must be called upon to liberate a virgin who has also been victimized
(at least symbolically) by the advances of one bent on her undoing.
Sabrina succeeds in liberating and implicitly repristinating the Lady
as the result of an incantatory power, accompanied by something that
resembles a baptismal ritual, which purifies the Lady and removes the
"gumms of glutenous heat" with which her "marble venom'd seat"
had been "smear'd" (ll. 909–18).

Given the occasion of Sabrina's act of purification, her success in
overcoming the effects of "insnared chastity" (l. 909) amounts to a
fantasy of repristination, a reversal of Comus's "rod" and the power
of his "dissevering" advances. Such is the result of Sabrina's enchantments (in effect, her disenchantments of Comus's enchantments),
manifested in her "backward mutters" and her baptismal rite. In the
world of masquery, such enchantments are perfectly appropriate. In
the real world, where Sabrinas are difficult to come by, such enchantments are out of place, however. Other means must be sought to ward
off the threats that one such as Comus with his crew represents.

III

Whether or not Milton's masque has ties to the various sexual
outrages scholars have seen to underlie its composition, Milton was
intensely conscious of and responsive to the dangers that beset those
votaries of chastity he held in such high esteem. Not long after the

35. Marcus, "Milieu of Milton's *Comus*," p. 319. See Milton's account in *The History of Britain*, YP, 5:18. In *A Mask*, the Attendant Spirit attributes the story to "*Melibaeus*," presum- ably Spenser (see *The Faerie Queene*, 2.10.14–19). There are other Renaissance versions as well. See Jack B. Oruch, "Imitation and Invention in the Sabrina Myths of Drayton and Milton," *Anglia* 90 (1972), 60–70.

performance of *A Mask*, Milton recorded with approval in his Commonplace Book: "The nun Ebba cut off her nose and lips and urged the other sisters to do the same thing so that, frustrated in this way, the Danes would make no attempt against their virtue [*Ebba monacha nasum sibi et labia truncavit, idemque caeteris sororibus suasit ut hoc modo elusi Dani nihil in earum pudicitiam tentarent*]" (*YP*, 1:370; *CM*, 18:133). Placing his observation under the heading *Castitas*, Milton implied that for him it represented the supreme response of the true virgin to the threat of anyone who might attempt to violate one's chastity.[36] Short of invoking a Sabrina with her enchantments to liberate "insnared chastity" from its perilous station, the alternative (an effective one at that) is to mutilate oneself beyond all recognition. The point is that underlying the figure of Sabrina is an awareness that will beset Milton throughout his career: in response to the "dissevering power" of Comus with his crew, the powers of Sabrina are finally ineffectual. It will take more than backward mutterings and baptismal rites to repristinate one subject to the violence that lies without.

Even after the Lady is liberated, the unsettling sense of her vulnerability persists. The masque ends triumphantly enough: the Lady and their brothers are presented to their parents, accompanied by dancing and festivity; and the Attendant Spirit returns to his "spheary" realm (ll. 957–1023). All is well within Ludlow Town and in the castle of the father's court. But this fantasy of release and return cannot dispel what lies without. Comus has escaped with his crew intact; he still possesses his powers, as well as that phallic wand through which his powers are made effective; his presence within the "cursed place" he calls home continues to represent a threat.

Despite its quality of celebration and closure, the action of the

36. Dated between 1639 and 1641, the entry in the Commonplace Book alludes to the account in John Stow, *The Annales, or Generall Chronicle of England* (London, 1615), p. 78: "An. 870. Saint Ebbe Abbesse of Coldingham vi miles North from Berwicke, cut off her nose & upperlip, & perswaded all her sisters to do yᵉ like that they being odible [*sic*] to the Danes, might the better keepe their Virginity, in despite whereof yᵉ Danes burned the Abbey, & the Nuns therein." In the margin, Stow has *"Flores Historiar. Chastity before beautie preferred,* a rare example." Concurring with Stow's estimate, Milton alludes to this marginal notation in his entry. For an elightening discussion of this practice of self-mutilation to counteract attempts at rape, see Jane Tibbetts Schulenburg, "The Heroics of Virginity: Brides of Christ and Sacrificial Mutilation," in *Women in the Middle Ages and the Renaissance: Literary and Historical Perspectives*, ed. Mary Beth Rose (Syracuse: Syracuse University Press, 1986), pp. 29–72. Compare as well Milton's entries under *De Libidine* (1639–41?) in the Commonplace Book, particularly that concerning "the examples of two Belgian virgins excellently avenging the dishonor done them" by killing those who sought to rape them (*YP*, 1:369–70; *CM*, 18:132).

masque gives rise to the nagging feeling that all is finally not right. The fantasy of release and return can be exploded by the troubling awareness that an alien world waits without: its terrors are not far to seek. Coming hard upon those of Sabrina, the enchantments created by the concluding festive moments in the masque are in their own way as delusive as hers. For all the promise afforded by the sudden, miraculous (but one might suggest, unscheduled) appearance of the nymph, the Lady remains subject to attack. Orpheus can still be violated by the Bacchantes. It is something of this ominous quality that pervades the awareness in *Lycidas* that the nymphs were helpless when "the remorseless deep" closed over the head of the poet; that the magic of the old bards proved futile; that the spirits of the "wisard stream" were nowhere to be found; that the Muse herself proved powerless to prevent the violation of her "inchanting son." All this, the poet of *Paradise Lost* would lament, is nothing but an empty dream. It is a dream Milton in his role as the Lady was made to experience as the enchantments of his fantasy were played out in production and survived in the memories of those who were aware that what they witnessed, after all, was that illusory world represented so well by the very title of Milton's work, *A Mask*.

When the work was published anonymously a few years later under the sponsorship of Henry Lawes, Milton inscribed his identity on the title page in the form of an epigraph from Virgil's second eclogue: *Eheu quid volui misero mihi! floribus austrum / Perditus* ("Alas! what have I brought on my miserable self? I have let the south wind ruin my flowers").[37] This was in effect a record of Milton's signature in a way that no official announcement of the author's name could be. It was also a highly personal commentary (the author's own, no doubt) on what otherwise was "not openly acknowledged by the Author."[38] That

37. The reference is to the 1637 edition in Sprott's *A Maske: The Earlier Versions*, p. 37. See also *Facsimile*, 1:265. The translation is Shawcross's in "Milton and Diodati," p. 153. "It may be significant," suggests Parker, "that Milton omitted this [epigraph] when he republished the masque in 1645" (*Milton Biography*, 2:795, n. 63). Included on the title page of the 1645 edition of the *Poems*, however, is an epigraph from Virgil's seventh eclogue: *Baccare frontem / Cingite, ne vati noceat mala lingua futuro* ("Wreathe my brow with foxglove, lest his evil tongue harm the bard that is to be").

38. According to Masson, Milton evidently supplied the motto (*Life of Milton*, 1:640), and Parker takes this as a given (*Milton Biography*, 1:143). The phrase "not openly acknowledged by the Author" is from Lawes's prefatory letter to the 1637 edition (*A Maske: The Earlier Versions*, p. 39).

otherwise not openly acknowledged might be said to be the predicaments encoded in the work this epigraph prefaces.[39]

The epigraph speaks of futility and failure. In the context of the eclogue from which it is taken, it speaks of the failure of the speaker, the shepherd Corydon, to gain the favors of the shepherd who is the object of his affections—the cold, aloof, and unresponsive Alexis, who simply refuses to be wooed. The failure is cast in the form of the exploding of an illusion. The speaker's dreams have been utterly shattered: boars have muddied his spring. Yet Corydon pursues: "Fierce lioness goes after wolf, wolf after goat, / The wanton goat goes after the flowering clover, and I / Go after you, Alexis—each towed by his own fancy [*torva leaena lupum sequitur, lupus ipse capellam, / florentem cytisum sequitur lasciva capella, / te Corydon, o Alexi: trahit sua quemque voluptas*]" (ll. 58–65).[40]

From the perspective of such a lament, what are we to make of the illusion generated by Milton's masque? It is an illusion that veils loss and futility; that masks the persistence of lascivious, wanton, and unlawful pursuit in the quest to destroy innocence; that betrays an awareness of the extent to which each of us is burdened with unfulfilled dreams. At the center of this illusion resides the Lady with her chastity, released momentarily through the fantasy of some higher power but forever "immanacl'd," "root-bound," as it were, to an illusory world where its "sun-clad" power is finally overwhelmed.

The predicament implied here, furthermore, is one that encodes gender as much as it suggests the conflict between the illusory and the real. For, as John T. Shawcross reminds us, the eclogue in question reflects an outlook in which male pursues male.[41] At the same time, however, each gender encodes its opposite: if male pursues male,

---

39. According to Parker, the epigraph "has been taken to mean that Milton deprecated any criticism of his masque—that he was reluctant to come out of privacy and run the risks of publication—but the quotation, in context, means that the shepherd accuses himself of *neglecting his proper business*" (*Milton Biography*, 1:142–43). As I argue, much more is implied here.

40. References are to Virgil, *The Eclogues and Georgics of Virgil* (Garden City, New York: Doubleday, 1964).

41. Shawcross's reading is in keeping with his analysis of the homoerotic dimensions of Milton's personality and work. According to Shawcross, "Milton would seem to be somewhere on the fringes of homosexuality through religious and ideological repressions of 'natural' attitudes toward sex, high-mindedness, and 'female' qualities of appearance, interests, and abilities" ("Milton and Diodati," pp. 152–53). My reading is not in conflict with Shawcross's; rather, it extends Shawcross's analysis into the area of bisexuality.

female pursues male, and male pursues female. Within the eclogue, the dialectics of pursuit and retreat, on the one hand, and gender specificity, on the other, are complex and shifting. Whether as male-male encounter, or male-female encounter, female-male encounter, the pursuit of Corydon for Alexis fails to come to fruition.[42] Corydon never does get his Alexis. Within the framework of Milton's masque, the articulation of these concerns is correspondingly complex. One fact, however, is certain: that feminine quality of which Milton as *the* Lady (whether of the *Mask*, or of Christ's) is the embodiment finds itself most at risk. He/she faces the fate of Orpheus at every turn. Nor, finally, can the Muse defend her son/daughter, despite momentary reprieves to the contrary.

Recalling the allusion to Caeneus in the sixth Prolusion, we are prompted to observe that, although Caenis may seek refuge in the identity of Caeneus, this transformation is insufficient to overcome the ravages of a hostile universe. Caenis as Caeneus remains vulnerable in her masculinity. Milton as the Lady is forever faced with the predicament of one who in his bisexuality confronts the possibility of his own undoing, an undoing with catastrophic consequences if the destructive forces that represent an ever-present threat are not overcome by a superior power in whom the prospective victim of these forces has complete faith.

As we have seen, both the reliability and the efficacy of that superior power are not always as they might appear. Calliope proves to be nothing more than an empty dream, and Sabrina herself provides only temporary aid within the immediate context of the illusory world of which she is a fleeting manifestation. In either case, the individual who is threatened by the ravages that beset him at every point is placed in a perilous situation indeed. Such is particularly true within the Miltonic universe. Centered in pervasive crisis of gender identification, that universe is constantly on the verge of disintegration before the "dissevering" powers it seeks to contain. Whether as male or as female, Milton feels himself besieged by an alien world that threatens to undo him. Victimized by that world, he faces the ever-present

---

42. Gender shifting occurs throughout the eclogue. On one level, the relationship between Corydon and Alexis is male-male. But it is also male-female, as Corydon (male pursuer) describes Alexis in female terms (*delicias domini*) with his "dazzling fairness" (ll. 2, 16). At the same time, it is female-male, as Corydon (fierce lioness: *torva leana*) pursues the wolf (*lupum*) (l. 63).

prospect of an impending *sparagmos*. Such is the fate of the Orphic poet delineated throughout Milton's works. Particularly from the bisexual perspective established here, this fate is discernible not only in the earlier poetry but in the later poetry as well. As I attempt to demonstrate in the following chapters, it is a fate that is dramatically discernible in the self-configurations of Milton's diffuse epic.

5

The Court of Belial

aving already examined the mythic dimensions of sparagmos as a crucial theme in the proem to the seventh
book of *Paradise Lost*, I now approach this theme from
the bisexual perspective established in the discussion of
such works as the sixth Prolusion and *A Mask*. Doing so, I can determine the extent to which the Miltonic other is made to encounter the
possibility of a sparagmos as momentous as any in the earlier works.
The immediate question is in what respect the Lady of the earlier
works manifests herself in *Paradise Lost*? To invoke Kerrigan's epithet:
wherein does the "poetess" of Milton's epic lie, particularly with respect to that primal scene centered in the dismemberment of Orpheus
by the Bacchantes?

The answer, I think, can be found if we move from the pagan
dimensions of *Paradise Lost* to the biblical dimensions. To do that is
to move from Bacchus to Belial. Underlying this movement is a situation in which the victimization of the male by a rout of uncontrollable females undergoes a gender reversal of the first magnitude. In
that reversal is depicted the brutal victimization of the female by a
rout of uncontrollable males. At the center of both victimizations
resides the Miltonic personality, at once terribly fearful of all that

sparagmos can inflict and inclined to visualize this horror in bisexual terms.

In *Paradise Lost*, such horror is nowhere felt more compellingly than in a passage that offers fit comparison with the proem to book 7. The passage in question appears within the context of Milton's account of the pagan deities in the first book of his epic. Culminating that portion of the account centered in the enumeration of biblical deities (1.384–85), this passage focuses on the figure of Belial, "then whom a Spirit more lewd / Fell not from Heaven, or more gross to love / Vice for it self" (1.490–92). Although cited last in the parade of false gods, Belial inspires in Milton his utmost contempt and loathing.

This feeling of revulsion permeates the passage in its entirety. Of Belial, Milton observes:

> To him no Temple stood
> Or Altar smoak'd; yet who more oft then hee
> In Temples and at Altars, when the Priest
> Turns Atheist, as did *Ely's* Sons, who fill'd
> With lust and violence the house of God.
> In Courts and Palaces he also Reigns
> And in luxurious Cities, where the noyse
> Of riot ascends above thir loftiest Towrs,
> And injury and outrage: And when Night
> Darkens the Streets, then wander forth the Sons
> Of *Belial*, flown with insolence and wine.
> Witness the Streets of *Sodom*, and that night
> In *Gibeah*, when th'hospitable door
> Expos'd a Matron to avoid worse rape. (1.492–505)

Crucial to an understanding of the relationship between lust and violence in Milton's thought, this passage provides renewed insight into the sparagmatic contexts explored in the foregoing discussion. With its focus upon Belial as a counterpart to Bacchus, moreover, the passage becomes a means of gaining greater insight into the bisexual concerns that have engaged us here.

That Belial for Milton represents the biblical counterpart of Bacchus, particularly as that figure is manifested in his son Comus, hardly needs extensive justification at this juncture. Belial's courts and palaces "where the noyse / Of riot ascends" recalls not only the "stately Palace" in which Comus immobilizes the Lady, but (in the words of the Lady herself) the noise of "riot and ill-managed merriment, / Such as the jocond flute or gamesom pipe / Stirs up amongst the loose unletter'd hinds" (*Mask*, ll.171–74). Just as the sons of Belial wander forth, "flown with insolence and wine," the sons of Comus, along with their master, are drunk with the "swill'd insolence" brought about by the "poyson of mis-used wine" (*Mask*, ll.178, 45–46). The passage concerning Belial, in short, reinscribes (but in much more ominous terms) those we associate with the son of Bacchus in *A Mask*. As Cedric Brown observes so well, Comus and Belial, as "perverters of the moral will," both "come out of the same stable."[1] For Milton, however, the transformation of Bacchus into Belial (in the movement from the masque to the epic) is accompanied by associations of a decidedly somber, even brutal sort. Such associations are very much in keeping with the conception of Belial as it emerges in the biblical traditions to which Milton was heir.

These traditions are founded upon the various meanings the term "Belial" comes to assume in the literature of the Old and New Testament. Appearing as a proper noun but not used as a proper name in the Old Testament, Belial implies "worthlessness," "lawlessness," "destruction."[2] In such phrases as "children of Belial," "sons [or

1. Cedric Brown, *John Milton's Aristocratic Entertainments* (Cambridge: Cambridge University Press, 1985), pp. 65–68. The name Comus as Komos appears directly in the Trinity College Manuscript in its association with Belial. See Milton's projected tragedy to be entitled "Comazontes or the Benjaminits or the Rioters. Jud. 19.20.&c" (*CM*, 18:236), discussed below. *Komazontes* is also used as a stage direction in connection with Comus in the Trinity College Manuscript (*Facsimile*, 1:400). Brown likewise demonstrates that in the exegetical literature Comus was associated with Chemos or Baal-Peor (pp. 71–72). As John M. Steadman has demonstrated, the association of Belial with Bacchus (particularly in the figure of Comus) is consistent with the Renaissance mythographical outlook and is implied on several levels in Milton's works; "A Mask at Ludlow: Comus and Dionysiac Revel," in *Nature into Myth: Medieval and Renaissance Moral Symbols* (Pittsburgh: Duquesne University Press, 1979), pp. 216–19.

2. What follows is largely indebted to Joseph A. Wittreich's informative entry on Belial in the *Milton Encyclopedia*, s.v. I have also consulted *A Hebrew and English Lexicon of the Old Testament*, ed. Francis Brown, S. R. Driver, and Charles A. Briggs (Oxford: Clarendon Press, 1907), s.v., and *A Greek-English Lexicon of the New Testament and Other Early Christian Literature*, ed. W. F. Arndt and F. W. Gingrich (Chicago: University of Chicago Press, 1957), s.v. On one level, the name Belial is a compound of the Hebrew terms *bli* or ("without") and *ya'al* or ("worth"). From this perspective, then, "Belial" is simply a noun that means "worthless." Among the many Old Testament passages in which these meanings emerge are Deuteronomy 13:13, 1 Samuel 25:25, 2 Samuel 16:7, 1 Kings. 21:13, Proverbs 19:28, Job 34:18, Nahum 1:11, 2:1. On another level, Belial has been connected with the Babylonian goddess of vegetation, who was also the goddess of the underworld. This makes Belial synonymous with the Abyss or Sheol, the place of no return. This view is underscored by Psalm 18:4–5, where Belial corresponds to death and Sheol in the parallelism of the verses; see Arthur E. Cundall,

daughters] of Belial," "man [or men] of Belial," the name Belial—used to designate particular classes of people—signifies the man of sin, the lawless one. Such constructions refer to individuals who have given themselves over to lewdness and licentiousness, to those who are notoriously evil and desperately wicked. Elsewhere in the Old Testament, Belial's name signifies one who gives false testimony or is guilty of plotting evil. In its most violent form, the word is used to designate a malevolent and destructive power. So it appears in Nahum, who speaks of one conspiring evil against God. Counseling "worthlessness" (*bliya'al*), this destructive being "dasheth in pieces" and utterly destroys all in his wake (1:11–2:1).[3] So Belial is conceived both in the apocryphal and pseudepigraphal writings as one given over fully to violence in its various forms but also associated with lust, fornication, covetousness, and rebellion as well as with destruction.

Undergoing a Pauline transformation in the New Testament, Belial is placed in a distinctly theological context. There, he comes to represent the very destructive forces of darkness and devastation Christ would overcome. So Paul appeals to those who desire to distance themselves from the children of Belial: "Be ye not unequally yoked together with unbelievers: for what fellowship hath righteousness with unrighteousness? and what communion hath light with darkness? And what concord hath Christ with Belial?" (2 Cor. 6:14–15). The appeal embraces a multitude of areas having to do with spiritual, ethical, and even cosmic considerations. Extending such considerations into the realm of worship, Paul asks, "And what agreement hath the temple of God with idols? for ye are the temple of the living God" (2 Cor. 6:16).

If in *Paradise Lost*, Milton observes that no temple stands or altar smokes to commemorate Belial, the tone of contempt is founded to a great extent on Paul's own sense of distaste for those who in their idolatry would create such places of worship. Such too is what underlies Milton's allusion to the sons of Ely, through whom Belial was indeed worshiped "in Temples and at Altars." The allusion is to 1

Judges: An Introduction and Commentary (Downers Grove: Inter-Varsity Press, 1968), p. 196. This view is confirmed by C. F. Burney, *The Book of Judges, with Introduction and Notes* (New York: Ktav, 1970), p. 468: in Psalm 18:4–5, *bliya'al* is parallel to Death and Sheol. It denotes the Abyss as the place from which one does not come up. The wickedness of Belial is "of an appalling and catastrophic character."

3. References to Hebrew scriptures are to the *Biblia Hebraica Stuttgartensia*, ed. K. Elliger and W. Rudolph (Stuttgart: Deutsche Bibelstiftung, 1967–77).

Samuel 2:12–17, which recounts the idolatrous practices of the sons of Ely, whose sin "was very great before the Lord," for through them "men abhorred the offering of the Lord." As a result of their idolatry, they are designated the "sons of Belial" (*bnay-bliya'al*). For Milton, their sin is compounded by those of lust and violence, with which they fill the house of God. This emphasis upon the collocation of lust and violence distinguishes Milton's understanding of Belial as not only the lewdest of all spirits that fell from Heaven but among the most destructive as well.[4]

From the perspective this emphasis upon lust and violence provides, we may proceed to the two major texts that underscore the culminating moment in the passage at hand: "Witness the Streets of *Sodom*, and that night / In *Gibeah*, when th'hospitable door / Expos'd a Matron to avoid worse rape." Alluding to both Genesis 19 and Judges 19, these lines bring into focus all that is implied by the transition from Bacchus to Belial (or, more specifically, from the the daughters of Bacchus to the sons of Belial) in Milton's thought. Doing so, they suggest the correspondence of Milton's sparagmatic outlook as reflected in the dismemberment of Orpheus with the violence perpetrated upon those central figures of the biblical accounts. At the heart of this correspondence is that all-important collocation of lust and violence so crucial to those overcome by the forces of an alien universe. In the execution of this collocation, we discover the gender reversals so fundamental to the Miltonic personality. As a counterpart to the male figure attacked by crazed women, we discover the female figure attacked by crazed men. Just as much in the latter case as in the former, this attack ultimately results in a dismemberment of the most savage and brutal sort. As a result of that sparagmos, the violent implications of the Miltonic bisexuality are fully and dramatically realized.

So important to Milton's outlook, Genesis 19 recounts God's vengeful destruction of Sodom and Gomorrah. A signal instance of the corruption found in these cities is the experience of the two angels who visit Sodom to determine the extent of its depravity. As the angels discover, the depravity is extensive indeed. Their encounter with Lot confirms them in the knowledge that, except for their host and his wife and daughters, no one in the city merits escape from destruction.

---

4. Such an outlook is confirmed by Milton's prose works. See the references to Belial in the *Doctrine and Discipline of Divorce* and in *The Likeliest Means* (*YP*, 2:225, 7:296).

In particular, the dramatization of the angels' encounter with Lot is at issue in Milton's allusion to the streets of Sodom. Persuading the angels to become guests in his house, Lot assumes the role of good host. But before the angels have the opportunity to retire for the night, "the men of the city, *even* the men of Sodom [*'anshay sdom*], compassed the house round, both old and young, all the people from every quarter: And they called unto Lot, and said unto him, Where are the men which came in to thee this night? bring them out unto us, that we may know them [*vned'ah 'otam*]" (Gen. 19:1–5). The idea of "knowing" here is clearly sexual and decidedly violent: the men of Sodom desire to overpower and to copulate with the angels.

In response to this demand, Lot is willing to make what for him is the ultimate sacrifice: he offers up his daughters. "Behold now," he says, "I have two daughters which have not known man [*lo'-yad'u 'ish*]; let me, I pray you, bring them out unto you, and do ye to them as is good in your eyes; only unto these men do nothing; for therefore came they under the shadow of my roof" (Gen. 19:8). Unappeased by this offer, the men of Sodom threaten further violence, and they in turn are smitten by the angels with blindness (Gen. 19:10–11). In retribution for the outrages committed in Sodom, as well as in Gomorrah, God rains upon them fire and brimstone out of heaven: "And he overthrew those cities, and all the plain, and all the inhabitants of the cities, and that which grew upon the ground" (Gen. 19:24–25).

The outrages committed in Sodom and Gomorrah had a profound effect on biblical thought even beyond the immediate context of the Genesis account. Traditionally, these outrages and their aftermath were associated with the fall of the rebel angels and the final punishment to be visited upon them. So, according to the Epistle of Jude, "the angels which kept not their first estate, but left their own habitation, he hath reserved in everlasting chains under darkness unto the judgment of the great day. Even as Sodom and Gomorrah, and the cities about them in like manner, giving themselves over to fornication, and going after strange flesh, are set forth for an example, suffering the vengeance of eternal fire" (Jude vv. 6–7). This emphasis upon the perverse desire to lust "after strange flesh," combined with the violence brought about by this desire, is the focus of the biblical understanding of the events that transpired at Sodom.[5] Placing that

5. So 2 Peter 2:4–10 refers to God's overthrow of Sodom and Gomorrah as retribution

understanding within the context of his account of Belial, Milton views this figure as the embodiment of all that the collocation of lust and violence comes to represent. At the core of the events at Sodom are the outrages perpetrated by Belial as manifested in his offspring.

Although the biblical account does not designate the men of Sodom specifically as the sons of Belial, the two are clearly synonymous for Milton. In their desire to commit unmentionable acts of the most extreme and outrageous sort, the men of Sodom epitomize for Milton everything he associates with Belial as not only the grossest and lewdest spirit to have fallen from Heaven but as a demon fully given over to acts of violence and destruction.[6] All that Belial epitomizes in his "sodomistic" presence here had a profound impact on Milton throughout his career. One need only examine the entries in his Commonplace Book to see the extent to which the Belial-like acts recorded in Genesis 19 influenced his thinking. Under the heading *De Libidine*, he singles out *paiderastia seu harrenokoitia* (lust for boys or men) as among the most abominable of sins. Citing Lactantius, he observes: "What can be sacred to those who would debase the age that is weak and in need of protection, so that it is destroyed and defiled through their own lust [*Quid potest esse sanctum iis qui aetatem imbecillam, et praesidio indigentem libidini suae depopulandam foedandamque prostraverint*]?" This entry is followed by others in the same vein, among them a reference to one King Mempricius, who in the English legends "is marked with the sin of sodomy [*notatur Sodomitici peccati*]" (*YP*, 1:369; *CM*, 17:132).[7] In his discussion of chastity in *De Doctrina Christiana* (2.10), Milton singles out sodomy, among other vices, as an act through which we sin against ourselves and injure ourselves exceedingly.

The extent of Milton's interest in the association of lust and violence implicit in the perversions suggested by Genesis 19 is most clearly demonstrated by his plans to write a drama based on the events of

---

for unnatural acts of the flesh. For Reformation responses, see Martin Luther, *Lectures on Genesis*, in *Luther's Works*, 55 vols., ed. Jaroslav Pelikan (St. Louis: Concordia, 1961), 3:255, and John Calvin, *Commentaries on the First Book of Moses called Genesis*, 3 vols., trans. Rev. John King (Edinburgh: Calvin Translation Society, 1897), 1:496–97.

6. In this respect, Belial has affinities with several of the fallen angels described in Book 1, including Moloch, Chemos (also known as Baal-Peor), Ashtaroth and Thammuz. See Jason Rosenblatt, " 'Audacious Neighborhood': Idolatry in *Paradise Lost*, Book I," *Philological Quarterly* 54 (1975), 553–68.

7. See Lactantius, *Seven Books on Divine Ordinances* (6.23), in *Opera* (Lyons, 1548), pp. 510–16.

Sodom. Titled "Cupids funeral pile. Sodom Burning," these plans are fully delineated in his outlines for tragedies in the Trinity College Manuscript.[8] In spirit, Milton's projected work is rooted in the sacred dramas to which he was exposed during his Continental journey, as well as in the host of Cupid plays and masques performed during the Renaissance.[9] The pageantry of these works accords with the processional background Milton had in mind for his proposed drama. In the detailed plans through which that drama is projected, we find the following description: Lot is seen returning from "his evening walk toward the citty gates." Accompanying him are the angels, described as "2 yong men or youths of noble form." Lot feeds and entertains them. "The Gallantry of the town passe by in Processi[on] with musick and song to the temple of Venus Urania or Peor." "Understanding of tow noble strangers arriv'd," the town "gallants" send "2 of thire choycest youth with the preist to invite them to thire citty solemnities" as "an honour that thire citty had decreed to all fair personages." The two angels demur and are inveighed at by the priest for their allegiance to "the strict raigned of Melchizedeck." In response to Lot's support of the angels, the members of the town assembly "taxe him of praesumption, singularity, breach of citty customs, in fine offer violence." The angels rescue Lot and warn him of the impending doom. "At last is describ'd the parting from the citty." "The Angels doe the deed with all dreadfull execution." The setting of the drama is one of great "solemnity."

Processions are everywhere. Before the city is destroyed, the Chorus relates how "each eveing every one with mistresse, or Ganymed, [goes] gitterning [strumming upon his instrument] along the streets, or solacing on the banks of Jordan or down the stream." The drama is also replete with debates, as the angels "dispute" with the Sodomite priests about "love & how it differs from lust." Even the destruction

---

8. The comments that follow draw upon my earlier study " 'Cupids funeral pile': Milton's Projected Drama on the Theme of Lust," in *Renaissance Papers*, ed. Dennis G. Donovan and A. Leigh Deneef (Durham: The Southeastern Renaissance Conference, 1977), pp. 29–41. For a treatment of the literary renderings of sodomy in the Renaissance, see Gregory W. Bredbeck's *Sodomy and Interpretation: Marlowe to Milton* (Ithaca: Cornell University Press, 1991), as well as his "Milton's Ganymede: Negotiations of Homoerotic Tradition in *Paradise Regained*," *PMLA* 106 (1991), 262–76.

9. See Christopher C. Love's unpublished doctoral dissertation, "The Scriptural Latin Plays of the Renaissance and Milton's Cambridge Manuscript" (University of Toronto, 1950), and John Arthos, *Milton and the Italian Cities* (New York: Barnes and Noble, 1968), pp. 134–54.

is in keeping with its tone of civility: "The firce thunders begin aloft the Angel appears all girt with flames which he saith are the flames of true love"; "then calling to ye thunders lightnings & fires he brings them down with some short warning to all other nations to take heed." With "the flames of true love," the angel destroys Sodom as a fit retribution for the sins of a city that heretofore burned in lust. The final conflagration is God's answer to the destruction Sodom has already brought upon itself (*CM*, 18:233–34). Such, in brief, is the nature of Milton's projected drama on the events narrated in Genesis 19. Reflecting an early interest in this narrative, "Cupids funeral pile" represents Milton's initial impulse to render Genesis 19 dramatically.

The projected dramatization is revealing as much for the similarites it shares with the epic rendering as it is for its departures in tone and substance. In both the drama and the epic, we find a fascination with the Sodom narrative as pageantry. In place of the pageantry of the Sodomites in his projected drama, Milton offers the pageantry of the fallen angels in his epic. The festivities on behalf of the pagan deities in "Cupids funeral pile" are transformed into the false worship of corresponding deities in *Paradise Lost*.[10] Milton's projected drama and his epic, then, share a concern with the opposition between true and false worship. They also share a concern with distinctions between love and lust. In the drama, the debates between the angels and the Sodomite priests about love and lust look forward, in part, to the dialogue between Adam and Raphael (although in a far different context) in *Paradise Lost* (e.g., 8.586–94). The philosophical predilections concerning such matters in "Cupids funeral pile" find their counterpart in the emphasis Milton's epic places throughout upon the role of love, as opposed to lust. An interest in these relationships was of fundamental concern to the Renaissance and to Milton both in the epic and in his other works. As we have seen, distinctions between love and lust certainly form the basis of the argument in *A Mask*, where they appear not only in the dialogue between the two brothers but between the Lady and Comus as well.

10. Significantly, the deity from "Cupids funeral pile" whose name appears in *Paradise Lost* as a symbol of false worship is Peor, a name Milton apparently inserted as an afterthought when he suggested the original name of Venus Urania. Although it is difficult to see how Venus Urania, a symbol of heavenly love in Milton's epic, and Peor, a symbol of sacrilege in Milton's epic, could be associated, they apparently are in the draft as we have it. Milton no doubt would have clarified the association had the drama been written.

In this regard, a sense of continuity develops between *A Mask*, "Cupids funeral pile," and *Paradise Lost*.

Corresponding similarities arise in connection with Milton's plans for a drama on the Fall in the Trinity College Manuscript. It is perhaps no accident that "Cupids funeral pile" immediately precedes "Adam unparadiz'd" in the arrangement of the plans.[11] In fact, judging by the writing, the two drafts almost seem to overlap, so much so that Milton had to draw a line between the ending of one and the beginning of the other to separate them. Were it not for that line, one might be inclined to think that Milton had planned to include a description of "Paradise" in his Sodom drama. Be that as it may, such an idea would not have been contrary to biblical precedence. Genesis 13:10 associates Sodom with "the garden of the Lord," and so it was looked upon thereafter.[12]

The idea is no less pertinent to *Paradise Lost*. Having associated the fallen angels with the Sodom milieu in Book 1, Milton completes the association in Book 10, where Eden finds its debased counterpart in an illusory "Grove" with "a multitude" of forbidden trees. Growing on those trees is "Fruitage fair to sight, like that which grew / Near that bituminous Lake where Sodom flam'd" (10.547–62). Forcibly transformed into serpents, the fallen angels devour the fruitage, which contains, to their dismay and disgust, "bitter Ashes" (10.565), the products of their own corruption. Whereas the fallen angels must presumably undergo this "humbling" annually (10.575–76), humans are able to escape from the Sodom they have created.

Such is precisely what the final lines of *Paradise Lost* suggest. Eden itself with its "torrid heat" (12.634) and "flaming Brand" (12.643) recalls the burning of Sodom (Gen. 19:24). Like Lot and his wife, Adam and Eve "linger" (12.639; Gen. 19:26). The angel must take them "in either hand" and lead them out to the "Plain" beyond (12.637–40; Gen.

11. See *Facsimile*, 2:16–29. Six New Testament subjects listed in the left-hand margin intervene. But I refer to the right-hand margin, where the material specifically involving the distinctions between love and lust seems to have been added after the initial draft was completed. Milton probably returned to the draft after having written "Adam unparadiz'd." If so, he had his paradise drama fresh in his mind when he made significant additions to the plans for his Sodom drama. James Holly Hanford and James G. Taafe suggest a similar idea in *A Milton Handbook*, 5th ed. (New York: Meredith Corp., 1970), pp. 150–51, n. 7.

12. In *Pilgrim's Progress*, Christian, having fled his own Sodom (cf. Isa. 19:18), echoes the biblical idea when he says that "the land of Sodom was ... [once] like the garden of Eden heretofore"; John Bunyan, *Pilgrim's Progress*, ed. Louis L. Martz (New York: Holt, Rinheart and Winston, 1949), p. 113.

19:16–17). Unlike Lot and his wife, however, Adam and Eve are permitted to look back (12.641; Gen. 19:17), perhaps as a dramatic reminder of all they have lost. The poignancy of the contrast is at least intriguing. Whether Milton would have incorporated it in his plans to recount Lot's "parting from the citty" remains to be seen. In any case, it is suggested in his epic, which finally embodies in more than one way his projected drama on Sodom.

As revealing as the connections between Milton's Sodom drama and his epic appear to be, the differences are even more pronounced. Both in tone and in substance "Cupids funeral pile. Sodom Burning" shares nothing of the grimness and the brutality Milton projects in the allusion to Belial and his milieu in *Paradise Lost*. Despite its references to the "offer[ing] of violence" (a rather vague threat, under the circumstances) and its concern with the nature of lust, Milton's projected drama is the very embodiment of civility compared with its epic counterpart. There is no sense of riot, injury, and outrage in the drama, no darkening of the streets, no wandering forth of the sons of Belial, "flown with insolence and wine." In fact, the Sodom of Milton's drama is a fairly pleasant place to be. Not so the dark, grim, and brutal city of the epic. No one wants to be caught unattended in that bad place.

There is, moreover, another difference of major import. Milton's projected drama says nothing of Lot's offer of his daughters in exchange for the angelic guests upon whom the sons of Belial seek to perpetrate unmentionable acts of lust and violence. The erasure of this detail from the drama as Milton conceives it relieves him of the responsibility of addressing an aspect of the narrative that is apparently self-sacrificing and noble (the father's willingness to offer up his daughters in his attempt to protect his male guests) but potentially disturbing in the extreme. What are we to make of Lot's offer, and what bearing does that offer have on the Miltonic point of view?

However else we might interpret the narrative of Sodom, Lot's offering up of his daughters remains a profoundly disturbing detail. In his treatment of the narrative, Robert Alter addresses that detail directly: "Some have thought to naturalize this outrageous offer by contending that in the ancient Near East the host-guest bond (someone coming under the shadow of your roof-beam) was sacred, conferring obligations that exeeded those of a man to his virgin daughters. The impassive narrator, as is his wont, offers no guidance on this question, but the unfolding of the story, and its contrastive connections with the surrounding narrative, cast doubt on this proposition that Lot was simply playing the perfect ancient Near Eastern host in rather trying circumstances." When we later learn that Lot's daughters are betrothed (Gen. 19:14), the problematic dimensions of the narrative are heightened even further, since "according to later biblical law, the rape of a betrothed woman is a crime punishable by death (cf. Deut. 22:23–27)." In his grand gesture of familial sacrifice, then, Lot exhibits "a disquieting readiness" to "serve as accomplice in the multiple enactment of a capital crime directed against his own daughters."[13]

As the narrative resolves itself, the profound dilemma suggested by Lot's offer is momentarily sidestepped: the rape of neither the male guests nor the virginal daughters comes about, and the appropriateness of Lot's gesture is never directly put to the test. Still, the disquietude brought about by the gesture continues to haunt the narrative and causes the action to focus itself upon the implications of the gender substitutions it brings to the fore. As a result of Lot's offer, we are constantly made to confront the irresolvable question with which the narrative assaults us: if homosexual gang rape is unthinkable, is the alternative proposed by Lot acceptable? Within the context of the narrative, the question fortunately does not need to be answered, but it retains a kind of subimperative presence, a trace, that refuses to release us.

From the Miltonic perspective, it brings to the fore the all-important dimension of gender shifting and gender substitution so crucial to his sense of self. Faced with the prospect of his own violent undoing, how might the "poetess" of *Paradise Lost* respond to the appalling dilemma encoded in the Genesis account? How does the "poetess" feel about Lot's offer of his virginal daughters to replace the male guests? Milton's response is in a sense as problematic as the dilemma it would seek to resolve. This response provides only the directive "Witness the Streets of *Sodom*." So we have witnessed those streets, and what are we to learn from the events that transpire on them?

The answer lies in the allusion with which the streets of Sodom

13. "Robert Alter, Sodom as Nexus: The Web of Design in Biblical Narrative," in *The Book and the Text: The Bible and Literary Theory*, ed. Regina M. Schwartz (Cambridge, Mass.: Basil Blackwell, 1990), pp. 151–52.

are conflated, that is, the streets of Gibeah, or, more to the point, "that night / In Gibeah, when th'hospitable door / Expos'd a Matron to avoid worse rape." In place of Genesis 19 with its unanswerable questions, we are given in this pivotal moment in the first book of Milton's epic another text: Judges 19, a text with problems at least as insurmountable. Crucial to the Miltonic outlook, Judges 19 brings to the fore those issues of gender-related violence culminating in sparagmos that are of fundamental concern to our study. In order to explore these issues further in the context of the allusion to Gibeah, we need first to summarize the main lines of the Judges account.

II

In Judges, a certain Levite sojourning on the side of Mount Ephraim takes a wife to himself, a concubine, from Bethlehem-judah. After they are married, the concubine departs from the Levite and returns to her father's house in Bethlehem-judah, where she remains four months. Her husband, in turn, seeks for her at her father's house, where he is treated with the utmost hospitality during his stay (Judg. 19:1–10). After his departure from the house of his father-in-law, he, along with his servants and his concubine, travels to Gibeah, the city of the Benjaminites. There, in the evening he is met by an old man (an Ephraimite), who takes him and his retinue into his house and feeds them much in the manner that Lot acted as a host for the two angels (Judg. 19:11–21).

"Now," the account relates, "as they [the host and guests] were making their hearts merry, behold, the men of the city, certain sons of Belial [*bnay-bliya'al*], beset the house round about, and beat at the door, and spake to the master of the house, the old man, saying, Bring forth the man that came into thine house, that we may know him [*vnedahe'nu*]." Appealing to the Benjaminites for pity, the master of the house responds: "Nay, my brethren, nay, I pray you, do not so wickedly; seeing that this man is come into mine house, do not this folly. Behold, *here is* my daughter a maiden, and his concubine; them I will bring out now, and humble ye them, and do with them what seemeth good unto you: but unto this man do not so vile a thing."[14]

14. The term the father uses for his daughter in Judges 19:24 is "virgin" (*btulah*), an allusion perhaps to Genesis 19:8: "I have two daughters which have not known man." The significance of the reference (in relation to the concubine) is discussed below in some depth.

The Benjaminites, however, disregard the appeal of the master of the house, so the Levite seizes his concubine and brings her forth unto them. They, in turn, "knew her, and abused her all the night until the morning: and when the day began to spring, they let her go." In the morning, the Levite finds her "fallen down at the door of the house" (Judg. 19:22–26).

In his cruelty, the Levite admonishes her to rise and prepare for departure, but she is unable to respond. So he places her on his ass, and when he comes to his house, "he took a knife, and laid hold on his concubine, and divided her *together* with her bones, into twelve pieces, and sent her into all the coasts of Israel" (Judg. 19:27–29). Those who become aware of this act are fully horrified by it, exclaiming: "There was no such deed done or seen from the day that the children of Israel came up out of the land of Egypt unto this day" (Judg. 19:30). As a prime instance of the biblical dimensions of sparagmos in its most devastating form, this narrative represented for Milton the extremes to which the lust and violence underlying the concept of Belial were capable of extending. In so doing, the narrative gave expression to his own deep-seated fears regarding the brutal effects of both rape and dismemberment upon the helpless female victim.

To understand the bearing of the narrative on Milton's outlook, we must first address the biblical account itself. As scholars generally agree, the portrayal of the incidents in Judges 19 represents a rewriting of those that occur in Genesis 19.[15] If such is the case, then this rewriting involves a brutalizing so extensive as to be almost unbearable in its implications. The threat of gang rape thwarted by the powerful angelic guests in Genesis 19 is not only realized in Judges 19 but, in that moment of realization, intensified effectively beyond comprehension. It is as if the author of Judges 19, upon reading the

---

15. See in particular here the detailed line-by-line comparisons of C. F. Burney, *Book of Judges*, pp. 444–45. In agreement are scholars such as Robert C. Culley, *Studies in the Structure of Hebrew Narrative* (Philadelphia: Fortress Press, 1976), pp. 56–59; J. Alberto Soggin, *Judges: A Commentary* (Philadelphia: Westminster Press, 1981), p. 288; and Phyllis Trible, *Texts of Terror* (Philadelphia: Fortress Press, 1984), pp. 75, 90n. According to Soggin, Genesis 19 is a much earlier story. For Robert G. Boling, the story of the Levite in Judges 19 "involves a calculated inversion of elements in the story of Lot"; see *Judges: Introduction, Translation, and Commentary*, The Anchor Bible (Garden City, New York: Doubleday, 1975), p. 277. Scholars are not in universal agreement, however. See Susan Niditch, "The 'Sodomite' Theme in Judges 19–20: Family, Community, and Social Disintegration," *Catholic Biblical Quarterly* 44 (1982), 365–78.

putatively earlier account, is prompted to ask himself, What would it be like if the *'anshay sdom*, now become the *bnay-bliya'al*, are allowed to have their way? Remove any pretense to divine intervention, and permit violence to take its course.

Such is indeed what happens. Whereas Genesis 19 generalizes the threat as an act of allowing the men of Sodom to perform upon Lot's daughters that which is "good in [their] eyes," Judges 19 particularizes the threat by inviting the sons of Belial to "humble" the Ephraimite's daughter and the Levite's concubine. The language of the account is revealing in its implications. The word "humble" (*'anu*, from *'anah*), for example, has about it not only the sexual idea of forced cohabitation but the related meaning of "doing violence to."[16] The author of Judges 19 takes nothing for granted: if rape is by its very nature a form of violence against the body, this rape will be of a particularly violent sort. Such ironically is "the good" (*hatob*) that the author of Judges 19 has in mind in his own reference to the men of Gibeah doing that which is "good in [their] eyes."

Moreover, that which haunts the Genesis account as an unrealized threat comes to fruition in the Judges account. Not only does the gender substitution actually occur (as the female concubine is substituted for the male guest), but the means of that substitution is unmitigatedly brutal. As Phyllis Trible remarks, "nothing has prepared us for the terror to come. Dialogue stops; bargaining ceases; the old man and his virgin daughter disappear. No one waits to learn what the dissatisfied Benjaminites might propose next." Instead, the Levite "seized [*vayahazak*] his concubine and pushed [*vayotse'*] to them outside" (Judg. 19:25). "So hurried is his [the Levite's] action," Trible observes, "that the Hebrew omits the direct object *her* for the second verb." In short, the Levite hurriedly and forcibly turns over the concubine to the enemy to save his own hide.[17]

All pretense to hospitality is undermined. What might have been construed in Genesis as the putatively noble willingness to sacrifice one's daughters for the sake of one's guests (a nobility in itself questionable) is completely erased in Judges. With the disappearance of the old man and his daughter and the sudden and unexpected action of the Levite, even the appearance of civility gives way to barbarity.

16. See *Hebrew and English Lexicon*, p. 776.
17. Trible, *Texts of Terror*, p. 76.

It is as if the author of Judges 19 has removed any lingering doubt about his own interpretive posture at this juncture. Nothing is left but the barbarity of the Levite's behavior and the horror to be perpetrated on the concubine. In the gender reversal this narrative encodes, all that remains is the woman as an object of sacrifice to the lusts of the *'anshay sdom*.

The horror does not end here, however: the enactment of the rape is intensified by its description. In their "humbling" of the concubine, the sons of Belial not only "knew her" (*vayed'u 'otah*) but, in that "knowing," violently "abused her" (*vayit'allu-bah*). In this context, the phrase *vayit'allu-bah* is particularly graphic. Deriving from the root *'ll*, it carries the reflexive sense of the *hitpa'el* as that which implies a sexually abusive act that takes place repeatedly through the "insertion" or "thrusting in" of one object into another.[18] In short, the sons of Belial abused the concubine by inserting or thrusting themselves into her in an act of ruthless gang rape. This they performed not only relentlessly as they passed her from one person to the next but unrelievedly, so the narrative insists, "all night until the morning." Only then did they "send her away," after which she is discovered by the Levite "fallen down at the door of the house," with her hands "upon the threshold." Her master's reaction upon finding her the following morning serves to reinforce the horror still further. Rather than respond in any sympathetic way to her desperate situation, he simply loads her like merchandise onto his ass and transports her to his house.

The sparagmos that follows is the most devastating aspect of the whole affair: "And when he was come into his house, he took a knife, and laid hold on his concubine, and divided her, *together* with her bones, into twelve pieces, and sent her into all the coasts of Israel." In the context of this rendering, some of the finer points of the original need to be clarified and elaborated.[19] First, the Hebrew specifies not "a knife" but "*the* knife" (*hama'khelet*; italics mine), an important distinction discussed in greater depth below. Second, the reference to the violent act of "laying hold" (*vayahazak*) on the concubine in order to dismember her is precisely that used to describe the act of seizing her in order to thrust her outside to the men of Gibeah. *Vayahazak*,

18. I here combine the first and third meanings of *'ll* from *Hebrew and English Lexicon*, pp. 759–60.
19. The rendering is that of the Authorized Version, which is not entirely accurate or in keeping with the nuances of the original.

from *hzk*, carries the sense of violently seizing or grasping.[20] Initially seized for the purpose of being brutally and relentlessly gang raped, the concubine is next seized for the sake of being divided.

The language used to describe the dissevering is likewise important: "divided her, *together* with her bones [*vaynatheah la'tsmeyah*]." *Vaynatheah*, from *nth*, indicates the act of cutting in pieces and dividing by joints. In other contexts, it is used to describe the dissevering of animals as sacrifices to God (e.g., Exod. 29:17: "And thou shalt cut the ram in pieces [*tnateah lintaha'v*]"; cf. Lev. 1:6, 12; 1 Kings 18:23, 33).[21] In the Judges account, the act is presumably committed to inspire outrage in and thus incite the Israelite forces (represented by the twelve tribes), here suggested by the fact that the concubine is divided into twelve pieces and distributed to all the coasts of Israel. As the final two chapters of Judges recount, the rape and slaughter of the concubine are followed by mass warfare and bloody carnage. Such an act of dividing the concubine in this manner is reflected in Saul's call to war in 1 Samuel 11:6–7: "And the Spirit of God came upon Saul . . . and his anger was kindled greatly. And he took a yoke of oxen, and hewed them in pieces [*vaynathehu*], and sent *them* throughout all the coasts of Israel."[22]

Like the sacrificial animals of which she is a type, the concubine becomes less than human, a commodity, the sole purpose of which is to satisfy the needs of those (whether of the men of Gibeah or the Levite) who would impose their will upon her. This fact is made all the more poignant in the use of the phrase *vaynatheah la'tsmeyah* ("divided her, *together* with her bones"). The literal rendering would be "and cut her to pieces *to* her bones": the cutting extends even to the bones themselves. *La'tsmeyah*, from *'tsm* ("bone"), signifies not just the physicality of the bodily frame, however. It also denotes the very substance or self, the "identity" of the concubine. To cut her to pieces to her bones is to obliterate her identity as a human being, to deprive her of her "beingness." It is an act that constitutes the immolation of the self.[23] As an expression of the outrage implied by the *sparagmos*

---

20. *Hebrew and English Lexicon*, pp. 304–5.
21. *Hebrew and English Lexicon*, p. 677.
22. See in this regard *The Interpreter's Bible*, 12 vols., gen. ed. George Arthur Buttrick, (New York: Abingdon Press, 1953), 2:813.
23. To reinforce the brutality of the situation even further, the Hebrew text leaves it unclear whether the concubine is dead before she is dismembered. In the Septuagint, the answer is clear: "for she was dead." This makes the men of Benjamin murderers as well as

of the concubine, the brutal fact of her dismemberment symbolizes what Mieke Bal so aptly calls *"the scandal of the speaking body."*[24] In the narrative that portrays this scandal, sparagmos becomes an act that constitutes the immolation of everything the concubine represents.

Exactly what the concubine does represent, that is, how she is to be read in the context of the Judges narrative, has been an issue of heated debate from the earliest times. In part, this debate centers on the function of the concubine, but, even more important, it centers on a detail concerning the "character" of the concubine herself as the result of her behavior toward her husband at the outset of the narrative. In biblical usage, the concubine, or *pilegesh*, assumed the role of a marital companion but one of inferior status to a wife. She was not a kept mistress or a woman who merely cohabited with a man while unmarried to him. Rather, she was a genuine wife, though of secondary rank. As such, she held an intermediate place between the wife of first rank and an ordinary slave. In the earliest forms of the institution, the *pilegesh* may have been a wife who remained in her father's house and received her husband, who lived elsewhere but visited her on occasion for conjugal relations. This marriage was genuine but without permanent cohabitation.[25] In her superb study of the Book of Judges, Bal argues that the term "concubine" (with its rather negative connotations) not be applied to the *pilegesh* at all. Rather, she should be called "patrilocal wife" to designate her role as "a wife living in the house of the father, a wife who remains a daugh-

---

rapists and torturers. As Trible observes, "the Hebrew text, on the other hand, is silent, allowing the interpretation that this abused woman is yet alive" (*Texts of Terror*, p. 79). Meir Sternberg comments: "The cause and time of death remain a permanent gap, the information having been elided to open an ambiguity for the reader to puzzle over throughout"; *The Poetics of Biblical Narrative: Ideological Literature and the Drama of Reading* (Bloomington: Indiana University Press, 1985), pp. 238–39. See further on this point Robert Polzin, *Moses and the Deuteronomist* (New York: Seabury Press, 1980), pp. 200–202. Compare also the Levite's own account of the men of Gibeah in Judges 20:5: "My concubine have they forced, that she is dead [*'inu vattamot*]." One must, of course, question here the Levite's own motives in fashioning his account, and even his statement does not clarify matters.

24. "Mieke Bal, Dealing/With/Women: Daughters in the Book of Judges," *Book and Text*, ed. Schwartz, p. 33.

25. *New Catholic Encyclopedia*, 16 vols. gen. ed. William J. McDonald. (New York: McGraw-Hill, 1967), 4:121. According to the *New Catholic Encyclopedia*, Samson's marriage to the Philistine woman (Judg. 15:1) appears to have been of this type. For additional discussion, see the *Encyclopedia Judaica*, 16 vols. (Jerusalem: Keter, 1971), 3:862–65. The term *pilegesh*, a non-Semitic loanword, was perhaps influenced by the Greek *pallakis* ("young girl"; cf. Latin, *pellex*). Its origin might also be Hittite. See *Hebrew and English Lexicon*, p. 811, and *The International Standard Bible Encyclopedia*, 4 vols., gen. ed. Geoffrey W. Bromiley (Grand Rapids: William B. Eerdmans, 1979–88), 1:759.

ter."[26] If the foregoing suggests something of the difficulty scholars have encountered in coming to terms with the function of the *pilegesh*, that difficulty is compounded by the apparently problematic behavior of the *pilegesh* toward her husband at the outset of the narrative.

According to the details of that narrative, after the Levite took a wife (*'ishah*), a concubine (*pilegesh*) out of Bethlehem-judah, she was unfaithful to him. As the Authorized Version renders it, "his concubine played the whore against him [*vatizneh 'alav*], and went away from him unto her father's house to Bethlehem-judah" (Judg. 19:2).[27] Given the extent to which it compromises the character of the *pilegesh* from the outset, what are we to make of this disquieting, indeed startling, revelation concerning her apparent infidelity? This revelation cannot be overlooked in any attempt to deal with the significance of the action and ultimate fate of the *pilegesh* as the innocent, brutalized female victim of an alien, male society.

The difficulties transcribers and readers of the text have had with this detail are already discernible in the earliest renderings, including versions of the Septuagint and the Vulgate. Either those versions avoided mention of the detail entirely or they provided a rendering completely at odds with the Hebrew that has come down to us. Rather than "his concubine played the whore against him," we have the following rendering in both the Greek and Latin texts: "His concubine became angry with him."[28] Shifting the onus from the *pilegesh* to the Levite, this rendering absolves the former of any taint of misbehavior that might compromise her standing in the narrative as a whole. She is not a whore (*zonah*) after all. She has not committed adultery; her virtue is thereby reclaimed. More than that, she is the offended one, he the offender. The guilt lies with her husband, not with her. Because

26. Mieke Bal, *Death and Dissymmetry: The Politics of Coherence in the Book of Judges* (Chicago: University of Chicago Press, 1988), pp. 86–90.

27. *Vatizneh 'alav* can be read as follows: "and she became a prostitute against him." See *Hebrew and English Lexicon*, pp. 275–76: "*zanah*: commit fornication, be a harlot."

28. *Interpreter's Bible*, 2:809: "The MT [Masoretic Text] says that 'she committed harlotry against him,' but the LXX [Septuagint] and the Vulgate more plausibly read that she *became angry with him*, and so returned home." One version of the Septuagint (LXX^A) has *orgisthe oto* ("scorned him"), another (LXX^B) *eporeuthe* ("he went away"). Medieval Jewish exegesis also took it in this sense; see Soggin, *Judges*, pp. 283–84. In his translation of the text, Boling has "But his concubine became angry with him and ran away to her father's house" (pp. 271). Justifying this rendering, Boling in effect accords primacy to LXX^A over the MT, which he calls "interpretive" (pp. 273–74n). For an early but informative discussion of the versions, see George F. Moore, *A Critical and Exegetical Commentary on Judges*, The International Critical Commentary (Edinburgh: T. & T. Clark, 1895), pp. 408–10.

of his offense, she leaves him, and he is obliged to seek her at her father's house. For various reasons, this reading is as problematic as the one it seeks to replace.[29] Whatever is to be made of the *pilegesh* as the offender or the offended, her character and her behavior became a cause célèbre in the exegetical traditions.

Characteristic of the outlook that distinguishes the seventeenth-century exegetical milieu are the deliberations of Milton's old adversary Joseph Hall. In his response to the behavior of the concubine, Hall observes:

> Shee whom ill custome had of a wife made a concubine, is now by her lust, of a concubine made an harlot; Her fornication, together with the change of her bed, hath changed her abode. Perhaps her owne conscience thrust her out of doores, perhaps the iust seuerity of her husband. Dismission was too easie a penalty for that which God had sentenced with death: She that had deserued to be abhorred of her husband, seeks shelter from her Father.

In short, Hall is uncompromising in his castigation of one whom he considers to be no better than a common whore and an adulteress to boot. No punishment for her offense would be too extreme. Both husband and father would be fully justified in casting her out:

> Why would her Father suffer his house to be defiled with an adultresse, tho out of his owne loynes? Why did he not rather say, What? Doost thou thinke to finde my house an harbor for thy sinne? Whiles thou wert a wife to thine husband, thou wert a daughter to me; Now, thou art neyther; Thou art not mine; I gaue thee to thy husband; Thou art not thy husbands, thou hast betrayed his bed; Thy filthinesse hath made thee thine owne, and thine adulterers; Goe seeke thine entertainment, where thou hast lost thine honesty.[30]

Commonplace among the exegetes of Milton's time, this outlook tends to compromise, if not vitiate, the standing of the concubine from the outset and therefore to render her terrible fate more palatable. Accordingly, Matthew Poole not only finds excuses for the

29. See the preceding note, as well as the cogent discussion of Bal, *Death and Dissymmetry*, pp. 72–73, 83–89.

30. Joseph Hall, *Contemplations upon the Principall Passages of Holy Storie* (London, 1620), p. 945.

offering up of the concubine but actually justifies her rape by ob-
serving: "Thus the Sin she formerly chose is now her Destruction;
and though her husband pardoned her, God would punish her, at
least as to this life." Poole thereby transforms a narrative of unmitigated horror and barbarity into an account of just, indeed divine,
retribution in response to the offences of one who finally deserves
what is meted out to her. Poole goes so far as to suggest that even
the mutilation of her body is undertaken for a justifiable cause: "This
might seem to be a Barbarous and inhuman act in it self," he observes,
"but may seem excusable, if it be considered that the sadness of the
Spectacle did highly contribute to stir up the zeal of all the *Israelites*"
to avenge the husband for the death of his concubine. The husband,
not the concubine, is the offended party: it is his honor and the abuse
of his property, tainted though it may be, for which the "profligate
Offenders" must answer.[31] Both the concubine and the horrors visited
upon her are totally deprived of meaning: having been sullied from
the outset, her presence is finally erased from the text. Such is the
nature of the response one encounters in the exegetical traditions to
which Milton was heir.

I have undertaken an examination both of the biblical texts underlying the references to Belial in the first book of *Paradise Lost* and
of the exegetical traditions to which the biblical texts gave rise in order
to establish an additional framework within which to examine the
nature of Milton's sparagmatic sensibility. Particularly as manifested
in the fate of the concubine of Judges, that sensibility bears directly
on the issue of gender in Milton's thought. In this sense, the movement
from Bacchus to Belial reflects a corresponding movement not only
from the pagan dimensions of Milton's epic to the biblical dimensions
but from the poet as defenseless male attacked by savage females to
the poet as defenseless female attacked by savage males. At the forefront of these configurations is the Miltonic portrayal of his own
identity. In our exploration of the biblical dimensions of that portrayal, we may now proceed to Milton's own view of the concubine
and the bearing of that view upon his sense of self.

31. Matthew Poole, *Annotations upon the Holy Bible*, 2 vols. (London, 1683), vol. 1, s.v.
For corresponding interpretations, see Richard Rogers, *A Commentary upon the Whole Book of
Judges* (London, 1615), p. 905; and John Diodati, *Pious Annotations Vpon the Holy Bible* (London,
1651), s.v.

6

The Exposure of the Matron

I

In contradistinction to the prevailing exegetical outlook concerning the concubine of Judges, Milton formulated a reading that had a profound impact not only upon his conduct as a writer but upon his sense of self. As Louise Simons cogently observes, the perplexities of the concubine's harrowing story seized his imagination: Milton, in effect, wrote her fate across his works.[1] The extent to which the concubine is crucial to Milton is discernible in both his prose and his poetry. In both forms of discourse, he transforms the concubine from the so-called adulteress and whore of the biblical account into the virginal matron of his epic. Underlying this transformation is a determination to cleanse the concubine of any possible taint of impropriety arising from the charge of sexual misconduct.[2] Such a determination is the foundation of Milton's stance as hermeneut and as poet, and it underlies his self-configuration.

---

1. Louise Simons, " 'An Immortality Rather Than a Life': Milton and the Concubine of *Judges* 19–21," in *Old Testament Women in Western Literature*, ed. Raymond-Jean Frontain and Jan Wojcik (Conway: University of Central Arkansas Press, 1991), pp. 145–73. Although my approach is quite different from Simons's, I am much indebted to her many insights.
2. Milton's attitude toward concubinage is largely negative. In the *Doctrine and Discipline of Divorce*, for example, he cites with approval Malachi's admonition against husbands' keeping "strange Concubines, to the vexation of their *Hebrew* wives" (*YP*, 2:354; cf. 2:616; Mal. 2:4–16). See also Milton's comments in *The History of Britain* (*YP*, 5:320, 326–27).

From the hermeneutic perspective, Milton's discussion of the meanings of fornication in the divorce tracts assumes crucial import. Thus, in *The Doctrine and Discipline of Divorce* and in *Tetrachordon*, Milton places fornication in a broader context than that customarily associated with it. In *Tetrachordon*, for example, he observes that "the language of Scripture signifies by fornication" not just "the trespas of body nor perhaps that between maried persons," that is, adultery. In marital relationships, fornication likewise includes "any notable disobedience, or intractable cariage of the wife to the husband." In matters of faith, moreover, fornication signifies "the apparent alienation of mind" that distinguishes idolatry, will worship, love of earthly things or worldy pleasures, even "in a right beleever." Although such "fornication" may be committed unwittingly, it may also include "willfull disobedience to any the least of Gods commandements," and therefore a distrust of God and a "withdrawing from that neernes of zeal and confidence which ought to be" accorded God (*YP*, 2:672–73).[3] Having bestowed upon fornication such a wide range of meanings, Milton invokes as his central prooftext for that mode of fornication arising in marital relationships the figure of the concubine and directs his reader to the discussion in *The Doctrine and Discipline of Divorce*.

In that discussion, Milton marshals an array of authorities to support a "liberal" interpretation of fornication based upon his own reading of the character of the concubine in Judges 19. He first calls upon Hugo Grotius as an unimpeachable authority on the subject. According to Grotius, fornication "is tak'n in Scripture for such a continual headstrong behaviour, as tends to plain contempt of the husband." This, observes Milton, Grotius "proves" from his analysis of Judges 19:2, "where the Levites wife is said to have playd the whoor against him." Interpreting this statement as a sign not of infidelity or adultery but of rebelliousness, Grotius, like Milton,

---

3. Compare Milton's discussion of *fornicatio* in *De Doctrina Christiana* (1.10): Fornication does not mean only adultery. "It can mean also either what is called *some shameful thing* (i.e., the lack of some quality which might reasonably be required in a wife)...or it can signify anything which is found to be persistently at variance with love, fidelity, help and society (i.e., with the original institution of marriage)." Having made this observation, Milton maintains that "the best text to demonstrate this [contention]...is Judg. xix.2: *she fornicated against him.* This was not by committing adultery [*non adulterando*], because then she would not have dared to run home to her father, but by behaving in an obstinate way towards her husband [*sed pervicaciter adversus maritum se gerendo*]" (*YP*, 6:378; *CM*, 15:170–74).

refuses to endorse a harsh sexual interpretation of the concubine. Milton accommodates the text to a reading that renders her behavior much more palatable. The act of having "playd the whoor" against her husband, Milton continues, is also viewed more liberally in the ancient texts: "*Josephus* and the *Septuagint*, with the *Chaldaean*," Milton maintains, "interpret only of stubbornnes and rebellion against her husband."[4]

Along with exegetes who endorse his position, Milton finds himself in accord both with earlier authorities and with ancient versions of the text. What is true of Grotius and Josephus before him is correspondingly true of the ancient rabbinical authorities: "And to this I adde that *Kimchi* and the two other Rabbies [Levi ben Gerson and Rashi] who glosse the text, are of the same opinion. *Ben Gerson* reasons that had it bin whoordom, a Jew and a Levite would have disdain'd to fetch her again." To this, Milton contributes his own observation "that had it bin whoordom she would have chosen any other place to run to, then to her fathers house, it being so infamous for an hebrew woman to play the harlot, and so opprobrious to the parents. Fornication then in this place of the *Judges*, is understood for stubborn disobedience against the husband, and not for adultery" (*YP*, 2:335–36).

The point is that, in Milton's liberal interpretration of fornication in the divorce tracts, the concubine emerges as a figure free of the taint of adultery and whoredom that customarily besmirches her character. She may be guilty of rebelliousness and stubborness in response to the imposition of authority—characteristically Miltonic traits, one might suggest—but not culpable of sexual impropriety of any sort. Milton is determined to cleanse her character of the imputation of any such misconduct. He has thus taken her under his wing: he becomes, as it were, her defender, she his cause. His hermeneutic outlook comes to represent an apologia for her character and finally for her behavior.

In his other works, such an outlook allows him to express his unmitigated outrage at the rape and his unqualified support for the

---

4. Milton alludes to Grotius's *Annotationes in Libros Evangeliorum* (Amsterdam, 1641). According to Lowell W. Coolidge, the editor of *The Doctrine and Discipline of Divorce* in the *YP*, Milton attributes to Grotius a more positive tone than the original warrants (*YP*, 2:335n). In effect, Milton is determined to find corroboration for his own views, even if it means misreading those of the authorities he calls upon to support his argument.

violence ultimately suffered by her violators. This expression of outrage coupled with support for justified violence, is discernible in *Eikonoklastes* and in the *Defensio Prima*. At issue in both works is the same
event: the Irish rebellion against the English occupation and the subsequent massacre of the Irish by the English in the early 1640s.[5] In
Eikonoklastes these events provide Milton the occasion to excoriate
Charles I for what Milton feels had been an unjustified softening of
the official stance against the atrocities of the Irish. The source of
Milton's rebuke is a passage in the *Eikon Basilike* (chap. 12), "in which
Charles blamed the desperate resistance of the Irish rebels on the
severity of the measures with which they had been threatened by
Parliament." According to the passage in question, "Parliament de-
served a curse such as Jacob had called down upon his sons Simeon
and Levi (Genesis 49:7) for their massacre of the men of Sechem
(Genesis 34: 25–26) in retaliation for the seduction of their sister
Dinah."[6]

In response to this passage, Milton launches an attack upon what
amounts to no more than an "affected mercy" in Charles toward the
Irish, when in fact the king had been barbaric all along in the treatment of his own countrymen. Milton's attitude toward the reference
to the seduction of Dinah and the curse leveled on those who attempted to revenge that seduction through an unjustified massacre
is correspondingly harsh. The parallel does not hold, he maintains,
because the offense represented by the seduction was atoned for by
"honorable love and offers of a most generous marriage settlement."[7]
The Irish, on the other hand, are guilty of much greater offenses
that warrant a violent reaction, one in which there is a "just Warr and
execution" upon them "who so barbarously had slaine whole Families
before."[8] To support his contention, Milton offers in opposition to

5. For a brief account of these events, see Don M. Wolfe's Introduction to *YP*, 1:168–
70.
6. The passage from *Eikon Basilike* is summarized by Merritt Y. Hughes in *YP*, 3:481n.
The seduction of Dinah is described in Genesis 34:1–3. Milton's interest in this text is discernible in his outlines for tragedies in the Trinity College Manuscript (*CM*, 18:235).
7. See Hughes, *YP*, 3:481n. Thus, Milton: "Neither is there the same cause to destroy
a whole City for the ravishing of a Sister." For the rape of Dinah was "not don out of Villany,"
and it was recompensed by the offer of marriage (*YP*, 3:481–82; cf. Gen. 34:4).
8. In his putative outrage at the massacre of the Irish, "Charles had likewise compared
the '*preposterous* and . . . *unevangelical Zeal*' of Parliament against the Irish rebels to 'that of the
rebuked Disciples,' James and John (Luke 9:52–56), who would have prayed for fire from
heaven to destroy 'a village of the Samaritans' for refusing to receive Jesus" (Hughes, *YP*,
3:482n). Milton likewise disputes this parallel (*YP*, 3:482).

the false example of the seduction of Dinah what he feels is the true rape, that of the concubine, which is met with a fully justified massacre, one that is the true type of the massacre of the Irish. "Did not all *Israel* doe as much against the *Benjamits*," he declares, "for one Rape committed by a few, and defended by the whole Tribe? And did they not the same to *Jabesh Gilead* for not assisting them in that revenge?"[9] The reference is to the terrible warfare in the aftermath of the rape and dismemberment of the concubine. That warfare involves two events in particular: first, the Israelite slaughter of twenty-five thousand Benjaminites and the destruction of their cities (Judg. 20:46–48); second, the massacre of the inhabitants (including the women and children) of Jabesh-gilead, simply because they did not support the Israelites against the Benjaminites (Judg. 21:10). Rather than question the extremity, indeed barbarity, of such responses, Milton is fully in accord with them. He endorses them not only because they serve to reinforce his immediate polemical agenda but because, in what amounts to his own emerging association with the concubine and her terrible plight, he feels that only by means of this sort of violence is it possible to vindicate the sufferings of one whose innocence has been wholly violated and whose very being has been completely destroyed.

Such an outlook resurfaces and in fact is further intensified in the *Defensio Prima*. Once again addressing the Irish rebellion and its aftermath, Milton draws upon the same text to justify the massacre of the Irish:

> Does it matter whether the enemy be foreign or domestic? Either one threatens the state with the same bitter and ruinous destruction. All Israel saw that without much shedding of blood she could not avenge the outrage and murder of the Levite's wife; did they think that for this reason they must hold their peace, avoid civil war however fierce, or allow the death of a single poor woman to go unpunished? [*Vidit totus Israel non posse se sine multo sanguine Levitae*

9. Milton attempts to tone this down: "I speak not this that such measure should be meted rigorously to all the Irish, or as remembering that the Parliament ever so Decreed, but to shew that this his [Charles's] Homily hath more of craft and affectation in it, then of sound Doctrin" (*YP*, 3:482). But his disclaimer does little to soften the harshness of his declaration. Milton fully supported the zeal underlying such massacres: he was a supporter of holy war in a just cause. See my chapter on warfare in *Poetics of the Holy: A Reading of "Paradise Lost"* (Chapel Hill: University of North Carolina Press, 1981), pp. 246–312.

uxorem stupro enectam ulcisci; num igitur quiescendum sibi esse duxit, num bello civili, quamvis truculentissimo supersedendum, num unam igitur mulierculam mori inultam est passus?] (*YP*, 4:431; *CM*, 7:286–89)

The assertion is significant for several reasons. Beginning as a political argument that justifies revenge upon those (both foreign and domestic) who threaten the stability of the state, it proceeds to the one lone figure of the concubine, whose terrible fate cried out for revenge of the most extreme sort.

The Latin is instructive. The concubine is referred to not as *concubina* or *paelex*; rather, she is deliberately dignified and elevated with the title of *uxor*: she already assumes a legal status in keeping with her high position. The outrage perpetrated upon her, moreover, is specified. Milton employs the harshest of terms: *stupro* (from *stuprare*, "to ravish," "rape," "defile") and *enectam* (from *enecare*, "to kill"). These outrages must be met with *ulcisci* (from *ulciscor*, "to avenge oneself on," "take vengeance on"). She becomes a *muliercula*, a "little woman," a "girl," defenseless against the onslaughts of those who would do her harm. The passage trumpets her innocence and cries out for the vengeance it feels is entirely justified. Any suggestion of culpability on the part of the concubine is totally obliterated. No longer is she associated with misdeeds of any sort: the earlier imputation of stubborness and rebelliousness against her husband has disappeared. In its place we encounter her purity, her fragility, and her vulnerability. It is as if she has undergone a transformation in Milton's determination to cleanse her. No longer *concubina* or *paelex*, she becomes *uxor* and *muliercula*, the first suggesting stateliness and dignity, the second, vulnerability and innocence; the first, age and wisdom, the second, youth and femininity.

All these meanings are implied by the term Milton adopts to designate the concubine in *Paradise Lost*. There, she assumes the form of a "matron" (1.504). This, in effect, is the final transformation she undergoes in Milton's treatment of the concubine from Bethlehemjudah. Both through its etymology and through Milton's use of the term in his own writings, "matron" is of crucial import to an understanding of the way the figure of the concubine assumes a profound significance to the poet of *Paradise Lost*. With its roots in the Latin *matrona*, "matron" gives rise to its own distinct connotations. The matrona is one who is at once a married woman and a woman of quality. She is "the lady of the house." In her is embodied all that is most estimable, virtuous, and chaste.[10] About her accrue associations of sanctity, indeed, saintliness.[11]

Given the extent of Milton's idealization of the *matrona* in this context, it is hardly surprising that she assumes numerous forms in his works, all of them suggesting a figure of the most exalted sort. Her idealized presence appears as early as the *Fair Infant* elegy in the role of "that crown'd Matron sage white-robed truth" (l. 54). There, she becomes part of that divine triad completed by the "just Maid" Astraea and "that sweet smiling Youth" Mercy. So conceived, she is a member of "that heav'nly brood / Let down in clowdie throne to do the world some good" (ll. 50–55). Milton's idealization of the virginal *matrona* does not end here, however. In *Il Penseroso*, for example, she is divinized as that "Goddes, sage and holy" whom Milton hails as "divinest Melancholy," a *matrona* "Whose Saintly visage is too bright / To hit the Sense of human sight; / And therfore to our weaker view, / O're laid with black staid Wisdoms hue" (ll. 11–16). The very embodiment of saintliness, she is even invoked in ecclesiastical terms: "Com pensive Nun, devout and pure, / Sober, stedfast, and demure." Attired "all in a robe of darkest grain," she has drawn over her "decent shoulders" that "sable stole" customarily worn by the chastest of matrons (ll. 31–36). In this guise, as well as in others, her presence is everywhere felt.

Assuming the form of the Countess Dowager of Derby in Arcades, for example, she is heralded with extravagant hyperbole: "Mark what radiant state she spreds / In circle round her shining throne, / Shooting her beams like silver threds. / This this is she alone, / Sitting like a Goddes bright / In the center of her light" (ll. 13–19). So conceived, the countess becomes the matron par excellence, a figure who rivals "the wise *Latona*" or Leto, mother of Apollo and Diana; "*Cybele*, / Mother of a hunderd gods"; and Juno herself (ll. 20–23).

If she has about her the sanctity of age in *Arcades*, she has about her all the innocence and vulnerability of youth in the elegies and the sonnets. A few examples suffice. In the elegies, she is depicted as the faithful uxor. She is Jane Paulet, in whose *Epitaph* Milton celebrates her as "the honour'd Wife of *Winchester*, / A Vicounts daughter, an

---

10. See "Matrona" in *A Latin Dictionary*, ed. Charlton T. Lewis and Charles Short (Oxford: Clarendon Press, 1879), s.v.

11. See the various definitions in the *Oxford English Dictionary*, s.v., to this effect.

Earls heir, / Besides what her vertues fair / Added to her noble birth, / More then she could own from Earth" (ll. 1–5). Having died in childbirth, she experiences a celestial apotheosis that allows this "bright Saint" to sit in glory next to "That fair Syrian Shepherdess" Rachel (ll. 62–63), the archetypal biblical matron who died giving birth to Benjamin (Gen. 29–37). Both for Milton are to be found beatified "Far within the boosom bright / Of blazing Majesty and Light" (ll. 69–70). On a much more personal note, she assumes in the sonnets the form of Milton's "late espoused saint" brought to the poet "like *Alcestis* from the grave." Whatever the identity of this saint, she too is a *matrona* who is both idealized and divinized. Appearing "vested all in white, pure as her mind," she is nonetheless "vail'd" as a symbol of the enduring mystery of her presence. Despite his inability to behold her face to face, the poet in his darkness is able to perceive that "Love, sweetness, goodness in her person shin'd / So clear, as in no face with more delight." But this perception is momentary. Until he has "Full sight of her in heav'n without restraint," the poet must remain in darkness: "But O as to imbrace me she enclin'd / I wak'd, she fled, and day brought back my night."[12]

Here, as elsewhere, the *matrona* for Milton assumes a mysterious, even sanctified bearing that situates her among the highest beings in the celestial realm. These are only some of the instances in which the *matrona* appears in the poetry. There are of others. The point is that in Milton's reference to the concubine as a matron in *Paradise Lost*, we encounter a profound transformation in the character of the concubine. She assumes a new identity, one that completely obliterates any taint that might have been associated with her former life.

Compounding this transformation is that through which Milton himself assumes the form of the *matrona* in his own writings. To witness such an "engendering," I return to the *Apology* for Smectymnuus. There, the transformation of the concubine into the concubine-become-matron is applicable to Milton's own sense of the gendered self as a matron par excellence. The entire situation in the *Apology*

---

12. The literature on this sonnet is immense. See Shawcross's full annotations and suggested readings in *Complete Poetry*, p. 246, as well as John R. Smart, ed., *The Sonnets of Milton* (London: Oxford University Press, 1966); E. A. J. Honigmann, ed., *Milton's Sonnets* (London: Macmillan, 1966); Anna K. Nardo, *Milton's Sonnets and the Ideal Community* (Lincoln: University of Nebraska Press, 1979), pp. 36–42.

implicitly plays upon the contexts established in the Sodom and Gibeah material. What results are reversals and counterreversals of those contexts through which Milton in his self-defense transforms himself from one who is associated with improprieties of sexual misconduct to one who is entirely above reproach. Undergoing that transformation, Milton responds to the onslaughts of an alien world. This is a world made up of rabble in the form of an adversary, a Confuter, who, in the fashion of the Belial-like sons of Sodom and Gibeah, is found constantly "barking at the doore" with his noisy and disruptive threats (*YP*, 1:892). In the face of those threats, Milton is obliged to defend his own chastity. He must cleanse himself of the taint of moral impropriety heaped upon him by his adversary, the Confuter.

Ironically, the Confuter places Milton in the position of one who is himself a son of Belial, for he charges that Milton is, among other things, a frequenter of bordellos, in effect, a whoremonger. Such role reversals Milton refuses to abide. It is the Confuter who is the whoremonger: he is the son of Belial. As a shameless prelate, in fact, he is among those "seene so oft upon the Stage writhing and unboning their Clergie limmes to all the antick and dishonest gestures of Trinculo's, Buffons, and Bawds; prostituting the shame of that ministery which either they had, or were nigh having, to the eyes of Courtiers and Court-Ladies, with their Groomes and *Madamoisellaes*" (*YP*, 1:887). A frequenter of bordellos himself, the Confuter "raps up without pitty the sage and rheumatick old *Prelatesse* with all her young *Corintian Laity*" (*YP*, 1:892). Casting aspersions upon the Confuter in this manner, Milton prepares us for a self-defense in which he absolves himself of those very taints with which the Confuter would besmirch him.

His self-defense is one in which he transforms ("refashions") himself into a virginal, indeed matronly figure whose character is entirely above reproach. In the act of such self-fashioning, he becomes in effect the very being he seeks to defend. That being is none other than a *matrona* of the most exalted sort. Purporting to defend this figure, Milton assumes her identity. The process of transformation (a kind of Miltonic *kenosis*) by which this assumption is effected is one in which the innocent but besmirched defender of his chastity offers to remove his attire. Doing so, he discloses himself so that he may appear completely naked before our eyes:

With me it fares now, as with him whose outward garment hath bin injur'd and ill bedighted; for having no other shift, what helpe but to turn the inside outwards, especially if the lining be of the same, or, as it is sometimes, much better. So if my name and outward demeanour be not evident anough to defend me, I must make tryall, if the discovery of my inmost thoughts can. (*YP*, 1:888–89)

Doffing his outward garment, his shift, and standing naked before us, he invites us to examine his body.

If such a gesture recalls that of the Domina in the sixth Prolusion, it is undertaken here not for the ostensible purpose of aligning oneself with one's audience in order ironically to generate acceptance and approval as *morosophos*. It is undertaken, rather, to proclaim one's purity as a *matrona* whose behavior is above reproach. In Milton's early poetry, the gesture finds its counterpart in (and comments implicitly upon) that of the female figure of Nature in the *Nativity* ode. In sympathy with the kenotic act of self-divestiture performed by "her great Master," she too removes her clothing ("her gawdy trim"), but, because she is fallen and polluted, her self-disclosure results only in her humiliation and shame. In effect, she is tantamount to a kind of whore, a fallen concubine: "Onely with speeches fair / She woos the gentle Air / To hide her guilty front with innocent Snow, / And on her naked shame, / Pollute with sinfull blame, / The Saintly Vail of Maiden white to throw, / Confounded, that her Makers eyes / Should look so neer upon her foul deformities" (ll. 32–44).[13]

Here, in a sense, is the obverse of the Miltonic act of self-disclosure in the *Apology*. I am not like *this* concubine, Milton proclaims in his own act of self-disclosure: Look, I shall gladly remove my clothing so that all can see! Behold my body, behold my inmost thoughts. I am pure. Moreover, I defend all those, like myself, who share my purity. In this regard, he holds up for admiration "the two famous renowners of *Beatrice* and *Laura*," Dante and Petrarch, "who never write but honour of them to whom they devote their verse, displaying sublime and pure thoughts, without transgression" (*YP*, 1:890).

Extolling such defenders of female purity, Milton avers that embodied in him is that very purity he would defend in other matrons

---

13. As I have argued elsewhere, this act of undressing represents a metaphorical reenactment of the theological concept of *kenosis*; see Michael Lieb, *The Sinews of Ulysses: Form and Convention in Milton's Works* (Pittsburgh: Duquesne University Press, 1989), pp. 38–52.

of the same kind. In his own character, he identifies himself with such matrons:

> These reasonings, together with a certaine niceness of nature, an honest haughtinesse, and self-esteem either of what I was, or what I might be, (which let envie call pride) and lastly that modesty, whereof... I may be excus'd to make some beseeming profession, all these uniting the supply of their naturall aide together, kept me still above those low descents of mind, beneath which he must deject and plunge himself, that can agree to salable and unlawfull prostitutions. (*YP*, 1:890)

I am neither the whoremonger nor the prostitute the Confuter makes me out to be, Milton proclaims. Examine me, examine my body: stripped of the clothing you have besmirched, this is a pure body. Like most matrons of my sort—perhaps, indeed, like Beatrice and Laura—I too am somewhat haughty, somewhat aloof, but I am pure. I am a *matrona* whose character is above reproach.

To underscore this posture of self-defense (which is also a posture of self-fashioning), Milton fabricates a kind of romance, one involving knights and ladies, as well as the perilous adventures they confront. If such damsels in the Miltonic romance are at risk of possible attack, their knights will certainly come to their aid. Participating in the very "lofty Fables and Romances" he creates to defend his own sense of self-purity, he declares: "There I read it in the oath of every Knight, that he should defend to the expence of his best blood, or of his life, if it so befell him, the honour and chastity of Virgin or Matron. From whence even then I learnt what a noble vertue chastity sure must be, to the defence of which so many worthies by such a deare adventure of themselves had sworne" (*YP*, 1:890–91). The entire romance in which Milton in the *Apology* finds himself an actor/actress becomes his own "deare adventure." Setting out on that adventure, he defends his honor and chastity by defending those of the "Virgin or Matron," of whom he himself is the prime representative.

If this sounds a bit haughty and lacking in modesty, so be it. In his virgin purity, Milton is one *matrona* who does not hesitate to come to his own defense with all the weapons at his disposal. He does not hesitate to disrobe in order to exhibit the purity of his body and to demonstrate that he is not like the fallen concubine of his *Nativity*

ode, whose "naked shame" is "Pollute with sinfull blame." He has no
fear of a "guilty front." *His* body is both innocent and beautiful. It is
that of the *matrona* in all her glory. Such is the romance of Milton's
concubine-become-matron as it is embodied in his own being, a being
he risks all to save from the "exposure" brought on by the disruptive
and noisy threats of the adversary "barking at the doore" of his own
retreat in the *Apology* for Smectymnuus.

Like all romances, this one will be exploded too. In *Paradise Lost*,
it is exploded by the terrible fate of the concubine-become-matron,
whose virginity, indeed, whose very body, Milton is at a loss to preserve
as it is gang raped all night and dismembered the following day. That
Milton was never able (or willing) to sustain the fantasy upon which
this romance is founded implies a pervasive awareness on his part
that he is a poet/poetess constantly at risk, constantly faced with the
prospect of a sparagmos.

II

The portent of sparagmos underlies the Sodom-Gibeah passage
that culminates the allusion to Belial in the first book of *Paradise Lost*.
As an expression both of the concubine's transformation in Milton's
works and of his association of the concubine-become-matron with
his own sense of self, this passage is seen to be of crucial import to
Milton's creation of gender identity. It is in effect a primal scene, a
moment of crisis in the Miltonic engendering of the self. Such an idea
gains even greater cogency if we take into account the significant
textual emendations the text itself underwent from its initial manuscript delineation to its final published form. These emendations reinforce our sense of the complexities surrounding the problematic
presence the evolving image of the concubine-become-matron assumes in Milton's works. Comparing the version that appears in the
1674 edition (cited above) with the surviving manuscript version of
the first book and the version that appears in the 1667 edition, we
are made aware not only how important the Sodom-Gibeah narratives
were to Milton but the extent to which he was at pains to render the
horrors embedded in those narratives as dramatically and succinctly
as possible.

The evolution of the emendations may best be determined in a text-by-text comparison, beginning with the manuscript version, proceeding to the first edition of 1667, and ending with the second edition of 1674.[14] The texts are as follows:

> *Manuscript version*
> Witnesse the Streets of Sodom, and that night
> In Gibeah, when hospitable doors
> Yeilded thir Matrons to avoid worse rape.

> *First edition (1667)*
> Witness the Streets of *Sodom*, and that night
> In *Gibeah*, when hospitable Dores
> Yielded thir Matrons to prevent worse rape.

> *Second edition (1674)*
> Witness the Streets of *Sodom*, and that night
> In *Gibeah*, when th'hospitable door
> Expos'd a Matron to avoid worse rape.
> (1.503–5)

Both the extent and the nature of the revisions reflected in these three versions are remarkable indeed. They suggest an evolution in Milton's thought that increasingly focuses attention on the concubine-become-matron and that emphasizes her importance as a figure made to endure horrors of the most unbearable sort.[15]

All three versions emphasize the way Milton, in keeping with earlier traditions, conflated Genesis 19 and Judges 19.[16] For him, these

14. References to all three versions are *Facsimile*, 2:74–75, 237; 3:107. For the manuscript version, see also *The Manuscript of Milton's "Paradise Lost". Book I*, ed. Helen Darbishire (Oxford: Oxford University Press, 1931). See also R. G. Moyles, *The Text of "Paradise Lost": A Study in Editorial Procedure* (Toronto: University of Toronto Press, 1985).

15. Throughout this discussion, one must keep in mind John T. Shawcross's caveat in his discussion of the changes that occurred between the 1667 and 1674 editions: "My aim has been to call in doubt hypotheses of the correctness of the text in terms of Milton's 'desires' or practices, to indicate the confusion of textual transmission and correction that must have occurred, and to suggest that the second edition has only some authority, not full authority, over the first edition"; Shawcross, "Orthography and the Text of *Paradise Lost*," in *Language and Style in Milton*, ed. Ronald David Emma and John T. Shawcross (New York: Frederick Ungar, 1967), p. 150.

16. Although Milton's early editors did not have access to the manuscript text, they were very much interested in the changes that occurred between the 1667 and 1674 editions. See in particular Patrick Hume's annotations in *The Poetical Works of Mr. John Milton* (London, 1695); Richard Bentley's annotations in *Milton's "Paradise Lost". A New Edition* (London, 1732); and the annotations of Jonathan Richardson, Father and Son, in *Explanatory Notes and Remarks on Milton's "Paradise Lost"* (London, 1734), among others.

biblical texts represent two accounts of the same story. In our own loathing for the barbarities with which Belial is customarily associated, we are invited to witness the events that constitute both accounts. As we have seen, the first account moves into the second as an intensification of the horrors that, if avoided in the first, are fully realized in the second, which is in effect a rewriting of the first. In that act of reinscription, Milton engages in his own rewriting as he moves from manuscript to earlier and then later published renderings of the same account. It mattered to him to get the wording right. In the process of doing so, he caused the Gibeah account, with its attendant brutalities, to become all-consuming.[17]

Thus, the "hospitable doors" of the manuscript version and the "hospitable Dores" of the 1667 edition are reduced from plural to singular in the 1674 edition. "Th'hospitable door" has a synecdochic force: it encodes the door that separates Lot, his family, and his guests from the men of Sodom, on the one hand, and the door that separates the nameless host, his family, and his guests from the men of Gibeah, on the other. Thus, "th'hospitable door" encapsulates the events surrounding Lot's offer of his daughters in Genesis 19 and the nameless host's offer of his daughter and the concubine in Judges 19. In this sense, the phrase has a metonymic force as well: embedded within it is the larger concept of what is implied by the kind of "hospitality"

_____

17. As one who worried the text as much as Milton, Richard Bentley (*Milton's "Paradise Lost,"* p. 23) provided annotations that not only call Milton's revisions into question but, in customary Bentleyesque fashion, rewrite Milton's own text. Bentley's annotations and revisions are worth quoting in full. Responding to the passage as it appears in the 1674 edition (as opposed to the 1667 edition), Bentley declares: "Here's an Alteration made here, varying from the First Edition, which gave it in the plural number, 'When the hospitable Doors / Yielded their Matrons *to avoid worse rape.' Agreeable to the Scriptures, and preferable to the present Reading. Doors*; both in *Sodom* and *Gibeah: Matrons*, because *Two were yielded* and offer'd in each place: in *Sodom*, Gen. xix.8. in *Gibeah, Judges* xix.24. The Editor has made three or four more Changes from the first Impression, and every one for the worse. In This, he confines the Fact to *Gibeah* alone: and so deserts the *Street of Sodom*, that are called on to *witness* nothing at all. But the Author too has incurr'd some blame; who after naming the *Streets of* One, says the *Night in* the Other; when there were equally concern'd *Streets of* Both, and *Night in* Both. Give the whole thus, with a slight Amendment on the First Edition: '*Witness the Streets of* Sodom; witness those / Of Gibeah; *when the hospitable* Doors / Yielded their Matrons *to avoid worse rape.*'" In short, Bentley insists on parity between Sodom and Gibeah, removes any reference to "night" in either, and largely retains the reading of the first edition. Doing so, he relieves the matron of the weight of the outrage she alone is made to bear. This, of course, is a splendid piece of misreading. Much more perceptive in their understanding of the Miltonic text and the implications of the revisions, the Richardsons defend the revisions. At the same time, they insist on distinctions between the virgin daughters of Genesis 19 and Judges 19, on the one hand, and the so-called matron of Judges 19, on the other (*Explanatory Notes*, p. 32).

both narratives portray. As Milton would no doubt aver, such hospitality is questionable at best and in fact devastatingly brutal and barbaric as it is finally put to the test. The movement from the phrase "hospitable Dores" to "th'hospitable door," then, focuses and intensifies both the metaphorical and ironic dimensions of this telling moment.[18]

Something of the same thing happens with the word "Matron." Reflecting the inclusiveness of "hospitable Dores" in the earlier versions, "Matron" likewise initially assumes the plural form. Included in the plural noun are not only Lot's daughters but the daughter of the nameless host and the concubine of his guest. As Milton conceives them, all these figures are virginal and therefore entirely innocent.[19] Transforming the noun from plural to singular in the 1674 edition, however, Milton causes the qualities associated with the virginity and innocence of the daughters to be embodied solely in the figure of the concubine-become-matron. She is made to stand alone and exposed in the final line of the description. In this sense the concubine-become-matron not only subsumes the virginal figures of the Genesis and Judges accounts; she also displaces them. The virgin daughters are no more: only the "Matron" remains to be violated and ultimately dismembered. The force of this displacement is especially felt in the substitution of the indefinite article for the possessive pronoun. No longer "*thir* Matrons," she becomes "*a* Matron." She belongs to no one: she is completely and desperately alone. She must bear the brunt of the horrors an alien world is determined to inflict. She has no compeer, no one to sustain her. Her plight is individual, unique; her experience one that totally obliterates the experience of those who would even faintly approach it. The fate of the nameless concubine-become-matron undermines all attempts to associate her with that of any other living being. Sodom and its events recede into the background, erased by the unthinkable barbarities perpetrated in Gibeah, where "a Matron" in her aloneness and vulnerability awaits the horrors to be visited upon her.

In the verbal changes Milton introduced between manuscript copy

---

18. Compare Milton's ironic use of the term "hospitable" in *A Mask*. There, the Lady with unself-conscious irony refers to the wilderness in which she finds herself as "the kind hospitable woods" (l. 187).

19. Interestingly, Lot's daughters, as we discover later in the Sodom narrative, are actually betrothed (Gen. 19:14).

and published text, these horrors are further reinforced by the word that describes the nature of her plight. Whereas the manuscript and the first edition have "Yielded" (or "Yeilded"), the second edition adopts the word "Expos'd." A distinction is thereby raised between "hospitable Dores / Yielded" in the earlier version and "th'hospitable door / Expos'd" in the later version. The alteration is significant. In Milton's poetic vocabulary the terms "yielded" and "expos'd" have very different connotations.[20] As applied to an individual, the first has about it the quality of the willing or unwilling surrender of that which one otherwise holds in one's possession. Implicit in the term is a volitional imperative that places the individual called upon to do the yielding in a position of assent or nonassent. These circumstances arise as the result of a relationship (usually one of power) that has been established between the individual called upon to yield and the individual to whose demands the yielder responds.

In the prelapsarian sexual economy of Milton's epic, the act of yielding initially has quite positive connotations. One thinks of the relationship engendered between Adam and Eve implicit in the description of Eve's "tresses": "Shee as a vail down to the slender waste / Her unadorned golden tresses wore / Dissheveld, but in wanton ringlets wav'd, / As the Vine curls her tendrils, which impli'd / Subjection, but requir'd with gentle sway, and by her yeilded, by him best receiv'd, / Yeilded with coy submission, modest pride, / And sweet reluctant amorous delay" (4.304–11; italics mine). The act of yielding here occurs in an environment of playful but innocent dalliance. Sexuality is entirely innocent: there is no hint of violence in the "subjection" and "submission" required of this unfallen being. That fact is reinforced moments later in Eve's account of her first encounter with Adam. Recalling Adam's declaration of his desire to be (re)united with her ("Part of my Soul I seek thee, and thee claim / My other

20. Compare the comments in the Todd variorum: "Milton did well in altering the passage; for it was not true of *Sodom*, that any *matron* was yielded there; see *Gen.* xix.8: And, as the women were only offered, not accepted, it is not proper to say that they were *yielded*. But observe that Milton, in the second edition changed *yielded* into *exposed*; because, in what was done at Gibeah, *Judges* xix.25, the Levite's *wife* was not only *yielded*, but put out of doors, and *expos'd* to the men's lewdness"; *The Poetical Works of John Milton: With Notes of Various Authors*, 6 vols., 3d ed., ed. H. J. Todd (London, 1826), 2:69–70. According to Patrick Hume, "expos'd" (from *exponere*) indicates "to set out to Publick View, to deliver into the Power of" (*Poetical Works*, p. 32). For the varying usage of individual words in Milton, see Laura E. Lockwood, *Lexicon to the English Poetical Works of John Milton* (1907; New York: Burt Franklin, 1968), s.v.

half"), Eve relates her experience of their (re)union: "with that thy gentle hand / Seis'd mine, I yeilded, and from that time see / How beauty is excelld by manly grace / And wisdom, which alone is truly fair" (4.487–91). In this context, the act of yielding is once again that of willing submission to a higher power in recognition of the superior virtues this power appears to possess. Whether we are inclined to agree that such an act of submission is warranted on the part of Eve, it is a voluntary act very much in keeping with the prelapsarian environment Milton portrays.

It hardly needs to be argued that in the postlapsarian world the experience of submission can assume an ominous and indeed brutal bearing. In this respect, the yielding up of the concubine-become-matron by the so-called hospitable door looks forward to the devastating experience she is forced to undergo in her own act of yielding. In the figure of the concubine-become-matron, the language that inscribes the prelapsarian sexual economy of Eve turns to indescribable horror, as the victimized matron yields her body to the overpowering demands of the men of Gibeah. The concubine-become-matron is yielded up by a hospitable door, a yielding that forces her into the position of having her own body itself yielded up. The notion is an interesting one but not quite to the point, for it suggests that the action of the hospitable door anticipates and is replicated in that of the individual who is so yielded.

What happens to the concubine-become-matron, however, is far more devastating than that of a yielding, enforced or otherwise. The helpless victim of gang rape, death, and finally outright dismemberment, she experiences horrors that extend well beyond the point of relinquishment, an enforced giving over of the will to a greater power. Hers is an experience that overgoes yielding of any sort. It is rather exposure that places her in the totally compromised and totally vulnerable position of finding herself without any possibility of preserving that which in the eyes of those who abuse her is in so sense hers either to give or to withhold. In their eyes, that is, she has nothing to yield, for she has nothing that is inherently her own, that constitutes her identity as a human being. Hers is an experience of complete and total victimization, one in which the relationship between the individual who overpowers and the individual who submits is not even at issue, because identity itself is not at issue. She is simply property, to be done with as her ravishers (and finally even her husband, to whom she is also property) see fit. Such is the "rape" to which the concubine-become-matron is "expos'd." Such is the tragedy of one whom Milton views in the highest terms but whom her abusers consider a thing to be disposed of at their will.

It is this exposure to the will of others that renders the experience of the matron so terrible. Milton's use of the term "expos'd" in the 1674 edition is precisely to the point. Reinforcing the biblical notion of the *pilegesh* as property, it heightens the tragedy of her utter vulnerability and total victimization. For Milton, the term is charged with just such a meaning, one that recalls the language of the antiprelatical tracts. There, he issues a lament over the fate of another matron, England herself, in the face of those sons of Belial, the prelates: "O Sir," he exclaims in *Of Reformation*, "if we could but see the shape of our deare Mother *England*, as Poets are wont to give a personal form to what they please, how would she appear, think ye, but in a mourning weed, with ashes upon her head, and teares abundantly flowing from her eyes, to behold so many of her children *expos'd* at once, and thrust from things of dearest necessity" (*YP*, 1:585; italics mine). The prelates who leave dear Mother England and her children so "expos'd" are the same who in *Animadversions* are guilty of "trampl[ing] upon" their "good Mother of *England*," that is, the church herself, in the manner that the sons of Belial abused the Levites wife in Gibeah" (*YP*, 1:713). In the context of *Paradise Lost*, it is just this kind of exposure to which the concubine-become-matron is subjected. As the result of such exposure, her victimization is complete and devastating. This fact reinforces the significance of the final set of alterations that appear between manuscript text and second edition.

In a sense, these alterations are the most interesting, for they suggest that Milton had been wrestling with the passage from the very beginning and that he kept struggling to get it right. Recalling the alterations in question, we have first the manuscript version: "*avoid* worse rape"; next the 1667 edition: "*prevent* worse rape"; finally, the 1674 edition: "*avoid* worse rape." What are we to make of these changes? What are we to make of the phrase as a whole—whether with "avoid" or "prevent"? First, the alterations. Milton began with "avoid" as a word that implies the idea of keeping away from, eluding.[21] For Milton, the word carried the same implications it carries

---

21. See *Oxford English Dictionary*, s.v., def. III: "to keep away from, keep from, keep

today. In this respect, it has about it the all-important quality of behaving expediently. Such behavior is undertaken as the result of responding in a practical manner to the demands of a given occasion. Acting in this manner becomes a way of not having to face the consequences of that which one otherwise seeks to elude. Avoidance, however, does not guarantee the absolute nonoccurrence of such consequences: to avoid may or may not prevent, and, even should prevention occur, the effects of avoidance may be momentary. As such, "avoid" has something of the provisional about it. Avoidance is at best precautionary.

"Prevent," by contrast, is a stronger word. In its Latinate sense, it carries the meaning of acting to anticipate (*praevenire*) that which might otherwise occur. It comes to assume, however, a much stronger, related meaning having to do with the idea of forestalling or obstructing. In the latter sense, one acts to keep something from occurring.[22] Although Milton used the term in both senses, he most often adopted the latter sense in both his poetry and his prose. As he employs it in the 1667 version of the passage in question, it has the force of acting to make certain that an event will not occur. Given these circumstances, his opting in the 1674 edition for the term "avoid" is significant, because it leaves open the possibility of occurrence, despite whatever precautionary steps one might take. It thereby suggests the presence of expediency. It invites the possibility of doubt. These unsettling qualities reinforce the problematic nature of the phrase as a whole.

As disturbing as "Yielded thir Matrons to prevent worse rape" might be, "Expos'd a Matron to avoid worse rape" is even more so: first, because it places the concubine-become-matron at the point of focus; second, because it views her as sole and helpless victim; third, because it calls into question both the motive and the efficacy of offering up the matron as sacrifice to "avoid" a victimization it implies

---

off." According to R. G. Moyles, "knowing that the word 'avoid' is also the manuscript reading, one might be tempted to conclude that the printer has here merely restored it from that source. Since, however, 'Expos'd a Matron' is completely new to the Octavo [1674 edition], it seems certain that Milton (or his agent) was responsible for the change" (*Text of "Paradise Lost,"* p. 21). Moyles's conclusions are in accord with those of Helen Darbishire, who considers all the verbal alterations from manuscript through published versions the result of deliberate planning. These alterations, she asserts, must be accepted without question as an indication of Milton's desire to refine his text (*Manuscript of "Paradise Lost,"* p. xlv).

22. See *Oxford English Dictionary*, s.v., defs. I and II: "To act before, in anticipation of"; "To forestall, balk, or baffle by previous or precautionary measures."

would be even worse were such an action not undertaken. "To avoid worse rape": what are we finally to think of this? What is worse than that which has already taken place? Is the expediency of offering up the concubine-become-matron as sacrifice to be preferred over the rape that threatens? If so, the best that can be said for the passage as a whole is that Milton shares in the complicity of those who do the offering up in order to save their own hides. Female rape, this act of complicity implies, is better than male rape. Better to encourage the one in order to "avoid" (the word begins to smell) the other. In a recent edition of Milton's works, the editors gloss this line with the appalling statement that "Milton's notion that there are preferable kinds of rape is entirely consistent with the biblical account."[23] Unless we attend to the tone of the passage as a whole, we are in danger of falling into the same trap.

Given the transformation the concubine undergoes in Milton's thought as well as the implications of the emendations sustained by the passage that inscribes her fate from manuscript text to final version, we are obliged to read the passage as an expression of unbearable irony. Milton condones neither the doings represented by that "hospitable door" nor the aftermath of the outrages once the Matron has been "expos'd." Hospitality of the sort that substitutes one form of rape in order to "avoid" another is hardly a concept Milton would have endorsed.[24] Nor would he agree that one form of rape is more preferable than another. The rape of the matron is as horrible as that which might have been perpetrated on those able to "avoid" such a fate. At some deeper level, one may even question whether that fate has been avoided at all.

If one assumes Milton's identification with the matron as a manifestation of his own bisexuality, then the poet who is also the poetess of *Paradise Lost* finds himself exposed by a door that is none too hospitable. The rape of the matron is the rape of Milton himself. He is as much the victim as is she. The "worse rape" is not avoided after

---

23. *John Milton*, The Oxford Authors, ed. Stephen Orgel and Jonathan Goldberg (Oxford: Oxford University Press, 1990), p. 860.

24. As I have argued above, the biblical account (Judges 19) itself calls into question the whole notion of the ethics of such a view of hospitality and what that view implies. In Milton's works, true hospitality is viewed as something of a sacred obligation. One thinks in *Paradise Lost* of Adam and Eve's hospitality toward Raphael as visitor (Books 4–8). In *The History of Britain*, Milton refers to the obligation "not to betray the Faith and inviolable Law of Hospitality and refuge giv'n" (5:197).

all: having occurred in all its brutality in the form of Milton as Orpheus attacked by maddened women (the daughters of Bacchus), it occurs as well in the form of Milton as the matron attacked by maddened men (the sons of Belial). These are deep-seated fears that extend into Milton's early life and underlie his fundamental sense of self.

Because of Milton's particular identification with the matron, the horrors she undergoes are that much more heinous in their implications. As I argue throughout, Milton as *the* Lady viewed himself in distinctly bisexual terms. He is not only the poet but the poetess of *Paradise Lost*, one whose personality encompasses both identities. A bisexuality that underscored Milton's entire career, it permeates the earlier works and manifests itself in dramatic form in the later writings, in particular the diffuse epic. Encompassing these identities, the Miltonic personality constantly felt itself at risk, constantly looked upon itself as an identity besieged, subject to forces beyond its control, forever in danger of being violated. The Miltonic body represents the sign of the horrors those forces, once unleashed, are able to perpetrate. As such, this body becomes a symbol of the objectification of the psyche beset by the forces of chaos, the forces of sparagmos.

Having explored the nature of those forces in the context of the bisexual self as it emerges both in Milton's earlier writings and in *Paradise Lost*, I next address a corresponding issue—what might be called the "theatricalization" of the self within the framework of Milton's polemic. Already implicit in the kinds of self-configuration one discerns in the sixth Prolusion, this theatricalization is of fundamental importance to the relationships established between body and self in the later prose. It is here that Milton's sparagmatic sensibility is most vividly and indeed dramatically portrayed.

Part III

STAGING THE BODY

7

The Theater of Assault

I f the fear of sparagmos permeates Milton's entire career, it
becomes particularly compelling in the context of the regicide
tracts. From the perspective of those tracts, the concept of
bodily rending and mutilation assumes consummate form. As
a victim and as a victimizer, Milton brought to bear in his regicide
writings a full awareness of what the experience of sparagmos entails.
In the portrayal of that awareness, one encounters an enactment of
violence that causes the polemical debates to assume the form of high
theater. As a prime actor in this theater of assault, Milton is forced
to react to the histrionics of his own bodily dismemberment first by
attempting to make his body whole and second by dismembering the
body of his antagonist. Such is the bodily *agon* of this Milton *agonistes.*

My focus in examining these tracts is the Miltonic Defenses of
1654 and 1655, specifically the *Defensio Secunda* (1654) and the *Pro Se
Defensio* (1655). Coming on the heels of the *Pro Populo Anglicano Defensio* (or *Defensio Prima*) of 1651, these later attempts by Milton to
respond to the virulent attacks upon his own body—and, by extension,
the body of the people whose cause he sought to uphold—provide a
unique opportunity to examine the dramatic bearing of sparagmos
as both a polemical and a theatrical event.

As a means of exploring the specifically bodily dimension the theater of assault enacted, I begin with the tract that set the later Miltonic Defenses into motion: the infamous *Regii Sanguinis Clamor ad Coelum Adversus Parricidas Anglicanos*.[1] Published anonymously at the Hague in 1652 but later acknowledged as the work of Peter Du Moulin, this tract, more than any other produced during that tumultuous period in Milton's life, served to focus his intense concern with the nature of his bodily well-being, with his sense of self, and with his ability to preserve his dignity in the face of the ad hominem (indeed, ad corporam) attacks mounted so effectively and indeed so scurrilously in the *Clamor*.[2]

Here was no dry and pedantic discourse on the nature of kingship and rule by jure divino, as made evident in the *Defensio regia pro Carolo I* (1649) of Salmasius.[3] Rather, here was an eloquent and uncompromisingly savage assault by an author capable of marshaling all the powers of rhetoric to produce a weapon that would effectively and mercilessly beat the enemy into complete submission. In the course of his polemical career, Milton had sustained numerous attacks against his person but never one against his character so vehement and virulent. What rendered the attack especially effective was the self-consciously theatrical nature of its approach. Its polemic becomes drama, in fact, high theater in which is enacted scenes of devastating cruelty. These scenes portray in explicit detail the march of events involved in the desecration and destruction of the martyred king, on the one hand, and the drama through which the perpetrators of these vile acts—most notably Milton himself—are undone as the result of a poetic act of retribution on the part of the anonymous author.[4]

1. References to the Latin original in my text are to the *Regii Sanguinis Clamor ad Coelum Adversus Parricidas Anglicanos* (The Hague, 1652). As appropriate, I have made use of the translations of selections from the *Clamor* by Paul W. Blackford in *YP* and by David Masson in *Life of Milton*. I have also had recourse to the complete translation of the *Clamor* by Harry G. Merrill, III, in "Milton's Secret Adversary: Du Moulin and the Politics of Protestant Humanism," unpublished doctoral dissertation, University of Tennessee, Knoxville, 1959.
2. For full discussion of Du Moulin, his family, his background, and his works, see Merrill, "Milton's Secret Adversary." See also *Life of Milton*, 4:454–59, 5:216–25; and the entry in the *Dictionary of National Biography*.
3. Parker's description is apt: "Except for an inflammatory preface," the *Defensio Regia* was largely a "tedious, laborious argument for absolute monarchy on the basis of historical precedent" (*Milton Biography*, 1:372). On the other hand, Parker's estimate of Milton's *Defensio Prima* in response to Salmasius is just as harsh. The controversy as a whole, Parker comments, "sounds like a bookish brawl, a quarrel in a library" (*Milton Biography*, 1:383).
4. The *Clamor*, to be sure, is not the only response Milton's *Defensio Prima* provoked. There was also the *Pro Rege et Populo Anglicano Apologia* (1651) of John Rowland, for exam-

Of initial concern is the author's treatment of the beheading of Charles I. From the outset of the *Clamor*, this event is viewed as a "spectacle" (*spectaculum*) and a "drama" (*drama*) perpetrated on the stage of the English nation. Such language permeates the tract as a whole. Thus, the beheading is termed specifically an "inhuman," that is, a savage or monstrous, "tragedy" that "was being acted" (*dum haec immanis agitur Tragoedia*) by those responsible for its perpetration (*YP*, 4:1042, 1058; *Clamor*, pp. 2, 46). Because of the heinous nature of their act, the perpetrators are, for lack of a better name, termed parricides and, worse, deicides. In killing the king, they are guilty of the worst possible form of sacrilege, one tantamount to killing God Himself. In fact, the author goes so far as to maintain that this murder was worse even than the Crucifixion: "Compared with this, the crime of the Jews in crucifying Christ was nothing." For, the author argues, the Jews would never have crucified Christ had they recognized him, whereas it was abundantly evident to the parricides whom it was they violated: it was "their own legitimate King" (*YP*, 4:1049).

In his impassioned portrayal of the beheading of the king, the author consciously looks upon himself as dramatist inspired by poetic fire, for this is a subject that warrants such a treatment. "Never did poetic fire," he proclaims, "burn with more vivid flames, never did it thunder with more fierce portents. But afflicted religion demanded a discourse unrestrained and frank, very full and vigorous, a learned defence; the church, made a prisoner by this hostile crime, demanded it; the sacred majesty of kings, subjected by a new and unspeakable precedent to the judgments of subjects and the axes of public executioners, demanded it" (*YP*, 4:1049). His *Clamor* is the outcome, one that "raises the Royal blood's outcry to heaven." In response to this outcry, those who are witnesses to the tragedy are exhorted to exclaim,

---

ple. Misattributing the work to others (Joseph Jane or John Bramhall), Milton's younger nephew John Phillips (no doubt along with Milton's help) responded with a *Responsio Ad Apologiam* (1651) (see *YP*, 4:887–961). Rowland later followed up his attack with *Polemica, sive Supplementum ad Apologian Anonymam* (1653). Among other attacks, the anonymous pamphlet *Carolus I. Britanniarum Rex, a Securi et Calamo Miltonii Vindicatus* (1652), attributed to the Frenchman Claude Barthelemy Morisot, is likewise of significance. The tract "alludes to Milton's views on divorce, and suggests that Milton put away his own wife from jealousy" (*Milton Biography*, 1:421, 433). Also of importance is Sir Robert Filmer's *Observations Concerning the Original of Government* (1652), as well as several German responses including those by Christian Woldenberg (1651), Nahum Bensen (1651), Casper Ziegler (1652), Jacob Schaller (1652), Erhard Kieffer (1652), and Martin Zeiller (1653). See the summary in John T. Shawcross's "The Life of Milton," in *The Cambridge Companion to Milton*, ed. Dennis Danielson (Cambridge: Cambridge University Press, 1989), p. 14.

"Arise, arise, God of vengeance, and avenge this parricide horrible and shameful to the Christian world!"[5] Such impassioned rhetoric is veritably Miltonic in its effectiveness. Self-consciously histrionic, it creates spectacle through the very rhetoric it marshals to portray the devastating events of the *tragoedia* it seeks to dramatize.

As high theater, this *tragoedia* is given every possible flourish. The account of the execution of the king bears ample witness to this fact. As dramatized, the execution is seen to be a particularly gruesome assault upon the king's body.[6] As he is led to the scaffold between files of soldiers, his garments are spat upon, and one soldier "even violated his august face with spittle." "This," the account continues, "because of the happier conformity with Christ, he [the king] placidly wiped away, saying, 'Christ for my sake endured much more.' " In keeping with the aura of what amounts to a martyrology, the account makes a point of sanctifying the king by associating his sufferings with those of Christ at the crucifixion: "Then, so that Charles might suffer many things like to Christ, the soldiers redoubled their mockery against him. The smoke of tobacco, which they knew was distasteful to him, they blew in his face, and they threw their broken pipes at his feet as he walked along" (*YP*, 4:1063). These are only the beginning of the indignities, however. In fact, those in the military council responsible for the execution purportedly "considered what disgraces might be added to capital punishment, since they thought for the king simply to die would be too little." It was thus decided that he would be humiliated by being "struck with an ax on a platform erected for the doleful drama" within Whitehall right opposite "a large chamber devoted to solemn feasts and state receptions, by far the most sumptuous in the whole kingdom." Enacting the drama of the execution in this manner would intensify the humiliation by subjecting Charles to "the greatest disgrace" in that very place "where he had been especially illustrious" (*YP*, 4:1063).

What governs the conduct of the affair is its underlying theatricality, a theme, in fact, that resonates throughout contemporary ac-

---

5. Merrill's translation, "Milton's Secret Adversary," p. 274.
6. Many of these and other details are derived from George Bate's *Elenchus Motuum Nuperorum in Anglia; Simul ac Juris Regii et Parlamentarii Brevis Enerratio* (Lyons, 1649). This popular Royalist tract was translated as *A Compendious Narrative of the Late Troubles in England. Or, Elenchus Englished* (London, 1652). See Harry G. Merrill, "Political Drama of the Salmasian Controversy," in *Studies in Honor of John C. Hodges and Alwin Thaler*, Tennessee Studies in Literature, Special Number (Knoxville: University of Tennessee Press, 1961), pp. 49–56.

counts of the event and has received ample and incisive commentary in recent scholarship.[7] In the handling of the execution by the author of the *Clamor*, that theatricality is especially reinforced as it extends even to an emphasis upon implements of torture as representations of stage machinery, here devised for the purpose of humiliating the king as much as possible and of depriving his body, if necessary, of any mobility. Accordingly, a machine is constructed with "iron hooks in which the head and arms" of the king might be held, should he attempt to resist (*YP*, 4:1067). Actor and victim in his own drama, the king is given every opportunity to fulfill his sacrificial role. For the parricides, that involves behavior by the king that would cause him to undermine any shred of personal dignity as he goes to his death. The author of the tract is quick to point out, however, that the king defies any such attempt to humiliate himself. Charles goes to his death with utmost composure, as well as with a sense of his own exalted station as royal actor par excellence. The protagonist of his own drama, he assumes full control of the occasion. One thinks of Andrew Marvell's account of the "Royal Actor" upon the "Tragick Scaffold": "*He* nothing common did or mean / Upon that memorable Scene: / But with his keener Eye / The Axes edge did try." Thereafter, he "bow'd his comely Head, / Down as upon a Bed."[8]

The author of the *Clamor* describes the event in similar terms. He has Charles lean forward on his knees, praying briefly, and then baring his "sacred neck" to the "wicked ax." "In a moment that wicked blow decapitated the august head of three kingdoms." The regal nature of the king's behavior is further reinforced by the Christ-like quality of his demeanor. He is beheld offering "his throat as king to the knives of his subjects no less worthily than Christ the king of kings had borne the heavy burden of the cross placed on him by his subjects" (*YP*, 4:1067). In keeping with this martyrological perspective, the author of the *Clamor* never abandons the Christocentric focus through which

7. The most perceptive treatment may be found in David Loewenstein, *Milton and the Drama of History* (Cambridge: Cambridge University Press, 1990), esp. pp. 55–57. Other works of the period overtly adopt the theatrical point of view. See, for example, the *Tragicum Theatrum Actorum, & Casuum Tragicorum Londini Publicae celebratorum* (Amsterdam, 1649), which portrays the beheading of Charles, among other executions of the period, as a tragic drama. An actor in that drama, Charles is conceived as being fully conscious of his theatrical role (pp. 184–94).

8. Andrew Marvell, "An Horatian Ode Upon Cromwell's Return From Ireland" (ll. 53–64), in *Seventeenth-Century Verse and Prose*, 2 vols., 2d ed., ed. Helen C. White et al. (New York: Macmillan, 1971), 1:490–91.

he enacts the drama of the suffering, humiliation, and, finally, execution of Charles. He is at pains to sacralize the person of the king as much as he is to impugn the character of those responsible for the king's undoing.[9]

The act of impugning the parricides is accomplished through an account of their barbaric behavior in violating the body of the king after his beheading. That violation is founded upon repeated acts of desecrating not just the body but the blood of the king, a desecration that reinforces the sense of barbarity and savagery of those who disregard all that the *sanguinis* of the king represents and are therefore responsible for what is implied by the cry of outrage implicit in the phrase *regii sanguinis clamor*:

> When the king had been killed, the savage assassins [*barbari sicarii*] jeered at his lifeless body; they smeared their hands with the warm blood [*cruore calido*] which was to hang on their heads; nor did they stop there, but dipped their very staffs in the king's blood [*Regio sanguini*] in mockery. . . . They even sold his hairs, mud colored with his blood [*sanguine imbutam*], and bloody chips of the block [*fragmenta stipitis sanguinolenta*] on which the royal neck had lain when it was about to be cut. (*YP*, 4:1067; *Clamor*, p. 65)

In this climactic moment, the author of the *Clamor* does all in his power to promote the sense of revulsion he desires his readers to feel. With his constant repetition of the terms for blood (*sanguinis, cruor*), he emphasizes what amounts to the blood lust of the parricides. Dishonoring the king's blood in this primitive act of frenzy, the parricides bring upon themselves the stain of irremissible shame and guilt.

The desecrations do not end there, however. Having violated the royal blood, the parricides would dismember the king's body even further in a final gesture of outrage. To that end, they arrange to give the body to "some quack medic" and to military surgeons "hostile to the royal name." These so-called physicians are directed to disembowel and then examine the body to determine whether it is infected with venereal disease or any other corresponding vileness. Whether

9. Such an act of sacralization is totally in accord with the portrayal of the king in what is putatively his own work but is actually the work of John Gauden, the king's chaplain: *Eikon Basilike: The True Portraiture of His Sacred Majesty in His Solitudes and Sufferings* (London, 1649). Immensely popular, this work reinforces, indeed, goes far to establish, the association of Charles with Christ.

or not they discover such a disease, they are commanded to lie about what they find and discredit the king. Although the intervention of an honest physician thwarts these plans and, in fact, demonstrates the health of the king's body, the very notion of disemboweling the body for the sake of defiling the king's reputation represents a final affront to the king and his body by those who are themselves savages worthy of utmost contempt and outrage (*YP*, 4:1067).

At the center of this contempt and outrage stands John Milton, who, as chief spokesman for the parricides, is the one individual worthy of all the abuse the author of the *Clamor* is able to marshal. In response to the parricidal attempt to defile the sacred person of the king, the author of the *Clamor* sets out to avenge Charles by brutalizing Milton in the most effective ways possible: principally, with an attack upon Milton's character and one upon his body. Such a mode of attack is understandable, if not inevitable. To undermine an individual most fully, one must assault both his character as the basis of ethical conduct and his body as the outward expression of what lies within. The idea is a commonplace of Renaissance thought. Character and body correspond to one another as that which constitutes the whole being of an individual. With attacks upon both character and body, the whole being will fall.

The impugning of Milton's character assumes a central focus in the first chapter. Beginning with extravagant praise of Salmasius, the author of the *Clamor* uses this as an occasion to defame Milton as the only representative of the parricides who was willing and able to defend their cause.[10] "Who he was and where he came from was in doubt," the author observes. It is not clear whether he was "a man or a worm voided lately from the dungpit," but this is the "dirt and filth" the parricides seized upon in order to throw "that insignificant piece of mud against Salmasius." Such denigration is reinforced by a perverse biographical account of Milton's life, gleaned no doubt from hearsay and cast in a form to undermine any claims to moral integrity on Milton's part. Beginning with the assertion that Milton was expelled from Cambridge for some disgrace, the account has him fleeing his country in shame and migrating as a traitor to Italy, that seat of corruption.

---

10. As far as finding an alternative to Milton, what could the parricides do? asks the author of the *Clamor*. "Selden cast the odious task from his shoulders; the universities were languishing, having been sedulously purged of learning by these very men" (*YP*, 4:1050).

Recalled from Italy by those instigating civil unrest, Milton wrote his divorce tracts to justify a breach in the relationship between husband and wife, as if the sacred ties of marriage were of no account. Advocating the violation of marital law, Milton next proceeded to endorse the violation of civil law, as he "passed from the disruption of marriage to the dissolution of kingdoms." Such a dissolution is that which forms the basis of his tracts against kingship, tracts that urge in particular the execution of the king. In his act of arguing on behalf of such a cause, Milton, the author of the *Clamor* maintains, is himself responsible for the beheading of King Charles: "Let the search cease for the man who finally cut through the sacred neck of the king with the unspeakable ax; we have the executioner who urged on the crime." It is John Milton: "He confesses the crime; he embraces it to himself; he defends it; he praises it." Doing so, "he paints with colors of piety and justice the most hideous and criminal parricide the world has ever seen" (*YP*, 4:1050–51).

Underlying this assault on Milton's character runs a common theme, the notion of a disruption or a breach brought about as the result of a moral flaw. The disruption begins with Milton's so-called expulsion from college. In his violation of the laws of his university, he finds himself cut off from the academic community, a breach so serious that he is forced to flee his own country. This pattern of disruption follows his every move; in fact, he endorses it in his own writings. Whether one considers his advocacy of a breach in the marital relationship or his endorsement of a violation in the relationship between subject and king, Milton's character is disruptive, destructive, and finally conducive to the disintegration of the union that binds human society. For this reason, his parricidal act of "cut[ting] through the sacred neck of the king with the unspeakable ax" is the most violent sign of his unstable character one can find. The only answer for such a destructive individual is the humiliation and final annihilation of his very being. That humiliation and annihilation must itself be of an uncompromisingly savage and violent sort. It must answer the physical violence of the beheading and disemboweling of the king with a corresponding kind of violence. Such violence, the author of the *Clamor* implies, must outdo Milton's own. Physical as well as moral in nature, it must give no ground. Answering blood for blood, it must make its victim bleed, and it must do so in the same theatrical manner the king himself was made to bleed. Inspired by the parricides' own blood lust, the author of the *Clamor* accordingly portrays the bodily undoing of Milton as a symbol of all the parricides themselves represent.

This undoing begins as early as the dedicatory epistle to Charles II that prefaces the *Clamor*. There, Milton is defamed as "a monster horrible, deformed, huge, and sightless [*Monstrum horrendum, informe, ingens, cui lumen ademptum*]."[11] In its brutal disfigurement of Milton's physical appearance, the defamation is important, for by means of it not just the adversary's reputation but his very body, the seat of his being, is undone. Implicit in the reference to Milton as a monster is Achaemenides' terrifying and graphic description of the Cyclops in the third book of Virgil's *Aeneid* (3.658).[12] According to Achaemenides, the Cyclops's very home "drips with gore" from disgusting banquets of men. The Cyclops himself is a giant "so tall that his head strikes the stars." Repulsive in appearance, "he dines upon black blood and entrails of miserable men." Achaemenides relates how the Cyclops seized two of his companions with his huge hand, smashed them on the rocks, and then wallowed in the gore he had spilled on the threshold. "I saw him," Achaemenides says, "devour their bodies all dripping / With dark blood; their warm limbs quivered beneath his teeth." As the Cyclops lay "Belching up blood in his sleep and the morsels of food / All mingled with gory wine," Ulysses and his men sprang upon him "And bored out his eye with a long sharpened piece of wood" (3.646–63). With its emphasis upon the brutality, bestiality, and cannibalism of the Cyclops, the description repeatedly signals that leitmotif so crucial to the *Clamor* as a whole, that is, the spilling of blood and all this act represents. Here, it is the Cyclops that is held responsible for such an act.

Within the framework of the allusion to Milton as a monster, both the horror of his presence and the repulsiveness of his behavior are poetically configured. More than that, however, the violence inflicted upon him as Cyclops through the gouging out of his eye renders the entire allusion particularly brutal and savage. As if commenting upon

11. *YP*, 4:1045, *Clamor*, p. 6. Although the epistle bears the name of the printer Adrian Vlacq, it was almost certainly written by Alexander More, the putative author of the *Clamor* and the object of Milton's assaults in the final two Defenses. According to Merrill, Du Moulin presumably did not approve of the epistle.

12. References are to Virgil, *The Aeneid*, trans. L. R. Lind (Bloomington: Indiana University Press, 1963).

all the allusion implies, however, the author is not content to leave it stand as it appears, for he immediately insists on qualifying the frightening aspects of the allusion by maintaining that Milton is not huge at all. Indeed, "nothing is more weak, more bloodless, more shriveled than little animals such as he, who the harder they fight, the less harmful they are." If one looks beneath the surface of this horror, one finds a contemptible being indeed. Accordingly, the author maintains that Charles II will be pleased to see Salmasius, the defender of kings, "tearing to pieces this disgrace to the human race [*Volupe tibi erit videre Virum tuum concerpentem istud generis humani de honestamentum*]" (*YP*, 4:1045, *Clamor*, p. 6).

It is precisely this idea of dismemberment (*concerpentem*) in which the polemic action of the *Clamor* culminates. As prose tract, this most devastating of works concludes with two poems, the first of which transforms its earlier idealization of Salmasius into a final celebratory gesture and the second of which transforms its earlier defamation of Milton into a supreme flyting. Although the second poem is of primary concern, I address the first as preparatory to the second. Titled *MAGNO SALMASIO Pro Defensione Regia Ode Eucharistica* ("To Great Salmasius, for the *Defensio Regia*, a Thanksgiving Ode"), the penultimate poem lauds Salmasius as a supreme hero in extravagantly hyperbolic terms. As such, the poem is not simply a thanksgiving: it is a eucharistic enactment in which the defender of monarchy undergoes sacralization. To compensate him for the assaults he sustained at the hands of Milton, he is made not only whole but holy. Such an enactment sacralizes Salmasius as a symbol of the repristination the author of the *Clamor* seeks to perform upon the body of the mutilated king in commemoration of his own divinity. By means of this eucharistic celebration of Salmasius, the author of the *Clamor* reenacts in poetic form his iconic worship of Charles I. During the course of some eighteen Horatian stanzas, Salmasius is accordingly invoked as one divinely inspired by the gods and dreaded by his enemies, a hero courageously overcoming all who foolishly stand in his path. Dragging the hellhounds into the light of complete exposure, this Herculean warrior displays his might, as his enemies are tried and judged before God.[13] In this eucharistic and indeed iconic transformation, the defender of monarchy reemerges as sacred and undefeatable. It is

13. See Merrill's translation of the poem in "Milton's Secret Adversary," pp. 384–87.

against such a poetic enactment that the final poem of the *Clamor* must be viewed.

Titled *In Impurissimum Nebulonem JOHANNEM MILTONUM Parricidarum & Parricidii Advocatum* ("Against That Foul Rascal JOHN MILTON the Advocate of Parricide & Parricides"), this poem is a virulent attack upon Milton's body, one that draws upon notions of physical violence invoked earlier in the tract as well as the concept of theatricality so crucial to its outlook. In this way, the poem does all in its power to excoriate the adversary through a rhetoric of savage abuse. As much as the poem that precedes it sacralizes its subject, the final poem defames and excoriates the subject of its abuse. Doing so, it stages a scene in which the speaker challenges his enemy to physical combat but then discovers that the enemy is too foul and loathsome to warrant the dignity of true battle. The outcome of this flyting is one in which the adversary is mortally wounded as a result of the humiliation he is obliged to sustain. The humiliation begins with the very title. Inscribed in capital letters, the name of the adversary (*JOHANNEM MILTONUM*) assumes major prominence as the mock epic hero (or antihero) of the song that will intone his dispraise in "lofty" iambics. Already in the title, this antihero is mired in a hyperbole of abuse, not simply as a "Foul Rascal" but as a "most filthy," "vile," and "impure" wretch.[14] The undoing of the antihero is effected in the very act of identifying him by name.

Reflecting the theatrical nature of the *Clamor* as a whole, the undoing of Milton assumes a distinctly dramatic form. The person of the antihero is subjected to the most humiliating of assaults, as the speaker transforms his poem into a weapon through which he cudgels his victim into submission. In one stanza after the next, this cudgeling proceeds unabated. Recalling the description of Milton in the dedicatory epistle, the antihero is depicted as a villain too vile to be touched. Totally depersonalized, this subject of abuse becomes once again a filthy little animal, in this instance "snapping with spiteful little teeth at the patron of great kings" (that is, Salmasius) "and at kings themselves." The contemptible creature at whom the speaker rails is conceived as an "evil poison" (*virus*) and a "cancerous ulcer" (*carcinoma*). So disgusting is this thing that it cannot be handled "except with a

---

14. The phrase "Foul Rascal" is Blackford's (*YP*, 4:1036). Masson has "Bestial Blackguard" (*Life of Milton*, 4:457); Merrill has "Deprav'd Wretch" ("Miltons Secret Adversary," p. 388).

hook." The only appropriate response to such slime is complete revulsion.

Although the speaker refuses to touch this slime, he would have
others completely and mercilessly rend its flesh. Addressing the subject
of his abuse in the most contemptuous of terms, the speaker declares:
"Though I hold off a fastidious hand, I shall not allow you, you
scoundrel, to obtain a welcome impunity for your villainy." Accordingly, he calls upon others to do his dirty work:

> Soho! Seize upon that wicked hangman of a scourger [*carnificem
> Lorarii*]. Seize him! Quick! Quick! Bind him up hands and feet. I
> owe him the sacred rites of the scourge [*Solemne debeo Virgidemiae
> sacrum*]. First, prod with a goad this future disciple to a gallows, this
> great bulwark of the people, this prop of Parliament! Soften his
> lying head with a cudgel; prepare him for flogging. Scourge his whole
> body to make it one big welt [*Lorisque totum facite sit tuber*]. Shall you
> ever stop? Beat him until he has evilly poured forth his fearful bile
> and diseased blood through his tears [*caedite dum diram male / Bilem
> saniemque per lacrymas affluderit*]. (*YP*, 4:1078)

What the speaker portrays is a solemnity of torture. In his ravaging
of Milton's body, he commissions his own executioner (*carnifex*) and
flogger (*lorarius*) to subject the victim to unspeakable indignities: seizing
his body, dragging him to the place of punishment, bashing his head,
and scourging his flesh incessantly until his very eyes bleed forth the
vileness that lies within. Such is the speaker's way of paying his respects
to the sacred powers of the whip (*Virgidemiae sacrum*).

In the enactment of this ritualized celebration of torture, the
speaker creates a theater of assault, at the center of which is the
victimized and brutalized body of that *Impurissimum Nebulonem JO-
HANNEM MILTONUM Parricidarum & Parricidii Advocatum*. At last,
"beautifully vermiculated with a mosaic of stripes, colored with a
scourge [*Tandem plagoso vermiculatum emblemate / Pulchre variatum vimine*]," the body of the victim becomes in effect a text upon which is
inscribed all the horrors the torturer is able to inflict. For the speaker,
who engages the torturer in his cause, that which results is truly (and
ironically) a work of rare beauty. The mutilated body of Milton stands
before us as a symbol of what the speaker's theater of assault is able
to effect. The final disposition of the body is in accord with the speaker's uncompromising brutality. Dragging Milton before the feet of

* Foucault . Kafka

Salmasius, the speaker leaves it to this Herculean figure to do with the body of the victim as he sees fit. "With his strong right hand," Salmasius accordingly whirls Milton into the air and savagely "bestrews the rocks far and wide with his [Milton's] shattered brain [*ille diffracto procul / Late cerebro saxa respersit cadens*]" (*YP*, 4:1078).

Such are the respects the speaker pays to the parricides in general and to Milton, the spokesman of the parricides, in particular. The body of Milton has been completely decimated. It has undergone a tearing to pieces or *concerpentem*, to use the language of the tract, from which it will never recover. The experience of mutilation and dismemberment lies at the heart of the *Regii Sanguinis Clamor ad Coelum*. Enacted within a theater of assault, it is a mutilation and rending that destroys both character and body as corresponding aspects of the single being it seeks to undermine. Nothing is left intact: all is decimated, all impugned, all defiled.

This, the author of the *Clamor* would argue, is the inevitable response to those sacrilegious defilers who besmirched, mutilated, and tore the king's own body to pieces within their own theater of assault. Represented by their chief spokesman John Milton, they have been treated in kind and in spades. Resacralizing and therefore repristinating the king in the very process of dramatizing the course of his martyrdom, the author of the *Clamor* performs precisely the opposite act upon the loathsome enemy. The result in effect is the sparagmos of John Milton, enacted savagely and brutally within the theatrical space the author of the *Clamor* so masterfully devises. We as spectators are eyewitnesses to the events dramatized in this theater. Like those who witnessed the solemn undoing of the martyred king, we are invited to participate in the counter-solemnity his enemies have brought upon themselves. The king's blood cries out for such revenge. The *Clamor* is the dramatic answer to that cry.

As it enacts the polemic and poetic undoing of Milton's very being, the *Regii Sanguinis Clamor ad Coelum* represents a landmark in the culture of sparagmos to which Milton was subjected throughout his career.[15] Although Milton had been attacked before and would be

---

15. For an account of the many attacks upon Milton and his works in the seventeenth century, see William Riley Parker, *Milton's Contemporary Reputation* (1940: Folcroft, Pa.: Folcroft Press, 1969). The most exhaustive bibliography of Miltoniana and allusions to Milton in the seventeenth century is John T. Shawcross, *Milton: A Bibliography for the Years 1624–1700* (Binghamton, N.Y.: Medieval and Renaissance Texts and Studies, 1984).

again, the *Clamor* proved especially frustrating not only because it was so effective as polemic but because its author refused to identify himself. By the time the tract's anonymity was fully and publicly dispelled, it was too late for its victim to respond. The act of complete disclosure occurred only after the passage of some twenty years when the author of the *Clamor* made his presence known through the publication of his collected poems, *Petri Molinaei P. F. PARERGA. Poematum Libelli Tres* (Cambridge, 1670).[16] In this collection, Peter Du Moulin published not only his companion poems on Salmasius and Milton but an *Epistolam quam Iambo in MILTONUM Author subjunxerat*, which represents both a justification of his poetic act of savagery against Milton and an account of the publication and reception of the *Clamor*. A consideration of Du Moulin's *Epistolam* should provide a perspective through which to consider Milton's Defenses.[17]

Beginning with an acknowledgment of the severe dangers (*periculum*) to his own person his poem against Milton would certainly have occasioned had his identity been publically disclosed, Du Moulin not only makes it abundantly clear that the stakes involved in assaults of this sort are exceedingly high but establishes that he is now in a secure position once again to attack Milton in his own name.[18] The *Epistolam* as a whole delights both in Du Moulin's fortune in escaping recrimination and in his freedom to launch additional assaults without fear of reprisal. As a revelatory document, the *Epistolam* freely recounts the circumstances surrounding the publication of the *Clamor*, including Du Moulin's sending his manuscript sheets to Salmasius, his entrusting them to Alexander More, or Morus, followed by More's delivering them to the printer Adrian Vlacq, and More's prefixing to the manuscript his epistle to Charles II in the name of Vlacq. This recounting of publication history prefaces the main section of the *Epistolam*, which focuses upon Milton and his reaction to the publication of the *Clamor*. Du Moulin conceives of Milton's commissioning spies of the regicides in Holland to discover the author of the *Clamor*, determining to his satisfaction that the author is Alexander More,

16. For an account of Du Moulin, as well as earlier disclosures of his authorship, see *Life of Milton*, 5:215–16. See also *Life Records*, 3:242–44.

17. References to the *Epistolam* in my text are to the 1670 edition of the *PARERGA*, pp. 141–42. The translation of the *Epistolam* is drawn from *Life of Milton*, 5:219–21.

18. See further, *Life Records*, 3:241. In a manuscript note, Du Moulin speaks elsewhere of being in an underground cellar where he "lay hid to avoyd warrants" that were issued against him from authorities to apprehend and bear him prisoner to Hull.

and launching into his *Defensio Secunda pro Populo Anglicano* against More.[19]

The effect was not simply to create enemies for More in Holland but to allow Du Moulin to escape recrimination and to revel in the pain he caused Milton. Du Moulin paints a vivid picture of what he considers must have been the anguish and futility of the adversary so mercilessly attacked in the *Clamor*:

> Meanwhile I looked on in silence, and not without a soft chuckle [*nec sine lento risu*], at seeing my bantling [*foetum meum*] laid at another man's door, and the blind and furious Milton [*coecum atque furiosum Miltonum*] fighting and slashing the air, like the hoodwinked horse-combatants in the old circus, not knowing by whom he was struck and whom he struck in return [*Andabatarum more pugnantem & aeromaxomenon a quo feriretur & quem contra feriret ignatum*]. (p. 141)

What makes the account so compelling is the almost sadistic delight in takes in another's pain. The fact of Milton's blindness simply serves to reinforce Du Moulin's pleasure. Du Moulin's depiction of Milton as a blindfolded gladiator (*Miltonum Andabatarum*) places the combatant's anguish and futility within the context of a circus spectacle or arena, one in which the gladiator is made to look foolish as he strikes out and "beats the air" (*aeromaxomenon*) at an adversary he is unable to behold. The use of the term *more* ("foolish") in the phrase *more pugnantem*, moreover, drives home the fact that it is not only Milton who is victimized by Du Moulin's assault: it is likewise More who must suffer. In his theater of torture, Du Moulin appears to have little remorse for the suffering he causes. Milton and More are seen almost as counterparts of one another.

The spectacle is reinforced by Du Moulin's account of the Milton-

19. See further, *Life Records*, 3:244: "The nameless Author of which being for a considerable time sought out, but in vain, by *Milton*, he at length learn'd by certain Ministers of State . . . that it [the *Clamor*] was written by one *Alex. More*, formerly a Professor and Minister at *Geneva*, then living in *Holland*." See also Kester Svendsen, "Milton's *Pro Se Defensio* and Alexander More," *Texas Studies in Literature and Language* 1 (1959), 11–29. Milton's known sources were Thurloe's agents, as well as Ezekiel Spanheim, John Dury, and Henry Oldenburg. In addition to these informants, Milton no doubt had information from other sources not yet disclosed (p. 16). See Milton's own references to John Thurloe in the *Pro Se Defensio* (*YP*, 4:740). Compare Wolfe, "Introduction," *YP*, 4:274–76: despite attempts to dissuade Milton from attacking More, Milton persisted, but he was supposed to have issued assurances "that he would let nothing proceed from his pen of an unbecoming nature." Given the tone of the *Defensio Secunda*, such assurances are ironic indeed.

More relationship subsequent to the publication of the *Defensio Secunda*. According to Du Moulin, More, "unable to stand out against so much ill-will, began to cool in the King's cause, and gave Milton to know who the author of the *Clamor* really was [*Clamoris Authorem Miltono indicavit*]."[20] If such is the case, Milton nonetheless refused to rectify his misunderstanding but persisted in his brutal attack on an enemy he was determined would bear the full blame for his own great suffering, whether or not that enemy warranted his wrath. In describing Milton's determination to persist in this manner, Du Moulin resorts to a language of violence and mutilation reminiscent of his poem against his adversary:

> For Milton, who had gone full tilt at Morus with his canine eloquence [*caninae eloquentiae*], and who had made it almost the sole object [*ferme unicum ... argumentum*] of his *Defensio Secunda* to cut up the life and reputation of Morus [*ut Mori vitam atque famam laceraret*], never could be brought to confess that he had been so grossly mistaken. (p. 142)

Du Moulin's observation is significant on several grounds. It astutely (if brutally) assesses the nature of Milton's futility in his unrelenting laceration of More (his tearing apart of More like a dog's tearing apart a morsel), despite what is undoubtedly his awareness of More's innocence. In the process of venturing this assessment, Du Moulin highlights the obsessive quality of Milton's vindictiveness as almost the sole object of his *Defensio Secunda* and, by implication, of his *Pro Se Defensio*.

Underscoring Du Moulin's emphasis upon the obsessive nature of Milton's behavior is the sense of futility to which his obsessiveness gives rise. For in presumably knowing who the true author was, Milton found himself helpless to rectify his misguided and misdirected ire, because he (as well as his fellow regicides) was afraid of the derision he would incur. That fear was particularly painful for Milton, who, Du Moulin suggests, was terrified "that the public would make fun

20. According to Masson, Milton probably did not know conclusively of Du Moulin's authorship until after the Restoration (*Life of Milton*, 5:222). According to Svendsen, More never disclosed anything about who the author really was. Du Moulin, John Aubrey, and Anthony à Wood were all convinced that Milton learned the truth but proceeded in the *Pro Se Defensio* with the attack on More in any case ("Milton's *Pro Se Defensio*," pp. 13–14). See also Kester Svendsen, "Milton and Alexander More: New Documents," *Journal of Germanic Philology* 60 (1961), 796–807.

of his blindness [*Scilicet metuens ne caecitati ejus populus illuderet*]." In short, the public would strike at his most vulnerable point: such derision Milton could not abide. Accordingly (and ironically), Du Moulin found himself secure in the very midst of danger: "As Milton preferred my getting off scatheless to being found in a ridiculous position himself, I had this reward for my pains, that Milton, whom I had treated so roughly, turned out my patron and sedulous body-guard" (p. 142).

Such is Peter Du Moulin's account of the publication and reception of the *Clamor* in general and his poem against Milton in particular. Graphic in its depiction of the suffering his work caused in his blind adversary, the account provides its own context through which Milton's later Defenses are to be read. Reinforcing the sense of assault its enemy is made to endure in that theater of torture known as the *Regii Sanguinis Clamor ad Coelum Adversus Parricidas Anglicanos*, the *Epistolam* to the *PARERGA* is crucial our understanding of Milton's precarious and perhaps even his untenable situation in attempting to defend himself, indeed, to make himself whole, in the later Defenses, particularly the *Defensio Secunda*.

II

As William Riley Parker, among others, has made clear, a full understanding of the *Defensio Secunda* must take into account not only the work to which Milton was responding but the circumstances of his own life during the period.[21] When the *Clamor* was published in the midsummer of 1652, Milton, as Secretary for Foreign Tongues to the Council of State, had already gained wide exposure, indeed, an international reputation, for his *Defensio Prima* (1651) in answer to Salmasius's *Defensio Regia Pro Carolo I* (1649).[22] Europe certainly did speak of Milton and his work "from side to side."[23] With that international exposure, however, came not just an awesome responsibility to defend the regime against any future attacks. More was at stake than that. As official spokesman of the new regime, Milton faced

---

21. In my account of the biographical matters, I am much indebted to the narrative in *Milton Biography*, esp. 1:412–61.
22. See *Milton Biography*, 1:386–89, 420.
23. The reference is to Sonnet 22 (l. 12).

the extreme likelihood that future attacks would be highly personal in nature. They would assault his character, his person, his very body, if necessary, in order to discredit the political entity, the body politic, he had sought to uphold. As a seasoned polemicist, Milton knew there would be no holds barred in such a warfare. He himself had engaged in ad hominem assaults against such enemies as Salmasius. Why should he expect any less from them? Having gained international exposure in mounting his assaults, he awaited Salmasius's response with a genuine sense of anticipation and with an awareness that much was at stake. When Salmasius's response finally did appear, circumstances had altered dramatically: the world was a very different place, and Milton was consumed with concerns of a wholly different order. Unknown to Milton at the time of the *Defensio Prima* was the fact that Salmasius's response would be many years in coming and that, with the old enemy dead some seven years, his answer to Milton would ironically be posthumous.[24]

Be that as it may, Milton was obliged to attend to his own circumstances during the crucial period between 1651 and 1652 as he awaited a response. That period was pivotal for him. Although the publication of the *Defensio Prima* was a high point in his public career, his personal circumstances placed him in a position of extreme vulnerability. Of utmost and ever-present concern was the complete loss of his sight in February 1652, an event that occurred a year after the appearance of the *Defensio Prima* and some six months before publication of the *Clamor*.[25] As Milton "suffered the rapid approach and then the arrival of total blindness, his health continued wretched. Probably, even to the last, he had dosed himself with medicines, and let his physicians take great quantities of blood, in an effort to delay the inevitable." Although there is no evidence to suspect that he was victimized by quacks, "standard cures in 1651 for diseases of the eye were, by all

24. Salmasius died in 1653, and his *Ad Ioannem Miltonum Responsio, Opus Posthumus* was not issued until 1660 by his son Claudius.

25. In 1650, Milton had effectively lost the sight in his left eye. The first *Defensio Prima* was published February 1651, and Milton was totally blind by February 1652. Milton describes his symptoms in full in his letter to his friend Leonard Philaras (September 28, 1654); see *YP*, 4:867–70. Among the numerous discussions of Milton's blindness, see Eleanor G. Brown, *Milton's Blindness* (New York: Columbia University Press, 1934), and William B. Hunter, "Some Speculations on the Nature of Milton's Blindness" (1962), in *The Descent of Urania: Studies in Milton, 1946–1988* (Lewisburg, Pa.: Bucknell University Press, 1989), pp. 184–92. See also Hunter's entry on Milton's blindness in *Milton Encyclopedia*, 1:194–95.

modern lights, barbaric."[26] In short, the very real assaults on his own body (however well-meaning) must have taken their toll. Compounding this were the trials brought by his domestic circumstances in 1652. "On Sunday, 2 May, somewhat before three o'clock in the morning, Milton's fourth child, another daughter, was born. The father was never to see her face. Nor could he see his wife's face when she died of childbirth three days later. Mary and he had been married for ten years, and had lived as man and wife for about six and a half. Now she was gone. She was but twenty-seven when she died. Her husband, weary, strangely old at forty-three, found himself alone with four motherless children: Anne, the lame one, almost six; little Mary, about three and a half; and two babies," John, a little more than a year old, and Deborah, newly born. The boy was not to last. He was fifteen months old when he died, some six weeks after his mother's death. Neither the exact date nor the cause is known. "A most pathetic aspect of the death," Parker comments, "is the fact that Milton himself did not know exactly when he lost his only son." Between the trauma of blindness and the tragedy of personal losses, this period was no doubt one of the darkest in Milton's life.[27]

26. *Milton Biography*, 1:393. See James Holly Hanford's illuminating study of seventeenth-century cures for optical illness, "John Milton Forswears Physic," *Bulletin of the Medical Library Association* 32 (1944), 23–34. The nature of these "cures" is based on a process known as "setoning" in which a thread or a piece of tape is "drawn through a fold of skin so as to maintain an issue or opening for discharges, or drawn through a sinus or cavity to keep this from healing up" (*Oxford English Dictionary*, s.v.). According to the Anonymous Biographer, this is what Milton underwent to treat his eyes, and Edward Phillips speaks of his uncle's "perpetual tampering with physic" to improve his condition (*Early Lives*, pp. 28, 72). A description of the tortures involved in the treatment of optical illnesses and headaches is given in the *Oeuvres* (1658) of Dr. François Thevinin, the physician Milton's friend Philaras might have consulted on the matter: "The patient is seated on a stool. He bends his head back a little so that the skin and fleshy panicle [swelling] may be loosened. Then an assistant, taking the skin with both hands just below the hair, either vertically or horizontally, lifts and pulls it up, and the surgeon with the seton pincers, formed like a waffle iron, broad at the ends and pierced, pinches the skin hard to deaden a little for the patient the pain of the burning, then passes through the holes in the pincers a hot cautery, having a diamond point; and when he draws out the cautery he passes with the needle through the same holes a four or five ply cotton thread dipped in white of egg and rose oil and puts a compress over it moistened with oxecrat [*sic*] and charged with the same remedy, continuing this till the suppuration [the formation or secretion of pus] is made and the inflammation past" (cited in Hanford, "Milton Forswears Physic," p. 31).

27. *Milton Biography*, 1:393, 412; 2:1012. In the *Pro Se Defensio*, Milton himself speaks of his vulnerability at the point when the *Clamor* was presented to him: "But, indeed, at this time especially, infirm health, distress over two deaths in my family, and the complete failure of my sight beset me [*Verum me, tum masime, & infirma simul valetudo, & duorum funerum luctus demesticus, & defectum jam penitus oculorum lumen diversa longe sollicitudine urgebat*]" (*YP*, 4:703; *CM*, 9:13–14).

It is precisely during this period that the *Regii Sanguinis Clamor ad Coelum Adversus Parricidas Anglicanos* appeared. During the long months of 1652, the author of the *Defensio Prima* waited for Salmasius's reply. "Reports from the Continent were emphatic: the rebuttal was in angry preparation; it might be published at any time. Milton regarded it as a daily threat."[28] Abroad, both Milton and his book continued to be discussed. In early July, it was becoming known in Europe that the Republic's champion was blind. In August, there were rumors that Milton was dead.[29] With the publication of the *Clamor*, events were brought to a head. Parker describes its appearance and its receipt by Milton in dramatic terms:

> Probably in late August . . . Milton was handed copies of the most brilliantly scathing rebuke he had ever received in print. He was attending a meeting of the Council when this work, scarcely complete in sheets, was first produced before his blind eyes. Its printer, Adrian Vlacq . . . had rushed the sheets, almost wet from the press, to his correspondent in England, Samuel Hartlib. Soon after the unstitched copy had been given him, Milton was sent another copy by the Council's Committee of Examinations, this time with an intimation that the Government expected him to make a suitable reply.[30]

As Parker observes in passing, "someone, of course, had the painful task of reading aloud to Milton the 188 pages of this vigorous and venomous rebuttal."[31] Who that someone was or even might have been is not known, and Parker offers no speculation on the matter. It is of small moment in any case. The point is that Milton as a blind man, one whose physical and emotional traumas were still fresh, was once again assaulted, this time by verbal attacks the virulence of which was unparalleled in the history of his career as a polemicist.

28. *Milton Biography*, 1:420. In the *Pro Se Defensio*, Milton refers to "that former adversary [Salmasius] abroad, far to be preferred to this one [Morus], was hovering [*impendebat*]; and at that very moment he daily threatened to assail me with all his force [*jamjamque se totis viribus incursurm indies minitabatur*]" (*YP*, 4:703; *CM*, 9:14).

29. *Milton Biography*, 1:420.

30. *Milton Biography*, 1:421. Compare Milton's own statement in the *Pro Se Defensio*: "Scarce was this book complete in the sheets before it was handed to me in the Council; soon after that session another copy was sent me by the court of inquisitions. It was also intimated that I was expected to serve the state and stop up the mouth of this troublesome crier [*ut huic importuno clamatori os obturarem*]" (*YP*, 4:703; *CM*, 9:12).

31. *Milton Biography*, 1:421.

Although it is not known who undertook the terrible job of reading the *Clamor* to Milton, the fact that he could not read it to himself warrants some consideration. The act of being able to see and assimilate what appears on a printed page is quite distinct from that which involves the condition of being obliged to hear what one has read to him. The circumstances in each case are entirely different, and the effects are correspondingly different as well. In the first case, an individual able to see what he reads has the advantage of that privacy which allows him to be in dialogue with the text free from the intrusion of another's presence. As the result of that privacy, such an individual is able to read and reread passages, establish contexts, and formulate responses as the occasion demands. His sight places him in control of the text he assimilates. When the text is particularly brutal and savage in tone, the seeing reader still has the opportunity to meet the text on an equal footing, to counter its devastating effects by imposing his will upon it.

When the reader is blind, on the other hand, the terrible fact of his victimization by a text that assaults becomes that much more pronounced. No longer in a position of being able to dialogue with a text in the privacy of a one-on-one encounter, he must depend upon an intermediary to read to him, to interpret for him the words of an otherwise-invisible enemy. Deriving his authority from the text he reads and interprets, the intermediary assumes the uncomfortable role of assaulter. The result is a theater of vocal assault, one in which the victim as audience is made to assimilate what he hears but cannot see. Within the darkness of this theater, the victim as audience must then recreate within his own mind the savage account of his own undoing.

One is reminded of Du Moulin's description in the *Epistolam* of "the blind and furious Milton fighting and slashing the air, like the hoodwinked horse-combatants in the old circus, not knowing by whom he was struck and whom he struck in return." One could not have a more graphic depiction of the blind man's plight under these circumstances. As Du Moulin was well aware, that plight was even further exacerbated by the fact that the attacker was doubly invisible. He could not be seen because his victim was blind, and he could not be known because he refused to announce his identity. All that remained were his words reverberating in the darkness of the victim's anguish and frustration. This double vexation transformed the victim into a true *agonistes*. As much as he might wish to respond to the assaults of his attacker with the demand, Let me *see* what he has written. Did he *really* say that? the victim is without recourse to the visible presence of his enemy. As much as he might wish to respond to these assaults with at least the knowledge of his attacker's identity, he is confounded by having to depend upon the assurances of those whose words he sees fit to trust. In both cases, he must rely upon the good offices of others. Milton's vulnerability could never have been greater. Fulfilling the obligation of an appropriate response, he no doubt was made to relive the moments of his laceration by having the text read to him repeatedly so that he could burn the words of his adversary into his memory. Only in this way could he prepare to answer the *Regii Sanguinis Clamor ad Coelum Adversus Parricidas Anglicanos*. What finally resulted is the *Pro Populo Anglicano Defensio Secunda* (1654).[32]

It is to this tract (the *Defensio Secunda*) and its counterpart, the *Pro Se Defensio Contra Alexandrum Morum Ecclesiasten* (1655), that I now turn. Because of the extent to which the *Pro Se Defensio* elaborates upon the polemical discourse initiated in the *Defensio Secunda*, I view these two works in conjunction. Since the second work (the *Pro Se Defensio*) itself responds to the *Fides Publica, Contra Ioannis Miltoni* (1654) of Alexander More, I attend to this additional voice in the sparagmatic chorus as occasion warrants. At the center of all responses is the undoing of Milton in the *Clamor* and his attempt to repristinate himself in his subsequent Defenses.

32. The reason for the long hiatus between the appearance of the *Clamor* in 1652 and the appearance of the *Defensio Secunda* in 1654 has been the subject of some speculation. Parker offers several convincing reasons, including the fact that Milton had been patiently awaiting the *Responsio* of Salmasius. Learning of Salmasius's death in 1653, Milton decided that, since the old adversary was no longer a threat, the new adversary required a response.

8

The Repristination of the Self

I

Milton's *Defensio Secunda* performs two functions: the announced one of defending the English people and the tacit one of defending the author's person against the attacks of an unknown enemy. Although these functions are not mutually exclusive, the second must constantly be kept in view in any consideration of this text. In this respect, the *Defensio Secunda* is as much a *Pro Se Defensio* as the work upon which Milton bestowed this highly personal title. As a work that undertakes to defend the English people, the *Defensio Secunda* announces this aspect in its title: *Pro Populo Anglicano Defensio*, a tag that recalls the title of the earlier work. In this respect, the *Defensio Secunda* conceives its role to be in accord with that undertaken in the *Defensio Prima*. The principal spokesman for those whose cause he champions, Milton as *Joannis MiltonI ANGLI* views himself as a warrior called upon to rally to the aid of his country yet once more. Attempting to demonstrate the nobility of the cause and the righteousness of the persons (himself among them) involved in the regicide, Milton in the *Defensio Secunda* assumes the exalted position as *rhetor*.[1] Even as *rhetor*, however, he is

---

1. His self-consciousness as *rhetor* is seen from the outset of his tract, which refers to

put to the expense of responding as effectively as possible to the highly personal attacks of the *Clamor*.

In its attempt to fulfill this tacit function, Milton's work does indeed become a *Pro Se Defensio* through which the author seeks to repristinate his being, so decimated by the author of the *Clamor*, and at the same time to assault an enemy he cannot see and whose identity he must take on faith. He must do this, moreover, within the international theater in which his own reputation has been torn asunder. Such an act of repristination, on the one hand, and counterattack, on the other, underlies Milton's polemical posture in the *Defensio Secunda* and provides compelling insight into the sparagmatic basis of his outlook. What is true of the *Clamor* is likewise true of the Miltonic Defenses: informing the violence and counterviolence, assault and counterassault, in which sparagmos and its aftermath are enacted is the ever-present sense of theater. It is within the confines of this theater that Miltonic polemic is staged. It is here that Milton fashions himself anew, and it is here that he would subject his enemy to the indignities that he has been made to undergo.

His attempt at repristination responds directly to the attacks in the *Clamor*. Recounting what was to him no doubt the most brutal affront to his precarious condition, he takes particular exception to the attack upon his blindness. That attack, as indicated, occurs in the dedicatory epistle to the *Clamor*. There, we recall, Milton is castigated as "a monster horrible, deformed, huge, and sightless." Whether or not the author was aware at the time of this castigation that Milton had indeed become completely blind, the allusion to the Cyclops causes Milton to engage in a long and detailed account of his appearance, his body, and his loss of sight.[2] It is essential to realize that the emphasis Milton places upon his physical presence is not simply a reflection of vanity, although this dimension of his personality certainly comes into play. His defensiveness, rather, springs from a desire—one might even say a desperation—to reclaim a body under siege.

---

itself as a speech (*orationis*) (*YP*, 4:557; *CM*, 8:2). Such an oratorical posture is discernible throughout. Reinforcing this posture is Milton's sense of himself as an exalted writer engaged in the production of a prose epic commemorating the great heroes of his country (*YP*, 4:685; *CM*, 8:252).

2. The nature of the reference is addressed in the discussion of the *Clamor* (see Chapter 7). In the *Fides Publica*, More maintains that he had originally been unaware of Milton's blindness, a disclaimer that is addressed below (*YP*, 4:1103).

The psychology at work is no less compelling than that which characterized his defensiveness concerning his physical well-being and moral rectitude in such works as the *Apology* for Smectymnuus. There, Milton as Domina sought to justify his chastity in terms that elevated himself, his body, and his behavior to the highest possible levels. One finds the same sensibility at work in the *Defensio Secunda*. There, however, self-justification is impelled by the added incentive of responding to an attack not just upon the body as the seat of virtue but upon the eyes as the vehicle of knowing. For Milton's enemies, deprivation of sight becomes a sign of the retribution against the blind man for unconscionable misdeeds. Such terms raise the stakes considerably. Uppermost in Milton's response to castigations against his body is the pervasive need to reclaim the self through a repristination of the body and its functions as attractive, virile, and serviceable. In defending the attractiveness and virility of his body, Milton seeks to uphold the conviction of his staunch manliness and irreproachable conduct; in defending the serviceableness of his body, he seeks to uphold the sense of himself as a being whose loss of sight is not the result of some moral breach but, paradoxically, a symbol of divine favor bestowed only upon the elect.

Initially, Milton adopts a tone of jocularity in response to the castigation of him as a monster—horrible, deformed, huge, and sightless." "Never," he says, "did I think that I should rival the Cyclops in appearance." Noting, however, that this castigation corrects itself by maintaining that he is not huge but feeble, bloodless, and pinched, Milton feels compelled to set the record straight. Apparent jocularity gives way to high seriousness, as Milton, with a certain self-consciousness and an awareness that his audience might well react adversely to an act of special pleading, focuses in detail upon his body—its form, appearance, and attractiveness:

> Although it ill befits a man to speak of his own appearance [*forma*], yet speak I shall, since here too there is reason for me to thank God and refute liars, lest anyone think me to be perhaps a dog-headed ape or a rhinoceros.... Ugly [*Deformis*] I have never been thought by anyone, to my knowledge, who has laid eyes on me. Whether I am handsome or not [*formosus necne*], I am less concerned. I admit that I am not tall, but my stature is closer to the medium than to the small. Yet what if it were small, as is the case with so many men of the greatest worth in both peace and war? (Although why is that

stature called small which is great enough for virtue [*quae ad virtutem satis magna est*]?) But neither am I especially feeble, having indeed such spirit and such strength [*animo iisque viribus*] that when my age and manner of life required it, I was not ignorant of how to handle or unsheathe a sword, nor unpractised in using it each day [*nec ferrum tractare, nec stringere quotidiano usu exercitatus nescirem*]. Girded with my sword, as I generally was, I thought myself equal to anyone, though he was far more sturdy, and I was fearless of any injury that one man could inflict on another. (*YP*, 4:582–83; *CM*, 8:60)

This is a remarkable performance indeed. Beginning with an oratorical gesture of modest self-denial, Milton proclaims his determination to address the nature of his appearance, despite the disapproval such a concern with one's own body might provoke. At the center of this discourse is a delineation of such matters as form, shape, and size. Milton first defends the attractiveness of his body. Hardly ugly, this is a body that has been deemed attractive, at least by some. Milton must approach this aspect of his self-defense with a certain amount of caution ("Whether I am handsome or not, I am less concerned"). Nonetheless, one detects here something of the fastidiousness that distinguishes the Domina of the *Apology* for Smectymnuus. Although charged with being "bloodless" by the author of the *Clamor*, Milton maintains that in his face "still lingers a color exactly opposite to the bloodless and pale." Even though he is "past forty," he continues, "there is scarcely anyone to whom I do not seem younger by about ten years." "Nor," he says, "is it true that either my body or my skin is shriveled" (*YP*, 4:583). There is a quality in this of preening, a quality that harkens back to the Lady of Milton's earlier persona. In the *Defensio Secunda*, that persona, once again under attack, does all in its power to reclaim itself on all fronts.

Especially crucial to Milton's self-reclamation is his insistence upon the ability of his body to demonstrate those qualities that distinguish him as a person of imposing virtue. Such "virtuousness" becomes a sign not only of Milton's ethical stature but of his strength and manliness (the Domina-become-male). By means of his oration on the dignity of his own body, Milton establishes at once his moral rectitude and his unimpeachable masculinity. His oration is as much a gender discourse as it is an ethical discourse. The language of maleness pervades the oration. At its center is that *ferrum* (both as "sword" and as "tool"), which Milton is able both to wield (*tractare*) and to unsheathe and draw forth (*stringere*), as occasion demands.[3] Although perhaps better equipped for such demonstrations in his youth, he is still a figure to contend with. In any case, his "self-display," his emphasis upon form, appearance, size, rectitude, virility, and sexual prowess, underlies Milton's determination to repristinate, as well as to purify, the body as self in the face of its undoing by the author of the *Clamor*. Milton's oration on the dignity of his body is tantamount to a poem upon the self. As such, it looks forward to that supreme epic moment when the poet of *Paradise Lost* takes the occasion to extol the bodies of the first man and the first woman, as they stand "erect and tall, / Godlike erect, with native Honour clad / In naked Majestie" before the eyes both of their maker and of the reader (4.288–311). Anticipating the epic, the Miltonic concern with the body reflects an awareness of audience.

In the case of the *Defensio Secunda*, that awareness, however, is intensified by the fact that the oration is uttered within the polemical context of the national and indeed international stage. Milton realizes what is involved in this most intimate of enactments, for he is at pains to round out his oration on the dignity of his body with the following disclaimer: "If I am in any way deceitful in respect to these matters, I should deserve the mockery [*ridiculus merito sim*] of many thousands of my fellow-citizens, who know me by sight, and not of a few foreigners as well" (*YP*, 4:584; *CM* 8:60). What renders the disclaimer so poignant is that it is issued by a blind man who stands exposed to the sight and therefore the possible derision of those whose approbation he so desperately seeks. Within this theater of darkness, Milton exposes at once his nakedness and his desire to clothe that nakedness as decorously as possible. He desires, that is, to remake, repristinate, refashion himself in the hope that the outcome will not result in his further undoing. Engaging in such an enactment, Milton is fully aware of the stakes: at any moment, he faces once again the likelihood of further opprobrium and final decimation by enemies who would not hesitate to subject his body to the tortures of a merciless *sparagmos*. Within the context of this moving defense of his body, Milton

---

3. Compare Milton's reference in his Letter to a Friend to his awareness of the individual who "cutts himselfe off from all action & becomes the most helplesse, pusilanimous & un-weapon'd creature in the [world]" (*YP*, 1:319). With a full awareness of the sexual punning implicit in his use of "pusilanimous" (from Latin *pusillus*, "very small") and "unweapon'd," Milton would distance himself from such individuals.

concerns himself with the terrible fact of his blindness. Recalling abilities of which he is now deprived, he observes: "Today I possess the same spirit [*animus*], the same strength [*eaedem vires*], but not the same eyes [*oculi non iidem*]. And yet they have as much the appearance of being uninjured [*extrinsecus illaesi*], and are as clear and bright, without a cloud [*ita sine nube clari ac lucidi*], as the eyes of men who see most keenly [*qui acutissimum cernunt*]. In this respect alone, against my will, do I deceive [*simulator sum*]" (*YP*, 4:583; *CM*, 8:60). Like the defense of the beauty of his body, the act of extolling his eyes immediately focuses upon their apparent wholeness, clarity, and brightness. In the act of repristination, it is important to Milton that, although his eyes, "Bereft of light thir seeing have forgot," are "clear / To outward view of blemish or of spot" (Sonnet 22, ll. 1–4). His orbs may "rowl in vain" (*Pardise Lost* 3:23–25), but, like his body, which is whole, his eyes, the inlets of the soul, are free from apparent injury: to outward appearances, they are unharmed. Underlying Milton's insistence upon the wholeness of his eyes is a reminder that the allusion to the Cyclops in the *Clamor* brings to mind the fate of that horrible monster: as the sleeping Cyclops lies belching up the blood of his victims, Ulysses and his men spring upon him and bore out his eye with "a long sharpened piece of wood." The brutality associated with this excruciating event echoes throughout Milton's attempt to dissociate himself as much as possible from that *Monstrum horrendum, informe, ingens, cui lumen ademptum* and its terrible fate.

In that attempt at dissociation, Milton takes the occasion to transform his plight into a sign of his own special election as 'a prophet-seer, one whose blindness elevates him to the highest possible levels of perception. A great deal of attention has already been accorded this aspect of his sense of himself as visionary.[4] From the perspective we are exploring here, his discourse on the nature of his blindness is to be understood in light of the attack upon him in the *Clamor* and his attempt to reemerge as a whole being from that attack. His undoing would then have the paradoxical effect of making him stronger. He would better be able to face the trials that continue to beset him in

4. See, among many studies, Michael Lieb, *Poetics of the Holy: A Reading of "Paradise Lost"* (Chapel Hill: University of North Carolina Press, 1981); William Kerrigan, *The Prophetic Milton* (Charlottesville: University Press of Virginia, 1974); and the books of Joseph Wittreich, including *Visionary Poetics: Milton's Tradition and His Legacy* (San Marino, Calif.: Huntington Library, 1979).

his blindness and that threaten to perpetrate further attacks upon his person. The discourse on his blindness, then, may be seen as a form of constructing barricades, of hedging himself about with barriers to future assaults. Such self-protectiveness will provide him the opportunity to ward off the possibility of yet another enemy's attempt to bore out an eye. At the same time, the discourse may be looked upon as an additional instance of self-justification and a determination to bear his affliction stoically.

With a heightened sense of his physical affliction, Milton responds to what he construes as a totally unwarranted attack by acknowledging his inability to countermand that which is an unfortunate reality: "Would that it were . . . possible to refute this brutish adversary on the subject of my blindness, but it is not possible [*Utinam de caecitate . . . liceret inhumanum hunc refellere adversarium; sed non licet*]. Let me bear it then [*feramus igitur*]. Not blindness but the inability to endure blindness is a source of misery [*non est miserum esse caecum; miserum est caecitatem non posse ferre*]. Why should I not bear that which every man ought to prepare himself to bear with equanimity, if it befall him" (*YP*, 4:584; *CM*, 8:62). With repeated emphasis upon the idea of bearing (*ferre*) the unbearable as patiently as possible, this agonistic figure confronts the fact of his suffering and the pain of feeling himself mocked and castigated because of it. His immersion in his suffering is uppermost in his mind. Cast into darkness, lacerated from without, lacerated from within, he must find a way to rise above the tumult of his own undoing.

This he does by looking upon his blindness as a sign of his membership among a select group who likewise bear this affliction. Although blindness has befallen many individuals, Milton declares, it "has indeed befallen certain men who are the most eminent and virtuous in all history [*& praestantissimis quibusdam, atque optimis omni memoria viris accidisse sciam*]." Milton calls upon this select group as witnesses of his secure and indeed transcendent membership. His litany of honored names assumes a ritual quality in its reconstruction of historical precedent. The reconstruction itself begins with a rhetorical flourish:

Shall I recall those ancient bards and wise men of the most distant past [*sive illos memorem vetustatis ultimae priscos vates, ac sapientissimos*], whose misfortune [*calamitatem*] the gods, it is said, recompensed with far more potent gifts [*multo potioribus donis compensarunt*], and whom

men treated with such respect [*& homines eo honore affecerunt*] that
they preferred to blame the very gods than to impute their blindness
to them as a crime [*ut ipsos inculpare maluerint deos, quam caecitatem
illis crimini dare*]? (*YP*, 4:584; *CM*, 8:62)

Having asked this question, Milton then invokes a series of names
ranging from ancient mythical figures (bards and wise men) to historical figures, including statesmen, soldiers, and theologians, who
shared his affliction. Reflecting his belief in the Bible itself as the source
of highest authority, his litany culminates in Old and New Testament
figures (*YP*, 4:584–87).

Throughout Milton's recitation, we can detect an ambivalence,
even a defensiveness, that we have seen before in his allusions to
various seers whose blindness, while affording them greater prophetic
knowledge, is somehow associated with violations of protocol (what
Milton calls *crimini*) with respect to the gods. As cited in the present
litany, the seers in question include Tiresias and Phineus. Blinded by
the gods for their effrontery, they nonetheless are able to achieve a
transcendent status among the gods and their fellow mortals.[5] They
are accordingly exonerated through divine dispensation. Milton justifies this act of exoneration in the following terms: "The more ver-
acious a man is in teaching truth to men, the more like must he be
to God and the more acceptable to him [*similior deo acceptiorque sit*]"
(*YP*, 4:585; *CM*, 8:64). Although possibly angering the gods as the
result of their behavior, these seers ultimately enjoy divine approbation and indeed protection, as they find acceptance before the powers of the other world. With his own sense of possibly having incurred
some sort of divine displeasure, Milton too seeks acceptance. Like the
blind seers he cites as his models, he desperately desires to be acceptable to God and in that state to be able to proclaim without hesitation that his blindness is ultimately a sign of divine favor.

Determined to view his blindness in this way, Milton looks upon
himself as one who corresponds to other holy men of the same sort.

5. Compare the earlier discussions of Tiresias in Chapters 2 and 4. Tiresias, Phineus,
Thamyris, and Maeonides (Homer) are cited in *Paradise Lost* as seers whom Milton extols
(3.31–36). Figures of this sort appear in the Latin elegies, the personal letters, and the
prolusions. Both before and after his blindness Milton was attracted to them, but particularly
after his blindness they became meaningful as at once exalted but potentially suspect because
of their putative culpability in offending the gods, who struck them with blindness as a
punishment yet allowed them greater spiritual sight as well.

They include such figures as Timoleon of Corinth, Appius Claudius, Caecilius Metellus, Dandolo, Zizka, and Zanchius. Grouping these individuals together, Milton creates an armory of defense against any who might attack him. To fortify his armory even further, however, he follows his litany of historical figures with such biblical patriarchs as Isaac and Jacob, against whom no one could impute blame. As if this were not enough, Milton culminates the recitation as a whole with the figure of the innocent blind man cured by Christ in the Gospel of John (9:1–41): "It is perfectly certain from the divine testimony [*divino testimonio*] of Christ our Savior," Milton asserts, "that the man who was healed [*sanatum*] by Him had been blind from the very womb, through no sin of his own or of his parents [*neque ob suum, neque ob parentum suorum aliquod peccatum, etiam ab utero caecum fuisse*]" (*YP*, 4:585–87; *CM*, 8:66).[6]

Such a recitation of authority (mythical, historical, and biblical) suggests the extent to which Milton was determined to discover any precedent that might justify himself before the world that stands in judgment of him and before those divine powers that visited this fate upon him. One can see him desperately searching his memory for such precedent, deciding which names to include and which to discard in his recitation. With his appeal to the biblical text as ultimate authority, it is surely significant that his final reference is to a figure whose blindness is ultimately healed, an event Milton in his darkness desired to enjoy but knew was beyond his immediate grasp. What he hoped was not beyond his grasp and what he pursued with utmost longing was the conviction that, in spite of the taunts of his enemies and his own fears, his darkness was imposed upon him with a purpose, indeed, as the result of a divine dispensation. Not to believe this was tantamount to a concession that would result in annihilation of the self, total and irremediable sparagmos.

Milton's awareness of this fact underlies the self-probing that follows his recitation. Just as that recitation begins with a rhetorical question concerning the need to invoke the names of those whose blindness must be looked upon as a sign of divine favor rather than of punishment for misdeeds, his litany ends with a prayer that he be

6. See John 9:1–7. The text was of supreme importance to Milton. The idea of the need to work during the light of day underlies the reference to "day labour" in Sonnet 19 (l. 7), and washing in the pool of Siloam looks forward to the allusion to "*Siloa's* Brook that flow'd / Fast by the Oracle of God" in *Paradise Lost* (1.11–12).

successful in dispelling any doubts regarding the occasion for his own blindness: "For my part," he proclaims, "I call upon Thee, my God, who knowest my inmost mind and all my thoughts [*mentis intinmae, cogitationumque*], to witness that (although I have repeatedly examined myself on this point as earnestly as I could, and have searched all the corners of my life [*quanquam hoc apud me saepius, & quam maxime potui, serio quaesivi, & recessus vitae omnes exussi*]), I am conscious of nothing, or of no deed, either recent or remote, whose wickedness [*atrocitas*] could justly occasion or invite upon me this supreme misfortune [*calamitatem*]" (*YP*, 4:587; *CM*, 8:68).

Displaying the turmoil he has undergone—indeed, enacting it in the form of an invocatory prayer—Milton lays himself bare to demonstrate his purity. The admission of constant and repeated self-interrogation, self-probing into his innermost recesses to discover there the least possible taint of some wickedness, hideousness, or repulsiveness (all suggested by *atrocitas*), becomes the psychological counterpart to that physical torture—the burning, the cauterizing, the bloodletting—to which Milton as blind man allowed himself to be subjected in the futile attempts to cure his afffliction, this supreme misfortune or *calamitatem*. Here, the admission of self-laceration provides the groundwork for what Milton hopes is the reestablishment of his own being.

Although the Royalists would argue that he is "now undergoing this suffering [*luere quasi piaculum*] as a penance [*existimant*], and they accordingly rejoice [*adeo triumphant*]," Milton calls upon God "to witness [*testor*]" his rectitude. (*YP*, 4:587; *CM*, 8:68). The very language of this proclamation confirms a reading of his suffering as involving an act of gleansing (*luere*) in order to absolve himself of all imputation of guilt. In that purification, Milton becomes a sacrifice or victim (*piaculum*) who must demonstrate his purity before the eyes of the world to repristinate himself. In this act, he invokes God to be his witness. Protesting the nobility of his calling, he recounts his willingness to undertake it despite his awareness that doing so will exacerbate his deteriorating health and hasten the onset of his blindness.

His reasons for this willing self-sacrifice, he avers, are the result of his having heeded the call of his own destiny (*fatum*) and his realization that, to be responsive to this call, he is obliged to sacrifice all to his own sense of sovereign duty (*summum officium*). The whole process of receiving this calling and being responsive to it Milton conceives in the most exalted, indeed oracular, of terms. Looking upon himself as a warrior commissioned by the gods to enter the field of battle with the knowledge that there is no denying his destiny, he is determined to view himself as the truly chosen one (*YP*, 4:588; *CM*, 8:68). Doing so, he protests that he is fully aware of the consequences of his actions.

Only by means of exalting himself in these oracular terms, then, is Milton able to remake himself from within the darkness of his own anguish—an anguish that is as much a consequence of his physical condition as a reaction to unconscionable castigations of the *Clamor*. It makes little difference to Milton that the purported author of the *Clamor* later protests his innocence in having any awareness of the terrible fact of Milton's blindness in the first place. All Milton requires is the accusation that his blindness is retribution for misdeeds.[7] This is reason enough to feel himself called upon to respond at length to what has been on his own mind, indeed, has no doubt been eating away at him throughout the course of his affliction, up to and even beyond its final onset. What may well have been inadvertency in the otherwise brutal castigations of the *Clamor* precipitated a long and torturous self-defense in which the blind polemicist struggles to justify his own blindness in order to make himself whole once again. This process of repristination culminates in Milton's most eloquent and moving statement concerning his exalted condition as one of the chosen of God.

Arguing that his blindness merely deprives him of the ability to see the color and superficial appearance of things (*colorem tantummodo rebus & superficiem demit*), he nonetheless has the power to behold their true and essential nature by means of an intellectual vision (*quod verum ac stabile in iis est, contemplationi mentis non adimit*). This contemplative ability sets him apart from those confined to a world of appearances. Although he may be seen by others as weak, he is really strong. Drawing upon the Pauline paradox that, for the truly faithful, one's strength is made perfect in weakness (2 Cor. 12:9–10; Heb. 11:34), Milton declares that he does not feel pain "at being classed with the blind, the afflicted, the suffering, and the weak," because he has hope that as the result of his afflictions he may "approach more closely the mercy and protection of the Father Almighty."

7. One might argue that even that suggestion is not present in the *Clamor* but that Milton was determined to find it there, because it represented the occasion through which he might give voice to his own internal misgivings and indeed his own very real anguish.

Developing the paradox as fully and effectively as possible, Milton observes:

> There is a certain road which leads through weakness, as the apostle teaches, to the greatest strength [*Est quoddam per imbecillitatem . . . ad maximas vires iter*]. May I be entirely helpless [*sim ego debillissimus*], provided that in my weakness there may arise all the more powerfully this immortal and more perfect strength [*immortalis ille & melior vigor*]; provided that in my shadows [*meis tenebris*] the light of the divine countenance may shine forth all the more clearly [*divini vultus lumen eo clarius eluceat*]. For then I shall be at once the weakest and the strongest, at the same time blind and most keen in vision [*tum enim infirmissimus ero simul & validissimus, caecus eodem tempore & perspicacissimus*]. By this infirmity may I be perfected, by this completed [*hac possim ego infirmitate consummari, hac perfici*]. So in this darkness, I may be clothed in light [*possim in hac obscuritate sic ego irradiari*]. (*YP*, 4:589–90; *CM*, 8:72)

As I have demonstrated elsewhere, the concept of having one's strength made perfect in weakness is one that exerted a profound influence on Milton throughout his career and had a particular cogency for him during the period of the regicide tracts.[8] For our purposes, the foregoing testament of faith, itself an eloquent prayer to the highest of all powers, is in effect an account of the process of repristination Milton seeks to experience in his blindness. It is a process of complete transformation, of becoming other. Milton conceives it as a journey (*iter*) from weakness to strength, from blindness to sight, from darkness to light, from sickness to health. In that journey, the individual whose being has been decimated through suffering becomes whole: the self undergoes an individuation, an apocatastasis (*hac perfici*) through which it is bathed in the light of a divine countenance. In this moment of consummation, the individual is purified, indeed sacralized, transformed into a state of ultimate vision (*perspicacissimus*).

---

8. See my full discussion (particularly with regard to *Samson Agonistes*) in Michael Lieb, *The Sinews of Ulysses: Form and Convention in Milton's Works* (Pittsburgh: Duquesne University Press, 1989), pp. 98–138. So taken was Milton with the reassurance the idea offered that he inscribed the text of 2 Cor. 12:9–10 as a self-reflexive motto in the autograph albums of Christopher Arnold in 1651 and John Zollikofer in 1656 (*CM*, 18:271). To know me, Milton suggests, is to understand the Pauline paradox by which strength is perfected in weakness, a perfection that permits the true Christian to glory in his infirmities (Lieb, *Sinews*, pp. 103–4).

Whatever the biblical foundations of this prayer for repristination, it is clear that Milton uses the occasion of his own dismemberment in the *Clamor* to engage in his most profound and eloquent appeal to be remade in wholeness.[9]

This is a moment of supreme intimacy, almost painful in its poignancy. In its self-defensiveness, it makes claims for those afflicted by blindness which presume to render such individuals sacrosanct, holy beyond the capacity of others to do them harm. To conceive of oneself as holy in this manner reflects a determination to remove oneself from the theater of assault. Such a person, Milton's argues, is simply not vulnerable to the ravages of sparagmos. On the contrary, those who attempt to engage in an assault upon the blind render themselves vulnerable instead. To support his contention, Milton utters a malediction that he would have all his enemies fear: "Woe to him who mocks us, woe to him who injures us [*Vae qui, vae qui laedit*]. He deserves to be cursed with a public malediction [*execratione publica devovendo*]. Divine law and divine favor have rendered us not only safe from the injuries of men, but almost sacred [*nos ab injuriis hominum no modo incolumes, sed paene sacros, divina lex rediddit, divinus favor*]." The shadows that surround us are those created as the result of being flanked by legions of celestial hosts (*quam coelestium alarum umbra has nobis fecisse tenebras videtur*). These shadows, in turn, are illuminated as the result of a divine favor that bestows upon the blind individual "an inner and far more enduring light [*interiore ac longe praestabiliore lumine*]" than any with which he was graced before he became blind (*YP*, 4:590; *CM*, 8:72).

At once repristinating himself and setting himself off in this manner, Milton fortifies his own identity within a protective enclosure that wards off any further attacks.[10] No one, he hopes, might be able to

9. For the biblical foundations, see, for example, Psalms 18:28 and 139:12.

10. Indeed, as he argues, rather than fearing the attacks of enemies, he is surrounded by friends: "To this circumstance I refer the fact that my friends now visit, esteem, and attend me more diligently even than before [*Huc refero, quod & amici officiousius nunc etiam quam solebant, colunt, observant, adsunt*]." He becomes the center of their attention, the object of their ministrations. Comparing himself respectively with the Orestes (*Orestes*, l. 795) and the Hercules (*Hercules Furens*, ll. 1398, 1402) of Euripides' two plays about besieged heroes, Milton views a world in which one who has been under attack is now secure. Far from being deserted even by those in power, he finds favor in their sight: they indulge him and continue to bestow their trust upon him. Although he is not as "useful" as he once was, he continues to be rewarded for his efforts and to enjoy the distinctions, honors, and prerogatives he once possessed (*YP*, 4:591; *CM*, 8:72–74). Milton's determination to refashion the self in visionary terms, then, is complemented by a determination to fortify the self against the attacks of

undermine him again. He is safe, secure, and sacrosanct. Free from all possibility of attack upon the one aspect of his being that renders him most vulnerable—not just to the attacks of others but to the anguish of his own inner turmoil—he no longer need be troubled by the prospect of sparagmos. If such an attempt at apocatastasis strikes us as overdetermined in the extent of its defensiveness, we need only be reminded once again of the circumstances out of which it has arisen: the defender of the regicides has himself been made the subject of extreme assault, of castigation, of defilement, of disfigurement, and finally of bodily mutilation and dismemberment. Such violence may exist only in the form of trope, but, as one who supported the decapitation of the king, Milton is fully aware that, given the opportunity, the enemies of those in power will gladly return the compliment. Compounding such circumstances is the unrelenting feeling that his darkness was brought about as the result of some *atrocitas* on his part. That is what his enemies would have him believe, and the possible validity of that belief is what he is so desperate to dispel as he attempts to deal with the terrible fact of his darkness.

II

In the *Defensio Secunda*, Milton's act of bodily repristination finds its counterpart in the remaking of his reputation, as he adopts the occasion to rewrite the events of his life in response to the attacks upon it in the *Clamor*. If these attacks are themselves a rewriting for the sake of defamation, Milton's rewriting counters this defamation with his own act of self-fashioning. Impugning Milton's character, the author of the *Clamor* does all in his power to pervert the details of his biographical account. According to this account, Milton, expelled from the university because he was disgraced, was made to flee England and migrate as a traitor to Italy. Returning home, he wrote his questionable prose tracts, all advocating disruptions and breaches of one sort of another, until he wound up supporting the regicides (or parricides, as the author of *Clamor* calls them). At the center of this fallacious act of rewriting is the prevailing assumption that the par-

---

enemies through a "staging" of the self as an entity that finds more than ample support within the outside world. Both internally and externally, Milton creates defenses.

ricide is inherently divisive or disruptive in all his dealings: whether as a divorcer or a king killer, Milton is a force for chaos. Destructive of himself, he attempts to destory the world around him. Such is the nature of this piece of filth "voided lately from the dungpit."

It is against aspersions of this nature that Milton must justify his behavior, salvage his reputation, and demonstrate his moral worthiness to act as a defender of his country in its time of need. Doing so, he acknowledges that, though he is unable to rescue his eyes from blindness or his name from oblivion or slander, he can at least bring his life "into the light out of that darkness which accompanies disgrace [*vitam tamen possim ab ea saltem obscuritate quae cum macula sit, in lucem vindicare*]." Such an act of self-vindication is one at which Milton, as experienced self-apologist, is thoroughly adept. Here, as elsewhere in his prose works, he proclaims his life "far removed from all vice and crime [*ab omni turpitudine ac flagitio remotam*]" (*YP*, 4:611; *CM*, 8:116–118). In contrast to earlier self-defenses, however, the present *apologia* arises out of circumstances that place Milton on an international stage. The stakes are thus far greater, and the exposure is such that, if the self-apologist is unable to vindicate his conduct before the eyes of the world, he shall have failed not only himself but the government whose cause he espouses as official spokesman. This is a theater in which the public act of self-fashioning, Milton would argue, might well have international repercussions. With his international exposure in mind, Milton sets about to repristinate (or to use his word, vindicate [*vindicare*]) himself.

His act of self-fashioning is decidedly formal, indeed oratorical. As orator, he engages in an "ethical proof" that obliges him to disclose all aspects of his curriculum vitae: his parentage, his upbringing, his education, his study habits, the honors and degrees he earned as a student, his period of self-study after graduation, his reasons for venturing abroad, along with the names of the estimable supporters of his venture, those equally estimable individuals who received him in his journey and whose names he recites as if he were engaging in an epic catalogue, his behavior while abroad, and a complete account of his itinerary.[11] Milton caps this recitation with a full disclaimer

---

11. For an enlightening interpretation of several of the issues addressed here, see Diana Treviño Benet, "The Escape from Rome: Milton's *Second Defense* and a Renaissance Genre," in *Milton in Italy: Contexts, Images, Contradictions*, ed. Mario A. Di Cesare (Binghamton, N.Y.: Medieval and Renaissance Texts and Studies, 1991), pp. 29–49. For a discussion of Milton's

concerning the irreproachable nature of his conduct both as a student and as a traveler abroad: "I lived free," he says, "and untouched by the slightest sin or reproach [*ab omni flagitio ac probro integrum atque intactum vixisse*]." His use of the terms *flagitio* and *probro* is particularly significant here, for it suggests once again his repugnance at characteristics that mark a form of behavior he makes every show of eschewing.

In this display of open repugnance, we are made to recall the figure in the *Apology* for Smectymnuus who reacts to the charge of frequenting brothels by protesting not only his innocence but the exalted nature of his ladylike purity. On occasions of this sort, what we hear in the *Defensio Secunda* is as much the voice of the Domina as it is the fearsome defender of the Commonwealth. As Domina, Milton would not deign to involve himself with the sexual disgrace implicit in *flagitio* and *probro*, for he knows all too well that, although he "might hide from the gaze of men," he could never "elude the sight of God [*si hominum latere oculos possem, Dei certe non posse*]," a knowledge that, as he himself openly attests, is the result of his contemplating such matters excessively (*illud perpetuo cogitantem*) (*YP*, 4:620; *CM*, 8:126).

The admission of his perpetual thinking about the results of sexual misconduct is fascinating: it tells us a great deal about the Miltonic personality as that which dwells upon itself (one might perhaps suggest "feeds" upon itself). In that act of *perpetuo cogitantem*, it does all in its power to ward off the temptations that beset it, for it knows that it cannot hide: it may elude the eyes (*oculos*) of the world, but the eyes of God are perpetually fixed upon it. For one who himself has the power of sight, such a prospect is frightening enough. For one who protests his purity from the depths of his blindness, the idea of conceiving oneself as the cynosure of divine eyes must certainly have had its terrifying moments. At the very least, this Domina of consummate purity must have felt the need (whether seeing or blind) to be forever on her guard against the possibility (indeed, the likelihood) of some attack.

Under such circumstances, then, the staging of the self in the theater of assault represented by the *Clamor* never allowed Milton a

journey, see Rose Clavering and John T. Shawcross, "Milton's European Itinerary and His Return Home," *Studies in English Literature* 5 (1965), 49–59.

moment's reprieve. Acknowledging the extreme self-consciousness to which his own sense of exposure drove him, he portrayed himself as one determined at all costs to keep to the true path. Only in this manner was he able to lay claim to his abiding purity. Refusing to tolerate impurity in himself, Milton refused to tolerate it in others. Maintaining such a high ground, he applied this outlook not only to matters of personal conduct but to matters of national conduct as well.

Once returned from his European journey, he felt obliged to fight against corruption on a national scale and to throw his support behind those who fought for liberty on their own soil. His determination to be of use in this way gave rise to his prose tracts, the kinds and titles of which he lays before the world as a testament to his unswerving dedication to the cause and his willingness to undertake the tasks he felt necessary to fulfill despite the considerable sacrifices he was obliged to sustain. Whether through the antiprelatical tracts, the divorce tracts, the tracts concerning the education of children and the freedom of the press, or the antimonarchical tracts and the Defenses, Milton argues that his writings are aimed not at being divisive or disruptive, as the author of the *Clamor* maintains, but at fostering constructive behavior. Their purpose has been to support the cause of Truth. The idealism with which Milton views his own career as writer of prose tracts is reinforced by a pervasive sense of self-righteousness. Fully committed to this view, he conceives his activities as the realization of a higher providential design (*YP*, 4:620–28; *CM*, 8:129–39).

Reflecting his abiding faith in that design, Milton's orderly putting together of his life exhibits a determination to view his accomplishments as the product of his unswerving dedication to the demands of his calling. In the attempt to fulfill those demands throughout his career, he wishes to demonstrate to the world (as well as to that divine "task-master" in whose eye he perpetually finds himself) that he has made use of his talents to the very best of his ability.[12] Such self-justification is hardly unique to Milton, but here it is particularly germaine to his argument against the author of the *Clamor*, for in showing himself serviceable in the recapitulation of his works and the

12. For a full discussion of the notion of talent in Milton (Sonnets 7 and 19, Letter to a Friend, etc.), see my entry in *Milton Encyclopedia*, s.v. On the subject of Milton and vocation, see John Spencer Hill, *John Milton: Poet, Priest and Prophet* (Totowa, N.J.: Rowman and Littlefield, 1979).

way in which his works fit into an overall providential scheme, Milton
is yet again refashioning himself, repristinating himself, and purifying
himself as a sign of his ability to recreate his identity from "the void
and formless infinite" into which it has been cast by Alexander More,
the putative author of the *Clamor*.

As an indication of the extent to which Milton views this self-
portrayal as an act of purification, we need only attend to the declaration in which he concludes his account:

> I have given an account of myself [*mei rationem reddidi*] to this extent
> in order to stop your mouth [*ad obturandum os tuum*], More, and
> refute your lies [*mendacia redarguenda*], chiefly for the sake of those
> good men who otherwise would know me not [*bonorum maxime vi-
> rorum in gratiam, qui me alias non norint*]. Do you then, I bid you,
> unclean More, be silent [*Tu, igitur, More, tibi dico immunde, phimotheti*].
> Hold your tongue, I say [*obmutesce inquam*]! For the more you abuse
> me [*quo enim magis mihi maledixeris*], the more copiously will you
> compel me to account for my conduct [*eo me rationes meas uberius
> explicare coegeris*]. From such accounting you can gain nothing save
> the reproach [*opprobrium*], already most severe of telling lies [*men-
> daciorum*], while for me you open the door to still higher praise of
> my own integrity [*mihi ad integritatis commendationem eo latius viam
> aperias*]. (*YP*, 4:628–629; *CM*, 8:138)

The thrust of this final admonition is particularly relevant: it provides
motive and justification for Milton's extensive self-portrayal, and it
enacts a silencing of the enemy that bears directly on that revelation
of the self. Milton's self-consciousness in having written so much about
his own life and accomplishments is reflected here. He is aware that
his act of saying so much about himself might be construed as a form
of self-indulgence, but, as suggested earlier, he views himself as official
spokesman for his country obliged to justify himself and his behavior
before an international audience that that has little or no knowledge
of his life (*qui me alias non norint*) and whose impressions have now,
Milton believes, been determined as a result of lies.

What is so fascinating in this need to set the record straight, however, is what might be construed as the almost compulsive sense not
only to say as much as possible but to warn that even more will be
forthcoming—and that with even greater copiousness (*uberius*). Milton
feels compelled to account for his conduct (*explicare coegeris*) and will

not hesitate to sing his own praises and extol his integrity (*mihi ad integritatis commendationem*) at the slightest provocation. By means of this act of incessant and unrelenting self-praise and self-justification, he will have accomplished two corresponding objectives: cleansing himself and silencing his enemy.

The extent to which those two objectives correspond may be seen in what might be called the speech act through which Milton forces his enemy to capitulate. Thus, Milton declares: "Do you then, I bid you, unclean More, be silent. Hold your tongue, I say!" Although on the surface Milton's declaration appears to be no more than an attempt to silence his enemy, the allusive context through which the cry is uttered brings into sharp and sudden focus the extent to which the idea of self-purification becomes the driving force behind Milton's account of his life and conduct. The context in question is that of Mark 1:23–27:

> And there was in their synagogue a man with an unclean spirit; and he cried out, Saying, Let us alone; what have we to do with thee, thou Jesus of Nazareth? art thou come to destroy us? I know thee who thou art, the Holy One of God. And Jesus rebuked him, saying, Hold thy peace, and come out of him. And when the unclean spirit had torn him, and cried with a loud voice, he came out of him. And they were all amazed insomuch that they questioned among themselves, saying, What thing is this? What new doctrine is this? for with authority commandeth he even the unclean spirits, and they do obey him.

The point is that, in silencing More by providing a true relation of who and what he is, Milton in effect assumes divine power and authority in being able to *exorcise* his enemy from the wracked body of one possessed by unclean spirits. The text in question must have been extremely important to Milton, for he quotes both the Greek and Latin versions (*phimotheti* and *obmutesce*) to make certain that the allusion and its full implications are not missed.

Repristination of the self, then, is an exorcism of the other: to refashion the self is to cleanse oneself of the taint of the other in an act of exorcism. The act becomes a purifying of the body, as the self is made whole. The process is not easy. As the unclean spirit is exorcised, the body of the possessed is "torn to pieces": it undergoes its own sparagmos in the process of repristination.[13] If Milton would have us stand amazed as much as those who witnessed the original exorcism, he nonetheless empowers himself with the authority to command unclean spirits. In Milton's case, however, it is his own body, his own reputation that he has cleansed in the process of exorcising from himself that unclean spirit, the individual to whom he attributes the authorship of the *Clamor*. In short, he performs the exorcism upon himself. More becomes, as it were, the Miltonic other, that aspect of himself which he must cleanse, exorcise, and finally destroy. Only in that way will he finally emerge as complete and whole. Having repristinated his own body, his own reputation, his own being, he must destroy More in order to be truly free of this unclean spirit. To that end, he devotes his energies to the aspersion and vilification of his enemy. This he does within that very theatrical context the author of the *Clamor* established in his own effort to dramatize the undoing of John Milton.

13. The Greek has *sparaxan*, the Latin *discerpens*. For the Greek, see the *Novum Testamentum Graece*, ed. Eberhard Nestle (Stuttgart: Württembergische Bibelanstalt, 1953); for the Latin, the *Biblia Sacra Iuxta Vulgatam Versionem*, ed. Robert Weber (Stuttgart: Deutsche Bibelgesellschaft, 1969).

9

The Humiliation of Priapus

I

In the *Defensio Secunda*, the destruction of Alexander More is a remarkable tour de force. Responding to the author of the *Clamor* as one who views his account as the reenactment of a tragedy (*tragoedia*), Milton transforms the author's work into nothing more than the lowest and perverse form of comedy. In Milton's hands, the *Clamor* is tantamount in fact to a travesty, replete with characters of the most comical sort. Conceiving the *Clamor* in this way, Milton declares: "Observe then, at the beginning, as is customary, the cast of characters [*dramatis personae*]: the 'Cry,' as prologue [*prologus*]; Vlacq, the buffoon (or if you prefer, Salmasius disguised in the mask and cloak of Vlacq the buffoon); two poetasters [*Duo Poetastri*], tipsy with stale beer; More the adulterer and seducer [*Morus adulter & stuprator*]. What splended actors for a tragedy [*Mirificos sane tragoedos*]!" This "troupe of actors [*grege histrionico*]" Milton attacks one by one (*YP*, 4:573–74; *CM*, 8:42–44). He does so by engaging in an assault upon their persons at the most primal level: that of refusing to acknowledge the tragic significance of the "cry" supposedly uttered by the "royal blood" that they have assembled at once to reenact and to lament. If there is a cry to be heard it all, its effect is to produce not horror but laughter. Listening to the clamor of the attacks upon him, the blind man turns that disruption back upon the attackers, silences them, and causes their noise, their assembled "cry," to confound itself in the form of a debased comedy.

The nature of that comedy is discernible in Milton's response to the two poems in which the *Clamor* culminates. As we recall, the *MAGNO SALMASIO Pro Defensione Regia Ode Eucharistica* ("To Great Salmasius, for the *Defensio Regia*, A Thanksgiving Ode") and the *In Impurissimum Nebulonem JOHANNEM MILTONUM Parricidarum & Parricidii Advocatum* ("Against That Foul Rascal JOHN MILTON the Advocate of Parricide & Parricides") encapsulate in poetic form the adulation of Salmasius and the contempt for Milton that characterize the polemic outlook of the *Clamor* as a whole. In his attempt to undermine that outlook, Milton does his utmost to counter these two poems, thereby setting the stage for his attack upon More as adulterer and seducer.

In keeping with the theatrical metaphor, Milton draws upon the formulation of the dramatis personae initiated early in the *Defensio Secunda*. Here, his concern is with the "two poetasters, tipsy with stale beer." Heralded like geese by their own discordant "cry" (*clamorem*), these two actors within their own "Tragedy of a Cry" are either two or a single figure, "twofold in appearance and of two colors [*biformi sane specie & bicolore*]." In fact, they are a single figure and monstrous at that. "Should I call it a sphinx," Milton asks, "or that monster which Horace describes in the *Ars Poetica*, with the head of a woman, the neck of an ass, clad in varied plumage, with limbs assembled from every source?" "Yes," he concludes, "this is that very monster" (*YP*, 4:592; *CM*, 8:76).

Answering a fool according to his own folly, the attack immediately establishes both the tone and the method of Milton's strategy. Stung as he might be by the poems in which the Clamor culminates, he refuses to grant his attacker the satisfaction of witnessing his discomfiture. Rather, the attacker must behold his "Tragedy of a Cry" transformed into low comedy and his poems trashed as the product of a monstrous poetaster, whose animality is such that not only its form but its gender is completely confused. With the head of a woman and the body assembled of bestial sources, this twofold creature is capable of producing nothing but "effeminate little verses [*versiculorum nuvigendos*]" that are totally impotent and despicable (*YP*, 4:592–93; *CM*, 8:78).

It is with such contempt that Milton treats both the penultimate

poem on Salmasius and the final poem on himself. The poem on
Salmasius he dismisses as hardly worthy of attention. Although the
poem extols Salmasius as a great "giant-fighting hero" (*Heroem Gigantomachum*) brandishing his weapons, Milton views him as "a mere
schoolmaster" (*Grammaticum*) who in his dotage has been taken in by
the nonsense this poetaster has written about him.[1] In Milton's hands,
the *MAGNO SALMASIO Pro Defensione Regia Ode Eucharistica* becomes
nothing more than a thanksgiving ode for a fool, who in turn has
been duped by a fool (*YP*, 4:593; *CM*, 8:80).

Precisely this attitude is reflected in Milton's treatment of the second
poem. Here, the poet is branded a madman who "does not write
verses, but simply raves, himself the most insane of all the possessed
whom he so rabidly assails." As such, he becomes "an executioner for
Salmasius [*Salmasii carnifex*]," one who assumes the role of a slave-
whipper (*Lorarios*) but who is himself the son of slaves. In an allusion
to Horace, Milton associates this *carnifex* overtly with Cadmus (an
ancient executioner, known especially for his cruelty) and implicitly
with those responsible for the casting of victims from the Tarpeian
rock.[2] In either case, Milton, as one subjected to the violence of this
assailant, is made to endure the indignities that such a scoundrel seeks
to inflict. Milton's response is to transform the violence enacted in this
sparagmatic drama into the foolishness of low comedy. Alluding to
such comic dramatists as Plautus, Milton views his assailant as a lowlife,
indeed, a member of the slave class, unable to muster reputable Latin
to carry out his attack. Resorting to "the filthy language of slaves and
scoundrels," this poetaster is capable of speaking nothing but Oscan,
the primitive dialect lacking the elegance of Latin. (In fact, Milton,
like a mock schoolmaster, does not hesitate to correct his opponent's
Latin in the implementation of his iambics.) Corresponding to the
frogs of Aristophanes, Milton's opponent can do little but croak. Mired
in "the hellish swamps in which he swims," he becomes a loathsome
creature whose croaking sends up a shrill clamor. He must be disposed
of accordingly (*YP*, 4:594–95; *CM*, 8:80–82).

Milton's decision concerning that disposition is a stroke of brilli-

---

1. In the *Defensio Prima*, Milton levels the same charge: Salmasius is nothing but a mere
grammarian (*Grammaticus*) (*YP*, 4:306; *CM*, 8:8).

2. See the annotations to this passage in *YP*, 4:594, nn. 201–2. The specific allusion is
to Horace, *Satires*, 1:6, 38–39: "Tune, Syri, Damae, aut Dionysi filius, audes / deicere e saxo
civis aut tradere Cadmo?"; *Horace: Satires and Epistles*, ed. Edward P. Morris (Norman: University of Oklahoma Press, 1939).

ance. Drawing upon the notion of the schoolmaster, Milton implicitly acknowledges his own earlier profession to castigate his opponent, a castigation he has just used against Salmasius. Under the present circumstances, Milton associates his opponent with a schoolmaster of the most notorious sort: "Meanwhile," Milton declares, "I hand you over, an Orbilius, to be executed by the 'harvest of rods' of your students [*interea te ego puerorum virgidemiis tuis caedendum trado Orbilium*]" (*YP*, 4:594–95; *CM*, 8:80–82). Branding his enemy an Orbilius, Milton effectively answers his enemy according to his own folly. As portrayed by Horace and Suetonius, among others, Orbilius Pupillus (ca. 112–117 B.C.) became known (in the words of Horace) as *Orbilium plagosum*, that is, "Orbilius full of blows or rods." Suetonius gives this account of him: "He was sour-tempered, not only towards rival scholars, whom he assailed at every opportunity, but also towards his pupils, as Horace implies when he calls him 'the flogger,' and Domitius Marsus in the line: 'Whomever Orbilius thrashed with rod or with whiplash of leather.'"[3] In response to his opponent as *"Orbilium plagosum,"* Milton hands him over to his students to be executed (*caedendum*) by their own "harvest of rods" (*virgidemiis*).[4] Judging by Milton's adoption of the term *caedendum*, the execution will be of a particularly brutal sort. As implied by *caedendum* (from *caedere*), this *Orbilium plagosum* will suffer a flogging that will effectively cut him to pieces.[5] Turning the torturer into the tortured, Milton provides a new understanding of his pedagogical principles, one hardly anticipated in *Of Education*.[6] What he envisions is a pedagogical program of an entirely unique

---

3. The explanatory note in *YP*, 4:594, n. 208 is helpful here. For Horace, see *Epistles*, 2:1, 70–71. For Suetonius, see *The Lives of Illustrious Men* (*Grammarians*), bk. 9, in *Suetonius*, 2 vols., trans. J. C. Rolfe (Cambridge: Harvard University Press, 1920), 2:410–11.

4. Compare Milton's reference in the *Defensio Prima* to Salmasius as a grammarian who is to be given over to his fellow grammarians to be flogged (*vapulandum*), as well as ridiculed (*deridendum*) (*YP*, 4:311; *CM*, 7:17).

5. *Caedendum* implies all these meanings, including killing and murdering; see *A Latin Dictionary*, ed. Charlton T. Lewis and Charles Short (Clarendon: Oxford University Press, 1975), s.v.

6. One should, however, take note of the charge of *plagosum* of which Milton as schoolmaster might well have been guilty, a charge that reinforces the complexity of the ironic and self-reflexive allusions to the profession of mere schoolmaster (and a brutal one at that) in the *Defensio Secunda*. The charge in question is made in the context of John Aubrey's observations concerning Mary Powell's decision to desert her new husband: "When she came to live wth her husband at Mr Russells in St Brides ch: yd, she found it very solitary: no company came to her, often-times heard his Nephews cry, and beaten. This life was irkesome to her; & so she went to her Parents at Fosthill"; "Minutes of the Life of Mr John Milton," in *Early Lives*, p. 14.

sort. If the tone of his attack is ostensibly comic, the clamor Milton has in mind is one in which his opponent is made to endure a sparagmos that is unbearably painful. Such is Milton's darker purpose, and such is what distinguishes the theater that he creates in his attack.

Moving from the *Duo Poetastri* who are really one creature, Milton focuses upon the creature itself. This, of course, is Alexander More, *adulter & stuprator*, whose indiscretions Milton seeks to expose in the most graphic form. As a result of that exposure, More is torn to pieces. Milton begins with the genre of the *Clamor* itself. Rather than having produced a tragic work in which the moans of the martyred can be heard redoubling from the vales to the hills, and they to heaven, he has created the basest of satyr plays (*satyram*), one entirely in keeping with his own lecherous and libidinous activities. Made abundantly evident in the chorus of cries these activities have provoked, More's indiscretions lend themselves to a comic catalogue that Milton invokes as a prologue to his own attack:

> Against you cries out (in case you do not know) that harlot of yours in the garden [*Clamat contra te, si nescis, Moecha illa tua hortensis*], who complained that she had been led astray chiefly by the example of you, her pastor. Against you cries out the husband whose bed you dishonored [*clamat contra te maritus, cujus torum violasti*]. Pontia cries out, whom you promised to marry and betrayed [*clamat Pontia, cui pactum nuptiale temerasti*]. If anyone cries out, it is the tiny baby whom you begot in shame and then abandoned [*clamat, siquis est, quem probro genitum, infantulum abdicasti*]. If you do not hear the cries of all these to Heaven against you, neither could you hear the Cry of the King's Blood [*horum omnium clamores ad coelum contra te, si non audi, neque illum regii sanguinis audiveris*]. (*YP*, 4:575; *CM*, 8:46)

The nature of these cries and the indiscretions they denounce will become clear, Milton implies, in his succeeding account. The point to be made in this prologue is that, as vocal testimony to More's true character, it completely undermines his credibility and therefore the credibility of the *Clamor*. Drowning out the sound of the king's cry, the cries More himself has caused transform the *Regii Sanguinis Clamor ad Coelum* into what Milton calls the *Lascivientis Mori hinnitus ad Pontiam*, that is, the "*Whinny of the Lustful More after His Pontia*." In that reinscription, tragedy becomes comedy, and the theater of assault is turned against the assaulter, who must abide the shame and scorn brought upon him by the whinnying or braying of all those he has violated.

The grim delight Milton takes in this enterprise has not gone unnoticed. In fact, it has proven at the very least disconcerting to modern critics. As much as one might wish to view the *Defensio Secunda* in particular as the sublime, epiclike defense of the English people that the work professes itself to be, there is definitely the underside to this work, as well as to the *Pro Se Defensio*, which must be taken into account as a revelation of what we have come to know as Milton's sparagmatic mentality. William Riley Parker for one is critical of this dimension of Milton's approach. Despite the fact that only about one-tenth of the *Defensio Secunda* is devoted to a personal attack upon More, this, Parker observes, is what attracts our attention. Although Milton might want to keep his work "on a higher plane than a petty quarrel or a scandalous exposé," he nonetheless fails. As a result of his "swallowing the gossip from abroad and regurgitating it with gusto," he succeeds in producing a few concentrated pages that "command fascinated attention." Both then and thereafter, readers "tended to focus upon the lurid parts, shocked or delighted by the verbal drubbing given Morus the corrupter of maid-servants, Morus the mass of impurity, Morus the goatherd pastor, Morus the lecher, the scoundrel, the perjurer."[7] What, Parker implies, could have prompted Milton to descend to such baseness? Such behavior for Parker, as for others, proved most disturbing.[8]

Not the least among those so disturbed was More himself. Attempting to counter Milton's theater of assault, More in his *Fides Publica* castigated his enemy for having "made a collection of villainies and taunts from old and new comedy" with which he "sprinkled" and "adorned" his "drama." More depicted Milton as "the only one sitting

7. *Milton Biography*, 1:449.

8. Among contemporary critics, see Don M. Wolfe's criticism of Milton's treatment of More. Responding to that treatment in the *Pro Se Defensio*, Wolfe views the work as "a polemic wasteland," one in which Milton is "a dwarf of himself." As much as it is able to avoid such a treatment, *Defensio Secunda*, on the other hand, is a great work (*YP*, 4:282–83). This is not, however, a view shared by Kester Svendsen, who appears to have understood this dimension of Milton's polemic best. See Svendsen's comments in the preface to his edition of the *Pro Se Defensio* (*YP*, 4:687–93), as well as his illuminating "Milton's *Pro Se Defensio* and Alexander More," *Texas Studies in Literature and Language* (1959), 11–29; and "Milton and Alexander More: New Documents," *Journal of English and Germanic Philology* 60 (1961), 796–807. See also his comments in *Milton and Science* (Cambridge, Mass.: Harvard University Press, 1956). During Milton's own time, the responses of his associates to his treatment of More in the *Defensio Secunda* are most illuminating; see *Milton Biography*, 1:451–52.

and applauding in a vacant theater," as he listened to the cries he engendered (*YP*, 4:1100, 1109). There is an eerie quality about this depiction: within the theatrical space of his own mental world, the blind polemicist, according to More, sits alone conjuring up a chorus of voices, of cries, whinnyings, brayings, through which he imagines the discomfiture of his adversary. The only sound to be heard, however, is Milton's own laughter and applause at the sounds he has created in his mind.

II

Whether Milton's theater of assault was in effect no more than a mental theater, he was absolutely convinced of the justness of his enterprise and felt assured that the collection of villainies and taunts with which he adorned his comedy first in the *Defensio Secunda* and then in the *Pro Se Defensio* would prove devastatingly effective. To assess the extent of its effectiveness, we need to entertain a willing suspension of disbelief and attempt to read Milton's discomfiture of More on its own terms. Those terms are founded upon the Miltonic notion of More's character. This character, Milton avers in the *Defensio Secunda* and in the *Pro Se Defensio*, is embodied in More's very name, *morus* or "fool" (*YP*, 4:565), one who will be accordingly treated according to his folly.[9] More's particular brand of folly is distinctly sexual: it is founded on sexual excess of the most profound sort. So excessive are More's escapades, in fact, that he becomes for Milton a veritable Priapus (*YP*, 4:631, 756). The association is hardly arbitrary. The son of Aphrodite and Dionysus, Priapus, as Milton was well aware, was customarily represented with a colossal penis.[10] The iconography of the penis is at the very heart of Milton's depiction of More as Priapus. From the perspective of both his parentage and his association with the phallus, Priapus recalls Milton's Comus with his magic wand. In either case, Priapus for Milton is a figure of lust and

9. In the *Fides Publica*, More returned the compliment and labeled Milton a "buffoon" engaged in the comic performance of his own theatrical production. More suggested that the *Defensio Secunda* be renamed *Antimorus* by one who is himself a *morus*. According to More, another title befitting the *Defensio Secunda* might well have been *Milton upon His Own Life* (*YP*, 4:1097).

10. See footnote references to Priapus in the *Defensio Secunda* and the *Pro Se Defensio*, in *YP*, 4:654 and 756, respectively.

debauchery.[11] In both Defenses, Milton's purpose is to unman More
by exposing him to ridicule. This Milton does in the most agressive
and indeed violent manner. Grasping hold of More's body, Milton
declares in the *Pro Se Defensio*: "See! I drag you out, violently by the
throat, reluctant as you are, into the sight of all, exposed to public
ridicule, a plague upon the people, in the church a boar, no less with
his tail [*cauda*] than with his slanting tusk [*dente*]" (*YP*, 4:746; *CM*,
9:116). In exposing to ridicule More's tail and his tusk, Milton deprives
his enemy of his sexuality, his virility, and his means of defending
himself.[12] So, one might suggest, Milton is finally able to "snatch"
Comus's wand.

Treating More as a fool according to his folly, Milton makes a
point of characterizing the kind of polemic he will bring to bear against
his enemy. Befitting this Comus-like Priapus, that polemic will be one
that portrays as graphically as possible the truly obscene nature of
More's escapades. Despite what others might think about the grossness
of his own depictions, Milton is perfectly comfortable with his polemic.
In the *Pro Se Defensio*, he stoutly defends what might be called the
"polemic of the penis." According to that polemic, the only way to
deal with one in whom is to be found "every vice and obscenity" is to
expose such foulness as frankly as possible: "He who describes you
and your villainies," Milton says to More, "must speak obscenely [*ne-
cesse est obscoena dicere*]." Such obscene speaking is totally in accord
with "the example of the gravest authors [*gravissimorum Authorum ex-
emplo defendissem*]. They have always thought that words unchaste and
plain thrust out with indignation signify not obscenity, but the vehemence of gravest censure [*non obscoenitatem, sed gravissimae repre-
hensionis vehementiam significare*]." Having ventured such assertions,
Milton cites a host of authorities, including Herodotus, Seneca, Suetonius, and Plutarch, among many others not only classical and biblical
but contemporary, to support his own polemical posture. All of them
had recourse to the polemic of the penis to counter the unchaste

11. More's affinity throughout with Milton's Comus may be seen in the contention that
More is a devotee of Cotytto, the goddess whom Comus celebrates in *A Mask*: "Hail goddess
of nocturnal sport, / Dark-vaild Cotytto, to' whom the secret flame / Of midnight torches
burns" (ll. 127–28). Comus, like More, is a priest of Cotytto. Milton also associates More, as
well as Vlacq, with Laverna, goddess of fraud and theft (see *Pro Se Defensio*, *YP*, 4:733).

12. Elsewhere in the *Pro Se Defensio*, Milton addresses More as follows: "Vile, prostituted
man, high priest of the stews. There is as much need for a buckle on your private parts, as
there is for one on your lips" (*YP*, 4:760).

habits of those "addicted to the penis [*penis deditos*]." As one most profoundly so addicted, More the fool, More the Priapus with his large, extended *cauda* must be unmanned, emasculated, exposed for the obscene "faun or naked satyr [*Fauno quovis aut nudo Satyro*]" he really is. Only in that way will his true nature and true offences come to light (*YP*, 4:743–45; *CM*, 9:108–11).

Milton had engaged in such defenses of his harsh polemic before, but never did he have the occasion to defend a polemic quite as gross and as violent as that which he employed against the Priapus of the *Lascivientis Mori hinnitus ad Pontiam.*[13] By means of this polemic, Milton invoked the various escapades of More in order to effect a sparagmos of the most extreme and brutal sort, certainly one as vicious as that launched against him in the *Clamor*. If the *Defensio Secunda* represents a signal instance of Milton's attempt to repristinate himself, his body and his character, it, along with its counterpart the *Pro Se Defensio*, also becomes the grand occasion for leaving the body and character of Alexander More mutilated and in shreds.

As suggested by Milton's catalogue of his enemy's indiscretions in the prologue to his attack, More both as man and as cleric had done much to cause himself shame. Milton was in possession of a good deal of information about More's sexual misadventures. They included some six or seven women with whom More became involved during an active career of debauchery.[14] Among these women, two in par-

---

13. For Milton's earlier defenses of his polemic, see, among other statements, the preface to *Animadversions upon the Remonstrants Defence, against Smectymnuus* (*YP*, 1:664; cf. *Apology* for Smectymnuus, *YP*, 1:894–95, 901–905). I treat this dimension at some length in Michael Lieb, "Milton's *Of Reformation* and the Dynamics of Controversy," in *Achievements of the Left Hand: Essays on the Prose of John Milton*, ed. Michael Lieb and John T. Shawcross (Amherst: University of Massachusetts Press, 1974). What Milton articulates in the *Pro Se Defensio*, however, is quite new. His justification of obscenity (the polemic of the penis) goes beyond anything else in the prose works.

14. See, in particular, Kester Svendsen's detailed notes to the *Pro Se Defensio*. Svendsen enumerates More's women as follows: "1) Claudia Pelletta (or Nicolarde Pelet) of Geneva; 2) Pontia of Leyden; 3) the heroine of the Tibaltiana; 4) perhaps the unknown maid whose fate is likened to Pontia's; 5) the strumpet of Amsterdam; 6) the widow; 7) the woman of Amsterdam who complained to the ecclesiastical authorities." Pontia is most certainly Elisabeth Guerret; the others can be identified with varying degrees of certainty. The official indictments against More include the "frequenting of brothels, imposture, and sodomy with one Herman Hendric de Doesburg of Amsterdam, in 1656. A repetition of this last offense with another boy in Middelburg in September, 1658, occasioned his [More's] arrest by the bailiff's deputy and his furtive withdrawal from Middelburg" (*YP*, 4:777–79). It is against Milton's own charges of such debauchery that More attempts to defend himself in the *Fides Publica* and *Supplementum*. In his assessment of More, Svendsen says dryly: "For it must be

ticular are the focus of Milton's attention in the *Defensio Secunda* and in the *Pro Se Defensio*.[15] They are one Claudia Pelletta (or Nicolarde Pelet) of Geneva and one Pontia (or Bontia) of Leyden, identified as Elisabeth Guerret, the maidservant of Madame Salmasius. Milton is unstinting in his scorn of More's treatment of these women.

Addressing our attention to them, we are made aware of one incontrovertible fact: the more we attempt to untangle the net of references Milton makes the more blurred the distinctions between them become. Claudia Pelletta (or Nicolarde Pelet) of Geneva becomes Pontia (or Bontia) of Leyden, that is, Elisabeth Guerret. Their identities, as well as their names, intermingle. We are thankful for the efforts of scholars in helping us keep them apart, but finally it matters little who is being tupped, where that tupping takes place, and precisely when it occurs. Our Priapus with his swollen member just seems to be everywhere: "In every bush, or under every tree; / Ther is noon other incubus but he," and as much as his victims may presume to "go safely up and doun," he "ne wol doon hem but dishonour." Claudia Pelletta, Nicolarde Pelet, Pontia, Bontia, Elisabeth Guerret: the litany of names rhymes and scans like a delightful refrain. Who can tell them apart or distinguish them by name? Who cares? They are all (or both) one, and Alexander More has tupped them all.[16]

For the sake of argument, we begin with Claudia Pelletta (or is it Nicolarde Pelet?) of Geneva. Alluded to by Milton in the *Defensio Secunda* simply as a certain maidservant of a host with whom More was residing at the time, this recently married young lady became the constant object of the amorous advances of our Priapus. Milton provides an account of their trysts in a manner tantamount to satisfying the curiosity of those whose inquiring minds want to know:

> The neighbors had often noticed that they entered all by themselves a certain summerhouse in the garden [*tuguriolum quoddam intrare hortuli*]. Not quite adultery [*adulterium*], you say. He could have done

---

admitted that with regard to the company of women he took little pains to mortify nature." Svendsen calls him a "belated Belial" in "Milton's *Pro Se Defensio* and Alexander More," p. 17.

15. For biographical accounts of More, see Peter Bayle, *The Dictionary of Mr. Peter Bayle*, 5 vols., 2d ed. (London, 1737), 4:271–76; and Archibald Bruce, *A Critical Account of the Life, Character, and Discourses of Mr. Alexander Morus* (London, 1813). Svendsen's full annotations to the *Pro Se Defensio* in the *YP*, as well as his articles, are a mine of information. Also of importance are Donald A. Roberts's annotations to the *Defensio Secunda* in the *YP*.

16. In the *Pro Se Defensio*, Milton does make a point of attempting to identify the objects of More's advances, see, for example, *YP*, 4:766.

anything else in the world. Certainly. He might have talked to her, no doubt about matters horticultural [*poterat confabulari nimirum de re hortensi*], or he might have drawn from the subject of gardens (say those of Alcinous or Adonis) certain of his lectures [*scoliae*] for this woman, who had perhaps a smattering of knowledge and a willing ear. He might now have praised the flower beds [*areolas laudere*], might have wished only for some shade [*umbram tantummodo desiderare*], were it possible merely to graft the mulberry on the fig [*licerat modo ficui morum inserere*], whence might come forth, with utmost speed, a grove of sycamores [*complures inde sycomoros quam citissime enasci*]—a very pleasant place to tread. He might then have demonstrated to his woman the method of grafting [*modum deinde insitionis mulieri poterat monstrare*]. These things and much else he could have done. Who denies it [*quis negat*]? (*YP*, 4:555–56; *CM*, 8:32)

Determined to make the most of this sordid little affair, Milton does all in his power to render it the object of scorn.[17] In his bathetic account, the summerhouse in the garden becomes a false paradise, a debased *hortus conclusus*. Into that *hortus* they "enter" (*intrare*) as a couple to find perfect bliss. Such an entrance, of course, is also a form of sexual penetration, one that More enacts upon the maidservant, whom he compromises without reservation. To highlight the ironies of the affair, Milton imbues his Latin with a multitude of double entendres. The idea of conversing (*confabulari*) is undermined by the nonsense (*fabulae*) that his *scoliae* contain. In any case, talking about "matters horticultural" is certainly something they did not do, unless it was preparatory to the penetration of the *hortus*, with its sweet *areola* or small garden bed, that became the object of his pursuit. As a result of that penetration, they learned together how to "graft the mulberry on the fig, whence might come forth, with utmost speed, a grove of sycamores." Implicit in this engrafting, to be sure, is that "union," that debased act of copulation, through which More both as fool

17. Milton elaborates further on the affair in the *Pro Se Defensio*: "There is a certain Claudia Pelletta, whom hereafter we shall call your mistress—I know not whether yours alone. When she was a maidservant in the house of an honorable man of Geneva, the same in which you were a most dishonorable guest, she was common to you, the footman, and the coachman. This poor woman, after she married, continued in adultery the commerce of lewdness which she had with you." As witnesses to the affair, Milton cites the gardener who saw More and the maidservant go into and come out of the garden cottage. There are other witnesses as well (*YP*, 4:756).

(*morus*) and as mulberry (*morum*) becomes one with the *ficus*, conceived here both as fig and as vagina. As a result of this union, little Mores, or "sycamores" burst forth.[18] Such is the method of engrafting More demonstrates to the maidservant in the garden.

Milton's depiction of More and the maidservant is fascinating not only on its own terms but for the larger contexts it implies. Alluding ironically to the gardens of Alcinous and Adonis, its portrayal of the false paradise inhabited by the debased couple looks forward to and becomes a perversion of the true *hortus* described so eloquently in *Paradise Lost*.[19] Reconceived there as the "blissful Bower" into which Adam and Eve retreat at nightfall to perform their "Rites / Mysterious of connubial Love" (4.689–775), the *tugurium* within the debased *hortus* of the polemical account suddenly assumes a new form. More and his maidservant thereby prefigure the Adam and Eve who appear before our eyes in naked splendor in the fourth book of Milton's epic (ll. 288–311). The anticipation of the entire scene throws into sharp contrast profane and sacred forms of paradisal conception, the first invoked to reinforce Milton's act of polemical debasement, the second to support his act of poetic idealization.

What particularly impresses us in the contrast between profane and sacred delineation is the extent to which the epic idealization of the unfallen couple so easily gives way to the obscene dimensions of the polemical rendering. A case in point is the apparently innocuous detail in the description of Eve as one whose tresses appeared "Dissheveld, but in wanton ringlets wav'd / As the Vine curls her tendrils, which impli'd / Subjection, but requir'd with gentle sway, / And by her yeilded, by him [Adam] best receiv'd, / Yeilded with coy submission, modest pride, / And sweet reluctant amorous delay" (4.304–11). It does not require an astute reader to see how those wanton ringlets and the subjection implied by the vine's curling of her tendrils find their counterpart in the activities that distinguish the obscene world inhabited by More and his maidservant. From the perspective of that world, we think immediately of the act of grafting the mulberry on

18. I am indebted to Roberts's notes to the passage in *YP*, 4:566, for this association. Other meanings of *ficus* can be found in *Latin Dictionary*. I have made use of this dictionary here as elsewhere in my treatment of the multiple meanings in Milton's Latin references.

19. For a brief account of the sources of Milton's references to the gardens of Alcinous and Adonis, see Roberts's notes to the passage in *YP*, 4:566. See *Paradise Lost* (1.446–52, 5.340–41, 9.439–41). Not only the Homeric and Ovidian background is at work here; the Spenserian background is at work too.

the fig and producing a grove of sycamores. Despite the sublimity of
the idealized world inhabited by Adam and Eve, the description of
them, their bodies, and their world is forever on the brink of "yielding"
to the debased environment we have come to associate with More and
his maidservant.

The polemicist and the poet in Milton are never far apart. It is,
after all, through Satan's eyes ("Saw undelighted all delight"; 4.286)
in Milton's epic that we view the unfallen couple in the first place.
Even in its epic context, such a viewing threatens to collapse the
depiction of those noble, naked creatures into something potentially
unsavory. We remember from Milton's depiction in the *Defensio Secunda* that we are invited to join those neighbors who often notice
how More and the maidservant enter that summerhouse "all by themselves." If inquiring minds want to know, that desire for knowledge
is amply, if perversely, rewarded in the prose tract. There, the demands of prurience are fully satisfied.

Milton's debasement of More can work both ways: in its desire to
distance itself from all that More represents, it must be constantly on
guard to keep itself in check, lest it suffer a similar fate. At some deep
level, Milton faced the prospect of implicating himself in the very
excesses with which he sought to castigate his opponent. Not that he
was actually guilty of such excesses; far from it. But thanks to an
almost obsessive preoccupation with and delight in the rehearsal of
More's sexual misadventures, Milton as voyeur became vulnerable. In
the *Fides Publica*, More charged Milton with being guilty of judging
the characters of other men from his own conduct and being "subject
to every vice" against which he inveighed (*YP*, 4:766). Outraged by
such castigations, Milton challenged his opponent to produce witnesses and evidence. Although More had neither the opportunity nor
the ability to do so, he did provide the occasion for Milton to protest
yet again what he found himself protesting so often throughout his
career, that is, his purity and chastity. For one who so delighted in
recounting detail the indiscretions of others, Milton was certainly at
pains to preserve against all possible onslaughts the abiding fact of
his own virginity.

His castigation of More's sexual misadventures with Claudia Pelletta extends even more graphically to More's relations with the so-
called Pontia (or Bontia) of Leyden, that is, Elisabeth Guerret. Initiated with gusto in the *Defensio Secunda*, this treatment is then further

developed in the *Pro Se Defensio*. We begin with the account in the *Defensio Secunda*. Although the accuracy of the chronology and circumstances narrated in the account is open to question, Milton as polemicist is concerned to establish cause and effect as simply and directly as possible.[20] When More arrived in Holland in 1649, he made it a point to visit Salmasius, at whose house More "cast lustful eyes" on Madame Salmasius's maid Pontia. After that initial visit, More, ever the opportunist, cultivated both Salmasius and Pontia. Winning Salmasius's confidence, More established a secret liaison with Pontia. What resulted was a sordid seduction, followed by a false promise of marriage.[21] "With this deluding hope," Milton observes, "he ruined her." As a result of this crime, "a minister of the holy gospel defiled even the house of his host" (*YP*, 4:568–69). Serving to heighten the low comedy of the affair, Milton's expression of mock outrage rounds out the first part of the account.

The second part of the account leads Milton into an extended, "metaphysical" speculation upon the outcome of the base copulation between More and Pontia. Cause gives rise to effect: "From the union resulted at length a marvellous and unnatural prodigy; not only the female but also the male conceived." Whereas Pontia gave birth to a little More, the father "conceived this empty wind-egg [*ovum hoc irritum & ventosum*], from which burst forth the swollen Cry of the King's Blood [*clamor regii sanguinis prorupit*]."[22] Portraying More's offspring as such a monster, Milton transforms his enemy's text (the *Clamor*) into an object of disgust and loathing. At first pleasant enough for the Royalists to suck on, the source of the *Clamor*, the egg itself, is (with its shell broken and its contents loosed) ultimately found to be "rotten and stinking [*vitiosum ac putridum*]," a thing that causes all to recoil in revulsion. As the offspring of More, the *Clamor* becomes the spawn of a corrupt and vile object, the *ovum*, traditionally viewed as

20. See Roberts's comments on the account in *YP*, 4:568, nn. 89–92.
21. Milton describes the pursuit and seduction ironically by alluding to the romance of Pyramus (More) and Thisbe (Pontia). With More and Pontia, Milton comments, there was "no need to seek a chink in the wall!" (*YP*, 4:569).
22. Compare Milton's account of Salmasius in the *Defensio Prima*. There, Milton portrays his adversary as Mount Salmasius (*Mons Salmasius*) in labor (*parturit*) and to be delivered of his offspring by a midwife: "There was reason in his being his wife's wife; watch out, ye mortals, for some monstrous birth [*foetum aliquem ingentem*]." But Milton concludes that there is little need to fear: "The mountain has really labored to bring forth this ridiculous mouse," that is, Salmasius's book. "Come all ye grammarians to help this grammarian in labor," for his work is only a grammar (*YP*, 4:454; *CM*, 7:348).

a source of spontaneous generation.[23] Such is the product of what Milton calls More's fetus (*foetu*), appropriately distended (*inflatus*) to produce these horrors (*YP*, 4:569–70; *CM*, 9:36).[24]

Portraying More and his offspring (his *Clamor*) in this manner, Milton adopts the occasion of More's relations with Pontia as a means of representing his enemy in bisexual terms. Underscoring that representation, Milton associates his act of gender transformation with the myth of Hermaphroditus as related by Ovid in the *Metamorphoses*. According to this myth, Hermaphroditus, the son of Hermes and Aphrodite, was pursued by the water nymph Salmacis. While he was wading in the spring she inhabited, he was attacked by her and proved unable to free himself from her grasp. He could not escape her amorous embraces. As she held him, she appealed to the gods: "May no day ever come / To separate us!" The gods heard her prayer, "And the two bodies seemed to merge together, / One face, one form. As when a twig is grafted / On parent stock, both knit, mature together, / So these two joined in close embrace, no longer / Two beings, and no longer man and woman, / But neither, and yet both" (4.283–389).[25] Such, according to Ovid, was the sad fate of Hermaphroditus in his enforced union with Salmacis.

Drawing upon the myth of Hermaphroditus and Salmacis, Milton extends his representation of More in bisexual terms to embrace the relationship between More and Salmasius. That relationship, Milton avers, is of a distinctly bisexual sort: it fulfills the expectations of those familiar with the story of Hermaphroditus and his transformation as a result of his union with the nymph Salmacis. Associating Salmasius with Salmacis through a comic pun, Milton observes: "Meanwhile, Salmasius, with a fate like that of Salmacis (for like the name, so too the fable is apt enough), unaware that in More he had associated with himself a hermaphrodite, as fit to give

23. Milton had used the wind-egg as polemical symbol on other occasions in his works, and the object was part of the pseudo-scientific lore of the Middle Ages and Renaissance. For a discussion of the background and significance of the wind-egg, see Svendsen, *Milton and Science*, pp. 141–43.

24. Centered in this role reversal of the male figure as a source of debased generation is a concept familiar to us with the begetting of Sin in *Paradise Lost*. Many of the elements we have come to associate with the epic account are already present in the prose tract. The springing forth of Sin, followed by that of Death and the Hell Hounds, is accompanied by a cry, a clamor of the most perverse sort (2.746–814).

25. References to Ovid are from *Metamorphoses*, trans. Rolfe Humphries (Bloomington: Indiana University Press, 1955).

birth as to beget [*tam gignendi, quam pariendi compotem*], ignorant too of what More had begotten in his home, fondled what he had brought forth, that book in which he found himself so often called 'the great' (in his own estimation just praise, perhaps, but foolish and absurd in the opinion of others)." To make certain that the book would see the light of day, Salmasius in turn found a printer (Vlacq), who agreed to act as midwife "in bringing to birth these encomia [*iis etiam divulgandis obstetricatur atque subservit*] or rather these rank flatteries of himself, which he had anxiously solicited from More and others" (*YP*, 4:571; *CM*, 8:38).[26]

In Milton's reinscription of the myth of Hermaphroditus and Salmacis, the events of the original Ovidian narrative are completely transformed and perverted. To begin with, the roles are effectively reversed: Hermaphroditus is no longer the innocent one victimized by the advances of an aggressive Salmacis. Already bisexual, More takes advantage of an unsuspecting Salmasius. As a result of this ironic rereading of Ovid, the original story is transformed into a sordid little

---

26. This is hardly Milton's first use of the myth of Hermaphroditus to defame his opponent. The very terms of his allusion to the myth in the *Defensio Secunda* are anticipated in the *Defensio Prima*. There, Milton attacks Salmasius's masculinity by associating him with Salmacis of the Ovidian source. In fact, he has Salmasius undergoing a veritable metamorphosis into Salmacis, "attempting by his fountain of false tears distilled by lamplight to draw the strength from manly hearts." Milton then cites Ovid's *Metamorphoses* (4.285–86) to demonstrate his point: "Lest wicked Salmacis should sap one's strength with waters strong to harm, / And he who came a man should leave unmanned, touched by the water's melting charm" (*YP*, 4:312; *CM*, 7:20). The *Defensio Secunda* extends and elaborates this act of bisexual gendering by including More in the transformation.

What Milton could not have known at the time of writing the *Defensio Prima* (or the *Defensio Secunda*, for that matter) is how much Salmasius would take offense at the Hermaphroditus-Salmacis allusion. Milton's association of Salmasius with Salmacis must have truly enraged the old adversary, for it becomes something of an obsession in Salmasius's *Ad Iohannem Miltonum Responsio, Opus Posthumus*. Calling Milton a "pigmy in stature," Salmasius maintains that not he but Milton is the nymph Salmacis, for the Italians did not believe him "to be a man": "They praised you indeed for the handsomeness of your form, and wrote verses to the effect that you would be Angelic, and not Anglic only, if your piety corresponded with your beauty. Who more deserves the name of a Salmacis than he who arrogates to himself what is special to women, and makes a boast of his beauty as his single endowment, who has even maligned his own engraver in published verses for having represented him as less beautiful than he really thought himself?" (cited in *Life of Milton*, 6:208–10).

Milton's reputation as "Lady" obviously followed him well into his career. The Vossius-Heinsius correspondence later intensifies the disparaging outlook reflected here. "In January 1653 Vossius learned (correctly) that Salmasius was planning to brand Milton as a catamite during his Italian journey." Replying from Italy to this putative allegation, Heinsius added fuel to the fire: Salmasius's statement "that his adversary sold his buttocks to Italians is pure calumny.... In fact, that Englishman was hated by the Italians, among whom he lived for a long time, because of his over-strict morals" (*Milton Biography*, 2:1027; *Life Records*, 3:316–20).

tale of sexual duplicity involving not only gender reversals but debased procreation. In More's pursuit of Salmasius, male pursues male. But as Hermaphroditus, More in the form of male/female pursues one who is also hermaphroditic (Salmasius as Salmacis). Here, the relationship is one of bisexual with bisexual. Compounding this perversion is that having to do with procreation. As Salmacis, Salmasius is unaware not only of his lover's bisexual gender but of his ability both to beget and to give birth to new offspring.

Considering the extent to which the whole issue of gender identity and gender reversals is significant to Milton's outlook, the articulation of these concerns in the present context once again refocuses the question of gender. In that act of refocusing, we must include the figure of Alexander More and the More-Salmasius "affair" as yet an additional dimension in our examination of Milton's sense of self-identity, his understanding of who and what he is, how he views himself in relation to the world, and how he sets about to establish his standing and selfhood in the face of those who would question his identity. The castigation of More's sordid affairs provides Milton the occasion to bring all these issues to the fore. If this is the form such castigations assume in the *Defensio Secunda*, they are no less compelling when rearticulated in the *Pro Se Defensio*. There, the More-Pontia relationship is pursued with renewed vigor.

At issue in the *Pro Se Defensio* is what transpired at More's final meeting with Pontia November 1652. Apparently, the episode, along with More's other affairs, was humiliating enough to have been chronicled in the literary correspondence of the day. In keeping with his own polemical purposes, Milton alters the particulars of the episode, which he relates in a manner to suggest a mock-epic battle. He portrays this battle in a way that gives free reign to his flair for the theatrical. In fact, what Milton creates in this portrayal is tantamount once again to a theater of assault. Within this theater, we behold to our great delight and edification a five-act drama in which More and Pontia undergo an *agon* that appropriately results in the undoing, indeed, mutilation of Alexander More.

The first act presents the occasion of the encounter of More and Pontia. They meet at Salmasius's house to discuss their future plans. Whereas Pontia is there to set a day for the wedding, More arrives to renounce his ties. With the second act, the battle commences. When Pontia perceives that More intends to dissolve the marriage pact made in the seduction, she, "impatient of such an injury," flies furiously at his "face and eyes with nails unpared [*in faciem tibi atque oculos, non sectis unguibus*]." With a reputation of being both *altier* and *feroculus*, the haughty, insolent, but finally effeminate More is one known to be equipped with his own "dreadful nails," which he does not hesitate to use for his protection (*terribiles ungues ad tui tutelam haberes*).[27] At the ready for the "womanish battle" that is to ensue, More prepares himself with nails extended, "quite in accordance," Milton ironically observes, with his "manly nature" (*pro virili tua parte ad foemineum hoc genus pugnae te comparas*). Presiding over the battle stands Juno Salmasia "as the umpire of the contest."[28] The fate of nations hangs in the balance. In the third act, the scene shifts to Salmasius, who is portrayed as lying ill with the gout in an adjoining chamber. Despite his illness, however, he nearly dies with laughter as he hears the battle begin.

The fourth act describes the battle itself. Poor More never has a chance. Overcome by the superior force of his Amazon-like opponent, this unwarlike Alexander (*imbellis Alexander*) falls defeated.[29] "Having already met with the lower parts [*Illa inferiorem nacta*]," she attacks "the upper parts of the man," including the forehead and the eyebrows and the nose (*in frontem & supercilia nasumque hominis*). With "strange arabesques [*miris capreolis*]," she inscribes her workmanship over the whole face of the prostrate warrior. "Never," declares Milton, "were the designs of Pontia [*lineamenta Pontiae*]" less pleasing to More. Completely "engraved on each border of the cheeks [*margine genarum, scriptus*]," More attempts with difficulty to rise up. "But be not aggrieved," Milton consoles More; "you that have been made a man down to the finishing touch of the sculptor's nail [*homo ad unguem*

27. Earlier in the *Pro Se Defensio* (*YP*, 4:727), Milton mentions More's reputation for being *altier*, a characteristic that apparently distinguished his deportment on many occasions. The effeminacy implicit in *altier* and *feroculus*, moreover, is reinforced by the references to More's nails, a detail John Diodati cites in his letter to Salmasius of May 9, 1648, and ironically included as a testimonial by More in his *Fides Publica*. Diodati says, *qui ne provoque point, mais aussi qui a de terribles ergots pour se defendre* (*YP*, 4:1112). Milton made the most of those "ergots."

28. Compare More's own references to Madame Salmasius as a Juno in the *Supplementum* to the *Fides Publica* (*YP*, 4:1120). In *Defensio Prima*, Milton has a great time poking fun at Salmasius as a husband ruled by a shrewish wife. As might be expected, his punning borders on the obscene (*YP*, 4:428; *CM*, 7:280).

29. Milton's actual references are a good deal more complex in their allusiveness than this summary suggests. See Roberts's comments in *YP*, 4:748, n. 120. Much of Roberts's discussion is based upon the findings of Svendsen.

factus]; you are no longer a mere professor, but a Doctor Pontificius; for by right you had been able, so to speak, to have written on the engraved tablet: 'This is Pontia's work [*picta tabula scripsisse*, Pontia fecit].' " So elaborately inscribed with Pontia's handiwork, More's face becomes a text, indeed a codex, "on which the avenging Pontia has set down her arguments with a new stilus [*stilo novo*]." His face is replete with her mournful ciphers. Thus the fourth act draws to a close with the transformation of More's face into a new and radiant work of art.

With the completion of the fourth act, the fifth and final act is one in which Milton, triumphantly addressing his opponent, recounts the aftermath of More's undoing. "Then, More, 'with face in tatters [*facia non integra*],' you snatched yourself away home," where you found yourself suddenly to be "much more deeply lettered [*multo literatior*]." At home, "you also hide yourself, so that you may be said to be a man of recondite letters [*reconditae literaturae*]." Do not hide yourself so, Milton implores; "show us your face, preacher, ancient indeed and venerable with furrows [*rugis venerandum*]. Why do you wish to be apocryphal [*cur apocryphus vis esse*]? since with Pontia herself as pontiff, you are now wholly canonical and rubricated [*canonicus iam maxime sis & rubricatus*]."[30] In short, with these new inscriptions on his face, More may be viewed as a venerable and wholly acceptable text, welcomed and embraced by all (*YP*, 4:747–50; *CM*, 9:120–22). Such in brief is the theater of assault through which Milton recounts in mock-epic terms the mutilation of his enemy. For Milton both as individual and polemicist, the implications of this event are signficant indeed.

Of central importance is Milton's rendering of the event itself. As is made apparent in the theater of assault through which that rendering is dramatized, the event is conceived in the most brutal, not to mention humiliating, form one can possibly imagine. Although contemporary accounts of the event suggest something of the comic violence underlying the encounter, Milton pushes such violence to

---

30. As Roberts points out, Milton's Latin is replete with puns on engraving and clawing. "Thus *lineamenta* means both the features of Pontia and the designs she cut into More's face." Echoes of both Horace and Martial lurk in the background. "*Novo stile* suggests new style as well as new stilus." "*Litteratior* means lettered or learned, but also branded, or even stigmatized." "*Apocryphal, canonical*, and *rubricated* refer at once to More's irregular religious opinions and to the list of his works given in *Fides Publica* [*YP*, 4:1104] (*YP*, 4:748–49, n. 121).

the extreme.[31] Taking his cue from the suggestion of More's reputation as one equipped with "dreadful nails" that he does not hesitate to use for his protection, Milton portrays his adversary in exceedingly effeminate terms. If More is *altier* and *feroculus*, his haughtiness and insolence are here entirely undermined in the "womanish battle" that ensues. He is, in short, once again unmanned, here by a feminine force, an Amazon, whose fingernails are more powerful than those of her lover-become-enemy. In this woman's world (a world of "feminine rule") presided over by the goddess Juno Salmasia, More is entirely at a loss. Pontia with her talons prevails, and More never has a chance to redeem himself, to reclaim any manhood he might otherwise have possessed. With his face in tatters, he may no longer appear to the world with that pride and ostentation he once was able to claim. He becomes a thing, a humiliating product of Pontia's making. His *sparagmos* deprives him of any claims to his former self, his former identity as he at least might wish to have it known.

Reconceived ironically in textual terms, More becomes a *picta tabula* upon which is inscribed the fate of his own undoing. He becomes a text that has undergone not simply deconstruction but complete and absolute mutilation, a new work with a *stile novo* that proclaims triumphantly the fact of his degendered self. No longer a threat to anyone (and therefore a text to which no one would take exception), this "venerable" codex is best consigned to oblivion, unworthy to be considered of consequence to any discerning reader. Both as man and as text, More finds himself mutilated, dismembered, in tatters, and completely neutered. This is Milton's final response to the indignities he has sustained at the hands of the putative author of the *Clamor*. Such a response, one might suggest, says at least as much about the victor as the victim.

---

31. The Vossius-Heinsius correspondence provides its own detailed account of the episode, which is conceived as comically but not brutally violent; *Life Records*, 3:278. In the *Mercurius Politicus* (no. 121, September 23–30, 1652, pp. 1907–10), there appeared the following distich: *Galli e Concubitu Gravidam Te, Pontia, Mori / Quis bene moratam, morigeramque neget?* (*Life Records*, 3:252). Milton cites the distich in the *Defensio Secunda*. The translation given in *YP* captures the puns as much as possible: "Who, Pontia, would deny that you, with child by Gallic More, / Are mor-ally pure and More-obliging?" (*YP*, 4:570). As a source of Continental gossip about More and Pontia, the distich enjoyed wide currency. In the *Fides Publica*, More made a frantic attempt to defend his behavior, impugn that of Madame Salmasius, and claim the unflinching support of Salmasius himself (*YP*, 4:1119–20).

III

To understand just what is implied by the relationship between victor and victim in the Miton-More scenario, we need to recall once again Milton's own reputation as the Lady, a reputation bestowed upon him by others which he himself acknowledged as an aspect of his personality from his earliest days. Based upon his own self-presentation, this reputation underscored his outlook at the very point that he was proclaiming his manhood, indeed his willingness and ability "to handle or unsheathe a sword" with which he boasted himself "equal to anyone." In defense of his Domina-like self-presentation, several Miltonic disclaimers come to mind and in fact are given new meaning in light of the scorn More must face as a result of *his* reputation for being *altier* and *feroculus*. We recall the protestations of the *altier* and *feroculus* Milton in the *Apology* for Smectymnuus: "These reasonings, together with a certaine niceness of nature, an honest haughtinesse, and self-esteem either of what I was, or what I might be, (which let envie call pride) and lastly that modesty, whereof . . . I may be excus'd to make some beseeming profession, all these uniting the supply of their naturall aide together, kept me still above those low descents of mind, beneath which he must deject and plunge himself, that can agree to salable and unlawfull prostitutions" (*YP*, 1:890). If Alexander More is the Miltonic other of the Defenses, this is certainly an other Milton must kill with as much scorn and ferocity as he can muster. I have spoken of Milton's adopting the occasion of those tracts to exorcise the unclean spirit of his enemy. Accompanied by an appropriate sparagmos, such exorcism occurs here as much with respect to the More-Pontia affair as it does anywhere else in Milton's Defenses.

As a result of this final brutalizing of More, Milton succeeds in doing to his enemy what he feels has been enacted upon his own body. Especially as it focuses upon the face as a sign of bodily wholeness, Milton's sensitivity to this enactment is no fantasy. Given Milton's brutal and indeed gruesome delight in the tearing asunder of More's face, this act of "defacement" assumes particular cogency in light of More's earlier statements regarding Milton's own face in the *Fides Publica*. In those statements, More ironically implicates himself in an act of "defacement" at the very point of proclaiming his innocence in ever having intended to do so. Although his disclaimer emphasizes his putative ignorance of Milton's blindness before he learned of it in the *Defensio Secunda*, his comments range significantly over Milton's entire face, which More succeeds "delicately" in defacing feature by feature:

> Neither is it possible to assert that other invidious opinion—that I reproached you with your blindness, as you covertly and less distinctly, but vehemently and almost tragically complain. Indeed, I can declare that I did not know that you had lost your eyesight before I read it in your book. For if by chance anything presented itself which seemed to point in that direction, I ascribed it to the blindness of your mind. See how wicked you are by reason of your zeal until you accomplish that which you wish. Never, I would have you know, have I discussed your *eyes*, since you see even that which nowhere exists; nor your *brow*, on which, like the sky on Atlas, your Commonwealth seemed to rest; nor your *nose*, which you turn up at all the best things; nor your wretched *tongue*, which you employ in the abuse of good men; nor your *teeth*, which you so often wish to sink into the fragile, but break off upon the solid.

Why, then, More concludes, "would I reproach you with blindness, who did not even know you are blind, or with deformity, who even believed you handsome, especially after I saw that elegant poem prefixed to your Poems?" At the very point of issuing this disclaimer, the disingenuous More cannot refrain from mocking Milton's most vital parts: "Yet, to be sure, you do have *eyes*, removable ones, like those of the Lamiae," which "blind self-love / And pride lifting its empty head too high" shut at home, when they have spitefully examined everything abroad (*YP*, 4:1103; italics mine).

This particular passage, we might suggest, accounted in large part for Milton's brutalizing of More's face in the *Pro Se Defensio*. After that act of brutalization, Milton, referring to the passage, says to More: "You reproach me with Cyclopsean blindness; and, what is more impudent, in the very act of denying that you did this, you do it again" by alluding to my eyes as "removable and witch's eyes." Centered on the figure of the Cyclops as the most repugnant of all blind, mutilated figures, Milton's outrage at his own defacement, his sparagmos at the hands of the effeminate More, reverberates throughout his final two Defenses and culminates here. Compounding the Cyclopsean insult is that which depicts the eyes as removable, like those of the Lamiae, a reference that once again underscores Milton's own vulnerability in response to attacks upon that feature which he is at greatest pains to defend.[32]

Such an act of defacement is only one aspect of More's attack. Addressing Milton's face feature by feature, More concretizes his attack by focusing upon what amounts to Milton's own poem of self-commentary prefixed to the William Marshall portrait that served as the frontispiece to the 1645 edition of Milton's poems.[33] Later entitled *In Effigiei Ejus Sculptorem*, this sardonic epigram (written in Greek) ostensibly ridicules the engraver but in fact comments on Milton's intense concern with his own appearance before the world at large.[34] Alluding to this poem in the very act of engaging in his defacement of Milton is a brilliant stroke on More's part, because it points up the highly self-reflexive quality of Milton's epigram. As one who is in his own way *altier*, Milton is very much concerned here as elsewhere with his facial beauty. Portraying Pontia as an "engraver" of More's face, Milton in a sense seeks vengeance upon his enemy in a manner that recalls his own distaste for the Marshall engraving. In that way, Milton repays his defacement with a corresponding defacement of More.

Attempting in the *Pro Se Defensio* to explain (and therefore justify) his response to the Marshall portrait, Milton is at pains to set the record straight: "If, at the suggestion and solicitation of a bookseller, I suffered myself to be crudely engraved by an unskillful engraver [*imperito Scalptori*] because there was no other in the city at that time,

---

32. For the basis of the allusion, see, among other works, Edward Topsell, *Historie of Serpents* (London, 1608), pp. 452–54, which describes Jupiter's bestowal upon Lamia "exemptile eyes that might be taken in and out at her pleasure" (*YP*, 4:750, n. 124). Svendsen explores additional sources (such as Plutarch's *Moralia* and Gesner's *Historia Animalium*) in *Milton and Science*, pp. 185–86.

33. Appearing before the portrait engraving of Milton in the 1645 edition of Milton's poems, *In Effigiei Eius Sculptorem* was reprinted (with the Latin title but without the engraving) in the 1673 editon. For comments on the poem, see Thomas O. Mabbott, "Milton's '*In Effigiei Eius Sculptorem*,' " *Explicator* 8 (1950), item 58, as well as the entry on the epigram in *Milton Encyclopedia*, 4:96–97. Milton's criticism of Marshall extends as well to the comments on the frontispiece to the *Eikon Basilike* as "the conceited portraiture before his Book, drawn out to the full measure of a Masking Scene, and sett there to catch fools and silly gazers" (*YP*, 4:342). See Masson's comments in *Life of Milton*, 4:135–36. Milton is also critical of Marshall in *Tetrachordon* (*YP*, 2:583).

34. As translated in the Shawcross edition, the epigram appears as follows: "This image [*eikona*] was drawn by an untaught hand, / you might perhaps say, looking at the form of the original [*eidos autophues*]. / But since here you do not recognize the modelled face [*ektupoton*], friends, / laugh at a bad imitation by a worthless artist."

that fact argues me rather more unwilling to trouble myself with matters of that kind than too fastidious, as you object [*id me neglexisse potius eam rem arguebat, cujus tu mihi nimium cultum objicis*]" (*YP*, 4:750– 51; *CM*, 9:124). Just the opposite is true. As More was well aware, Milton's fastidiousness (*cultum*) is precisely what is at issue here. His defensiveness does little but lend further credence to a reading that attributes to Milton a heightened sense of fastidiousness (however ironically projected) in response to an engraving the poet feels does not do his appearance appropriate justice. It is within the context of these concerns, finally, that Milton's brutal defacement of More must be understood.

I began my treatment of the concept of staging the body in the final two Miltonic Defenses from the perspective of the *Regii Sanguinis Clamor ad Coelum Adversus Parricidas Anglicanos*. That work provided the impetus for what might be considered the most revelatory of Milton's sense of self, his need to protect his body and his reputation from the onslaughts of an alien world. Moving from the arena of international politics established in the *Clamor* to the highly, in fact, painfully personal confines of his own world, Milton responded in his final two Defenses to what he construed as the theater of his undoing by an anonymous author, in effect, an anonymous playwright. Upon this playwright, Milton in his darkness was determined to bestow a local habitation and a name. Dismembered in the theater of assault by an adversary who refused to divulge his identity, Milton forged an identity for him and then proceeded to enact a sparagmos upon it in almost ritual fashion within his own theater of assault. The international stage of Charles's undoing became the domestic stage of the undoing of a *morus*, a satyrlike Priapus, humiliated, mutilated, emasculated, transformed into a new being deprived of self, identity, bodily integrity, and wholeness.

If this *morus*, this fool, is the Miltonic other that must be exorcised and destroyed in an act of self-purification, the devastation involved in such an act is not simply the result of a desire to "get even." Rather, it represents, as we have seen, the counterpart of a corresponding act of self-repristination, a remaking the self within that world of darkness, the theater of bodily deprivation and pain, in which the seer (despite his misgivings, his self-doubts, his sense of guilt for having been struck blind) creates himself anew. Such, I would argue, is the psychic drama encoded in the final two Defenses.

As we see in the chapter that concludes this book, that drama finds a final and indeed consummate poetic expression in the biblical theater of assault Milton creates for it in *Samson Agonistes*. In our exploration of Milton's sparagmatic mentality, it is to this dramatic poem that we now attend.

Conclusion: The Politics of Violence

I

William Riley Parker observes that at some point in 1652–53 Milton may have continued work on an "unfinished *Samson Agonistes*" begun possibly some six or seven years earlier. "No other literary design, not even *Paradise Lost*," suggests Parker, "could have had more relevance for him in this period of personal crisis. Samson's plight was more than ever his own plight. If Milton, too, could achieve fortitude, could find renewed strength, could glimpse with sightless eyes God's final use of him, all might be well. The working out of the drama was, in a sense, the working out of his own problem." Parker even goes so far as to suggest that a draft of the tragedy might have been completed before September 1653.[1] To assert that such observations are conjectural is

1. *Milton Biography*, 1:432. For Parker's argument concerning the inception of *Samson*, see 1:313–21. Additional discussion of dating is to be found in 2:903–17. See also Parker's other studies, including "The Date of *Samson Agonistes*," *Philological Quarterly* 28 (1949), 145–66; and "The Date of *Samson Agonistes* Again," in *Calm of Mind: Tercentenary Essays on "Paradise Regained" and "Samson Agonistes" in Honor of John S. Diekhoff*, ed. Joseph Anthony Wittreich, Jr. (Cleveland: The Press of Case Western Reserve, 1971), pp. 163–74. Of corresponding importance is Allen H. Gilbert, "Is *Samson Agonistes* Unfinished?" *Philological Quarterly* 28 (1949), 98–106; and John T. Shawcross, "The Chronology of Milton's Major Poems," *PMLA* 76 (1961), 345–58.

certainly to venture an understatement. Parker himself is very much aware of the provisional nature of his suggestions, and there has been as much convincing argument for the later, traditional, dating of *Samson* as there has been the earlier one.[2] Despite all the debate concerning such matters, I still do not think it possible to know conclusively either when the work was written or what the immediate occasion of its composition was. At this time, I am frankly uncertain whether the problem will ever be resolved.

Having issued this disclaimer, I nonetheless wish to place *Samson Agonistes* in the context of the period of the Defenses. I do so not to argue for categorical dates of composition through which to determine the political and biographical circumstances underlying the action of Milton's drama. (If the drama as finally published were in fact revised at various times during Milton's career, the attempt to "fix" it at any given juncture is moot in any case.[3]) Rather, I adopt such a position in order to propose an interpretive hypothesis: assuming for the sake of argument that Samson (possibly at some stage of its composition, retrospectively or otherwise) encodes the struggles of this critical period, what then are the implications of such an assumption? Proceeding on that assumption through a willing suspension of disbelief, I explore *Samson* as the expression of Milton's attempt to deal in poetic form with the crisis that faced him during the time the Defenses were produced. To approach *Samson* in this way will at once deepen our understanding of the impact of sparagmos upon Milton's thought and provide interpretive closure to the discussion of this phenonenon undertaken both in the previous three chapters and in the book as a whole.

To pursue this line of thought, it would be appropriate to remind ourselves of the extent to which Samson assumed a political presence in Milton's prose works from the period of the antiprelatical tracts through the period of the Defenses, that is, from the early 1640s to

2. See in particular the arguments of Mary Ann Radzinowicz in *Toward "Samson Agonistes": The Growth of Milton's Mind* (Princeton: Princeton University Press, 1978), esp. pp. 387–407; and Ernest Sirluck, "Milton's Idle Right Hand," *Journal of English and Germanic Philology* 60 (1961), 749–85, esp. the Appendix to the article. As Radzinowicz notes, four dates have been proposed by twentieth-century Miltonists for the composition of *Samson Agonistes*: 1640–41, 1647–53, 1660–61, and 1667–70.

3. If the drama as finally published were in fact revised at various times during Milton's career, the attempt to "fix" it at any given juncture is moot in any case. Sirluck's dismissive arguments to the contrary, I find Gilbert's arguments really compelling here.

the early 1650s. Recalling this fact reinforces the idea of Milton's own inclination to politicize Samson, especially during that tumultuous period.[4] Such an approach is hardly without precedent. The inclination to embed *Samson* in the politics of a given period has a long history. Critics tend to read the political dimensions of Milton's drama according to their interpretations of the events arising from the times through which they would contextualize it. Two of the most important studies of *Samson Agonistes* within the past two decades have approached Milton's drama from this perspective. Although each study has its own agenda, both have made clear the significance of an approach that takes into account not just the political dimensions of Samson but in particular those aspects that reflect the period between the early 1640s and the early 1650s.

As an aspect of her masterly study of the emergence of the Samson narrative in Milton's developing sensibility, Mary Ann Radzinowicz has plotted the course of Milton's incorporation of Samson into his political outlook. Arguing that Milton's drama is the culmination of his entire career, Radzinowicz explores the political underpinnings of *Samson* in order to demonstrate that, as she maintains, the work is very much a "political document."[5] Approaching *Samson Agonistes* from an entirely different perspective, Joseph Wittreich offers a cogent and indeed brilliant reading of the revolutionary culture of the period in question to make clear the fact that *Samson* "is a poem of, and partly about, the Puritan Revolution: it has its deepest roots in that experience and is, in the largest sense, an emanation of the spirit of its age."[6] Whatever its date of composition, it is no longer possible

4. It hardly needs to be reiterated that most of Milton's direct allusions in his prose tracts to Samson occur during this critical period. The notebook jottings in the Trinity College Manuscript provide further evidence of the extent of his interest in Samson as a subject for poetic reenactment (*CM*, 18:236).

5. Radzinowicz, *Toward "Samson Agonistes"*, p. 117. See in particular the discussion on the political dimensions of the drama, pp. 71–86, 111–79. See also her important essay, "*Samson Agonistes* and Milton the Politician in Defeat," *Philological Quarterly* 44 (1965), 454–71.

6. Joseph Wittreich, Jr., *Interpreting "Samson Agonistes"* (Princeton: Princeton University Press, 1986), p. 218. Arguing against a regenerationist reading of *Samson*, Wittreich explores in depth the Miltonic allusions to the Samson narrative not only during the period in question but throughout Milton's career. More than that, Wittreich reconstructs the political climate in which the figure of Samson became a focal point of attention among Milton's contemporaries (see, in particular, pp. 174–238, 296–328). On the regenerationist question Wittreich confronts, see also the important essays in *Calm of Mind*. For a discussion of the figure of Samson as a culture hero in the seventeenth century, see Jackie DiSalvo, " 'The Lord's Battells': *Samson Agonistes* and the Puritan Revolution," *Milton Studies* 4 (1972), 39–62.

to divorce *Samson* from the political circumstances out of which it arises.

In an earlier exploration of the political dimensions of *Samson*, I sought in particular to contextualize the drama through an analysis of the significance of "strength" as a phenomenon in Milton's thought. Such an undertaking involved the attempt to demonstrate in part how extensively Milton drew upon the Samson narrative in Judges 13–16 in order to reinforce his evolving political point of view.[7] As early as *The Reason of Church-Government* (1642), Milton adopted the narrative of Samson to construct an allegory of the way the strength of king and commonwealth is liable to be undermined by prelatical enemies bent on pursuing their own ends. At the forefront of the allegory is the figure of "that mighty Nazarite *Samson*." Disciplined from his birth in the Nazaritical precepts and practices that would keep him strong, Samson "grows up to a noble strength and perfection with those his illustrious and sunny locks the laws waving and curling about his godlike shoulders." As long as he keeps his locks about him "undiminisht and unshorn," his strength remains intact: "he may with the jaw-bone of an Asse, that is, with the word of his meanest officer suppresse and put to confusion thousands of those that rise against his just power" (cf. Judg. 15:15–16). But the moment he succumbs to the Delilah-like "strumpet flatteries of Prelats," they "wickedly shaving off all those bright and waighty tresses of his laws, and just prerogatives which were his ornament and strength," he is blinded and made to grind in the prison house of his Philistian prelates. Even this situation is not irremediable, however. Recalling that Samson experienced renewed strength with the growth of his hair even after he had fallen (cf. Judg. 16:22), Milton foresees the nourishing again of the "puissant hair" ("the golden beames of Law and Right") of his allegorical Samson, whose locks "sternly shook, thunder with ruin upon the heads of those his evil counsellors," although, Milton concedes, "not without great affliction to himselfe" (*YP*, 1:858–859; cf. Judg. 19:28–30).

In his allegorical depiction of the prelatical attempt to undermine king and commonwealth, Milton focuses on both the solar and the

---

7. The following summary is drawn from the chapter "The Theology of Strength," in Michael Lieb, *The Sinews of Ulysses: Form and Convention in Milton's Works* (Pittsburgh: Duquesne University Press, 1989), pp. 117–20; the entire chapter (pp. 98–138) is relevant to the present undertaking.

Nazaritical dimensions of Samson's strength as manifested in the un-shorn hair. From the solar perspective, Milton calls upon the com-monplace association of Samson as sun figure (*shemesh*) whose strength and authority are resplendent in "those bright and waighty tresses of his laws." When he betrays his solar authority and his "sunny locks" are cut, he is left in darkness: "those Philistims put out the fair, and farre-sighted eyes of his natural discerning." The solar perspective, in turn, is reinforced by the Nazaritical. From this perspective, Milton invokes that dimension of the narrative in which strength assumes a cultic bearing. As ceremonially sacred, strength becomes the distin-guishing feature of one who as Nazarite is set apart or separated (*nazir*) to God, and thereby crowned with the blessings of God. As Nazarite, Samson is crowned with the strength that resides in his locks. With the violation of his Nazarate, Samson loses this distinguishing regal feature: the "prelatical rasor" berefts him of "his wonted might." From both the solar and the Nazaritical perspectives, however, Samson's strength returns. Newly empowered, he sternly shakes "the golden beames of Law and Right," with devastating results to those who misled him (and, by extension, with unavoidable affliction on himself). The foregoing political allegory demonstrates the extent to which Milton was inclined to draw upon the Samson narrative as an ex-emplum of the nature of divine strength, its unfortunate loss and its eventual triumphant (if devastating) resuscitation. As medium of di-vine empowerment, strength, in Milton's interpretation of the Samson narrative, assumes a mythical (solar) and a sacred (cultic) bearing, both of which contribute to Milton's delineation of political power and prelatical corruption in *The Reason of Church-Government*.

Milton's antiprelatical tract, however, is not the only example of the politicization of Samson as a symbol of divine power. The ref-erence in *Areopagitica* has been cited so often as to be almost legion. For our purposes, its importance resides in the additional emphasis it places upon renewed strength as in effect restorative in its force. Once again, the figure of Samson is invoked to reinforce a political statement. In this case, it is Milton's vision of a resuscitated England imbued with that Reformation fervor Milton sees stirring in his com-patriots who have cast off "the old and wrincl'd skin of corruption" in order to overcome their "pangs and wax young again, entring the glorious waies of Truth and prosperous vertue destin'd to become great and honourable in these latter ages." Within the context of this sense of rebirth Milton proclaims:

> Methinks I see in my mind a noble and puissant Nation rousing herself like a strong man after sleep, and shaking her invincible locks; Methinks I see her as an Eagle muing her mighty youth, and kindling her undazl'd eyes at the full midday beam; purging and unscaling her long abused sight at the fountain it self of heavenly radiance; while the whole noise of timorous and flocking birds, with those also that love the twilight, flutter about, amaz'd at what she means, and in their envious gabble would prognosticat a year of sects and schisms. (*YP*, 2:557–58)

The vision brings into play an entire range of associations that augment and enhance the concept of strength embodied in the figure of Samson. Drawing upon biblical narrative, the vision alludes most immediately to Judg. 16:13–14, which recounts Samson's awakening out of his sleep still a strong man, despite Delilah's third attempt to bind him by weaving together the seven locks of his head. In the reference to Samson's shaking his invincible locks, however, the vision includes both the subsequent loss of strength after the shaving of his hair (Judg. 16:19–20: "And he awoke out of his sleep, and said, I will go out as at other times before and shake myself. And he wist not that the Lord was departed from him") and its eventual resuscitation (Judg. 16:22: "Howbeit the hair of his head began to grow again after he was shaven"), followed by that final demonstration of remarkable prowess (Judg. 16:30: "And he bowed himself with all his might: and the house fell upon the Lords, and upon all the people that *were* therein. So the dead which he slew at his death were more than *they* which he slew in his life").[8]

This very idea is anticipated in *The Reason of Church-Government* with the reference to the nourishing again of the "puissant hair" of Samson, whose locks "sternly shook, thunder with ruin upon the heads" of the enemy. What the Samson of *Areopagitica* experiences,

---

8. Compare the reference to Samson in *Paradise Lost*. After Adam and Eve have fallen, they copulate in lust until they are enveloped by "dewie sleep." When Adam and Eve awaken, Adam's plight in particular is delineated in terms of Samson's: "So rose the *Danite* strong / *Herculean Samson* from the Harlot-lap / Of *Philistean Delilah*, and wak'd / Shorn of his strength." (9:1059–63). This regaining of strength is the focus of the final two books of *Paradise Lost*.

however, is the kind of regenerative shaking that betokens renewal and resuscitation. In political terms, this occurs "when God shakes a Kingdome with strong and healthfull commotions to a generall re-forming" (*YP*, 2:566; cf. Hag. 2:6–7; Heb. 12:26–29). Further rein-forcing the resuscitative dimension are the references to the serpentlike casting off of one's "old and wrincl'd skin of corruption" in order to overcome one's "pangs and wax young again" and the eaglelike "muing" or renewing of one's "mighty youth." This act of renewal is accompanied by a "kindling" of one's "undazl'd eyes at the full midday beam" and a "purging and unscaling" of one's "long abused sight at the fountain it self of heav'nly radiance." Both ref-erences take into account the experience of vigor that comes with the renewal of one's strength: overcoming the pangs of torment that accompany corruption, one becomes young again in might; and, pu-rifying sight from the darkness that surrounds it, one is able to see again as he has never seen before. Like a bird of God, he is able to behold the sun, the fountain of celestial radiance. He is, in effect, reborn in the sun. All this is implicit in the return of strength from weakness (cf. Heb. 11:34).

If such is the outlook manifested in the antiprelatical and the tract upholding the liberty of unlicensed printing, Milton's appropriation of Samson to reinforce his polemical views during the period in ques-tion extended into his tracts against monarchy as well. In his splendid exploration of the iconoclastic impulse in Milton's concept of history, David Loewenstein has already done much to focus attention on this dimension of the politicized Samson. As Loewenstein has made clear, a full understanding of the drama involves an awareness of the "cru-cial intersection in Milton's work between iconoclasm and a dramatic sense of historical process." As such, the drama is as much that of a "Samson Iconoclastes" as it is that of a "Samson Agonistes." Imple-menting the former configuration both in his polemic and in his drama, Milton portrayed a "Samson Iconoclastes as the militant activist who displays the spectacular power of heavenly wrath against his and God's enemies." For a militant figure of this sort, Loewenstein cogently observes, "violence and vehemence become an essential and dramatic means of historical liberation." Representing that event in "violent, turbulent, and iconoclastic terms," Milton believed that "great icon-oclastic disturbances, though deeply violent and unsettling, could also have healthful and purgative effects."[9] Such, as we have seen through-out this took, is crucial to the Miltonic notion of sparagmos as an essentially paradoxical phenomenon, one that conceives violence in regenerative terms.

Having explored those terms in the emergence of a politicized Samson in *The Reason of Church-Government* and in *Areopagitica*, we may now proceed to *Eikonoklastes* (1649) and the Defenses. The ap-propriation of Samson in *Eikonoklastes* is interesting as it reverses Mil-ton's own earlier association of the biblical figure with the king in *The Reason of Church-Government*. There, Milton invoked Samson to con-struct an allegory of the undermining by prelatical enemies of the king and commonwealth. In Milton's hands, this became an allegory of power, how it is threatened and how it is to be preserved. With Charles I as the object of his polemic in *Eikonoklastes*, Milton makes a point of dissociating Samson from the monarch. The dissociation is important, for through it Milton himself is at pains to undermine any claims to power Charles might attempt to appropriate in the name of Samson. Milton has in mind precisely that attempt in the *Eikon Basilike*, in which the king speaks of "eclipsing" his "beams" to satisfy the fears of his enemies, "who think they must needs be scorched or blinded" if he should "shine in the full lustre of kingly power wherewith God and the laws have invested [him]."[10] In *Eikonoklastes* Milton counters such an arrogation of power by conceiving Charles as an individual completely deprived of royal authority: "*The words of a King*, as they are *full of power*, in the autority and strength of Law, so like *Sampson*, without the strength of that *Nazarites* lock, they have no more power in them then the words of another man" (*YP*, 3:546; cf. 461). Charles is certainly no Samson, Milton implies, and, if he has any association

9. David Loewenstein, *Milton and the Drama of History: Historical Vision, Iconoclasm, and the Literary Imagination* (Cambridge: Cambridge University Press, 1990), esp. pp. 126–28, 140–41. In contradistinction to the portrait of Samson drawn in his study, Loewenstein also acknowledges (p. 128) the presence in Milton's controversial prose of this period another, negative dimension to Samson, especially discernible in *The Doctrine and Discipline of Divorce*. Here, one finds a lonely, wretched figure with whom Milton compares the husband tragically entrapped in a burdensome marriage. Such a figure grinds with horror and bitterness "in the mill of an undelighted and servil copulation" (*YP*, 2: 258). It is very much this dimension that Wittreich's own study *Interpreting "Samson Agonistes"* expounds.

10. *Eikon Basilike* (Oxford and London: James Parker, 1869), p. 67. According to Loew-enstein, John Gauden, "the secret coadjutor of *Eikon Basilike*," likewise associated Parliament with Delilah and the Philistines and Charles with Samson in *A Just Invective against those of the Army, And their Abettors, who murthered King Charles I* (London, 1662), p. 8.

with the biblical figure at all, that association is one that deprives him of power rather than imbues him with it. In this way, Charles becomes a fallen Samson shorn of his strength.

Far from calling Samson's own power into question, this depiction is one through which Milton as iconoclast reasserts his faith in that power by undermining any claims to it that Charles might assert. Power, in this sense, is invoked to demolish pretension and to explode presumption. It is brought to bear in the cause for which Milton views himself as iconoclast from the outset of his tract as one who in his "zeal to the command of God" and in response to the corruptions of idolatry "took courage, and broke all superstitious Images to peeces" (*YP*, 3:343). This, as Milton makes clear in *Eikonoklastes*, is tantamount to subjecting all tyrants to a bodily rending of the most profound sort. Such tyrants, Milton proclaims, are to be torn "to peeces" for their tyranny (*YP*, 3:361). In his adoption of the role of iconoclast, Milton performs precisely that function throughout his regicide tracts and the Defenses. At the center of that iconoclastic enactment stands the biblical figure of Samson replete with power.

The extent to which Milton conceives Samson in this way is particularly discernible in the *Defensio Prima*. There, Milton's animus against Salmasius as a defender of tyrants is given full expression. For our purposes, that animus is most effectively manifested in Milton's response to Salmasius's detailed arguments in the fourth book of the *Defensio Regia* (1649) that among the ancient Jews and Christians one finds no precedent for the kind of barbarous fate visited upon Charles. Resorting to examples from the Old and New Testaments, as well as from early patristic authority, Salmasius attempts to establish his case for unswerving respect for the Lord's anointed. From the Old Testament, Salmasius cites such examples as David, who, in deference to his king, refrained from killing Saul, although both provocation and opportunity presented themselves. Likewise, no one raised his hand against Solomon, even though he had broken the commands laid upon him. These and other examples are cited to demonstrate that biblical history affords no precedent for the treatment Charles suffered among his own people.[11]

In response to arguments of this sort, Milton sought support in the premonarchical history of the book of Judges. As if drawing in-

11. This summary is indebted to the full annotations in *YP*, 4:399–400.

spiration from the culture of a formative period, Milton once again invoked Samson to drive his point home. All the fervor and energy reflected in the allusions to the Samson of the earlier tracts is once again discernible here. True to his convictions even among countrymen who do not appreciate him, Samson strikes out courageously and uncompromisingly against those who would subject him and his people. So Milton declares that

> even the heroic Samson [*heros*], though his countrymen reproached him saying, Judges 15, "Knowest thou not that the Philistines are rulers over us?," still made war single-handed [*solus*]on his masters, and, whether prompted by God or by his own valor, slew at one stroke not one but a host of his country's tyrants [*neque unum sed multos simul patriae suae tyrannos*], having first made prayer to God for his aid. Samson therefore thought it not impious but pious to kill those masters who were tyrants over his country [*Non impium ergo sed pium Sampsoni visum est, dominos, patriae tyrannos occidere*], even though most of her citizens did not balk at slavery. (*YP*, 4:402; *CM*, 7:218)

Here Samson appears as a heroic figure, alone among a multitude unacknowledged and even held as suspect by those he is attempting to protect and who are content to remain in bondage. Not only is he cast as a regicide, he is viewed as one who kills an entire host of tyrants in one stroke. There is no equivocation on Milton's part in his depiction of Samson's act here. The act is conceived not just with approval but with applause: Milton celebrates it.[12] The energy of the act, indeed its uncompromising barbarity, is held up as a model of heroism and courage on the part of one who refuses to be subjected by tyrants of whatever stamp. The only equivocators are the people, and they are

12. My view departs from that of Joseph Wittreich, who sees in Milton's portrayal of Samson an underlying ambivalence. Wittreich finds Milton to be "deliberately evasive and hesitant," characteristics that call into question the extent and nature of Samson's triumph. In fact, Wittreich argues that "in virtually every citation of Samson, Milton speaks guardedly; and more, he equivocates on every accepted touchstone to Samson's heroism—his stature as national leader and deliverer, his supposedly authorized slayings of others, even his self-slaying, and most of all his ostensible promptings from God" (*Interpreting "Samson Agonistes,"* p. 306). Although I agree that Samson is a problematic figure for Milton—and therefore apt for tragic representation—in the present context the determination to justify the actions of the regicides in the form of Samson's heroism outweighs any possible tendency toward evasiveness or hesitancy on Milton's part. If anything, those are qualities that for Milton would describe the people who refused to recognize Samson's heroism for what it was.

cowards. In his depiction of the event, moreover, Milton emphasizes at this pivotal juncture that the individual responsible for the enactment of the slaughter carries it out alone, single-handedly. His actions are the true mark of a hero indeed.

Here, as elsewhere, Milton projects himself into the figure of Samson, views himself as one who, in the act of defending the regicides, adopts their cause with all the fervor and conviction of those who carried out the act in the first place. Milton's defense of the regicides is a defense of himself, his support of their cause, a support of his own. In that defense, he himself becomes the strong man, one among a multitude prepared to overcome tyranny and all who would condone it. Fulfilling this responsibility courageously and unstintingly, Milton does battle face-to-face with his own enemy, his own tyrant, whom he too slaughters at one stroke. As Loewenstein wisely observes in his essay on Milton's poetics of defense, it is on occasions of this sort that "the defensive polemicist presents himself as a militant champion, engaging in a highly active, strenuous mode of confrontation no less hazardous, courageous, and aggressive than that of his warfaring contemporaries."[13] If *their* enemy was Charles, whom they so soundly defeated, in effect, tore "to peeces" in their righteous zeal, *his* enemy is Salmasius, whom Milton as Samson-like strongman slaughters with the force of his own power and the courage that impels it.

This passage in the *Defensio Prima* brings to closure a series of passages in works ranging from *The Reason of Church-Government* and *Areopagitica*, on the one hand, to *Eikonoklastes* and the *Pro Populo Anglicano Defensio*, on the other. In each of these works, Milton does not hesitate to reconceptualize the Samson narrative in political terms. That narrative serves to focus the political circumstances surrounding the work in question. Whether those circumstances concern the corruptions of the prelates, the deleterious effects of censorship, the duplicitous claims of a fallen monarch, or the threats of an alien foe, the figure of Samson, his history, his activities, and his fate, underscores Milton's polemical posture at every turn. Although the Samson narrative is not invoked without qualification and without a sense that Samson is himself a source of anxiety and disruption, it represents

13. David Loewenstein, "Milton and the Poetics of Defense," in *Politics, Poetics, and Hermeneutics in Milton's Prose*, ed. David Loewenstein and James Grantham Turner (Cambridge: Cambridge University Press, 1990), p. 181.

for Milton the occasion to bring to bear in the crucial period between the antiprelatical tracts and the Defenses his sense of himself as warrior faced with the need to overcome dilemmas of the most profound sort. At no other time have these dilemmas assumed greater moment than in the circumstances out of which the final two Defenses emerged. Providing the impetus for these dilemmas, we recall, is the infamous *Regii Sanguinis Clamor ad Coelum Adversus Parricidas Anglicanos.*

II

In the foregoing chapters, I have already discussed at length the impact upon Milton of the *Clamor*. Responding to this work in the *Defensio Secunda*, Milton was at pains both to repristinate himself (his body and his being) and to undo his putative enemy, a program even further implemented in the *Pro Se Defensio*. In this respect, the latter two Defenses become the arena, indeed the theater, in which the corresponding process of sparagmos and apocatastasis takes place. What results is a staging of the body both as victim of assault and as locus of counterassault. With that counterassault, the body of the enemy is undone and the body of the self is reborn. Violence thereby fulfills its paradoxical potential of becoming at once the source of devastating destruction and ultimate renewal. By situating *Samson Agonistes* within the economy of such a process, I look upon the drama as a work in which the sparagmatic sensibility of the supremest of poets transmutes into a new form the elements of violence and brutality embodied in the *Clamor* and that triumphantly reasserts the politicization undergone by the figure of Samson in Milton's earlier prose works. With that transmutation, *Samson Agonistes* provides the most dramatic occasion through which Milton's incorporation of the phenomenon of sparagmos is able to occur.

In no other work of Milton is the sparagmatic experience more germane than in *Samson Agonistes*. The drama is a work of violence to its very core. It extols violence. Indeed, it exults in violence. The nature of that violence in *Samson Agonistes* is distinctly sparagmatic. The idea of sparagmos is sounded from the outset when the Chorus distinguishes between what it perceives as Samson in his present condition and the Samson of old. "Can this be hee, / That Heroic, that

Renown'd, / Irresistible Samson?" the Chorus asks incredulously upon first beholding him in such disarray. Oh, for the good old days, when he was not simply a pillar of strength but was the very embodiment of the glorious forces of violence! Recalling these heady days, the Chorus declares that this is the hero "whom unarm'd / No strength of man, or fiercest wild beast could withstand; / Who tore the Lion, as the Lion tears the Kid, / And weaponless himself, / Made arms ridiculous" (ll. 124–31). A most devastating source of sparagmos, this one: he had been a hero of consummate but immensely destructive power. Even without weapons, he went about tearing apart the mightiest of animals (cf. Judg. 14:5–6). The violence he enacted upon animals he was fiercely capable of enacting upon all beings. He was a true *anthroporraistes*, "render of men."

If weapons did come into play, they were appropriated only as a sign of how little they were needed. So the Chorus recalls that equipped only with a "trivial weapon, the Jaw of a dead Ass, his sword of bone," Samson managed to crush the hosts of the Philistines (Judg. 15:15–17). This act too is conceived in sparagmatic terms: "A thousand fore-skins fell, the flower of Palestin / In *Ramath-lechi* famous to this day" (ll. 141–45). The synecdoche ironically transforms the act of conquest into a brutal and massive circumcision of an entire army. Mass slaughter is conceived sparagmatically as wholesale circumcision. It also becomes the occasion for demonstrating Samson's sexual prowess. Recalling Milton's boast in the *Defensio Secunda* of his ability "to handle or unsheathe a sword [*ferrum*]," the trope telescopes the boast into an event of momentous proportions. Wielding his "trivial weapon," his *ferrum*, the circumcised hero cuts down that foreskinned race, derprives them of their own source of power and virility.[14] In effect, he emasculates them, an act that subjects them to a sparagmos of the most humiliating and devastating sort. Such, the Chorus declares, is the kind of power Samson as Nazarite, as the holy, chosen one of God, once possessed.

14. As a source of power and virility, then, his "trivial weapon" as *ferrum* is not so trivial after all. Although it may appear to be trivial, it is transformed from that which is "vulgar" (*trivialis*) into that which is splendid indeed. Milton, of course, plays on the Latinate meaning of "trivial" as *trivialis*, literally, that which "belongs to the cross-roads or public streets" and therefore "common" and "vulgar"; see *A Latin Dictionary*, comp. Charlton T. Lewis and Charles Short (Oxford; Claredon Press, 1879), s.v.

With its source in the idea of rending, that power assumes for the Chorus cosmic proportions. So the Chorus's account of Samson's past culminates in an attestation to what once had been his ability to rend the very fabric of the earth in order to perform feats of gigantic proportions: "Then by main force pull'd up, and on his shoulders bore / The Gates of Azza, Post and massie Bar / Up to the Hill of Hebron, seat of Giants old, / No journey of a Sabbath day, and loaded so; / Like whom the Gentiles feign to bear up Heav'n" (ll. 146–50; cf. Judg. 16:3). Atlas-like in his bearing, Samson then was seen to rival the most powerful of figures. Then, no one could defeat him: he was truly "irresistible," indeed triumphantly violent.

In his present condition, however, he appears to be entirely changed. No longer the *anthroporraistes* of old, he becomes a render of himself, a self-torturer, one whose sense of desertion, defeat, and alienation causes him to suffer the fate of one whose sparagmatic mentality has been turned inwardly upon itself as it rends its own being. In this sense, the body is internalized: it becomes the body of the mind, the body of the self. As one who undergoes the agon of the mutilation of that body, Samson laments his own sparagmos:

> O that torment should not be confin'd
> To the bodies wounds and sores
> With maladies innumerable
> In heart, head, brest, and reins;
> But must secret passage find
> To th' inmost mind,
> There exercise all his fierce accidents,
> And on her purest spirts prey,
> As on entrails, joints, and limbs,
> With answerable pains, but more intense,
> Though void of corporal sense.
>   My griefs not only pain me
> As a lingring disease,
> But finding no redress, ferment and rage,
> Ranckle, and fester, and gangrene,
> To black mortification
> Thoughts my Tormentors arm'd with deadly stings
> Mangle my apprehensive tenderest parts,

> Exasperate, exulcerate, and raise
> Dire inflammation which no cooling herb
> Or medcinal liquor can asswage. (ll. 606–27)

Having suffered the ravaging, the laceration, the rending of his own being, Samson must now discover some means of self-reclamation, indeed, repristination in the act of countering those forces that seek to undo him utterly. As agonistes he must do battle with the demons of the self.[15] In the context of Milton's drama, such a battle assumes complex overtones. Each of the figures Samson confronts becomes a contestant in what amounts to his attempt to regain his former standing as "render of men." What he truly desires is to be able once again to enact that process of sparagmos upon anyone who would oppose him. He wishes, in effect, to become the executor of violence rather than the recipient of it. In this way, he would become once again a victimizer rather than a victim. This, I take it, is a rather disturbing reading of what transpires in Milton's drama, but from the sparagmatic perspective the drama encodes it is a reading that assumes particular cogency within the political framework to which the *Regii Sanguinis Clamor ad Coelum Adversus Parricidas Anglicanos* might be seen to give rise.

Approaching Milton's drama from this point of view, I consider once again the two poems appended to the *Clamor*: the *MAGNO SAL-MASIO Pro Defensione Regia Ode Eucharistica* and the *In Impurissimum Nebulonem JOHANNEM MILTONUM Parricidarum & Parricidii Advo-catum*. In the theater represented by these poems and the work they append, *Samson Agonistes* may be seen as Milton's act of transforming his hostilities into a poetic manifestation of his own sparagmatic sensibility, one that responds to the extravagant praise of his enemy in the *MAGNO SALMASIO* and to the merciless undoing of his own body in the *In Impurissimum Nebulonem JOHANNEM MILTONUM*. Viewed in this way, the drama becomes a weapon for launching a counter-attack as powerful and as complex as any that Milton's Defenses might be said to have mounted. To view Samson in such a manner is, of course, to contextualize it polemically, an act entirely consistent with

15. For a discussion of the concept of *agonistes* in Milton's Samson, see in particular Paul Sellin, "Milton's Epithet *Agonistes*," *Studies in English Literature* 4 (1964), 137–62. The typological dimensions of the term *agonistes* are explored in Michael Krouse, *Milton's Samson and the Christian Tradition* (1949; New York: Farrar, Straus and Giroux, 1974), pp. 108–18.

Milton's own corresponding behavior in the prose. In accord with that behavior, I view the Samson of Milton's drama in political terms. Doing so allows his drama to release some of its most primitive and disturbingly violent elements. Such is necessary in order to understand the full impact of the apocatastasis the poem likewise encodes. This approach should provide crucial insight into the sparagmatic outlook that informs and in fact determines the action of Milton's *Samson Agonistes*.

As I discussed earlier, the *MAGNO SALMASIO* is a poem in which Salmasius is celebrated (in effect, sacralized in "eucharistic" fashion) as a magnificent hero and an invincible warrior, divinely inspired by the gods and feared by his enemies. The Muse is invoked to inscribe his name on adamant. Surpassing all others in prowess, this priest of the Muses is extolled in the highest possible terms. As he champions the cause of monarchs, the Herculean figure "charge[s] into the shields and swords" of his enemies, whom he fully overwhelms with his courage and might. The poem celebrates Salmasius's victories, the power of his blows, as his enemies are dragged in chains into the light of judgment, where they are tried and convicted for their crimes before the Highest Judge. "Arise Avenger," the poet proclaims, and, "with your right hand become crimson, spear the sacrilegious band [*Exurge vindex, & rubente / Sacrilegos jaculare dextra*]"; uproot them, and "squeeze out this noisome pus / The guilty Parricides, Earth's dross [*Piaculares parricidas / Pus olidum, scoriamque Terrae*]." After that, these Hell Hounds will be sent down to the realm of Pluto. Thus, the guilty parricides, dross of the earth, are uprooted by the great and triumphant Salmasius. In attestation to the overcoming of the enemy, the poem concludes with the vision of Salmasius's making his triumphal entry on his chariot, followed on foot by his devoted admirers: *Tu Magne Salmasi triumpha / Nos pedibus sequimur quadrigam*.[16]

Complementing this penultimate poem of thanksgiving on the great defender Salmasius is the final poem of denunciation, the *In Impurissimum Nebulonem JOHANNEM MILTONUM*. This poem, we

16. Accompanied by my own silent emendations, citations in English are from the translation in Harry G. Merrill III, "Milton's Secret Adversary: Du Moulin and the Politics of Protestant Humanism," unpublished doctoral dissertation, University of Tennessee, Knoxville, 1959, pp. 384–87. Latin interpolations are from the original poem appended to the *Clamor*. See Chapter 7 for an earlier discussion of this poem. From an entirely different point of view, Salmasius on his chariot offers ironic comparison with the Son on his chariot in *Paradise Lost* (6:723–912).

recall, is a virulent attack upon Milton's body, one in which the "parricide" is subjected to a rhetoric of savage abuse. In its enactment of that abuse, the poem stages a scene (a theatrical representation of torture) in which the speaker (as defender of Salmasius) challenges his enemy to physical combat but then discovers that the enemy is too foul and loathsome to warrant the dignity of true battle. "Soho!" the speaker cries, "Seize upon that wicked hangman of a scourger [*carnificem Lorarii*]. Seize him! Quick! Quick! Quick! Bind him up hands and feet. I owe him the sacred rites of the scourge [*Solemne debeo Virgidemiae sacrum*]." So debased, the enemy is humiliated through a series of merciless assaults upon his body. Called into service, an executioner completely and vindictively causes Milton's flesh to be lashed and rent to the point that it resembles "one big welt" (*Lorisque totum facite sit tuber*). Bound hand and foot, Milton is then further goaded and finally cudgeled, until he has been made to pour forth his bile and diseased blood through his tears. "Beautifully vermiculated with a mosaic of stripes [*Tandem plagoso vermiculatum emblemate / Pulchre variatum vimine*]," the mutilated body of the debased victim is finally dragged before the feet of Salmasius, who, "with his strong right hand," whirls the body into the air and savagely "bestrews the rocks far and wide" with the poor victim's "shattered brain" (*ille diffracto procul / Late cerebro saxa respersit cadens*).[17]

Such in brief are the terms upon which the final two poems of the *Clamor* are fashioned. Sacralization and vilification, eucharistic adulation and savage mutilation: these are what underscore the "poetic" moments in which the *Clamor* culminates. Our discussion of the Defenses has already recorded Milton's expression of contempt and outrage in response to these poems. In the *Defensio Secunda*, Milton transforms them into nothing more than low comedy, a form of debased theater characterized by gross buffoonery and pomposity. For Milton, the poems become "effeminate little verses" that are completely impotent and worthy only to be despised. The poet of these verses is a bizarre, even monstrous figure, who is quite mad. The hero whom this poet extols is, in turn, nothing but "a mere schoolmaster," old, foolish, and impotent. Milton, in fact, makes a particular point

17. Citations in English are from the the translation in the *YP*, 1078. Latin interpolations are once again from the original poem appended to the *Clamor*. See Chapter 7 for an earlier discussion of this poem.

of deriding the portrayal of Salmasius with which the penultimate poem commences.

Accordingly, Milton marvels that the poet "brings on in a 'triumphal' chariot, no less, the giant-fighting hero [*Heroem Gigantomachum*], brandishing his 'javelins and boxing-gloves' and all manner of trifling weapons, with all the scholars following the chariot on foot, but a tremendous distance to the rear, since he is the one 'whom divine providence has raised up in evil times for the salvation of the world.' " Such a description of the *Heroem Gigantomachum* Milton is particularly at pains to undermine. "Salmasius," he comments, "must have been mad and in his second childhood not only to have been so hugely gratified by such praises but also to have taken such pains to have them printed with all possible haste." At the same time, the poet too must have been "wretched and ignorant of propriety" if he thought "a mere schoolmaster worthy of such immoderate eulogy" (*YP*, 4:592–93; *CM*, 8:78). For all his efforts, this poet invites not just derision but bodily pain. As a slave-whipping executioner for Salmasius, the poet should himself be mercilessly whipped and tortured. In that way, he will be taught a lesson he will never forget. Such is what Milton himself sets out to do in the Defenses, as the loathsome More is humiliated, bodily mutilated, and effectively emasculated.

To view *Samson Agonistes* in the context of this polemic is to encounter a rereading of the two appended poems of the *Clamor* that at once draws upon and refashions the dynamics that energize the brutal polemic and that represents a fitting counterpart to corresponding acts of politicization in the prose. In his poetic, Milton's drama infuses the scathing jocularity of the Defenses with a profound sense of tragic self-awareness. Informed as it is by the precariousness of its own situation, that self-awareness provides renewed insight into Milton's sparagmatic sensibility and invites an interpretation of his drama that more fully accords with the experience of violence that infuses his works. To no other incident that distinguishes the action of *Samson Agonistes* is this observation more nearly applicable than that which portrays Samson's verbal combat with Harapha of Gath. It is in the primitive articulations of this combat that Milton's sparagmatic outlook at its most archaic comes into play. It is here that Milton as blind, suffering hero finally has his opportunity to play out in poetic form his violent response to both the extravagant elevation of his old enemy and the savage mutilation and dismemberment of his own body.

III

To suggest that the portrayal of Samson's encounter with Harapha finds its counterpart in Milton's struggles with Salmasius is hardly new to Milton criticism. The idea was enunciated at least as early as David Masson, reasserted by E. H. Visiak, elaborated upon in depth by Christian Edzard Kreipe, and reconfirmed by Theodor Seibert.[18] Perhaps because of our understandable determination to eschew easy identifications of this sort, we tend to overlook their potential relevance. A one-to-one identification between Salmasius and Harapha is reductionist at best, but the attempt to contextualize the encounter between Samson and Harapha through recourse to the poetic fictions of the *MAGNO SALMASIO* and the *In Impurissimum Nebulonem JO-HANNEM MILTONUM* suggests a polemical bearing consistent with Milton's own tendency to politicize the Samson narrative during the revolutionary period under consideration. Milton's own scathing response to the Salmasius of the *MAGNO SALMASIO* as a *Heroem Gigantomachum* is very much in accord with his ironic portrayal of Harapha of Gath in the drama.

In that portrayal, Milton makes us aware of the bearing and demeanor of his character in a manner that complements his satirical denunciation of Salmasius as the mock-hero of the *MAGNO SALMASIO*. Like the coming of Salmasius, Harapha's arrival, for example, is announced with all due pomp and circumstance. Although not borne like his counterpart on a triumphal chariot, Harapha nonetheless makes a grand, if ominous, entrance. Comparing that entrance to the onset of a storm, the Chorus issues the following warning:

> Look now for no inchanting voice, nor fear
> The bait of honied words; a rougher tongue
> Draws hitherward, I know him by his stride,

18. See *Life of Milton*, 6:675; E. H. Visiak, *Milton Agonistes* (London: A. M. Philpot, 1923), p. 99; Christian Edzard Kreipe, *Milton's "Samson Agonistes"* (Halle: Verlag von Max Niemeyer, 1926), pp. 54–57; and Theodor Seibert, "Egozentrisches in Miltons Schreibweise," *Anglia* 54 (1930), 64.

The Giant *Harapha* of *Gath*, his look
Haughty as is his pile high-built and proud.
Comes he in peace? what wind hath blown him hither
I less conjecture then when first I saw
The sumptuous *Dalila* floating this way:
His habit carries peace, his brow defiance. (ll. 1061–73)

As if the manifestation of the tempestuous elements of nature, Harapha suddenly comes into view. On the surface at least, his appearance is initially daunting and, based on the Chorus's "riddling" description of it, a source of confusion to Samson.[19] The Chorus heralds Harapha's approach by implicitly comparing it to that of Dalila, "floating this way." Whereas Dalila's coming was "Like a stately Ship / Of Tarsus" sailing into view (ll. 713–15), Harapha's arrival is implicitly that of a frigate frought with at least the threat of peril. As it "draws hitherward," that threat, moreover, assumes a synecdotal force in the comparison between Dalila's "inchanting voice" and "honied words," on the one hand, and Harapha's "rougher tongue," on the other. Although Harapha's "habit carries peace," his face bears all the marks of defiance.

As a counterstatement to the depiction of Salmasius in the *MAGNO SALMASIO*, the portrayal of Harapha in the drama, moreover, brings into focus Milton's own ironic response to his old enemy as "the giant-fighting hero" in the Defensio Secunda. The epithet is one that comments implicitly on the significance of Harapha. In *Samson Agonistes*, Harapha appropriately assumes the role of what his name implies. Both in name and in form, he becomes *the giant*. So he is described by the Chorus specifically as "The Giant *Harapha* of *Gath*" (l. 1068). A cunning transliteration of the Hebrew, the name Harapha is an onomastic signature of what the character himself represents: *Haraphah*, means quite literally "the giant."[20] Encoded in this name is the

19. Of importance to the interchange between Samson and the Chorus here and to the drama in its entirety is the whole question of the riddle. As Mieke Bal makes abundantly and brilliantly clear in *Death and Dissymmetry: The Politics of Coherence in the Book of Judges* (Chicago: University of Chicago Press, 1988), pp. 75–80, 135–43, the riddle in the original biblical account is a speech act that encodes both power relations and acts of violence. This represents a dimension of Milton's drama that I do not have the opportunity to discuss here.

20. See my examination of the etymologies not only of Harapha but of the other figures in *Samson Agonistes* in *Sinews of Ulysses*, pp. 98–138, esp. pp. 127–29. See also Rabbi Jack Goldman, "The Name and Function of Harapha in Milton's *Samson Agonistes*," *English Language Notes* 12 (1974), 84–91. Informative are the entries on *rapha*, *ha-rapha*, and *rephaim* in

Hebraic obverse of Salmasius's own mockingly poetic signature in the *Defensio Secunda*. In Milton's reconceptualization of that signature for the purposes of his drama, it is Samson who becomes the true *Heroem Gigantomachum*, a role he comes to assume as a result of his encounter with the "tongue-doughtie Giant" (l. 1181). As portrayed in *Samson Agonistes*, that encounter is tantamount to a warfare as fierce as any Milton waged in the Defenses.

The mode of conducting that warfare suggests the concurrence of verbal and physical violence. At the center of this violence is the body as a thing to be attacked, mutilated, and rent asunder. These elements are present from the outset of the encounter, which pits strongman against strongman. The terms of the encounter are initiated by Harapha himself. Establishing his credentials as a being in whom supreme power dwells, Harapha begins by tracing his genealogy to the world of giants, after which he moves to issue what appears to be a challenge to physical combat: "I am of *Gath*," he boasts;

> Men call me *Harapha*, of stock renown'd
> As *Og* or *Anak* and the *Emims* old
> That *Kiriathaim* held; thou knowst me now
> If thou at all art known. Much have I heard
> Of thy prodigious might and feats perform'd
> Incredible to me, in this displeas'd,
> That I was never present on the place
> Of those encounters, where we might have tri'd
> Each others force in camp or listed field:
> And now am come to see of whom such noise
> Hath walk'd about, and each limb to survey,
> If thy appearance answer loud report. (ll. 1078–90)

Both the way Harapha establishes his credentials and the means by which he issues his challenge reinforce the notion of physical violence so crucial to the conception and the portrayal of the *agon*. Although such violence is interwoven within the very fabric of the biblical account, it assumes an especially telling presence here, precisely because

---

A Hebrew and English Lexicon of the Old Testament, ed. Francis Brown (Oxford: Clarendon Press, 1907), 950–52. Under *rapha*, one finds multiple meanings, including ironically the idea of "losing heart" and becoming weak and feeble, the very paradox implicit in the character of Milton's Harapha.

of the absence of a "Harapha" in the Judges narrative. That absence affords Milton the opportunity to import into the narrative not only a whole new character but the possibility of a whole new combat. Conceived as an *agon* in which Samson adopts the role of *Heroem Gigantomachum*, this combat assumes particular cogency within the context of Milton's drama.

Harapha's act of establishing his credentials brings the nature of the combat into focus. He begins by announcing not simply that his name is Harapha but that he is called Harapha by others. In an gesture of onomastic self-legitimation, Harapha justifies his claim to power by maintaining that his name has been bestowed upon him as the result not only of who he is but of what he is. The idea of who he is grounds itself in the notion of appearances, a notion manifested entirely in the trappings of power. The idea of what he is grounds itself in the notion of lineage, a notion manifested entirely in the names and places through which lineage is established. Intimately intertwined, both the belief in appearance and the assertion of lineage determine Harapha's self-identity. Both underscore his claim to power, and both are exploded during the course of the battle.

The references to "*Og* or *Anak* and the *Emims* old / That *Kiriathaim* held" situate Harapha in the world of ancient biblical story that extends from the period of Abraham onward. The lore surrounding the giants, or *rephaim* is so engrained in the biblical consciousness that it is part of the fabric of the myths that entail prodigious feats of beings whose reputation in battle is legion. It is a daunting lineage that Harapha claims indeed. Despite the power associated with these beings, however, their names are characteristically invoked not as symbols of indomitable might but as representations of those who have challenged God's power and have lost. They are, in short, symbols of a race that embodies an ignoble history of warfare through which those who attempted to assert power against the divine will were finally discomfited. Thus, the Emim and the Anakim, for example, are designated an ancient race of giants and a great people, whom "the Lord destroyed" and are deprived of power (Deut. 2:10, 20–21). Repeatedly, the *rephaim* are overwhelmed in battle by the forces of God (cf. Gen. 14:5; 1 Chron. 20:4–8).

Of the myths surrounding the *rephaim*, the most famous recounts the battle between David and Goliath. As John M. Steadman has so effectively demonstrated, that battle represents the biblical foundation for the Samson-Harapha *agon* in Milton's drama.[21] The biblical account of the battle between David and Goliath is too well known to need recapitulation here. But, perhaps because of its very currency as a locus classicus of biblical lore, we might tend to overlook its significance for the Samson-Harapha *agon*. From the perspective of that *agon*, the David-Goliath battle assumes importance as a profound symbol of the way faith in the power of God is sufficient to overcome the mightiest of enemies. In the defeat of such enemies, the trappings of power on the part of God's enemies are undermined. Like Harapha, whose look is "haughty as is his pile high-built and proud," Goliath is conceived as a symbol of presumption, a tower ready to be toppled:

> And there went out a champion out of the camp of the Philistines, named Goliath of Gath, whose height *was* six cubits and a span. And *he had* an helmet of brass upon his head, and he was armed with a coat of mail; and the weight of the coat was five thousand shekels of brass. And *he had* greaves of brass upon his legs, and a target of brass between his shoulders. And the staff of his spear *was* like a weaver's beam; and his spear's head *weighed* six hundred shekels of iron: and one bearing a shield went before him. (1 Sam. 17:4–7)

The hyperbolic dressing of Goliath in the trappings of power (helmet, armor, shield, weapon) cries out for that divestiture, that stripping bare, effected by the shepherd lad who refuses to be attired

21. John M. Steadman, "Milton's Harapha and Goliath," *Journal of English and Germanic Philology* 60 (1961), 786–95. According to Steadman, the mortal duel between David and Goliath became a common theme in Renaissance Biblical epic, and Milton might have come across the theme of the *monomachia* of David and Goliath in several heroic poems (p. 788). See also Steadman's other important studies bearing on this theme, especially " 'Men of Renown': Heroic Virtue and the Biblical Giants," in *Milton's Epic Characters: Image and Idol* (Chapel Hill: University of North Carolina Press, 1968), pp. 177–93. Also of interest is George Waggoner, "The Challenge to Single Combat in *Samson Agonistes*," *Philological Quarterly* 39 (1960), 82–92. In "Milton's Harapha and Renaissance Comedy," *ELH* 11 (1944), 297–306, Daniel C. Boughner places Harapha in the context of the traditions of the *commedia del l'arte*. He associates Harapha as well with Spenser's Braggadocchio, to which one might likewise add the figure of Orgoglio. William Riley Parker, in turn, views Harapha from the perspective of the blusterers in Euripidean drama; *Milton's Debt to Greek Tragedy in "Samson Agonistes"* (Baltimore: Johns Hopkins University Press, 1937), pp. 122–24. As comic figure, Harapha finds corresponding types in the *miles gloriosus*. Most recently, see Noam Flinker, "Typological Parody: Samson in Confrontation with Harapha," *Milton Quarterly* 24 (1990), 136–40, and the response and counterresponse by Anthony Low and Noam Flinker in *Milton Quarterly* 25 (1991), 143–49.

in such accoutrements but proclaims against the Philistine: "Thou comest to me with a sword, and with a spear, and with a shield: but I come to thee in the name of the Lord of hosts, the God of the armies of Israel, whom thou hast defied" (1 Sam. 17:38–39, 45). Placing his entire faith in the power of God, David is prepared to engage Goliath in combat to the death:

> This day will the Lord deliver thee into mine hand; and I will smite thee, and take thine head from thee; and I will give the carcases of the host of the Philistines this day unto the fowls of the air, and to the wild beasts of the earth; that all the earth may know that there is a God in Israel. And all this assembly shall know that the Lord saveth not with sword and spear: for the battle is the Lord's, and he will give you into our hands. (1 Sam. 17: 46–47).

The language of David's challenge transforms the terms of the impending battle into a warfare between two concepts of power: that which derives its impetus from a reliance on the world of physical might and the accoutrements that adorn it and that which derives its impetus from a belief in forces that extend beyond the boundaries of the physical to make their presence known. These forces are of the highest sort: they are those of the God of Israel. His conquest of the Philistines and their host is effected through the offices of one who at first blush appears least likely to fulfill that role. When he does fulfill it, his mode of bringing it to bear assumes the most violent of forms: having smitten the Philistine in the forehead with his stone, he concludes the job by performing what in effect is an act of dismemberment: "David ran, and stood upon the Philistine, and took his sword, and drew it out of the sheath thereof, and slew him, and cut off his head therewith. And when the Philistines saw their champion was dead, they fled" (I Sam. 17:49–50). What might be called the defacement of Goliath here represents the biblical formulation of that consummate moment of sparagmos in which the power of God makes itself known in the undoing of that presumption represented by the giant Goliath. With the dismemberment of Goliath, all the trappings of power upon which he relied are undone. The tower is toppled, and appearance is exploded.

Although quite understandable, it is nonetheless ironic that in the roll call of names that constitute his lineage, as well as his offspring, the giant of Milton's drama neglects to mention this most famous of giants. The omission is rectified by Samson himself at the conclusion of his own combat with Harapha. Having exposed Harapha for the coward he is, Samson declares, "I dread him not, nor all his Giant-brood, / Though Fame divulge him Father of five Sons / All of Gigantic size, Goliah chief" (ll. 1244–49). Recalling the discomfiture of Goliath by the youthful shepherd, the allusion to Harapha as the putative father of five sons, Goliath chief among them, glances at the battles David waged later in his career as king, when "the Philistines had yet war again with Israel." In these wars, David, along with his servants, is made once again to encounter giants and the sons of giants. Recounting how these giants (four in particular) were defeated in battle, the biblical narrative concludes with the statement that "these four were born to the giant in Gath and fell by the hand of David, and by the hand of his servants" (2 Sam. 21:15–22). Although the precise identities of the giants, as well as their respective genealogies, is open to question, they all may be seen as types of Milton's own Harapha. Perhaps in some way related to the unnamed "giant in Gath" as progenitor of four gigantic sons, Milton's Harapha, as the result of Samson's dismissive gesture, finds himself putatively and perhaps hyperbolically the progenitor of *five* sons, "all of Gigantic size, *Goliah* chief." Despite the chronological problems raised by Samson's reference, the point is that the ignoble history of Goliath is one Milton's Harapha would just as soon overlook.[22] It is a history, however, to which he is inevitably tied, and the events surrounding it represent a subtext of the *agon* between Samson and Harapha in Milton's drama.

The association of the encounter between Samson and Harapha, and that between David and Goliath goes far to justify a reading that places the *agon* in the context of the Defenses. Milton does much to encourage such a reading in the *Defensio Secunda*. There, he portrays himself as a kind of David made to do battle with the giant Goliath. Whereas Salmasius at the time of his writing the *Defensio Regia* was perceived as a giant of erudition, "which he had been fostering for

---

22. David Masson has the following comments on the anachronistic problems in Samson's allusion to Goliath: "As the date of the death of Samson, in the Biblical chronology, is some eighty years before the accession of David to the throne, it is only on the supposition that the giants were unusually long-lived that Milton's accuracy in making the five sons of Harapha, who were all slain in David's time, full-grown in Samson's time, can be defended" *The Poetical Works of John Milton*, 3 vols., ed. David Masson (London: Macmillan, 1890), 3:614.

many years by writing a great many books, and very thick ones," Milton was virtually unknown: "I could excite no interest in myself," he says. "In fact, many persons tried to discourage me from undertaking the task, on the ground that I was a tyro about to join battle with a veteran. Some were jealous, lest it might somehow prove glorious for me to have engaged so great a foe, some fearful both for me and for our cause, lest I be conquered and leave the field with serious damage to both." All these things worked against him, yet like David, he prevailed (*YP*, 4:602–3). What is implied by the analogy in the *Defensio Secunda* is stated overtly by Milton's nephew Edward Phillips in "The Life of Mr. John Milton" (1694). Depicting Salmasius as a pompous and inflated Goliath, Phillips observes "that there could no where have been found a Champion that durst lift up the Pen against so formidable an Adversary, had not our little *English David* had the Courage to undertake this great *French Goliah*, to whom he gave such a hit in the Forehead, that he presently staggered, and soon after fell," so that "he was glad to have recourse to Death, the remedy of Evils, and ender of Controversies."[23]

An awareness of such contexts helps to establish a sense of the political overtones implicit in the Samson / Harapha encounter. Delineating that encounter by means of the *agon* between David and Goliath, the battle between Samson and Harapha draws upon this biblical prototype to suggest the way Samson assumes the role Milton ironically associates with Salmasius but in fact attributes to Samson himself, that of *Heroem Gigantomachum*. In the enactment of this role, Samson as hero does noble battle against the giant that would dispatch him if he possibly could. What Harapha discovers is that such an attempt would result in ultimate disaster to himself. The nature of this discovery is founded upon a concept of physical violence and bodily rending as graphic as any the biblical prototypes have to offer. Although actual combat between Samson and Harapha never comes to pass, the implications of such combat are very much present in the dialogue that ensues between the two characters. Harapha begins by issuing an implied call to combat, a testing as it were of Samson's mettle. Asserting that he has heard of Samson's prodigious might and feats of strength, Harapha regrets that he was not present at the time to witness and to challenge his

23. *Early Lives*, p. 70.

enemy, so that each might test the other's "force in camp or listed field." Having missed that opportunity, Harapha now takes the occasion to "survey" every "limb" of Samson's body. Immediately, the body itself becomes the subject of focus and possible attack. It is as if the whole drama is made to center on this object, how it is constituted, how it is sustained, how it is invigorated, how it behaves, and, what is most important, how it responds to the threat of attack.

Samson's response is the correct one: he meets the threat of physical violence with an equal threat of counter-violence. There is nothing spiritual in this response; rather, it is entirely, unabashedly, and indeed triumphantly physical: "The way to know were not to see but taste" (l. 1091). Don't simply "survey" my body, Samson implies; instead, you should "taste" its power. Undermining all pretension, this terse counter to Harapha's challenge is a hammer blow, one inspired by the desire to get even for the bodily suffering one has been made to endure as the result of the uncompromising mutilation of one's own body by his enemies. In this sense, Harapha represents a perfect opportunity to realize that desire were the giant only foolhardy enough to take Samson up on his offer. Harapha would then be forced to taste the fruits of Samson's power.

In contradistinction to the act of beholding as the result of surveying, the act of tasting implies a direct involvement in all that bodily power entails. As opposed to seeing (that capacity of which Samson is deprived), tasting is tactile: it implies touching, an act inherent in *tangere* ("to taste," "to touch"). It also implies knowing, an act inherent in *sapere* ("to know," "to taste"). As Samson is aware, such tasting is the best way of knowing, of gaining true wisdom, for the knowledge he imparts is born of violence in its most brutal form. Had Dalila persisted in her pursuit, Samson would certainly have imparted such knowledge to her. "Let me approach at least, and touch thy hand" (l. 951), Dalila had earlier implored. "Not for thy life," Samson responds, knowing full well the horrors that would result: "lest fierce remembrance wake / My sudden rage to tear thee joint by joint" (ll. 952–953).[24]

24. Space does not permit consideration of the role of Dalila in the context of Milton's sparagmatic sensibility. Of immense importance to the consideration of Dalila as a manifestation of Samson's outlook is Jackie DiSalvo, "Intestine Thorn: Samson's Struggle with the Woman Within," in *Milton and the Idea of Woman*, ed. Julia Walker (Urbana: University of Illinois Press, 1988), pp. 211–29. DiSalvo's article is crucial to an understanding of the bearing of gender in Milton's drama. From the sparagmatic perspective addressed in the present study, Dalila is "the Lady" whom Milton must overcome. By extension, Harapha and Dalila

If he is capable of enacting such a sparagmos on his sometime lover, one can only imagine what he would do to Harapha, who has come openly to gloat over Samson's sufferings and whose very presence represents an unbearable affront to the fallen figure.

Samson's counterchallenge to Harapha provokes not action but a further slight against Samson's claim to power: "Dost thou already single me; I thought / Gyves and the Mill had tam'd thee?" Already on the defensive, Harapha seeks refuge in Samson's apparent physical incapacity as one who has been bound by the shackles of imprisonment and forced labor, for Harapha a condition of humiliation that renders Samson impotent. Viewing Samson in contempt and at a safe distance, Harapha is in a condition of allowing himself the luxury of yet another idle boast. If only he had been present when Samson to was to have "wrought such wonders with an Asses jaw," Harapha exclaims. Had Harapha been there, he would have forced Samson to take up stronger arms than that or face the prospect of having his "carkass where the Ass lay thrown." Such contempt for and denigration of the body is Harapha's hallmark. At the very point that Samson would oppose his bodily strength against Harapha's, the giant would deface and humiliate his enemy's body further as a means of glorifying his own. In this way, Harapha seeks to reempower his own nation, which had been disempowered and disgraced at the hands of Samson: "So had the glory of Prowess been recover'd / To *Palestine*, won by a Philistine / From the unforeskinn'd race" (ll. 1092–1103).

Harapha's act of self-aggrandizement is as much a political gesture as a personal one. He is a representative of those "foreskinned" (as opposed to "unforeskinn'd") people whose "noble" cause he represents. As valiant defender of that cause, Harapha maintains that he would have welcomed the opportunity to engage in a mortal duel with Samson when he had the power, as well as the visual ability, to fight. Prevented now from engaging in such a duel because of the loss of his eyes, Samson has deprived Harapha as warrior and political spokesman from upholding the cause of his people. Duplicitous and self-indulgent as it is, Harapha's response to Samson's counterchallenge makes clear the political dimensions of his bearing. In his own way, Harapha becomes an advocate on behalf of those whose claims

---

should be viewed as counterparts, both subject to the sparagmos Samson would enact, both aspects of Samson's personality.

against Samson include the humiliation *they* were made to endure
when he defeated their armies single-handedly. As champion of his
people, Harapha would maintain that his claim to be able to defeat
Samson is a matter of national pride as well as personal glory. The
political dimensions of the proposed combat are as much a part of
the fabric of the encounter as are the personal dimensions. In both
respects, Samson is made to endure the kind of bombast we have
already seen as that which provides the impetus for the extolling of
Milton's enemy in the *Ode Eucharistica.* "Arise Avenger," and, "with
your right hand become crimson, spear the sacrilegious band"; uproot
them, and "squeeze out" the "noisome pus," the source of all offen-
siveness. Harapha does not heed the call: all he says is nothing but
an idle boast. A duplicitous upholder of a groundless cause, Harapha
is one whose attempt at self-aggrandizement falls flat.

Samson's response to Harapha's *Ode Eucharistica* explodes all such
pretension: "Boast not of what thou wouldst have done, but do / What
then thou wouldst, thou see it in thy hand" (ll. 1104–05). This is but
another version (indeed, a concretizing) of "The way to know were
not to see but taste." If Harapha has the ability to see at all, he should
know that the only way of proving himself is in hand-to-hand combat
with his adversary. At the center of Samson's challenge once again is
that source of power, the "hand" itself as an instrument of destruction,
a means of tearing the enemy "joint by joint" in an unmitigated act
of sparagmos. "Thou see it in thy hand": it is in the power of either
or both to dispose of the other as each sees fit. No room for compromise here: brute hand-to-hand combat is the only option that
remains to resolve the question of power. Whose "right hand," after
all, will prevail after each has bloodied his hand?[25] The answer is in
the tasting, in the act itself.

Harapha refuses to accept such terms. His bluff has been called.
He is put to the expense of disgusting subterfuge that transforms the
pure violence implicit in Samson's challenge of the hand into a ques-

25. In biblical terms, "hand" (*yod*) finds its figurative counterpart in the idea of strength
and power: the meanings are practically synonymous. See *Hebrew and English Lexicon*, pp. 388–
91. Especially as descriptive of God's power, the right hand is the seat of power. Compare
Exod. 15:6: "Thy right hand, O Lord, is become glorious in power: thy right hand, O Lord,
hath dashed in pieces the enemy." Milton was fully aware of such meanings and implemented
them throughout his works.

tion of false propriety and mock-fastidiousness as the basis of Harapha's rejoinder: "To combat with a blind man I disdain, / And thou hast need much washing to be toucht" (ll. 1106–07). The rejoinder brings into focus the terms we have already encountered in that poem of consummate violence through which Milton's own body was subjected to such humiliation: the *In Impurissimum Nebulonem JOHANNEM MILTONUM.* The savage abuse this poem encodes suggests a context for Harapha's own abusiveness and invites the kind of virulence that characterizes Samson's response. Recalling the contempt exhibited by Harapha, the poet of the polemical tract proclaims: "Shall I touch this evil poison, this cancerous ulcer? Oh, it is disgusting, a thing which the beadle can scare bear to touch." Although the poet of the polemical tract "hold[s] off a fastidious hand" from coming into contact with this defiled and loathsome thing, he commissions the executioner to perform the honors. These include, we remember, binding the victim hand and foot, lashing and rending his flesh, cudgeling him, and then, after this series of humiliations, dragging the debased body of the victim before the feet of his enemy Salmasius himself, who, "with his strong right hand," whirls the body into the air and savagely "bestrews the rocks far and wide" with the poor victim's "shattered brain" (*YP*, 4:1078). At some primal level, Samson's encounter with Harapha allows Milton to return the compliment.

He does so by adopting the role assigned to Salmasius in the *Ode Eucharistica.* This role, once again, is that of the *Heroem Gigantomachum.* In that role, Samson challenges Harapha to attire himself in the armor of the one giant missing from Harapha's own earlier roll call, Goliath of Gath. The nature of this armor has already been addressed in our discussion of the Davidic dimension of the Samson-Harapha encounter. So Goliath appears in all his pride: "And *he had* an helmet of brass upon his head, and he *was* armed with a coat of mail; and the weight of the coat *was* five thousand shekels of brass. And *he had* greaves of brass upon his legs, and a target of brass between his shoulders. And the staff of his spear *was* like a weaver's beam; and his spear's head *weighed* six hundred shekels of iron: and one bearing a shield went before him" (1 Sam. 17: 4–7). In the same spirit, Samson calls upon Harapha to "put on all thy gorgeous arms, thy Helmet / And Brigandine of brass, thy broad Habergeon, / Vant-brass and Greves, and Gauntlet, add thy Spear / A Weavers beam, and seven-times-folded shield" (ll. 1119–22).[26] In this act of attiring, the giant is challenged to outfit himself in his war gear not only to prepare for battle but to demonstrate the extent of his prowess through an exhibition of his military finery. Exhibiting himself in this manner, he will thereby distinguish himself even further from the miserable and abject situation of one whose condition the giant dismisses as beneath contempt. At the same time, the giant will distance himself even further from the circumstances of one so lowly and indeed so vitiated that he "hast need much washing to be toucht." In contradistinction to himself, Samson desires Harapha to be decked out in this manner so that when he attacks the giant he will be able to bring down all the pretension, pomposity, and claims to superiority the giant represents. Like David in his discomfiture of Goliath, Samson will strip Harapha of the trappings of power and expose him for what he is.

If David accomplished such a discomfiture with a sling, Samson will accomplish it "only with an Oak'n staff," a symbol of his faith in the power of God. With this weapon, Samson says to Harapha, I "will meet thee, / And raise such out-cries on thy clatter'd Iron, / Which long shall not with-hold mee from thy head, / That in a little time while breath remains thee, / Thou oft shalt wish thy self at *Gath* to boast / Again in safety what thou wouldst have done / To *Samson*, but shalt never see *Gath* more" (ll. 1123–29). The idea of "withholding" Samson from Harapha's "head" is particularly apposite here, for underlying this threat is the reminiscence of that dismemberment Goliath himself was made to undergo at the hands of his adversary. It is in the spirit of this defacement that Samson would do battle with Harapha.

Although deriving its inspiration from the biblical account, such an act of mutilation is appropriately in keeping with the language of the *In Impurissimum Nebulonem JOHANNEM MILTONUM*. This fact becomes clear after Samson has issued yet another challenge to Harapha. That challenge culminates what in effect becomes Samson's act of self-justification in the face of Harapha's attempt to undermine his faith in the power of God. The purpose of such an attempt is to convince Samson that the source of his power has been illusory from the very beginning. Samson would not be so inclined to "disparage"

---

26. As I have suggested in *Sinews of Ulysses* (p. 129), this passage ironically parodies the Pauline call to arms in Ephesians 6.

the "glorious arms" in which warriors like Harapha put their trust "had not spells / And black enchantments, some Magicians Art / Arm'd [him] or charm'd [him] strong" (ll. 1130–34). Imputing to Samson the same confidence in the world of illusion that is the source of his own power, Harapha would vitiate whatever confidence in the divine Samson still possesses.

Such a temptation affords Samson the opportunity to reaffirm his faith in the true source of power, God Himself: "I know no Spells, use no forbidden Arts; / My trust is in the living God who gave me / At my Nativity this strength, diffus'd / No less through all my sinews, joints and bones / Then thine, while I preserv'd these locks unshorn, / The pledge of my unviolated vow" (ll. 1139–44). That this vow was in fact violated accounts for Samson's misery now. Nonetheless, his faith in the source of strength remains. It is a source as powerful as any Harapha has ever known. If Harapha has any doubts of this, he should call upon Dagon for aid as the two of them do battle to determine "whose God is strongest," Harapha's or Samson's (ll. 1145–55). In this respect, the battle would resolve itself into a combat of supernatural forces, one in which the representative of each divinity would demonstrate his respective prowess. Founded in a manifestation of divine strength, the terms of the combat would nonetheless be entirely and brutally physical. They would confirm the Miltonic emphasis upon the need to make the body whole through a corresponding act of violence upon the body of the adversary.

It is, of course, Harapha's purpose to undermine Samson's faith in the efficacy of this act by persuading the fallen hero to believe that his God has deserted him. "Presume not on thy God, what e're he be, / Thee he regards not, owns not, hath cut off / Quite from his people, and deliver'd up / Into thy Enemies hand, permitted them / To put out both thine eyes, and fetter'd send thee / Into the common Prison, there to grind / Among the Slaves and Asses thy comrades" (ll. 1156–62). Such aspersions represent Harapha's bringing to the fore (in effect, verbally reenacting) the sparagmos Samson has endured as the result of his own violations. The rending of Samson both from his God and from his people is symbolized in his facial mutilation (his defacement), and bodily degradations (his binding and imprisonment). This condition is further exacerbated by the internalization of these sufferings. Both externally and internally, such a condition of having been rendered impure by a multiple sparagmos is one Samson as Nazarite must attempt to overcome in his reassertion of his faith in the ultimate source of both his power and his wholeness. He accomplishes this reassertion by acknowledging his culpability but also by maintaining that he despairs not of God's "final pardon / Whose ear is ever open; and his eye / Gracious to re-admit the suppliant" (ll. 1169–73).

Only after Samson is brought to the point of engaging in such a reassertion is he able once more to repeat the challenge to Harapha: "In confidence whereof I once again / Defie thee to the trial of mortal fight, / By combat to decide whose god is God, / Thine or whom I with Israel's Sons adore" (ll. 1174–77). Such a challenge has moved Samson to a new plane of understanding, one that allows him to see that his combat with Harapha transcends the immediate circumstances of pitting one strongman against the other. Violence assumes a theological bearing: it speaks to the very nature of godhead. At the source of that godhead is sparagmos at its most extreme. Inspired by that awareness in what amounts to a renewal of his faith in the source of all power, indeed, the source of all violence, Samson renews his assaults upon his enemy until the giant is brought low. Despite all the subterfuges Harapha invents to delay the inevitable, he can do nothing to prevent his undoing. All his shifts are vain. "Answer thy appellant," Samson cries: "Who now defies thee thrice to single fight, / As a petty enterprise of small enforce" (ll. 1220–23). Harapha can do nothing but reiterate the terms of his former disclaimer: "With thee a Man condemn'd, a Slave enrol'd / Due by the Law to capital punishment? / To fight with thee no man of arms will deign" (ll. 1224–26). The posture adopted by the poet of the *In Impurissimum Nebulonem JO-HANNEM MILTONUM* will no longer serve the giant, however. Despite his fallen condition, Samson has proved himself worthy of combat, worthy to take up God's cause. All that remains is for Samson to repeat his battery of assaults: "Come nearer, part not hence so slight inform'd"; "bring up thy van, / My heels are fetter'd, but my fist is free" (ll. 1228–29; 1234–35).

With Harapha in retreat, Samson is finally in a position to threaten him with precisely that fate Milton himself endured at the hands of Salmasius in that poem of violent bodily undoing: "Go baffl'd coward, lest I run upon thee, / Though in these chains, bulk without spirit vast, / And with one buffet lay thy structure low, / Or swing thee in the Air, then dash thee down / To th'hazard of thy brains and shatter'd sides" (ll. 1237–42). This is the ultimate revenge, the ultimate act of violence, that the Miltonic Samson is able to enact upon his enemy. It is his way of responding to all the indignities of the *In Impurissimum Nebulonem JOHANNEM MILTONUM*, where Milton found himself bound, lashed, cudgeled, and then whirled into the air by an enemy who savagely "bestrews the rocks far and wide" with his victim's "shattered brain." Such is precisely the fate Harapha himself would sustain at the hands of the Miltonic Samson were the giant foolish enough to take Samson up on his offer. The fact that this event does not actually come about is of little concern. The giant is discomfited: his sparagmos is effected in the very language that projects his fate. Verbal assault becomes physical assault. Samson has his way: he repays his enemy in kind for the undoing of his body. Milton has his way too: as champion of God, he projects a situation in which the undoing of his body in the form of poetic abuse is answered by his own poetic weapon, the drama in which he stages the sparagmos of the giant against whom he has already done battle in his fierce prose. There can be no greater satisfaction than this.

Almost as if in response to both situations (the immediate one of Samson's responding in kind to Harapha and the implied one of Milton's adopting the occasion to respond to his own personal enemies), the Chorus celebrates the triumph of violence it has just witnessed: "Oh how comely it is and how reviving / To the Spirits of just men long opprest!" they proclaim, "When God into the hands of thir deliverer / Puts invincible might / To quell the mighty of the Earth, th' oppressour, / The brute and boist'rous force of violent men / Hardy and industrious to support / Tyrannic power." Responding with his own form of violence, the deliverer renders his enemies useless, as "he executes / His errand on the wicked, who surpris'd / Lose thir defence, distracted and amaz'd" (ll. 1268–86). Samson's discomfiture of Harapha reminds the Chorus of those glory days when in the triumph of his might he was able to destroy all who would oppose. In contradistinction to this form of response, however, the Chorus proposes another alternative for Samson, one consistent with the debilitating fact of his blindness: "But patience is more oft the exercise / Of Saints, the trial of thir fortitude, / Making them each his own Deliverer, / And Victor over all / That tyrannie or fortune can inflict." Either of these alternatives, the Chorus suggests, is Samson's lot: that of violent deliverer or that of suffering saint. Because of his blindness, the Chorus concludes that perhaps patience is ultimately the alternative that Samson must adopt: as saint, Samson will be crowned with patience (ll. 1287–97). He will, that is, continue to undergo the role of sufferer as a kind of Samson *patiens*. Nothing could be further from the truth: Samson is no saint. The outcome of his *agon* with Harapha is one that moves him to an ultimate act of glorious and triumphant violence.

IV

Samson is now prepared to bring down the edifice, the true tower, of the Philistines themselves. Doing so, he fulfills that mission Milton portrays for him in the *Defensio Prima*: "whether prompted by God or by his own valor," Samson "slew at one stroke not one but a host of his country's tyrants [*neque unum sed multos simul patriae suae tyrannos*], having first made prayer to God for his aid. Samson therefore thought it not impious but pious to kill those masters who were tyrants over his country [*Non impium ergo sed pium Sampsoni visum est, dominos, patriae tyrannos occidere*]." This incident represents the culminating moment of Milton's drama. Performing as an actor before the assembled Philistines, Samson first reveals not just his strength but his ability to fulfill his role as *anthroporraistes* (ll. 1623–28). That accomplished, Samson fulfills all the sparagmatic potential latent in his vast might. His demonstration of that might is consummately destructive.

As the Messenger relates it, this demonstration moves to the point of natural catastrophe. It is almost impersonal in its all-encompassing destructiveness. In the theater of destruction, Samson embodies all the forces of sparagmos as he grasps the pillars that support the edifice he seeks to destroy: "As with the force of winds and waters pent, / When Mountains tremble, those two massie Pillars / With horrible convulsion to and fro, / He tugg'd, he shook, till down they came and drew / The whole roof after them, with burst of thunder / Upon the heads of all who sate beneath" (ll. 1647–52). The act assumes an elemental cast: the sparagmos Samson executes finds its correspondence in the forces of nature. But this is a personal victory as well, one through which Samson realizes on a national scale the full potential of his sparagmatic mission. All his former activities of tearing apart animals, crushing armies, rending the fabric of the earth, and pulling up posts are summed up in this one final act of devastation. Having overcome Harapha as the culminating moment in a series of encounters (including those with Manoa and Dalila), Samson has reached the point in which sparagmos may be given free reign against the assembled enemy. The act of destruction is not only politically justified (*neque unum sed multos simul patriae suae tyrannos*) but personally fulfilling. With all its violence and devastation, the act purifies Samson: it is a pious act (*Non impium ergo sed pium Sampsoni visum est*), an act through which Samson demonstrates his piety to his "living Dread," his God (cf. l. 1673). By means of it, the formerly impure Nazarite regains his purity.

Despite the imputation of what Manoa calls "self-violence" (l. 1584), it matters little that Samson is consumed by his own destructive act. Such, to cite the Messenger, was the "Inevitable cause / At once both to destroy and be destroy'd" (ll. 1587–88). All that matters finally is that Samson is afforded once again the opportunity to allow the forces of sparagmos to be released against the enemies of God. As a result of that release, sparagmos as a phenomenon at once violently destructive but potentially restorative is allowed to find full and triumphant expression. So the Semichorus confirms the celebratory nature of the event: "Though blind of sight, / Despis'd and thought extinguish't quite, / With inward eyes illuminated," Samson as a fiery dragon experiences that renewal through which his former violence and destructiveness are "rouz'd / From under ashes into sudden flame." Whether as an eagle, the bird of God, or a phoenix, "that self-begott'n bird," he realizes his holocaustal destiny as not simply a redeemer but a violent destroyer (ll. 1687–1707).

Manoa is right: "Come, come, no time for lamentation now, / Nor much more cause, Samson hath quit himself / Like Samson, and heroicly hath finish'd / A life Heroic, on his Enemies / Fully reveng'd" (ll. 1708–12). Samson's end is a new beginning, a cause for celebration, not despair. The successful enactment of violence in God's cause becomes its own reward. As the way in which violence is executed upon God's enemies, Samson regains his former stature. From the very beginning his purpose was that of revenge, his means of fulfilling that purpose violence. The situation is no different now. Violence has brought forth violence; all is as it should be. Like the Samson Milton conceived as early as *The Reason of Church-Government*, the Samson of the drama fulfills his mission nobly. Allowing that his act results in "great affliction to himselfe," Milton•portrays a Samson whose locks in effect "sternly [shake] thunder with ruin upon the heads" of the enemy. If anything, the drama exults even more openly in the sparagmos this "thunder with ruin" entails.

As a symbol of all that the repristination of Samson implies, Manoa seeks to reclaim the body in order to cleanse it and memorialize it: "Let us go find the body where it lies / Soak't in his enemies blood, and from the stream / With lavers pure and cleansing herbs wash off / The clotted gore." From there, the body will be fetched hence and solemnly attended with "silent obsequie and funeral train" as it is returned to its native home, where a monument will be built to commemorate Samson's conquests (ll. 1725–46). This is as it should be. As a sign of the repristination of the hero, the body is cleansed of all impurities that might accrue to it by virtue not of the undoing it has enacted upon itself but of the undoing it has executed upon others. It is not its own blood but the blood of its enemies from which it must be cleansed.

Nor is the undoing it has executed upon others viewed as an emblem of blame. Quite the contrary: the blood spilled in this act of violence is an emblem of the heroism it has attained. It is a signature of the body's triumph, a signature of the triumph of sparagmos, the triumph of revenge. Cleansing the blood thereby becomes a symbol of the homage those who worship the body seek to bestow. This homage finds its correspondence in the solemnities that surround the monument built to commemorate the heroism brought about by the successful enactment of sparagmos. All who bear witness to this "great event" come to recognize, in the words of the Chorus, that it is fruitless "to resist" God's "uncontroulable intent" (ll. 1753–54). As the consummate manifestation of that intent, Samson has fulfilled his role admirably and indeed triumphantly. In its most profound form ever, violence prevails: sparagmos has done its work.

Whether or not *Samson Agonistes* is the product of the years leading up to and culminating in the Defenses, the drama clearly reflects the sparagmatic mentality that distinguishes this crucial period. It is a work in which all the energies underlying Milton's concern with the nature of violence and the significance of the body in the face of that violence are brought to the fore. From the perspective of the period in question, the drama is a work in which the Miltonic Samson as hero reflects that process of politicization undergone by the biblical counterpart in the prose works. In keeping with that process, the encounter between Samson and Harapha demonstrates the extent to which *Samson Agonistes* is responsive to the humiliation and undoing of Milton's own body enacted in the polemic of the period. Taking that polemic into account, Milton conceived his own work of violence, one in which his enemies were undone in the most brutal and devastating form. Transmuting this brutality and devastation into a supreme work of poetic discourse, Milton created his own theater of violence, his own *agon*, one in which his hero as *anthroporraistes* was given the opportunity to fulfill his destiny.

My analysis of *Samson Agonistes* represents a fitting closure to my study of sparagmos as a whole. In my discussion of Milton's works, I have taken into account the emergence of what I call a "sparagmatic sensibility," one in which an underlying concern with the body and the forces that threaten to assault and dismember it assume profound importance. In his response to those forces, Milton provides the occasion through which the body is imbued with a new meaning and a new life. As phenomenon, indeed, as event, the body is configured and reconfigured within the contexts (poetic and polemic) Milton envisions for it. Whatever form it assumes and, by extension, whatever gender distinguishes it, the body is portrayed as a phenomenon beset by a world of violence in which it must sustain itself, assert itself, maintain its integrity lest it be torn asunder, violated, and destroyed.

In the theater of assault by means of which the body is staged, the being who inhabits this body is faced with a terrible choice. He may either allow himself to undergo a sparagmos of the most brutal and devastating kind, or he may marshal those very forces through which sparagmos is executed in order to repristinate himself, his being, his body anew. If Milton was victimized by the forces of sparagmos, he also overcame those forces. He did find a means through which sparagmos was able to realize its paradoxical potential. Violence was triumphant in him. It became a source of renewal as well as a source of devastation. Throughout Milton's career the dilemma represented by the undoing of the body made itself known time and again in his works, in fact, in his very being. Violence was his signature. *Samson Agonistes* may end in a spirit of "peace and consolation" with "calm of mind all passion spent," but Milton himself was never able to gain such composure for very long. Indeed, judging by the events surrounding the afterlife of his body in the grave, such composure might well have eluded him even then.

Index

Abyss, the, 116n.2
Achaemenides (*Aeneid*), 167
Adam, 122, 123–24, 150–51, 185, 212–13, 231n.8
"Adam unparadiz'd," 123
Ad Iohannem Miltonum Responsio, Opus Posthumus (Salmasius), 216n.26
Adonis, 212
Ad Patrem, 39–40
Adultery, 132–34. *See also* Fornication
Adversus Haereses (Irenaeus), 19n.13
Aeneid (Virgil), 167, 182, 183, 186
Aeschylus, 42n.10
"Against That Foul Rascal JOHN MILTON the Advocate of Parricide & Parricides" (Du Moulin), 169–71, 202–3, 240–42, 255, 256, 258–59. *See also Regii Sanguinis Clamor ad Coelum Adversus Parricidas Anglicanos*
Alcinous, 212
Aleian plain, the, 67
Alexis (*A Mask*), 111–12
Alter, Robert, 124–25
Amphion, 88
Anderson, W. S., 42n.9
Androgyny. *See* Bisexuality; Gender
Aphrodite, 207, 215
Apocalypse, 27–29, 33, 35, 56
Apocatastasis, defined, 15–16. *See also* Sparagmos

Apollo, 104
Apology for Smectymnuus, 102, 183, 184, 196, 209n.13, 221; Milton as matron in, 142–46
Arcades, 141
Archer, Stanley, 105n.32
Areopagitica, 5, 17–22, 35, 230–33; apocalyptic perspective of, 27–29; historical context of, 22–25
Arion, 53–55
Arnold, Christopher, 192n.8
Ascough, William, 4
Ashton, John, 3n.3, 7n.6
"At a Vacation Exercise in the Colledge," 86. *See also* Sixth Prolusion
Atropos, 50n.29
Attendant Spirit (*A Mask*), 61n.1, 107–8, 109
Aubrey, John, 85n.4, 174n.20, 204n.6
Avoiding, and preventing, distinguished, 152–55

Bacchantes, the, 42–43, 48n.28, 60
Bacchus, 43n.11, 115–16. *See also* Dionysus
Bal, Mieke, 131–32, 245n.19
Banquet imagery, 91–92, 97–98
Bassarids (Aeschylus), 42n.10
Bastwick, John, 22–25, 50n.29
Bate, George, 162n.6

265